A GRAMMAR OF THE SANTHAL LANGUAGE

A GRAMMAR OF THE SANTHAL LANGUAGE

BY THE

REV. L. O. SKREFSRUD, M.A.S.B.
MISSIONARY TO THE SANTHALS.

GYAN

ISBN: 978-81-212-1385-1(PB)

First Published in 1873
Indian Reprint in 2017

Published by

Gyan Publishing House
5, Ansari Road
Daryaganj, New Delhi-110002
Phone: 9811692060
E-mail: books@gyanbooks.com

Cataloging in Publication Data—DK
Courtesy: D.K. Agencies (P) Ltd. <docinfo@dkagencies.com>

Skrefsrud, L. O. (Lars Olsen), 1840-1910, **author.**
A grammar of the Santhal language / by the Rev. L.O. Skrefsrud.
pages cm
Reprint. Originally published: Calcutta : Calcutta School Book and Vernacular Literature Society, 1873.
ISBN 9788121213851 (PB)

1. Santali language—Grammar. I. Title.

PL4563.1.S57 2017 DDC 495.95 23

INTRODUCTION.

SANTHALI is the language spoken by a people called by foreigners the Santhals or Santals, inhabiting the western frontier of Lower Bengal, from Orissa in the south to Bhagulpore in the north, of late made so prominent to the public by the Lieutenant-Governor of Bengal, Sir George Campbell's famous "Enactment for the better Government of the Santhals," Dr. Hunter's highly interesting "Rural Bengal," his suggestive "Comparative Dictionary of the Languages of India and High Asia," and the Commissioner of Chutia Nagpore, Colonel Dalton's able "Ethnology of India."

It is spoken with hardly more than a dialectical difference, in common by Santhals, Kolhes, *Koḍas, Mahles, Birhọrs, Muṇdas, Hos* and *Koṛkos;* but in grammatical structure Santhali is as superior to the others as is Sanskrit to its cognate languages.

It belongs to what is called the "Turanian family of speech," or what is denominated by August Schleicher, as "compounding languages," and will, I believe, be found to be second to none of these (not even to the Turkish, which is deemed to be one of the most philosophical of languages) in grammatical structure.

At what period the Santhal language attained its present copiousness is not easily ascertained; but certain it seems from the traditions of the people (which I hope soon to publish with their institutions and poetry) that they had arrived at a not inconsiderable state of culture in the Punjab, when the Aryans entered India, although there are no indications showing that it had *that* richness which it now manifests in a degree far above what might be expected from a language of the same group as itself.

The name by which the Santhals call themselves is *Hoṛ*, man. Now this word is, according to the Santhal traditions, connected with the very origin of the human race. *Pilchu Haḍ-am* (or *Haṛam*, the Santhal Adam,) says the tradition, is the father of all mankind, and his first-born was *Hũsd-ak̇*, which means *of Hũsd*, the *ak̇* being the old genitive-sign in Santhali. It is evident that *Haḍ* in the words *Pilchu Haḍam*, and *Hũsd* in *Hũs-dak̇* belong to the same root, *sd* and *ḍ* being interchangeable as *sth* is with *ṭh* (in *sthan*=*ṭhañ*, *etc.*,

It is true that the nasal in *Hũsd-ak̇* would have to be accounted for, as *Hũsd* would not give *Haḍ*, but *Hanḍ;* but the interchange of *ṇḍ* and *ḍ* is quite common in Santhali; as *oṇḍ-oṅ=oḍ-oṅ*, to take out; *huṇḍin=huḍiṅ=huṛiṅ* (all of which are at present in use among the Santhals) small. *Khond* and Gond are probably instances of the same change.

Haḍ is the root cf a very large number of the names o the aboriginal tribes of India:— *Haḍ-i*, *Haṛ-i*, (a low caste Hindu); *Hoḍ*, *Hoṛ*, (the Santhals); *Ho*, (the *Hos*); *Kar*, (the Kar-ens); *Koḍ*, (the Kod-as); *Koṛ*, (the Kor-kos); *Kol*, (the Kolhes and Kols); *Kul-i*, (a low workman); *Khair*, (Khairgar, Khairs); *Kher*, (Kher-o-ar=Kherwar, the ancient name of the Santhals); *Ker*, (the Kerus); *Gar*, (the Garos); *Gour*, *Gur*, (Gours, Gurka); *Khond*, (the Konds); *Gond*, (the Gonds). *Hãs*, *Hãs-in*, two birds, who, according to the Santhal traditions, were the parents of *Pilchu Haṛam* and *Pilchu Buḍhi*, will be found to be from the same root.

With regard to the ancient home of the Santhals, the traditions say, that the cradle of the human race (before the flood) was in the East (not east from the Santhal Parganas, but from the place whence the traditions took their rise); that the two first human beings were carried to the west to *Hihiṛi-pipiṛi* (a reduplication of *Hiṛi-piṛi*, which again is a jingle from *Hiṛi* (like *Hako-pako*) where seven sons and seven daughters were born to them; that they proceeded to *Sasaṅbeḍa*, from whence they removed to *Khojkaman,* where God, on account of their sins, destroyed the whole human race with fire-rain, two, however, being saved in the cave of *Har-a,* or *Har-a-ta* mountain.

After the flood, so run the traditions, the Santhals, a part of the new race, took an easterly direction and came to *Jarpi,* whence (passing the *Siṅpass* and the *Bahīpass*) they proceeded to *Aere.* (Iran ?)

From *Aere* they came to *Khaṇḍe* (Afghanistan ?) and from *Khaṇḍe,* taking a north-easterly direction, they entered *Chae* (the Chinic Tartary ?), and turning south-eastward, and passing the *Chae* and *Champa* passes, they arrived at *Champa* with the seven rivers, (Saptasind, the present Panjab ?) where they lived for generations, and where many of their institutions were formed.

From this place of prosperity and power (they had also kings of their own) they were driven by powerful enemies, and wandering through many places they came at last to Nagpore, from whence they removed to Sikhar (Hazaribagh District) and finally to the Santhal Parganas. They have lived near many rivers, they say, among which are the *Maha nai, Siṅjo nai,* the *Giru nai* the *Suṛa nai,* the *Gaṅ nai* and the *Gua nai.*

They are divided into twelve tribes, each of which is subdivided into twelve families. They were originally composed of only seven tribes, and the five additional are deemed inferior. One of the tribes is lost. The remaining eleven are as follows :—1, *Hũsdak̕*; 2, *Kishu*; 3, *Murmu*; 4, *Manḍri*; 5, *Hemrom*; 6, *Soren*; 7, *Ṭuḍu*; 8, *Baske*; 9, *Chõṛe*; 10, *Puõria* 11, *Besra*.

The construction and arrangement of a Grammar of such an intricate language as Santhali is necessarily beset with many difficulties, especially when one has to collect the materials chiefly from the mouths of the people; and moreover to write in a foreign tongue, hence imperfections are inevitable; yet one thing I may say, and that is, that I have spared no trouble in endeavouring to make the Santhal part of the Grammar as accurate as possible, and I am sure that my Missionary brethren, who themselves feel the common difficulty in learning Santhali, will bear with me for any error which they may discover in the book.

To those who are not acquainted with the language a few hints as to what parts of the Grammar they ought first to learn may not be unacceptable. After having learnt the first 20 pages, they should commit the full and abridged form of the Pronoun to memory; and having mastered which they would do well in learning the table of the tense-signs (page 144). The auxiliary verbs (page 146) should next be learnt, and then the regular verb (pages 156-270). It is of the highest importance, however, for the student to learn well the abridged Pronoun and the tense-signs, for these are as it were the very key to the language.

In conclusion, I would here beg to offer my most sincere thanks to my highly esteemed and learned friend Dr. Wenger for his very valuable assistance in the arrangement and correction of the Grammar; to Dr. Lazarus, of Benares, for his personal care and skilful management in the printing of it; and last, but not least, to my aged and much respected friend Dr. Phillips, *Sr.*, of the American F. W. B. Mission in Orissa, who is the oldest Missionary among the Santhals, and who published an outline of a Santhal Grammar 21 years ago, for the encouragement he has given me in my work, and for the recommendation given by him to the C. S. B S. in favor of these pages instead of a reprint of his own outlines.

L. O. SKREFSRUD.

P. S.—I am in possession of a large number of songs composed in a very old dialect of Hinde, and which may prove valuable to the Philologist. They have been handed down from Sage to Sage among the Santhals. I hope soon to publish them. L. S.

CONTENTS.

Tables of the formation of the verb.

Reciprocal.

Reciprocal continuative. 65

Tables of the formation of the tenses.

A.—ON THE DERIVATION OF WORDS.

B.—ON THE COMPOSITION OF WORDS.

PART II.—Of Syntax.

CHAPTER I.

SECTION I.—OF THE LETTERS.

The Santals being destitute of any signs or characters of their own, by which to express their language in writing, we are obliged to borrow them from some other language. And as the Roman character presents the fewest difficulties to the European Student, it appears advisable to adopt that character, with certain diacritical signs, to represent sounds peculiar to the Santal language.

Vowels.	Consonants.	Semi Vowels.	Semi Consonants.
Long. *ā ē̱ ē ī ō̱ ō ū*	Faucal, *h*		
Short. *ă ĕ̱ ĕ ĭ ŏ̱ ŏ ŭ*	Gutturals, *k kh g gh ṅ*		*k'*
Neutral. *ḁ i̥ o̥ u̥*	Palatals, *ch chh j jh ń*	*y*	*ch'*
Nasal. *ã ẽ̱ ẽ ĩ õ̱ õ ũ*	Cerebrals, *ṭ ṭh ḍ ḍh ṇ*	*ṛ ṛh*	—
Diphthongs.	Dentals, *t th d dh n*	*r l*	*t'*
ae, ao, e̱i, e̱o, eo, eu, iu, o̱e, oe, oi,	Labials, *p ph b bh m*	*w*	*p'*
ua, ui, ḁi, ḁu, o̥i.	Sibilant, *s*		

SECTION II.—OF THE PRONUNCIATION OF LETTERS.

VOWELS.

ā, is pronounced like the English *a* in father; as *dāl*, to strike.

ẹ, is pronounced like the German *ä* in *ähnlich*, or somewhat like the English *a* in fat; as *ẹ̄r*, to sow.

e, is pronounced a little more i.-(ee) like, than the English *a* in fate, or the German *e* in *Segen;* as *jēl*, meat.

i, is pronounced like the English *i* in police; as *siń*, day.

ọ, is pronounced like the English *a* in fall; as *ọ̄l*, to write.

o, is pronounced a little more *u*-like, than the English *o* in note; as *oni*, he, or she; *kōl*, to send.

u, is pronounced like the English *u* in prune, or full; as *ūl*, mango; *ūsŭl*, high.

ą, is a neutral a, and is distinguished from the English *o* in nation, and the German *e* in Verstand, by being a deep guttural. It is probably the same sound, which Dr. Lepsius mentions, as existing in the Bornu language.

į and *ų* are only used as forming the second vowel in a

diphthong in connection with *q̥*, as far as I have been able to ascertain.

ã, ẽ̥, ẽ, ĩ, õ̥, õ, ũ, are nasal vowels. *ã* is pronounced like the French *an* or *en*, and *õ* is pronounced like the French *on*. Each of these vowels retains its respective sound with the nasal element added to it; as *ãṛgatre*, early (before the usual time); *hẽ̥*, yes; *hõ̥*, also.

ae. In this diphthong, as well as in all the others, the vowels retain their respective sounds, like in German, and are not like in English, where *ai* is pronounced like *e** in hair, *oa* like *o* in load; as, *paera*, to swim.

ao, as in *kadrao*; *e̥i*, as in *e̥i!* *e̥o*, as in *chhe̥ok*, and *ke̥o*; *eo*, as in *le-ohae*; *eu*, as in *ḍheu*; *iu*, as in *diuhe*; *o̥e*, as in *ho̥e*; *oe*, as in *hoe keda*; *oi*, as in *koiṇḍa*; *ua*, as in *sikuar*; *ui*, as in *uihar*; *q̥i*, as in *q̥imq̥i*, *q̥u*, as in *kq̥umq̥u*, *q̥i*, as in *hejukme q̥i!*

CONSONANTS.

k, is pronounced like the English *k* in king, so that no aspiration is heard; as *kq̥i*, crime.

kh, is the aspirated form of the preceding consonant; as *kho̥n*, from. It is pronounced like *kh* in *ink-horn*.

g, is pronounced like *g* in give; as *gapa*, to-morrow.

---

* The *e* is pronounced in the Italian way, as well as the other vowels.

gh, is the aspirate of the preceding consonant; as *ghasao*, to scour.

ṅ, is prounced like the English *ng* in ring; as *baṅ*, (bang) no.

ch, the Santal palatals differ a little from the English in pronunciation. The former are pure, uncompounded letters, pronounced like the Hindui, Bengalee* and Ooria palatals (with the exception of *ń* used as an initial), namely by placing the tongue quite flat up to the palate, a little behind the upper teeth, and allowing no concavation of the tongue by its striking against the lower teeth again at the reopening of the organ: there is nothing of that hissing sound heard in the pronunciation of the Santal palatals, which is slightly heard, when an Englishman pronounces *ch*, or *j*.

chh, is the aspirate of the preceding consonant.

j, stands exactly in the same relation to the English *j*, as the Santal *ch* to the English *ch*, namely by there being nothing of that hissing sound in the Santal *j*.

jh, is the aspirate of the preceding consonant.

ń, this nasal, unlike the Sanscrit ञ ń, may be both initial, final, and joined to other palatals. The Sanscrit letter, when pronounced in connection with other palatals, is pronounced just like the Santal; but when pronounced alone (as by the Hindus at present) it differs from the Santal *ń* by the

---

* I do not mean the corrupt pronunciation of some Bengalies, who pronounce *ch* like *tse*.

tongue being a little hollow, when it strikes against the lower teeth again. This Santal nasal is pronounced by placing the tongue quite *flat* up to the palate and not allowing any concavation of the tongue at its leaving the gum and striking against the lower teeth again. This being a palatal nasal, it sounds, when preceded by a vowel, as if an *i* was inserted; as *ań* (ainy, the *y* being pronounced as in yes)—*ńam* (sounds somewhat like nyam).

ṭ, this cerebral (lingual) letter differs considerably from the English, and still more from the pure dental German *t*, in the pronunciation. It is pronounced by turning the tip of the tongue up against the hard palate and pronouncing the *t*, with, the tongue in that position; as *ṭanga,* an axe.

ṭh, is the aspirate of the preceding consonant; as *ṭhen* near, to, by, from.

ḍ, stands in the same relation to the English, as the Santal *ṭ* to the English *t;* as *ḍaṭa,* tooth.

ḍh, is the aspirate of the preceding consonant.

ṇ, stands in the same relation to the English *n*, as the Santal *ṭ* to the English *t*. This nasal is never initial or final, but only joined to other cerebrals. (linguals).

t, is a pure dental, not like the English *t* in take, but the German *t* in tief, only with the exception, that the Santal *t* has no aspiration whatever.

th, is the aspirate of the preceding consonant.

d, is also a pure dental and sounds like the German *d* in denken not like the English *d*, in did; as *dāl*, to strike.

dh, is the aspirate of the preceding consonant.

n, is a pure dental, when joined to other dentals, but when initial or final it is not a pure dental, it is then pronounced just where the English *n* is pronounced, *i. e.* between the dental and cerebral (lingual), the tongue by closing the organs touches at the root of the teeth, *i, e.* on the gum, instead of the teeth themselves; as *nẹs*, this year; *sahan*, wood.

p, is pronounced like the English *p*, with the exception of there being no aspiration in it.

ph, is the aspirate of the preceding consonant.

b, is like the English *b*; as *bọtọr*, to fear.

bh, is the aspirate form of the preceding consonant.

m, is pronounced like the English *m*; as *mọlọṅ*, the forehead.

h, is pronounced like the English *h* in have; as *hạ̃s* pleasure.

s, is not a dental, nor yet a cerebral, but a palatal. It is pronounced by drawing the tip of the tongue a little back from the lower teeth, and the middle of it touching the palate, expelling the breath through the concavity of the tongue, in that position:—thus the Santal *s* is produced.

SEMI-VOWELS.

---

y, is pronounced like the English *y* in yes. This letter is used instead of *e*, when pronounced between two other vowels; as *taean*=tayan, *maeam*=mayam, *toeo*=toyo.

ṛ, the sound, which this letter represents, is exceedingly difficult to pronounce for a European generally, there being only two countries in Europe (so far as I know) Sweden and Norway, (and even there only amongst the peasants) where it is to be found. It differs very much from the English *r*, in world, and still more from the dental or guttural *r*. It stands in the same relation to *ṭ* as the dental *r* to *t*; it is a cerebral (lingual) *r*, pronounced by turning the tip of the tongue back against the hard palate, and letting the tongue glide quickly toward the root of the upper teeth on its way, when striking down against the lower teeth again. The Bengalees have also the sound; as for instance in *bọṛọ*. It is very necessary indeed to learn to pronounce this letter correctly, else the greatest confusion will be the result, which a few examples will show: *Họr*, is a road, but *họṛ*, a man; *arak̔*, is red, but *aṛak̔*, is to set at liberty, *etc.*

ṛh, is the aspirate of the preceding semi-vowel.

w, is pronounced a little more *o*-like, than the English *w*. It is used instead of *o*, when it is placed between two other vowels; as *heoa*=hewa, *coer*=ewer.

SEMI-CONSONANTS.

k̓, ch̓, t̓, p̓. The sounds, which these letters represent are peculiar to the Santal language; the first is a guttural, the second a palatal, the third a dental, or rather between dental and cerebral (lingual), and the fourth a labial. They have the peculiarity in common of never being initials, but only finals, and in certain cases middle letters.

When succeeded by a vowel, as in the conjugation of the verb, they are changed into their respective soft sounds; as *senok̓*=sonogo, *raṛech̓*=raṛejo, *aṭet̓*=aṭedo, *chahap̓*=chahabo. An exception to this rule is caused by the vowel *a;* as *chàhap̓aǹ* (not chahabaǹ)—, still this exception is very often disregarded.

These sounds are not pronounced like other consonants by successively "closing and opening," and allowing the breath to touch the respective organs at their reopening, but by partly inhaling the breath and simultaneously closing the throat and the respective organs, and not allowing the breath to touch them at their reopening, but letting it pass unarrested out of the throat: thus an abrupt half consonant is produced.

The "Schnalz-laute" (click-sounds) mentioned by Dr. Lepsius, as existing in some of the African languages, appear to have some similarity to these Santal jerks; but according to Boyce's description, they are not alike.

These sounds are hard and pronounced very sharply and abruptly, so that it would be impossible to use the soft letters *g*, *j*, *t*, *b* as bases—, and as the hard guttural in English is *k*, the hard palatal *ch*, the hard dental (not pure) *t*, and the hard labial *p*,—I therefore have thought myself justified in adopting *k*, *ch*, *t*, and *p* as the basis for these four Santal sounds, they being respectively a guttural, palatal, dental, and labial. It is true that the Santal guttural jerk is pronounced further back in the throat, than the English *k*, nay even further than the Arabic ق *q*;* still, as in English *k* is the hard sound for *g*, *p* for *b*, and *t* for *d* &c., it seems, that no better basis can be had for it. The Sanscrit visarga (:) might (as it has been) be used; but that sound, as pronounced by the Hindus of Bengal and the North West, is no nearer to the Santal guttural sound, than *k*, it being a slight aspirate, which the former is not at all; on the contrary, it is an inspirate. And if we adopted (:) for the Santal guttural, what should we adopt for the palatal? the same? It might be done (as it also has been, and would be no greater irregularity, than the Germans using the same letter *ch* both as a guttural and palatal, as in *ach* and *ich*; but as we are compelled to use *t* as the basis for the dental, and *p* for the labial, it seems to be more consistent also to use *k* as the basis for the guttural, and *ch* for the palatal; for if *p*, which changes into *b*, when succeeded by a vowel, is the right basis for the labial (and we cannot use any other), and *t*, which changes into *d*, for

---

* The Arabic 'ain when having the tashdid is very much like it; as فعّل

the dental :—then also *ch*, which changes into *j*, and *k*, which changes into *g*, must be right as the basis for the palatal and guttural respectively.

Besides this, if visarga (:) were used for both the guttural and palatal Santal sounds, an *i* would have to be inserted in the latter case, in order to make it sound somewhat like the Santal *cḱ*. For instance *raṛecḱ* would have to be written *raṛei :*, which would be incorrect, there being no *i* in the word; because, if there were, then, instead of being *raṛejo* in the middle voice, present and future tenses, it would be *rareijo ;* for it is the visarga (I mean the Santal palatal jerk) not the *i*, which should be changed into *j*, in the same manner, as it is changed into *g*, not taking away the preceding vowel, when used as a guttural in *seno:*=senog-o; *tio:*= tiogo, not *tigo*, which would be the case if the preceding *i* in *raṛei:* changed into *j*.

ḱ, is pronounced by sharply inhaling the breath, and quickly closing the throat below the guttural point, by which the breath is suddenly stopped, and on re-opening it, allowing the breath free passage through the mouth :—Thus an abrupt guttural jerk is produced ; as *aḱ*, a bow.

It is as if the *k* were cut off: only with the difference that it is pronounced below the guttural point, instead of where the English *k* is pronounced.

cḱ, is pronounced by sharply inhaling the breath, and suddenly closing the throat (as by *ḱ*) and at the same time striking with the flat of the tongue sharply against the palate, and re-opening it without allowing the breath to touch that organ, (for in that case a pure palatal—with the exception of the closing of the throat—would be pronounced) :—thus an abrupt half *ch* is produced.

t', is pronounced by sharply inhaling the breath, and suddenly closing the throat (as by *k'*) and at the same time striking with the tip of the tongue at the root of the upper teeth, and re-opening the mouth without allowing the breath to touch there (at the root of the upper teeth), but letting it have free passage through the mouth :—thus an abrupt half *t* is produced.

p', is pronounced by sharply inhaling the breath, and suddenly closing the throat (as by *k'*) and at the same time sharply closing the lips, and re-opening them without allowing the breath to touch them, but letting it free passage through the mouth :—thus a half *p* is produced.

SECTION III.—OF ACCENTUATION.

All monosyllabic words, when doubled, have the accent on the last syllable; as *dāl, dadā́l*. This is also the case when the "mutual" *p* is inserted; as *dāl, dapā́l*.

In words of two syllables the penultima is generally accented; as *kó̦ṅka, sérma*. An exception to this rule attends the four semi-consonants; as *rehet', chaháp', raréch', senok'*. Also words ending in a diphthong; as *sarháo*. And finally, words terminating in *ń ; tehéń, seréń* Besides these there are many other exceptions.

Words of three syllables are not very common in the Santal language, and when occurring, the accent varies ; as *pắriu pợrắeni, sariắo.*

Jingling words of four syllables retain the accent they have, when separate.

By the declension of nouns the accent is not altered.

In the conjugation, the vowel preceding the semi-consonants *k'* and *t'*, is accented. But when those inspirations are followed by a vowel, and *k'* consequently changes into *g*, and *t'* into *d*, then the succeeding vowel has the accent ; as *dāl két' ;* dalkedéa.

SECTION IV.—OF THE PERMUTATION OF LETTERS.

The four semi-consonants, when followed by a vowel, are, as above mentioned, changed into the respective softer sounds, *viz. k'* into *g*, *ch'* into *j*, *t'* into *d*, and *p'* into *b*. An exception from this rule is, that where one of those semi-consonants is followed by *a* it ought *not* to be changed into the softer sound. It is true, that many Santals do not adhere to this rule, but the best-speaking Santals do, and analogy shows, that it ought to be done ; as *dālakắt'a,* instead of *dālakada.*

o, is sometimes changed into *w*, and *e* into *y*, *i. e.* when they are inserted between two vowels ; as *heoa*=hewa, *taea* =taya.

CHAPTER II.

OF NOUNS.

To Nouns belong Gender, Number, Case and Declension.

SECTION I.—OF GENDER.

The genders are three, masculine, feminine and neuter.

The names of males are masculine; the names of females, feminine; and the names of inanimate objects, neuter.

The Santals have three methods of distinguishing sex, *viz.*

a. By difference of words; as *herel,* a man; *mai̥ju,* a woman; *aṇḍia,* a male; *eṅga,* a female.

b. By difference of termination; as *koṛa,* a boy; *koṛi,* a girl.

c. By prefixing a word indicative of the gender; as *aṇḍia kūl,* a tiger; *eṅga kūl,* a tigress.

SECTION II.—OF NUMBER.

Santal nouns have three numbers, *viz.* Singular, Dual and Plural. The dual is formed by adding *kin,* and the plural, by adding *ko* to the root. The neuter receives also *kin* in the dual, and *ko* in the plural.

SECTION III.—OF CASE.

The Santal noun has properly speaking no cases, at least not in the classical sense, as the word never changes, but takes various affixes which give the required meaning; still, those affixes being so constantly used, they may be regarded as forming cases, thus facilitating the comprehension of the European student.

By those affixes eight cases may be formed, *viz.* the Nominative, the Genitive or Possessive, the Instrumental, the Dative, the Accusative or Objective, the Ablative, the Locative, and the Vocative.

The nominative is the *root.*

The genitive is formed by affixing to the root *ren,* or *ak̔,* or *aṅ,* or *reak̔,* or *reaṅ.* The first of these is used, when the succeeding noun designates an animate object, whereas the four last are used, when the following noun is a neuter. *Ren* is formed from *re,* in, and *on,* that (as in *on-i, on-kin, on-ko, on-parom*)=*re-on*=ren; as *Iṅ-re-on-ko*=Iṅrenko—, and *ak̔* is formed from *a,* at, to, and *k̔,* which latter is the sign of the neuter, as shown when *a,* at, to, is used in connection with the verb; as *em-a-e-a-ko: em,* to give, *a,* to, *e,* him, *a,* it, or it is, *ko,* they=they will give him, or *lit.* to give to him it is they. In the above example the *a* is undoubtedly a preposition, and the *e* the 3rd. person singular. *Dak̔-ak̔-me!* *dak̔,* water, *a,* to, at, *k̔* it (neuter), *me,* thou (imperative)=water to it thou=water it! (*i. e.* the tree). *Aṅ* comes from *a* at, to, and *ṅ*, sign of the neuter like *k̔*. *Reak̔* comes from *re*, in, and *ak̔*, and *reaṅ* comes from *re*, in, and *aṅ* (*vide* declensions of Pronouns).

The instrumental case is formed by *te*, into, *ho̱tete* by means of, or *ṭhen* or *ṭhech̔*, which two latter come from *ṭhãi*, a place.

The dative case is formed by adding *ṭhen, ṭhech̔* to the nominative.

The accusative is like the nominative.

The ablative is formed by *kho̱n, kho̱ch̔, kho̱nak̔*, from.

The locative is formed by *re* in, on, or *talare*, in the midst, or *mo̱to̱re*, among.

The vocative is formed by prefixing interjections such as *e̱ !, e̱ho ! O !*

It will be seen by the above, that the genitive, instrumental and dative are really all locatives.

SECTION IV.—OF DECLENSION.

The Santal language may be said to have three declensions, one belonging to masculine and feminine, and the other two to the neuter. Their respective terminations are as follows:—

	I. Declension.	II. Declension.	III. Declension.
Nom.	——	——	——
Gen.	*ren*	*reak̇, ak̇, reaṅ, aṅ*	*reak̇, ak̇, reaṅ, aṅ*
Instr.	*ṭhen, te, hotete*	*te*	*te*
Dat.	*ṭhen*	*ṭhen, theck̇*	*te*
Acc.	——	——	——
Abl.	*khon*	*khon, khonak̇, khock̇*	*khon, khonak̇, khock̇*
Loc.	*re*	*re*	*re*
Voc.	*e!*	*e!*	*e!*

The only difference between these three declensions is, that the instrumental of the first declension generally has *ṭhen;* as *koṛa ṭhen e dalocholena,* he was struck by the boy, and that the dative in the second declension has *ṭhen,* whereas in the third it has *te.*

Te, is however also used to form the instrumental in the first declension.

FIRST DECLENSION.

Singular.

Nom.	*Koṛa,*	the boy.
Gen.	*Koṛa-ren,*	of the boy (as the mother—)
Instr.	*Koṛa-ṭhen, te, hotete,*	by the boy.
Dat.	*Koṛa-ṭhen,*	to the boy.
Acc.	*Koṛa,*	the boy.
Abl.	*Koṛa-khon, khonak̇,*	from the boy.
Loc.	*Koṛa-re,*	in, on the boy.
Voc.	*e Koṛa!*	O, boy!

Dual

Nom.	*Koṛakin,*	the two boys.
Gen.	*Koṛakin-ren,**	of the two boys.
Instr.	*Koṛakin-ṭhen, te, hotete,*	by the two boys.
Dat.	*Koṛakin-ṭhen,*	to the two boys.
Acc.	*Koṛakin,*	the two boys.
Abl.	*Koṛakin-khon,*	from the two boys.
Loc.	*Koṛakin-re,*	in, on the two boys.
Voc.	*e Koṛakin,*	O, two boys!

Plural.

Nom.	*Koṛako,*	the boys.
Gen.	*Koṛako-ren,**	of the boys.
Instr.	*Koṛako-ṭhen, te, hotete,*	by the boys.
Dat.	*Koṛako-ṭhen,*	to the boys.
Acc.	*Koṛako,*	the boys.
Abl.	*Koṛako-khon,*	from the boys.
Loc.	*Koṛako-re,*	in, on the boys.
Voc.	*e Koṛako!*	O, boys!

SECOND DECLENSION.

Singular.

Nom.	*Ṭaṅga,*	the axe.
Gen.	*Ṭaṅga-reak',* etc.,†	of the axe (as the iron of—)

* If the succeeding noun is to express a duality, then *kin* is added to *ren* and if a plurality, then *ko is* added.

† It must be borne in mind, that the succeeding noun (in the nominative) decides whether *ren*, or *reak'* shall be used, not the word to which the genitive sign is affixed. When the succeeding noun (in the nominative) is an animate object, then *ren* is used, whether the word in the genitive be ani-

B

Instr. *Ṭaṅga-te,* by, with, the axe.
Dat. *Ṭaṅga-ṭhen,* to the axe.
Acc. *Ṭaṅga,* the axe.
Abl. *Ṭaṅga-khon, khoc̆,* etc., from the axe.
Loc. *Ṭaṅga-re,* in, on the axe.
Voc. *e Ṭaṅga!* O, axe!

Dual.

Nom. *Ṭaṅgakin,* the two axes.
Gen. *Ṭaṅgakin-reak̆,* etc., of the two axes.
Instr. *Ṭaṅgakin-te,* by the two axes.
Dat. *Ṭaṅgakin-ṭhen,* to the two axes.
Acc. *Ṭaṅgakin,* the two axes.
Abl. *Ṭaṅgakin-khon,* etc., from the two axes.
Loc. *Ṭaṅgakin-re,* in, on the two axes.
Voc. *e Ṭaṅgakin!* O, two axes!

Plural.

Nom. *Ṭaṅgako,* the axes.
Gen. *Ṭaṅgako-reak̆,* etc., of the axes.
Instr. *Ṭaṅgako-te,* by the axes.
Dat. *Ṭaṅgako-ṭhen,* to the axes.
Acc. *Ṭaṅgako,* the axes.
Abl. *Ṭaṅgako-khon,* etc., from the axes.
Loc. *Ṭaṅgako-re,* in, on the axes.
Voc. *e Ṭaṅgako,* O, axes!

---

mate or inanimate; and when the succeeding noun is a neuter, then *ren* cannot be used, even if the noun in genitive is an animate object.

THIRD DECLENSION.

Singular.

Nom.	*Buru,*	the mountain.
Gen.	*Buru-reaḱ, ren,* etc.,	of the mountain.
Instr.	*Buru-te,*	by the mountain.
Dat.	*Buru-te,*	to the mountain.
Acc.	*Buru,*	the mountain.
Abl.	*Buru-khon,* etc.,	from the mountain.
Loc.	*Buru-re,*	in, on the mountain.
Voc.	*e Buru!*	O, mountain!

Dual.

Nom.	*Burukin,*	the two mountains.
Gen.	*Burukin-reaḱ,* etc.,	of the two mountains.
Instr.	*Burukin-te,*	by the two mountains.
Dat.	*Burukin-te,*	to the two mountains.
Acc.	*Burukin,*	the two mountains.
Abl.	*Burukin-khon,*	from the two mountains.
Loc.	*Burukin-re,*	in, on the two mountains.
Voc.	*e Burukin!*	O, two mountains!

Plural.

Nom.	*Buruko,*	the mountains.
Gen.	*Buruko-reaḱ,* etc.,	of the mountains.
Instr.	*Buruko-te,*	by the mountains.
Dat.	*Buruko-te,*	to the mountains.
Acc.	*Buruko,*	the mountains.
Abl.	*Buruko-khon,* etc.,	from the mountains.

Loc. *Buruko-re*, in, on the mountains.
Voc. *e̱ Buruko*! O, mountains!

CHAPTER III.

OF ADJECTIVES.

SECTION I.—OF GENDER.

Adjectives sometimes vary in gender and number, but not in case. A number of adjectives terminate in *a*, when used in connection with a masculine, and in *i*, when in connection with a feminine; as *lelha koṛa*, a foolish boy; *lelhi koṛi*, a foolish girl. Besides this the adjectives make no distinction of gender.

SECTION II.—OF THE COMPARISON OF ADJECTIVES.

Santal adjectives are not compared by regular inflexions, but by affixing the ablative termination *kho̱n* to the word which in English would be preceded by *than*, in order to form the comparative; as *iṅ-kho̱n amem maraṅa*, you are greater than I; andby prefixing *sanamkho̱n*, in order to form the superlative; as *sanamkho̱n onie maraṅa*, he is greater than all=greatest. The comparative is sometimes expressed by *arhõ*, more; as *oni arhõe maraṅa*, he is greater; and the superlative is often formed by *utạr*, exceedingly; as *oni do maraṅ utạr*, or *sanam kho̱n maraṅ utạr*, he is greatest.

SECTION III.—OF NUMERICAL ADJECTIVES.

The Santals are not far advanced in mathematics, their numerals only amounting to twenty.

	CARDINALS.	ORDINALS.
1	mit́, *one.*	laha-ren* *or* reaḱ, *the first.*
2	bārea *or* bar, *two* &c.	laha-tayom-ren, reaḱ, *or* tala-ren.
3	pēa *or* pe.	talatayom-ren, reaḱ, *or* bāreatayom-ren
4	po̱nea *or* po̱n.	peatayom-ren, reaḱ.
5	mo̱ṛe.	po̱neatayom-ren, reaḱ.
6	tūrui.	mo̱ṛetayom-ren, reaḱ.
7	ēae.	turui tayom-ren, reaḱ.
8	irāl.	ēae tayom-ren, reaḱ.
9	āre.	iral tayom-ren, reaḱ.
10	gēl.	are tayom-ren, reaḱ.
11	gēlmit́.	gēl tayom-ren, reaḱ.
12	gēlbarea *or* gēlbar.	gēlmit́ tayom-ren, reaḱ.
13	gēlpēa *or* gēlpe.	gēlbar tayom-ren, reaḱ.
14	gēlpo̱nea, *or* gēlpo̱n.	gēlpe tayom-ren, reaḱ.
15	gēlmo̱ṛe.	gēlpo̱n tayom-ren, reaḱ.
16	gēltūrui.	gēlmo̱ṛe tayom-ren, reaḱ.
17	gēlēae.	gēlturui tayom-ren, reaḱ.
18	gēlirāl.	gēlēae tayom-ren, reaḱ.
19	gēlāre.	gēlirāl tayom-ren, reaḱ.
20	mit́isi.	gēlāre tayom-ren, reaḱ.

* When the succeeding noun is an animate object, then *ren* is used, and when an innimate object, then *reak'*, *ak'*, *reaṅ*, or *aṅ* are used.

By combination the Santals may count so far as upward to 400; as *mit' isi* 20, *bar isi*, 40, *pe isi* 60, *pon isi* 80, *mõre isi* 100, *turui isi* 120 etc. The Santals do not say three tens= thirty, but *mit'isi gēl*, one twenty and ten=30, etc. Upwards from twenty they say; *mit'isi mit'* 21, *mit'isi barea* 22: mit'si *pēa* 23, etc.

MISCELLANEOUS REMARKS ON THE ADJECTIVES.

By affixing the pronominal suffixes, any adjective may become a verb, and be conjugated through the different tenses and moods; as *marań*, great; *marań meań*, I shall make you great; *marań ok kanae*, he is making himself great.

The oblique cases may also be conjugated as a verb; as *ińrenkedeań*, I made him mine; *ackthenkedeae*, he made him his adherent.

NOTE.—From ten, instead of saying gelmit' &c., gēl khon mit' &c., may be used.

CHAPTER IV.

OF PRONOUNS.

Pronouns are of six kinds, Personal, Possessive, Demonstrative, Interrogative, Relative, and Indefinite; all of which have three numbers, *viz.*, the Singular, Dual and the Plural.

SECTION I.—OF PERSONAL PRONOUNS.

The personal pronouns have two forms, the full and the abridged, the latter of which may be annexed to any part of speech.

FULL PRONOUNS.

Singular.	*Dual.*	*Plural.*
1 *Iń*, I.	*Aliń*, *Alań*, we two.	*Ale*, *Abon*, *Abo*, we
2 *Am*, thou.	*Aben*, you two.	*Ape*, you.
3 *Ack*, self.	*Akin*, they two. them-selves.	*Ako*, they themselves
4 *Oni*,* he or she	*Onkin*, they two.	*Onko*, they.
Neuter *Ona*, it	*Onakin*, they two.	*Onako*, they.

Alań in the Dual, and *abon* and *abo* in the Plural are used, when the person addressed is *included*; whereas *aliń* in the Dual and *ale* in the Plural are used, when the person addressed is *excluded*.

* Oni, Onkin and Onko, are strictly speaking demonstrative pronouns from *on*, that, and *i*, *kin*, *ko*.

*Acĥ** self, is sometimes incorrectly written *ai*, as there is no *i* in the word, but the *i*-like sound is produced by the semi-consonant *cĥ* being a palatal. *Acĥ*, self, is only used in the 3rd person. For the 1st and 2nd person there is no special form for *self*, but the personal pronouns with the addition of *tege*, are used as substitutes, when requisite.

The Santals have no honorific pronouns, neither do they use the plural of the personal pronouns as such, in the way it is used in other languages; and yet they use both Dual and Plural in addressing a single person, but in a very peculiar and rather patriarchal way. The Dual is used between the son or daughter-in-law, and their respective father and mother-in-law, and all the older members of the family;† and the Plural is used between the husband's and wife's parents, and their brothers and sisters with their respective wives and husbands.

But the most strange of all is, that the addressed person answers in the same number; as *duṛup'ben Jawae!* sit (*lit.* you two) down, son-in-law. *Maliṅ* (not *laṅ* or *iṅ*) *duṛup'a*, yes, I (*lit.* we two) will sit down. *Duṛup'pe sumdhi!* sit (*lit.* many of you) down, my child's father-in-law. *Male* (not *bon* or *bo* or *iṅ*) *duṛup'kana*, yes, I (*lit.* we many) am sitting down.

When two persons, being parents-in-law, speak about themselves, they do not use *laṅ*, as every body else would do,

* Dual Akin, and Plural Ako.

† As elder brothers and sisters with their wives and husbands, etc.

but thy use *bon*, or *bo;* as, *e sumdhi, oṛakte bon chalaka, sebon baṅa.* O, my child's father-in-law, shall we (you and I (lit. we all) go home or not ?

I cannot account for this singular way of using the dual and plural otherwise, than by assuming that it has sprung from the very correct notion of the husband and wife being *one* inseparable duality, so that when one is addressed, the other ought to be included; that the husband and wife suppose their respective parents, and elder brothers and sisters-in-law, etc. to be so *entirely* one with the person they have married, that when they address any of them they include that person and use the dual; and that when parents-in-law address each other (or each others brothers and sisters with their respective wives and husbands) they think each other so interested in, and one with the married couple and their children, that they mentally combine them all with one person and use the plural.

The Dual is never used to those who are younger than the married persons.

Persons, who are not related to one another may also by mutual agreement address one another in the above manner.

DECLENSION OF THE FULL PERSONAL PRONOUN

(vide Declension of nouns.)

1st *Person Singular.*

Nom.	*Iń*, I.
Gen.	*Iń-ren,* renkin, renko; ak̓, ań, reak̓, reań*, my, mine.
Instr.	*Iń-te, hotete, ṭhen, ṭhek̓*, by me.
Dat.	*Iń-ṭhen, ṭhek̓, sen, sek̓*, to or near or from me.
Acc.	*Iń*, me.
Abl.	*Iń-khon, khonak̓ khok̓*, from me.
Loc.	*Iń-re, talare*, in, on me.

2nd Person.

Nom.	*Am*, Thou.
Gen.	*Am-ren, renkin, renko; ak̓, ań, reak̓, reań* thy, thine.
Instr.	*Am-te, hotete, ṭhen, ṭhek̓*, by thee.
Dat.	*Am-ṭhen, thek̓, sen, sek̓*, to thee.
Acc.	*Am*, thee.
Abl.	*Am-khon, khonak̓*, from thee.
Loc.	*Am-re, talare*, in, on thee.

3rd Person.

Nom.	*Ak̓*† self.
Gen.	*Ak̓-ren, renkin, renko ; ak̓, ań, reak̓, reań*, own.
Instr.	*Ak̓-te, hotete, ṭhen, thek̓*, by self.
Dat.	*Ak̓-ṭhen, ṭhek̓, sen, sek̓*, to self.

---

* Ren. (dual renkin and plural renko) is used, when the succeeding nominative is an animate object, whereas all the others denote inanimate objects

† Oni and ona declined in the same way.

Acc. *Ach*, self.

Abl. *Ach-khonak*, from self.

Loc. *Ach-re, talare*, in, on self.

1st *Person, Dual.*

Nom. *Aliń*, or *alań*, we two.

Gen. *Aliń-ren, renkin, renko; ak, ań, reak, reań*, our, ours.

Instr. *Aliń-te, hotete, then, thech*, by us two.

Dat. *Aliń-then, thech, sen, sech*, to us two.

Acc. *Aliń*, us two.

Abl. *Aliń-khon, khonak*, from us two.

Loc. *Aliń-re, talare*, in, on us two.

2nd *Person.*

Nom. *Aben*, you two.

Gen. *Aben-ren, renkin, renko; ak, ań, reak, reań*, your, yours.

Instr. *Aben-te, hotete, then, thech*, you two.

Dat. *Aben-then, thech, sen, sech*, to you two.

Acc. *Aben*, you two.

Abl. *Aben-khon, khonak*, from you two.

Loc. *Aben-re, talare'* in, on you two.

3rd *Person.*

Nom. *Akin*, they two themselves.

Gen. *Akin-ren, renkin, renko; ak, ań, reań, reak*, their own.

Instr. *Akin-te, hotete, then, thech*, by themselves.

Dat. *Akin-ṭhen, ṭhek̓*, to themselves.

Acc. *Akin*, themselves.

Abl. *Akin-kho̱n, kho̱nak̓*, from themselves.

Loc. *Akin-re, talare*, in, on themselves.

1st *Person, Plural.*

Nom. *Ale, abon* or *abo*, we.

Gen. *Ale-ren, renkin, renko ; ak̓, aṅ, reak̓, reaṅ*, our, ours.

Instr. *Ale-te, ho̱tete, ṭhen, ṭhek̓*, by us.

Dat. *Ale-ṭhen, ṭhek̓, sen, sek̓*, to us.

Acc. *Ale*, us.

Abl. *Ale-kho̱n, khonak̓*, from us.

Loc. *Ale-re, talare*, in, on us.

2nd *Person.*

Nom. *Ape*, you.

Gen. *Ape-ren, renkin, renko ; ak̓, aṅ, reak̓, reaṅ*, you yours.

Instr. *Ape-te, ho̱tete, ṭhen, ṭhek̓*, by you.

Dat. *Ape-ṭhen, ṭhek̓, sen, sek̓*, to you.

Acc. *Ape*, you.

Abl. *Ape-kho̱n, kho̱nak̓*, from you.

Loc. *Ape-re, talare*, in, on you.

3rd *Person.*

Nom. *Ako*, they themselves.

Gen. *Ako-ren, renkin, renko; ak̓, aṅ, reak̓*, their own.

Instr. *Ako-te, ho̱tete, ṭhen ṭhek̓*, by themselves.

Dat.	*Ako-ṭhen, ṭheck, sen, seck,* to themselves.
Acc.	*Ako,* themselves.
Abl.	*Ako-khon, khonak,* from themselves.
Loc.	*Ako-re, talare,* in, on themselves.

SUFFIXES, OR ABRIDGED PRONOUNS.

	Singular.		*Dual.*		*Plural.*	
1.	*ń,*	I	*liń* or *lań,*	we two.	*le, bon, bo,*	we.
2.	*m,*	thou	*ben,*	you two.	*pe*	you.
3.	*e,*	he or she.	*kin,*	they two.	*ko*	they.

When the words to which these suffixes are annexed terminate in a consonant, the full pronoun is used in the 1st person Singular, and an *e* is either prefixed or affixed to the 2nd person Singular.

They are declined as follows :—

1st *Person.*

	Singular.	*Dual.*	*Plural.*
Nom.	*ń,* I.	*liń, lań,* we two.	*le, bon, bo,* we.
Gen.	*t-i-ń,* My.	*ta-liń, ta-lań,* our.	*tale, ta-bon, ta-bo,* our.
Dat.	*a-ń,* to or for me.	*a-liń, a-lań,* to, or for us two.	*a-le, a-bon, a-bo,* to or for us.
Acc.	*ń,* or *iń,* me.	*liń, lań,* us two.	*le, bon, bo,* us.

2nd Person.

N. *m* or *em*, thou.	*ben*, you two.	*pe*, you.
G. *ta-m*, thy.	*ta-ben*, your (two.)	*ta-pe*, your.
D. *a-m*, to or for thee.	*a-ben*, to or for you two.	*a-pe*, to or for you.
Ac. *m* or *me*, thee.	*ben*, you two.	*pe*, you.

3rd Person.

N. *e*, he, she.	*kin*, they two.	*ko*, they.
G. *ta-e*, his, her.	*ta-kin*, their (two.)	*ta-ko*, their.
D. *a-e*, to or for his or her.	*a-kin*, to for or them two.	*a-ko*, to or for them.
Ac. *e*, him, her.	*kin*, them two.	*ko*, them.

SECTION II.—OF POSSESSIVE PRONOUNS.

These are supplied by the genitive case of the full personal pronouns.

1st Person, Singular.

N. *Iṅren*,* *Iṅak̓*, *Iṅaṅ*, *Iṅreak̓*, *Iṅreaṅ*, my, mine.
G. *Iṅren-reak̓*, *or Iṅreak̓,-ren*, etc., of my or mine.

---

* In the dual renkin and in the plural renko is used, though not always, as the sign of number is often added to the succeeding word; as *iṅren hoponе ṅama, amren hoponkin ṅama, iṅren hopon ko ṅama.*

These pronouns are used both as adjectives and substantives.

Instr.	*Ińren-te, hotete, then*, or *Ińreak-te*, by mine.	
Dat.	*Ińren-then* or *Ińreak-te*, to mine.	
Acc.	*Ińren, Ińreak, my*.	
Abl.	*Ińren-khon*, or *Ińreak-khon* or *khonak*, from mine.	
Loc.	*Inren-re, talare*, or *Ińreak-re, talare*, in or on mine.	

2nd Person.

Nom.	*Amren, Amak*, etc.,	thy, thine.
Gen.	*Amren-reak*, etc.,	of thine.
Instr.	*Amren-te*, etc.,	by thine.
Dat.	*Amren-then*, etc.,	to thine.
Acc.	*Amren, Amreak*, etc.,	thine.
Abl.	*Amren-khon*, etc.,	from thine.
Loc.	*Amren-re*, etc.,	in, on thine.

3rd Person.

Nom.	*Acren, Acreak*, etc.,	his or her own.
Gen.	*Acren-reak*, etc.,	of his own.
Instr.	*Acren-te, then*, etc.,	by his own.
Dat.	*Acren-then*, etc.,	to his own.
Acc.	*Acren, Acreak*, etc.,	his or her own.
Abl.	*Acren-khon*, etc.,	from his own.
Loc.	*Acren-re*, etc.,	in, on his own.

1st Person, Dual.

Nom.	*Alińren** *Alań reak, alińak*, etc.,	our, ours	(two)
Gen.	*Alińren-reak* or *alań reak-ren*, etc.,	of ours	"
Instr.	*Alińren-te* or *alińreakte*, etc.,	by ours	"

* Or Dual Alińrenkin, and Plural Aliń renko. (vide note on the preceding page.)

Dat.	*Alińren-ṭhen,* or *alińreaḱ-ṭhen,*	to ours	(two)
Acc.	*Alińren, aliń reaḱ*	our, ours	〃
Abl.	*Alińren-kho̱n,* or *alińreaḱ-kho̱n,*	from ours	〃
Loc.	*Alińren-re,* or *alińreaḱ-re,*	in, on ours	〃

2nd Person.

Nom.	*Aben ren, abenreaḱ,* etc.,	your, yours	(two)
Gen.	*Aben ren-reaḱ,* etc.,	of yours	〃
Instr.	*Abenren-te,* etc.,	by yours	〃
Dat.	*Abenren-ṭhen,* etc.,	to yours	〃
Acc.	*Abenren, abenreaḱ* etc.,	your, yours	〃
Abl.	*Abenren kho̱n,* etc.,	from yours	〃
Loc.	*Abenren-re,* etc.,	in, on yours	〃

3rd Person.

Nom.	*Akinren, akin reaḱ,* etc.,	their own	(two)
Gen.	*Akinren-reaḱ,* etc.,	of their own	〃
Instr.	*Akínren-te, ṭhen,* etc.,	by their own	〃
Dat.	*Akinren-ṭhen,* etc.,	to their own	〃
Acc.	*Akinren, akin reaḱ,*	their own	〃
Abl.	*Akinren-kho̱n,* etc.,	from their own	〃
Loc.	*Akinren-re,* etc.,	in, on their own	〃

1st Person Plural.

Nom.	*Aleren,* alereaḱ,* etc.,	our, ours.
Gen.	*Aleren-reaḱ,* or *alereaḱren,* etc.,	of ours.
Instr.	*Aleren-te, ṭhen,* or *alereaḱ-te,* etc.,	by ours.
Dat.	*Aleren-ṭhen* or *alereaḱ-ṭhen,*	to ours.
Acc.	*Aleren, alereaḱ,* ete.,	our, ours.
Abl.	*Aleren-kho̱n,* or *alereaḱ-kho̱n,*	from ours.
Loc.	*Aleren-re* or *alereaḱ-re,* etc.,	in, on ours.

2nd Person.

Nom.	*Aperen, apereak̇,** etc.,	your, yours.
Gen.	*Aperen-reak̇*, or *apereak̇-ren*, etc.,	of yours.
Instr.	*Aperen-te, ṭhen*, or *apereak̇-te*, etc.,	by yours.
Dat.	*Aperen-ṭhen*, or *apereak̇-ṭhen*, etc.,	to yours.
Acc.	*Aperen, apereak̇*, etc.,	your, yours.
Abl.	*Aperen-khon*, or *apereak̇-khon*,	from yours.
Loc.	*Aperen-re*, or *apereak̇-re*,	in, on yours.

3rd Person.

Nom.	*Akoren, akoreak̇*, etc.,	their own.
Gen.	*Akoren-reak̇*, or *akoreak̇-ren*,	of their own.
Instr.	*Akoren-te*, or *akoreak̇te*,	by their own.
Datv.	*Akoren-ṭhen*, or *akoreak̇-ṭhen*,	to their own.
Acc.	*Akoren-akoreak̇* etc.,	their own.
Abl.	*Akoren-khon*, or *akoreak̇-khon*,	from their own.
Loc.	*Akoren-re*, or *akoreak̇-re*,	in, on their own.

Ren, as already mentioned, denotes that the following noun is an animate abject; as *Iṅren hopon* my son. If the following noun is in the dual, then *kin* is added to it, and if in the plural, then *ko;* as *Iṅrenkin hopon*, my two sons; *Iṅren ko hopon*, my sons. On the south side of the Damuda river, towards Orissa, the singular has also a suffix, namely *ick̇;* as *Iṅrenick̇ hopon*, my son.

Ak̇, aṅ, reak̇, reaṅ are used when the following noun is a neuter; as *Iṅak̇ ṭaṅga*, my axe etc. Amongst old people

* Remarks.—The first is used, when the Nominative is animate, and the second, when it is inanimate.

re is sometimes used instead of *ren*; as *bohure eṅgat,* the bride's mother.

The genitive case of the suffixes, although its principal use is in connection with the verb, is often employed in connection with nouns; as *oṛaḱtiń,* my house.

But Santals very often dispense with possessive pronouns altogether, and simply use the personal pronouns to express that relation; as *hopon iń* or *ińhopon,* my son; *am hopon,* thy son, etc.

Another possessive form *tet'* † is often used in connection with nouns, which makes no distinction between gender and number; as *hopon tet',* his or their son; *ḍartet',* its branch.

In accordance with the possessive case, the instrumental, ablative, and dative cases are also declined. *Ren* is formed from the locative *re,* ἐν, by affixing an *n,* which shows the object to be animate. *Te,* εἰς, is also changed into *ten* for the same reason; *ṭhen* comes from *ṭhãi* a place.

The Instrumental case.

Nom. *Ińhoteten,* or *Ińhotete,* the one* through or by me.
Gen. *Ińhoteten-ren, reaḱ,* or *Ińhotete-ren, reaḱ,* of the one by me.
Instr. *Ińhoteten-te,* etc., by the one through me.

---

* When *kin* or *ko* are affixed to *ten,* or *ṭhen,* then of course "ones" must be written. *Ińhoteten,* and *Ińṭhen* are used as substantives.

† This *tet'* is also used as a difinite article; as *hoṛtet'* do *bugigia,* the man is good. At other times it is used like itself; as *atotet'regi* in the village itself.

Dat. *Iṅhoteten-ṭhen*, etc., to the one through me.
Acc. *Iṅhoteten*, *Iṅhotete*, etc., the one through me.
Abl. *Iṅhoteten-khon*, from the one through me.
Loc. *Iṅhoteten-re*, in the one through me.

The Dative case:

Nom. *Iṅṭhen*, the one near me.
Gen. *Iṅṭhen-ren or reak'*, etc., of the one near me.
Instr. *Iṅṭhen-te*, by the one near me.
Dat. *Iṅṭhen-ṭhen*, to the one near me.
Acc. *Iṅṭhen*, the one near me,
Abl. *Iṅṭhen-khon*, from the one near me or from near me.
Loc. *Iṅṭhen-re*, in the one near me.

The Ablative case has only *Iṅkhon ren*, which is declined like *Iṅren*; as *Iṅkhonrente*, by the one of (them) from me, etc. The genitive case of the instrumental and dative cases is also declined like *Iṅren*; as *Iṅhoteteren ṭhen* to the one of (them) through me; *Iṅṭhenrente*, by the one of (them) near me. In fact these cases may be declined, and re-declined *ad infinitum*.

SECTION III.—OF DEMONSTRATIVE PRONOUNS.

Singular.	*Dual.*	*Plural.*
Noi,* this (near).	*Nokin*, these two.	*Noko*, these.
Oni, that (farther distant or absent).	*Onkin*, those two.	*Onko*, those.

* This *o* in *noi* sounds very much like an oo (ù)—in fact many Santhals pronounce ǔni (oonee).

Honi, that (still farther distant).	*Honkin*, those two.	*Honko*, those.
Hani, that (furthest distant).	*Hankin*, those two.	*Hanko*, those.
Ni, this (same) (near).	*Nikin*, these two.	*Niko*, these.
Ini, that (further distant.) [distant.)	*Inkin*, these two.	*Inko*, those.
Hini, that (furthest	*Hinkin*, those two.	*Hinko*, those.
Noa, this (near) (neuter.) [tant.)	*Noakin*, these two.	*Noako*, these.
Ona, that (further dis-	*Onakin*, those two.	*Onako*, those.
Hona, that (still further distant.)	*Honakin*, those two.	*Honako*, those.
Hana, that (furthest distant.)	*Hanakin*, those two.	*Hanako*, those.
Nia, this (same) (near).	*Niakin*, these two.	*Niako*, these.
Ina, that (further distant.) [distance.)	*Inakin*, those two.	*Inako*, those.
Hina, that (furthest	*Hinakin*, those two.	*Hinako*, those.

The first seven of these pronouns relate to animate objects ; and the last seven to inanimate ones.

These pronouns may be used both as adjectives and substantives.

Nonkan, such as this one, etc.	*Nonkankin*, such as these two.	*Nonkanko*, such as these.
Onkan, such as that.	*Onkankin*, " "	*Onkanko*, " "
Honkan, such as that.	*Honkankin*, " "	*Honkanko*, "

Hankan, such as that.	*Hankankin*, . .	*Hankanko*, . .
Nenkan, such as this.	*Nenkankin*, . .	*Nenkanko*, . .
Enkan, such as that.	*Enkankin*, . .	*Enkanko*, . .
Henkan, such as that.	*Henkankin*, . .	*Henkanko*, .
Nonkanak', such as this.	*Nonkanak'kin*, .	*Nonkanak'ko*, .
Onkanak', such as that.	*Onkanak'kin*, .	*Onkanak'ko*, .
Honkanak', such as that.	*Honkanak'kin*, .	*Honkanak'ko*, .
Hankanak', such as that.	*Hankanak'kin*, .	*Hankanak'ko*, .
Nenkanak', such as this.	*Nenkanak'kin*, .	*Nenkanak'ko*, .
Enkanak', such as that.	*Enkanak'kin*, .	*Enkanak'ko*, .
Henkanak', such as that.	*Henkanak'kin*, .	*Henkanak'ko*, .

In the last seven pronouns *ak'*, added to *kan* to denote the neuter, may be dispensed with, as also *nonkan, onkan*, etc., may be used as neuter. These pronouns may be used both as adjectives and substantives.

SECTION IV—OF INTERROGATIVE PRONOUNS.

Singular.	*Dual.*	*Plural.*
Okoe? who?	*Okoekin?* what?	*Okoeko?* who?
Chele? what?	*Ohelekin?* what?	*Cheleko?* what?
Oka? which?	*Okakin?* which?	*Okako?* which?
Chet'? what?	*Chet'kin?* what?	*Chet'ko?* what?

The two first of these apply to animate objects, and the two last to inanimate ones. They are all declined like the personal pronouns.

SECTION V.—OF RELATIVE PRONOUNS.

The Santal language has no special relative pronouns for animate objects, but supplies their place by the personal (full and abridged), the interrogative, and demonstrative pronouns; as *holako heclLlen, onkodo okaena?* they who came yesterday, what has become of them? what has become of them who came yesterday? *Hopon em rānade tae, oni joharam lagit'e hecLakana,* whose son you gave medicine to, he has come to thank you. *Enbetarem rānade, oni do phariaoena,* to whom you gave medicine at that time, he has recovered. *Hola jēlem kiriṅkede oni do okare menaea?* the deer which you bought yesterday, where is it?

Here are four examples, one for each of the four cases in connection with the verb.

The interrogative pronouns *chele* and *chet'* are never used as relatives, only *okoe* and *oka* or *okaṭa* are used as such; as *okoe ṅaṅam ko senakan, onie hejuLkana,* whom they have gone in search of, he is coming. *oni kiriṅem metadiṅ onie gocLena,* whom you told me to buy, he has died. The *interrogative* pronouns are used as relatives, when the object is *uncertain*, whereas the *personal* and *demonstrative* pronouns are used as such, when the object is *certain;* as *okoeko daṛeaLa, onko ko tūlma,* they who are (may be) able, let them lift. *Onko ko daṛeaLa, onko baṛe tūlochoakom,* they who are (in reality) able, let (allow) them (to) lift. Instead of relative pronouns the numerous participles and gerunds are extensively used; *as ńēldāllede ko onkoko men dareak'a, iń do bań baraeet'a,* they who saw him strike, they are (will be) able to say; I do not know. *Hola hećlen ko hor, on ko do okaena?* what has become of the people who came yesterday?

In the neuter the pronoun is often dropped altogether; as *holam agulet', onado okare?* where is that which you brought yesterday?

There is another class of pronouns implying that the object is neuter, which combine demonstrative and relative meaning, and are indeclinable. They are as follows:—

Singular.		*Dual.*		*Plural.*	
nok'oe,	this which	*nok'oekin,*	these two wh.	*nok'oeko,*	these wh.
one,	that "	*onekin,*	those two "	*oneko,*	those "
hone,	that "	*honekin,*	those two "	*honeko,*	those "
hane,	that "	*hanekin,*	those two "	*haneko,*	those "
neke,	this "	*nekekin,*	these two "	*nekeko,*	these "
ene,	that "	*enekin,*	those two "	*eneko,*	those "
hene,	that "	*henekin,*	those two "	*heneko,*	those "

These pronouns are very often succeeded by the demonstratives; as *one onam agulet',* that which thou didst bring, etc.

The same difference exists between *nok'oe* and *neke, one* and *ene,* and *hone, hane* and *hene,* as between *noi* and *ni, onkan* and *enkan,* etc.

SECTION VI.—OF INDEFINITE PRONOUNS.

The following are some of the principal indefinite pronouns:

Mit',	one, a.	*Aḍi*,	much, many.
Banar,	both.	*Uḍi*,	much, many.
Jọtọ,	all, the whole.	*Uṛi*,	much, many.
Sanam,	all.	*Okoe*,	somebody.
Goṭa,	the whole.	*Okoe hõbaṅ*,	nobody.
Adom,	some.	*Okoeko*,	some.
Eṭak',	other.	*Jahãe okoe*,	any one.
Tinak',	some.	*Ar, arhõ*,	more.

CHAPTER V.

OF VERBS.

The Santal verb, in connection with the pronominal suffixes, (which constitute an essential element of its formation), is unquestionably the most important part of Speech in the language; and so extremely artificial and complex, and yet so simple and transparent, is it in its construction, that it does not even yield to the Turkish, which hitherto, with all its Voices, Negatives, Impossibles and Causatives, its Tenses, Participles and Gerunds, has been deemed to be one of the most philosophical of languages; for what the Santal verb lacks in Negatives and Impossibles, it more than makes up for in cases.

To Santal verbs belong Voice, Mood, Tense, Gender, Number, Person, Case, Forms and Conjugation.

a. Voices.

The voices are five in number, viz:

1. Active.

a. The General Form;* as *Dal-et'-ko-kan-a-e,* he is striking them; *Dạṛ-et'-kan-a-e,* he is fleeing.

b. The Reservative Form; as *Dal-ka-ko-kan-a-e,* he is striking them; (and leaves them).

c. The Intensive Form; as *Am-e Da-dal-kan-a,* he is striking thee.

2. Reciprocal Active.

a. The General Form; as *Dapal-et'-kan-a-e,* he is striking together (something).

b. The Reservative Form; as *Dapal-ka-k'-kan-a-e,* he is striking together (and leaves it).

c. The Intensive Form; as *Da-k'-pal-kan-a-e,* he is striking together.

3. Reflexive.

a. The General Form; as *Dal-ok'-kan-a-e,* he is striking himself; *Gujuk'-kan-a-e,* he is dying.

b. The Reservative Form; as *Dal-k-ok'-kan-a-e,* he is striking himself.

c. The Intensive Form; as *Dal-og-ok'-kan-a-e,* he is striking himself.

4. Reciprocal Reflexive.

---

* Vide Explanation of the different Forms, p. 45.

a. The General Form ; as *Dapal-ok̇-kan-a-e,* he is striking mutually = fighting.

b. The Reservative Form ; as *Dapal-k-ok̇-kan-a-e,* he is fighting.

c. The Intensive Form is wanting.

5. DEPONENTS ; as *Hoṛo-e-irok̇-kan-a,* he is cutting Dhan.

Remark 1. The Intensive Form and the Deponents have only six* tenses, the Future, the Present, and the Imperfect, and the three Inchoatives.

Remark 2. The Reflexive voice is extensively used as a Passive both with the Common and Neuter Gender ; the Simple Reflexive being generally used in connection with the Neuter, and the Reflexive Causative with the common Gender ; as *Dal-ok̇-kana,* it is being struck ; *Dal-ochok̇-kanae,* he is being struck. (lit. he lets himself be struck.) But the simple Reflexive is also employed for the common Gender ; as *Sab-ok̇-a-e,* he will be caught.

Remark 3. In the Santal language there are a number of impersonal verbs with the accusative case ; as *tetaṅet'-ko-a,* they are thirsty (lit. it thirsteth them) ; *menak̇-ko-a,* they are ; *banuk̇-ko-a,* they are not.

Remark 4. There are verbs in the Santal language, which would seem to belong to the Neuter voice ; but, so far

* With certain verbs many of the other tenses are also used ; as *ọhọṅ emlena,* I will not give (this or that).

as I have been able to ascertain, they are all in reality either Reflexive or Deponent or Impersonal verbs.

b. *Moods.*

There may be said to be five moods in Santalee, viz., the Indicative, the Subjunctive, the Benedictive, (or Precative) the Imperative, and the Infinitive ; as *Dal-a-e,* he will strike ; *Dal-khan-e,* if he will strike ; or *Dal-chǫ-e,* he may strike, or *Paset'e dal,* perhaps he will strike (these are different *particles used in connection with the Subjunctive) ; *Dal-ma-m !* mayest thou strike, or that thou strikest ; *Dal-me !* strike thou ! *Janhe dal e senakana,* he has gone to thrash out Janhe.

Remark. Besides these moods there are two participles (adjective or relative and adverbial), and one Gerund for each tense.

c. *Tenses.*

Of tenses there are twenty three, viz. the Future, the General Incomplete Present, the Special Incomplete Present, the Recent Past, the Anterior Past, the Perfect, the General Incomplete Past, the Special Incomplete Past, the Indecisive Pluperfect, the Decisive Pluperfect, the Inchoative Future, the Inchoative Present, the Inchoative Past, the Optative, the Conditional, the Contingent, the Preliminary Future, the Preliminary Expostulative, the Preliminary Persuasive, the Preliminary Admissive, the Continuative Future, the

---

* The subjunctive is also expressed without any particle, as *Senkate ar ńelkoe, chet'e mena?* going and (if) he sees them, what will he say ?

Continuative Present, and the Continuative Past: each of which has *a Causative* throughout all voices, moods, numbers, persons, and cases.

d. Genders.

There are two genders in connection with the verb, the common and the neuter; as *ńur-ok̇-ae,* he will fall; *ńur-ok̇-a,* it will fall. (Nom-case) *Dal-ka-e-a-ko,* they will strike him; *Dal-ka-k̇-a-ko,* they will strike it; (Acc. case) *Dal-a-e-a-ko,* they will strike for him; *Dal-a-k̇-a-ko,* they will strike at it. (Dat. case)

e. Number.

Santal verbs have three numbers in the common gender, viz., the Singular, the Dual and the Plural; whereas the neuter Gender has only one, the Singular. When Duality or Plurality is to be expressed in the neuter gender, then pronouns must be prefixed; as *Dala-e,* he will strike; *Dal-a-kin,* they two will strike; *Dal-a-ko,* they will strike, *Ona ńurok̇a* it will fall; *onakin ńurok̇a* they (neuter) two will fall; *onako ńur-ok̇a,* they (neuter) will fall.

f. Persons.

There are three persons in Santali, 1st the speaker, 2nd the person spoken to, and 3rd the person spoken of. The 1st person dual has two forms, one used when the person addressed is excluded (as *aliń,* we two)—, and one when he is included (as *alaṅ,* we two)—, and the 1st person plural has three forms, one employed when the addressed person is excluded (as *ale,* we), and two, when he is included (as *abon* or *abo*) (vide Pronouns).

g. Cases.

In many languages, cases have no connection with the conjugation of verbs, but in Santali the verb is influenced by four cases, the Nominative, the Genitive, the Dative and the Accusative, which moreover may be joined and rejoined, till it makes in all nine ; as 1. the Nominative, 2. the Nominative with Genitive, 3. the Nominative with two Genitives, 4. the Nominative with Dative, 5. the Nominative with Dative and Genitive, 6. the Nominative with Dative and two Genitives ; 7. the Nominative with Accusative, 8. the Nominative with Accusative and Genitive, 9. the Nominative with Accusative and two Genitives ; as *Dalae,* he will strike ; *Daltaeae* he will strike his ; *Daltaetiñae,* he will strike his who is mine ; *Dalaeae,* he will strike for him ; *Dalaetaeae,* he will strike for him who is his ; *Dalae-tae-tiñae,* he will strike for him who is his, who is mine ; *Daleae,* he will strike him ; *Daletaeae,* he will strike him who is his ; *Daletaetiñae,* he will strike him, who is his, who is mine.

Remark. It will be observed, that the oblique cases are infixed between the root and the final a,* whereas the Nominative case is affixed to *it.*

h. Forms.

There are four forms, viz. the General, the Reservative, the Intensive, and the Continuative ; as, *ñel-a-e,* he will see ;

* As *Dal-ko-a-e,* He will strike them, *dal* being the root, *ko* the oblique (acc.) case, *a,* the "final a" and *e* the nominative case.

ńel-kak̇-a-e, he will see (and leave it for a while); *ńeńel-a-e* he will look at it; *ńam-a-e,* he will get; *ńam-ka-k̇-a-e,* he will get (and keep till further); *ńa-ńam-a-e,* he will seek; *Dal-akae-tahen-a-e,* he will continue striking.

i. CONJUGATION.

Conjugations there are two *viz.*, the Inflective and Uninflective; as *Dal-ko-a-e,* he will strike them; *onko-e Da-dal-a,* he will strike them. Only the Intensive Form is conjugated according to the 2nd, the General, Reservative and Continuative forms being conjugated according to the 1st conjugation.

Remark. To these forms may be added a Repetitive which follows the General, the Reservative and the Intensive forms; as *Daldalkedeań,* I repeatedly struck him; *Daldalkadeae,* he repeatedly struck him (and left him there); *Dak̇dal-kan-a-e,* He is striking.

TABLES OF THE FORMATION OF THE VERB.

GENERAL FORM.

ACTIVE VOICE.	REFLEXIVE VOICE.
NOM (OBJECT INANIMATE.)	
Dal-a-e, He will strike (it).	*Dal-ok̄-a*, It will be struck.
GEN. WITH NOM.	
Dal-tae-a-e,* He will strike (it) his.	*Dal-ok̄-tae-a*, What is his will be struck.
GEN. WITH GEN. AND NOM.	
Dal-tae-tiń-a-e, He will strike (it) his who is mine.	*Dal-ok̄-tae-tiń-a*, What is his, who is mine will be struck.
NOM. CAUSATIVE.	
Dal-ochoe-a-e, He will cause (it) to be struck.	*Dal-ochok̄-a*, It will be caused to be struck.
GEN. WITH NOM.	
Dal-ocho-tae-a-e He will cause (it) his to be struck.	*Dal-ochok̄-tae-a*, What is his will be caused to be struck.
GEN. WITH GEN. AND NOM.	
Dal-ocho-tae-tiń-a-e, He will cause (it) his who is mine, to be struck.	*Dal-ochok̄-tae-tiń-a*, What is his, who is mine will be caused to be struck.

* This may also be translated : he will strike *for* him.

ACTIVE VOICE.	REFLEXIVE VOICE.
Acc. with Nom. (object animate.)	
Dal-e-a-e, He will strike him.	*Dal-oḱ-a-e,* He will strike himself.
Acc. with Gen. and Nom.	
Dal-e-tae-a-e, He will strike him, who is his.	*Dal-oḱ-tae-a-e,* He, who is his, will strike himself.
Acc. with Gen. Gen. and Nom.	
Dal-e-tae-tiń-a-e, He will strike him, who is his, who (again) is mine.	*Dal-oḱ-tae-tiń-a-e,* He, who is his, who is mine, will strike himself.
Acc. Causative.	
Dal-ocho-e-a-e, He will cause him to strike or to be struck.	*Dal-ochoḱ-a-e,* He will let himself be struck.
Acc. with Gen. and Nom.	
Dal-ocho-e-tae-a-e, He will cause him, who is his, to strike or to be struck.	*Dal-ochoḱ-tae-a-e,* He, who is his, will let himself be struck.
Acc. with Gen. Gen. and Nom.	
Dal-ocho-e-tae-tiń-a-e, He will cause him, who is his, who is mine, to strike or to be struck.	*Dal-ochoḱ-tae-tiń-a-e,* He, who is his, who is mine, will let himself be struck.

ACTIVE VOICE.

DAT. WITH NOM. (OBJECT INANIMATE.)

Dal-a-ḱ-a-e, He will strike at or on it.

DAT. WITH GEN. AND NOM.

Dal-aḱ-tae-a-e, He will strike at (it) his.

DAT. WITH GEN. GEN. AND NOM.

Dal-a-ḱ-tae-tiń-a-e, He will strike at (it) his, who is mine.

DAT. CAUSATIVE.

Dal-ocho-a-ḱ-a-e, He will cause (it) to be struck at, or allow it to be struck.

DAT. WITH GEN. AND NOM.

Dal-ocho-a-ḱ-tae-a-e, He will cause (it) his to be struck at, etc.

DAT. WITH GEN. GEN. AND NOM.

Dal-ocho·a-ḱ-tae-tiń-a-e, He will cause (it) his, who is mine, to be struck at, etc.

REFLEXIVE VOICE.

Is wanting.

ACTIVE VOICE.	REFLEXIVE VOICE.
DAT. (OBJECT ANIMATE.)	
Dal-a-e-a-e, He will strike for or towards him.	*Dal-joṅ-a-e,* He will strike for himself.
DAT. WITH GEN. AND NOM.	
Dal-a-e-tae-a-e, He will strike for or towards him, who is his.	*Dal-joṅ-tae-a-e,* He, who is his, will strike for himself.
DAT. WITH GEN. GEN. AND NOM.	
Dal-a-e-tae-tiṅ-a-e, He will strike for or towards him, who is his, who (again) is mine.	*Dal-joṅ-tae-tiṅ-a-e,* He, who is his, who is mine, will strike for himself.
DAT. CAUSATIVE.	
Dal-ocho-a-e-a-e, He will cause to be struck for, or allow him to strike or be struck.	*Dal-ocho-joṅ-a-e,* He will cause to be struck for himself.
DAT. WITH GEN. AND NOM.	
Dal-ocho-a-e-tae-a-e, He will cause to be struck for or allow him who is his, to strike or be struck.	*Dal-ocho-joṅ-tae-a-e,* He, who is his, will cause to be struck for himself.
DAT. WITH GEN. GEN. AND NOM.	
Dal-ocho-a-e-tae-tiṅ-a-e, He will cause to be struck for or allow him who is his, who is mine to strike or be struck.	*Dal-ocho-joṅ-tae-tiṅ-a-e,* He who is his, who is mine, will cause to be struck for himself.

THE RESERVATIVE FORM.

ACTIVE VOICE.

Acc. with Nom. (Inanimate.)

Dal-ka-k̓-a-e, He will strike it [and leave it (till further)]

Acc. with Gen. and Nom.

Dal-ka-k̓-tae-a-e, He will strike what is his.

Acc. with Gen. Gen. and Nom.

Dal-ka-k̓-tae-tiń-a-e, He will strike what is his, who is mine.

Acc. Causative.

Dal-ocho-ka-k̓-a-e, He will cause it to be struck.

Acc. with. Gen. and Nom.

Dal-ocho-ka-k̓-tae-a-e, He will cause what is his to be struck.

Acc. with Gen. Gen. and Nom.

Dal-ocho-ka-k̓-tae-tiń-a-e, He will cause what is his, who is mine, to be struck.

REFLEXIVE VOICE.

Dal-kok̓-a, It will be struck (and left till further.)

Dal-kok̓-tae-a, What is his will be struck.

Dal-kok̓-tae-tiń-a, What is his, who is mine will be struck.

Dal-ocho-kok̓-a, It will be caused to be struck.

Dal-ocho-kok̓-tae-a, What is his will be caused to be struck.

Dal-ocho-kok̓-tae-tiń-a, What is his, who is mine will be caused to be struck.

ACTIVE VOICE.	REFLEXIVE VOICE.
ACC. (ANIMATE.) (him).	
Dal-ka-e-a-e, He will strike him (and leave	*Dal-kok-a-e,* He will strike himself.
ACC. WITH GEN. AND NOM.	
Dal-ka-e-tae-a-e, He will strike him, who is his.	*Dal-kok-tae-a-e,* He, who is his, will strike himself.
ACC. WITH GEN. GEN. AND NOM.	
Dal-ka-e-tae-tiń-a-e, He will strike him, who is his, who is mine.	*Dal-kok-tae-tiń-a-e,* He, who is his, who is mine, will strike himself.
ACC. CAUSATIVE.	
Dal-ocho-ka-e-a-e, He will cause him to strike or be struck.	*Dal-ocho-kok-a-e,* He will let himself be struck.
ACC. WITH GEN. AND NOM.	
Dal-ocho-ka-e-tae-a-e, He will cause him, who is his, to strike or be struck.	*Dal-ocho-kok-tae-a-e,* He who is his, will let himself be struck.
ACC. WITH GEN. GEN. AND NOM.	
Dal-ocho-ka-e-tae-tiń-a-e, He will cause him who is his, who is mine, to strike or be struck.	*Dal-ocho-kok-tae-tiń-a-e,* He, who is his, who is mine, will let himself be struck.

THE INTENSIVE FORM.

ACTIVE VOICE.	REFLEXIVE VOICE.
Nom. (Object in Active to precede* the Verb.)	
Da-dal-a-e, He will strike.	*Dal-og-ok̓-a-e,* ‡ He will strike himself or be struck.
Nom. with Gen.	
Da-dal-tae-a-e, He who is his will strike.	*Dal-og-ok̓-tae-a-e,* He, who is his will strike himself or be struck.
Nom. with Gen. and Gen.	
Da-dal-tae-tiń-a-e, He who is his, who is mine will strike.	*Dal-og-ok̓-tae-tiń-a-e,* He who is his, who is mine, will strike himself, or be struck.
† Nom. Causative.	
Da-dal-ok̓cho-a-e, He will cause to strike.	*Dal-ochog-ok̓-a-e,* He will let himself be struck etc.
Nom. with Gen.	
Da-dal-ok̓cho-tae-a-e, He, who is his will cause to strike.	*Dal-ochog-ok̓-tae-a-e,* He, who is his will let himself be struck.
Nom. with Gen. and Gen.	
Da-dal-ok̓cho-tae-tiń-a-e, He who is his, who is mine, will cause to strike.	*Dal-ochog-ok̓-tae-tiń-a-e,* He, who is his, who is mine, will let himself be struck.

* As *oni-ń dadal-a,* I will strike him ; *ona-ń dadal-a,* I will strike it.
† This causative has also another form : *Dal-ok̓cho-a-e,* He will cause to be struck.
‡ Or (inanimate) *Dal-og ok̓-a,* It will be struck.

RECIPROCAL.

GENERAL FORM.

ACTIVE VOICE.

NOM. (INANIMATE.)

Dapal-a-e, He will strike together.

NOM. WITH GEN.

Dapal-tae-a-e, He will strike his together.

NOM. WITH GEN. AND GEN.

Dapal-tae-tiń-a-e, He will strike his, who is mine, together.

NOM. CAUSATIVE.

Dapal-ochoe-a-e, He will cause to strike or be struck together

NOM. WITH GEN.

Dapal-ochoe-tae-a-e, He will cause his to strike or be struck together.

NOM. WITH GEN. AND GEN.

Dapal-ochoe-tae-tiń-a-e, He will cause his, who is mine, to strike or be struck together.

REFLEXIVE VOICE.

Dapal-oǩ-a, I will be struck together.

Dapal-oǩ-tae-a, What is his will be struck. together.

Dapal-oǩ-tae-tiń-a, What is his, who is mine will be struck together.

Dapal-ochoǩ-a, It will be caused to be struck, together.

Dapal-ochoǩ-tae-a, What is his will be caused to be struck together.

Dapalochoǩ-tae-tiń-a, What is his, who is mine will be caused to be struck together.

ACTIVE VOICE.	REFLEXIVE VOICE.
ACC. (ANIMATE.)	
Dapal-e-a-e, He will cover* him.	*Dapal-ok̇-a-e*, He will strike mutually=fight
ACC. WITH GEN. AND NOM.	
Dapal e-tae-a-e, He will cover him who is his.	*Dapal-ok̇-tae-a-e*, He, who is his, will fight.
ACC. WITH GEN. GEN. AND NOM.	
Dapal-e-tae-tiṅ-a-e, He will cover him, who is his, who is mine.	*Dapal-ok̇-tae-tiṅ-a-e*, He who is his, who is mine, will fight.
ACC. CAUSATIVE.	
Dapal-ocho-e-a-e, He will cause him to strike mutually=fight.	*Dapal-ochok̇-a-e*, He will let himself be caused to fight.
ACC. WITH GEN. AND NOM.	
Dapal-ocho-e-tae-a-e, He will cause him, who is his to fight.	*Dapal-ochok̇-tae-a-e*, He who is his, will let himself be caused to fight.
ACC. WITH GEN. GEN. AND NOM.	
Dapal-ocho-e-tae-tiṅ-a-e, He will cause him who is his, who is mine, to fight.	*Dapal-ochok̇-tae-tiṅ-a-e*, He, who is his, who is mine, will let himself be caused to fight.

* The direct meaning of the Reciprocal is not used in connnection with Dal, in the three first cases, whereas it is with other verbs; as *ṅam-e a-e*, he will get him, *ṅapam-e-a-e*, he will get him together with another.

ACTIVE VOICE.

DAT. (INANIMATE.)

Dapal-a-k̓-a-e, He will strike (them) against one * another.

DAT. WITH GEN. AND NOM.

Dapal-a-k̓-tae-a-e, He will strike what is his, against one another.

DAT. WITH GEN. GEN. AND NOM.

Dapal-a-k̓-tae-tiń-a-e, He will strike what is his, who is mine, against one another.

DAT. CAUSATIVE.

Dapal-ocho-a-k̓-a-e, He will allow it to strike or be struck together or cause it to get cover.

DAT. WITH GEN. AND NOM.

Dapal-ocho-ak̓-tae-a-e, He will allow his to strike or be struck together etc.

DAT. WITH GEN. GEN. AND NOM.

Dapal-ocho-a-k̓-tae-tiń-a-e, He will allow his, who is mine, to strike or be struck together etc.

REFLEXIVE VOICE.

Is wanting.

* Or put a cover on it

ACTIVE VOICE.	REFLEXIVE VOICE.
DAT. (ANIMATE.) *Dapal-a-e-a-e,* He will strike together for him.	*Dapal-joṅ-a-kin,* They two will fight for themselves (quitely alone.)
DAT. WITH GEN. AND NOM. *Dapal-a-e-tae-a-e,* He will strike together for him, who is his.	*Dapal-joṅ-tae-a-kin,* They two who are his will fight for themselves.
DAT. WITH GEN. GEN. AND NOM. *Dapal-a-e-tae-tiṅ-a-e,* He will stike together for him, who is his, who is mine.	*Dapal-joṅ-tae-tiṅ-a-kin,* They two, who are his, who is mine, will fight for themselves.
DAT. CAUSATIVE. *Dapal-ocho-a-e-a-e,* He will allow him to fight, or strike together.	*Dapal-ocho-joṅ-a-e,* * He will cause to fight or be fought for himself.
DAT. WITH GEN. AND NOM. *Dapal-ocho-a-e-tae-a-e,* He will allow him, who is his, to fight, or strike together.	*Dapal-ocho-joṅ-tae-a-e,* He who is his will cause to be fought for himself.
DAT. WITH GEN. AND NOM. *Dapal-ocho-a-e-tae-tiṅ-a-e,* He will allow him, who is his, who is mine, to fight etc.	*Dapal-ocho-joṅ-tae-tiṅ-a-e,* He who is his, who is mine, will cause to be fought for himself.

* The Reflexive causative in connection with Dapal is seldom heard, whereas it is often used in connection with other verbs; as *khuṇṭi-c-tepen-ocho-joṅ-kan-a,* he causes posts to be put together for himself.

THE RESERVATIVE FORM.

ACTIVE VOICE.	REFLEXIVE VOICE.
ACC. WITH NOM. (INANIMATE).	
Dapal-kaḱ-a-e, He will strike it together (and leave it)	*Dapal-koḱ-a,* It will strike or be struck together (and left till further.)
ACC. WITH GEN. AND NOM.	
Dapal-kaḱ-tae-a-e, He will strike his together.	*Dapal-koḱ-tae-a,* What is his will strike or be struck together.
ACC. WITH GEN. GEN. AND NOM.	
Dapal-kaḱ-tae-tiń-a-e, He will strike his who is mine, together.	*Dapal-koḱ-tae-tiń-a,* What is his, who is mine, will strike or be struck together.
ACC. CAUSATIVE.	
Dapal-ocho-kaḱ-a-e, He will cause to strike or be struck together.	*Dapal-ocho-koḱ-a,* It will be caused to be struck together.
ACC. WITH GEN AND NOM.	
Dapal-ocho-kaḱ-tae-a-e, He will cause his to strike or be struck together.	*Dapal-ocho-koḱ-tae-a,* What is his will be caused to be struck together.
ACC. WITH GEN. GEN. AND NOM.	
Dapal-ocho-kaḱ-tae-tiń-a-e, He will cause his, who is mine, to strike, or to be struck together.	*Dapal-ocho-koḱ-tae-tiń-a,* What is his mine, will be caused to be struck together.

ACTIVE VOICE.	REFLEXIVE VOICE.
Acc. with Nom. (Animate).	
Dapal-ka-e-a-e, He will cover* him.	*Dapal koǩ-a-e,* He will fight.
Acc. with Gen. and Nom.	
Dapal-ka-e-tae-a-e, He will cover him, who is his.	*Dapal-koǩ-tae-a-e,* He, who is his will fight.
Acc. with Gen. Gen. and Nom.	
Dapal-ka-e-tae-tiń-a-e, He will cover him, who is his, who is mine.	*Dapal-koǩ-tae-tiń-a-e,* He, who is his, who is mine, will fight.
Acc. Causative.	
Dapal-ocho-ka-e-a-e, He will cause him to fight.	*Dapal-ocho-koǩ-a-e,* He will let himself be caused to fight.
Acc. with Gen. and Nom.	
Dapal-ocho-ka-e-tae-a-e, He will cause him, who is his, to fight.	*Dapal-ocho-koǩ-tae-a-e,* He, who is his, will let himself be caused to fight.
Acc. wieh Gen. Gen. and Nom.	
Dapal-ocho-ka-e-tae-tiń-a-e, He will cause him, who is his, who is mine, to fight.	*Dapal-ocho-koǩ-tae-tiń-a-e,* He, who is his, who is mine, will let himself be caused to fight.

* The direct meaning is used in connection with other Verbs ; as *onituluch' iń ńepel-ka-e-a* (from *ńel* to see) I wil give him an interview with him (and leave him there.)

THE INTENSIVE FORM.*

ACTIVE VOICE.

NOM.

Daḱpal-a-e, He will strike together.

NOM. WITH GEN.

Daḱpal-tae-a-e, He, who is his, will stike together.

NOM. WITH GEN. AND GEN.

Daḱpal tae-tiń-a-e, He, who is his, who is mine, will strike together.

‡ NOM. CAUSATIVE.

Daḱpal-oḱchoe-a-e, He will cause to strike together.

NOM. WITH GEN.

Daḱpal-oḱcho-tae-a-e, He who is his, will cause to strike together.

NOM. WITH GEN. AND GEN.

Daḱpal-oḱcho-tae-tiń-a-e, He who is his, who is mine, will cause to strike together.

REFLEXIVE VOICE.

Dapal-og-oḱ-a, It will be struck together.

Dapal-og-oḱ-tae-a, What is his will be struck together.

Dapal-og-oḱ-tae-tiń-a, What is his, who is mine, will be struck together.

Dapal-ochog-oḱ-a†, It will be caused to be struck together.

Dapal-ochog-oḱ-tae-a, What is will be caused to be struck together.

Dapal-ochog-oḱ-tae-tiń-a, What is his, who is mine will be caused to be struck together.

---

* The real force of the Instensive form can not so well be shown in the verb *dal* as in *ńel.* and *ńam.* It shows rather an effort made for gaining the object, than the gaining of the object itself : *ńam-et'-kan-a-e*, he is getting, *ńa-ńam-kan-a-e*, he is seeking to get ; *Si-et'kan-a-e* he is ploughing, *Si si-kan-a-e*, he is learning to plough (said about children). It thus coinsides in some cases with the form which in other languages *(E. g. in Sanskrit)* is called desiderative.

† The causative may also be used in connection with *the common gender* with the direct meaning, (as *dapal-ochog-ok'-a-e*, We will be caused to fight) and in the simple Reflexive with the meaning of covering oneself.

Remark. It will be observed, that the first *ok'* has been changed into *og.* As the first syllable is doubled in the active voice Intensive Form, in the same manner is the last syllable doubled in the Reflexive voice Intension Form ; as *Da-dal-a-e*, *Dal-ok'-ok'-a-*=*Dal-og-ok'-a.*

‡ There is a second form *Dapal-ok'-choe-a-e*, He will cause to be struck together (things.)

THE CONTINUATIVE FORM.

ACTIVE VOICE.	REFLEXIVE VOICE.
NOM. (OBJECT INANIMATE.)	
Dal-akae-tahen-a-e, He will continue to strike.	*Dal-akan-tahen-a*, It will remain struck.
NOM. WITH GEN.	
Dal-akae-tahen-tae-a-e, He will continue to strike his.	*Dal-akan-tahen-tae-a*, What is his will remain struck.
NOM. WITH GEN. AND GEN.	
Dal-akae-tahen-tae-tiń-a-e, He will continue to strike his, who is mine.	*Dal-akan-tahen-tae-tiń-a*, What is his, who is mine, will remain struck.
NOM. CAUSATIVE.	
Dal-ocho-akae-tahen-a-e, He will continue causing to be struck.	*Dal-ocho-akan-tahen-a*, It will remain caused to be struck.
NOM. WITH GEN.	
Dal-ocho-akae-tahen-tae-a-e, He will continue causing his to be struck.	*Dal-ocho-akan-tahen-tae-a*, What is his will remain caused to be struck.
NOM. WITH GEN. AND GEN.	
Dal-ocho-akae-tahen-tae-tiń-a-e, He will continue causing his, who is mine, to be struck.	*Dal-ocho-akan-tahen-tae-tiń-a*, What is his, who is mine, will remain caused to be struck.

ACTIVE VOICE.

Acc. with Nom. (Animate.)

Dal-aka-e-tahen-a-e, He will continue to strike him.

Acc. with Gen. and Nom.

Dal-aka-e-tahen-tae-a-e, He will continue to strike him, who is his.

Acc. with Gen. and Now.

Dal-aka-e-tahen-tae-tiń-a-e, He will continue to strike him, who is his, who is mine.

Acc. Causative.

Dal-ocho-aka-e-tahen-a-e, He will continue causing him to strike, or be struck.

Acc. with Gen. and Nom.

Dal-ocho-aka-e-tahen-tae-a-e, He will continue causing him, who is his to strike etc.

Acc. with Gen. Gen. hnd Non.

Dal-ocho-aka-e-tahen-tae-tiń-a-e, He will continue causing him, who is his who is mine etc.

REFLEXIVE VOICE.

Dal-akan-tahen-a-e, He, will continue to strike himself.

Dal-akan-tahen-tae-a-e, He, who is his, will continue to strike himself.

Dal-akan-tahen-tae-tiń-a-e, He, who is his, who is mine, will continue to strike himself.

Dal-ocho-akan-tahen-a-e, He, will continue letting himself be struck.

Dal-ocho-akan-tahen-tae-a-e, He, who is his, will continue letting himself be struck.

Dal-ocho-akan-tahen-tae-tiń-a-e, He, who is his, who is mine, will continue letting himself be struck.

ACTIVE VOICE.

DAT. WITH NOM. (INANIMATE.)

Dal-akao-ak̓-tahen-a-e, He will continue to strike on it.

DAT. WITH GEN. AND NOM.

Dal-akao-ak̓-tahen-tae-a-e, He will continue to strike on his.

DAT. WITH GEN. GEN. AND NOM.

Dal-akao-ak̓-tahen-tae-tiń-a-e, He will continue to strike on his, who is mine.

DAT. CAUSATIVE.

Dal-ocho-akao-ak̓-tahen-a-e, He will continue causing to be struck on.

DAT. WITH GEN. AND NOM.

Dal-ocho-akao-ak̓-tahen-tae-a-e, He will continue causing his, to be stıucke on.

DAT. WITH GEN. GEN. AND NOM.

Dal-ocho-akao-ak̓-tahen-tae-tiń-a-e, He will continue causing his, who is mine, to be struck on.

REFLEXIVE VOICE.

Is wanting.

ACTIVE VOICE.	REFLEXIVE VOICE.
DAT. (ANIMATE.) *Dal-akao-a-e-tahen-a-e*, He will continue to strike for him.	*Dal-akao-an-tahen-a-e*, He will continue to strike for himself.
DAT. WITH GEN. AND NOM. *Dal-akao-a-e-tahen-tae-a-e*, He will continue to strike for him, who is his.	*Dal-akao-an-tahen-tae-a-e*, He who is his, will continue to strike for himself.
DAT. WITH GEN. GEN. AND NOM. *Dal-akao-a-e-tahen-tae-tiń-a-e*. He will continue to strike for him, who is his who is mine.	*Dal-akao-an-tahen-tae-tiń-a-e*, He, who is his, who is mine, will continue to strike for himself.
DAT. CAUSATIVE. *Dal-ocho-akao-a-e-tahen-a-e*, * He will continue causing to be struck for him.	*Dal-ocho-akao-an-tahen-a-e*, He will continue causing to be struck for himself.
DAT. WITH GEN. AND NOM. *Dal-ocho-akao-a-e-tahen-tae-a-e*, He will continue causing to be struck for him, * who is his.	*Dal-ocho-akao-an-tahen-tae-a-e*, He, who is his, will continue causing to be struck for himself.
DAT. WITH GEN. GEN. AND NOM. *Dal-ocho-akao-a-e-tahen-tae-tiń-a-e*, He will continue causing to be struck for * him, who is his who is mine.	*Dal-ocho-akao-an-tahen-tae-tiń-a-e*, He, who is his, who is mine, will continue causing to be struck for himself.

* Or allow him to strike.

CONTINUATIVE FORM.

RECIPROCAL.

ACTIVE VOICE.	REFLEXIVE VOICE.
NOM. (OBJECT INANIMATE.) *Dapal-akae-tahen-a-e,* He will continue to strike together.	*Dapal-akan-tahen-a,* It will remain struck together.
NOM. WITH GEN. *Dapal-akae-tahen-tae-a-e,* He will continue to strike together what is his.	*Dapal-akan-tahen-tae-a,* What is his will remain struck together.
NOM. WITH GEN. AND GEN. *Dapal-akae-tahen-tae-tiń-a-e,* He will continue to strike together his, who is mine.	*Dapal-akan-tahen-tae-tiń-a,* What is his, who is mine will remain struck together.
NOM. CAUSATIVE. *Dapal-ocho-akae-tahen-a-e,* He will continue causing to strike or be struck together.	*Dapal-ocho-akan-tahen-a,* It will remain caused to be struck together.
NOM. WITH GEN. *Dapal-ocho-akae-tahen-tae-a-e,* He will continue causing his, etc.	*Dapal-ocho-akan-tahen-tae-a,* What is his will remain caused to be struck together.
NOM. WITH GEN. AND GEN. *Dapal-ocho-akae-tahen-tae-tiń-a-e,* He will continue causing his, who is mine, etc.	*Dapal-ocho-akan-tahen-tae-tiń-a,* What is his who is mine., will remain caused to be struck together.

ACTIVE VOICE.	REFLEXIVE VOICE.
ACC. (ANIMATE.) *Dapal-aka-e-tahen-a-e,* He will continue to cover* him.	*Dapal-akan-tahen-a-e,* He will continue to fight.
ACC. WITH GEN. AND NOM. *Dapal-akae-tahen-tae-a-e,* He will continue to cover him, who is his.	*Dapal-akan-tahen-tae-a-e,* He, who as his, will continue to fight.
ACC. WITH GEN. GEN. AND NOM. *Dapal-aka-e-tahen-tae-tiń-a-e,* He will continue to cover him, who is his, who is mine.	*Dapal-akan-tahen-tae-tiń-a-e,* He, who is his who is mine, will continue to fight.
ACC. CAUSATIVE. *Dapal-ocho-aka-e-tahen-a-e,* He will continue causing him to fight.	*Dapal-acho-akan-tahen-a-e,* He will continue letting himself be caused to fight.
ACC. WITH GEN. AND NOM. *Dapal-ocho-aka-e-tahen-tae-a-e,* He will continue causing him, who is his, to fight.	*Dapal-ocho-akan-tahen-tae-a-e,* He, who his will continue letting himself etc.
ACC. WITH GEN. GEN. AND NOM. *Dapal-ocho-aka-e-tahen-tae-tiń-a-e,* He will continue causing him, who is his, who is mine, to fight.	*Dapal-ocho-akan-tahen-tae-tiń-a-e,* He who is his, who is mine, will continue letting etc.

* The direct meaning is used in connection with other verbs; as *ńapam-aka-e-tahen-a-e,* he will continue giving him interviews (with such and such a person) (from *ńam* to get.)

ACTIVE VOICE.

DAT. (INANIMATE.)

Dapal-akao-a-k̇-tuhen-a-e, He will continue to strike against one another.

DAT. WITH GEN. AND NOM.

Dapal-akao-ak̇-tuhen-tae-a-e, He will continue striking what is his against one another.

DAT. WITH GEN. GEN. AND NOM.

Dapal-akao-a-k̇-tuhen-tae-tiṅ-a-e, He will continue to strike against one another what is his, who is mine.

DAT. CAUSATIVE.

Dapal-ocho-akao-a-k̇-tahen-a-e, He will continue to allow it to strike or be struck together.

DAT. WITH GEN. AND NOM.

Dapal-ocho-ak̇ao-a-k̇-tahen-tae-a-e, He will continue to allow his to strike or be struck together.

DAT. WITH GEN. GEN. AND NOM.

Dapal-ocho-akao-a-k̇-tahen-tae-tiṅ-a-e, He will continue to allow his, who is mine to strike or be struck together.

REFLEXIVE VOICE.

Is wanting.

ACTIVE VOICE.	REFLEXIVE VOICE.
DAT. (ANIMATE.)	
Dapal-akao-a-e-taheń-a-e, He will continue to strike together for him.	*Dapal-akao-an-tahen-a-kin,* They two will continue fighting† by themselves.
DAT. WITH GEN. AND NOM.	
Dapal-akao-a-e-tahen-tae-a-e, He will continue to strike together for him, who is his.	*Dapla-akao-an-tahen-tae-a-kin,* They two who are his will continue etc.
DAT. WITH GEN. GEN. AND NOM.	
Dapal-akao-a-e-tahen-tae-tiń-a-e, He will continue to strike together for him, who is his, who is mine.	*Dapal-akao-an-tahen-tae-tiń-a-kin,* They two who are his, who is mine, will contiuue etc.
DAT. CAUSATIVE.	
Dapal-ocho-akao-a-e-tahen-a-e, He will continue to allow him to fight.*	*Dapal-ocho-akao-an-tahen-a-e,* He will continue causing to fight ‡ or be fought for himself.
DAT. WITH GEN. AND NOM.	
Dapal-ocho-akao-a-e-tahen-a-e, He will continue to allow him, who is his, to fight.*	*Dapal-ocho-okao-an-tahen-tae-a-e,* He who is his well continue causing to fight ‡ etc.
DAT. WITH GEN. GEN. AND NOM.	
Dapal-ocho-akao-a-e-tahen-tae-tiń-a-e, He will continue to allow him who is his, who is mine to fight.*	*Dapal-ocho-akao-an-tahen-tae-tińa-e,* He who is his, who is mine will continue etc.

Remark. Deponents are verbs with Reflexive form and Active meaning and need no special Table.

* Or strike together.

† Or covering for themselves.

‡ Or be struck together.

TABLES OF THE FORMATION OF THE TENSES.

ACTIVE.

NOMINATIVE CASE

(OBJECT INANIMATE)

TENSES.	ADJECTIVE PARTICIPLES.	ADVERBIAL PARTICIPLES.	GERUNDS.
FUTURE. *Dal-a-e,* He will strike.	*Dal,* Struck.	*Dal-khan,* Willing to strike.	*Dal-reak̇, te, ṭhen, khon, re,* * Of, by, in (etc.) striking (general.)
GENERAL INCOMPLETE PRESENT. *Dal-et'-a-e,* He strikes.	*Dal-et',* Who strikes.	*Dal-et'-khan,* Striking.	*Dal-et'-reak̇, te, ṭhen, khon re,* Of, by, in (etc.) striking.
SPECIAL INCOMPLETE PRESENT. *Dal-et'-kan-a-e,* He is striking.	*Dal-et'-kan,* Who is striking.	*Dal-et'-kan-khan,* Striking now.	*Dal-et'-kan-reak̇, te, ṭhen, khon, re,* Of, by, in (etc.) striking now.
RESENT PAST. *Dal-ket'-a-e,* He struck, or has struck.	*Dal-ket',* Who struck, or has struck.	*Dal-ket'-khan,* Having struck.	*Dal-ket'-reak̇, te, ṭhen, khon, re,* Of, by, in (etc.) having struck.
ANTERIOR PAST. *Dal-let'-a-e,* He struck or had struck.	*Dal-let',* Who struck, or had struck.	*Dal-let'-khan,* Having struck.	*Dal-let'-reak̇, te, ṭhen, khon, re,* Of, by, in (etc.) having struck.

* The Gerund are declined like nouns. (Vide declension of nouns.)

Tenses.	Adjective Participles.	Adverbial Participles.	Gerunds.
General incomplete Past.			
Dal-et'-tahĕkan-a-e, He used to strike, or was striking.	*Dal-et'-tahĕkan*, Who used to strike, or was striking.	*Dal-et'-tahĕkan-khan*, Using to strike.	*Dal-et'-tahĕkan-reak̓*, *te*, *then*, *khon*, *re*, Of, by, in (etc.) using to strike.
Special incomplete Past.			
Dal-et'-kan-tahĕ-kan-a-e, He was striking.	*Dal-et'-kan-tahĕkan*, Who was striking.	*Dal-et'-kan-tahĕkan-khan*, Being (then) striking.	*Dal-et'-kan-tahĕkan-reak̓*, *te*, *then*, *khon*, *re*, Of, in (etc.) striking then.
Indecisive Pluperfect.			
Dal-let'-tahĕkan-a-e, He had struck.	*Dal-let'-tahĕkan*, Who had struck.	*Dal-let'-tahĕkan-khan*, Having struck.	*Dal-let'-tahĕkan-reak̓*, *te*, *re*, *etc.*, Of, by, in (etc.) having struck.
Inchoative Future.			
Dal-lagit'-e, He will be about to strike.	*Dal-lagit'*, Who will be about to strike.	*Dal-lagit'-khan*, Being about to strike.	*Dal-lagit'-reak̓*, *te*, *re*, *etc.*, Of, by, in (etc.) being about to strike.
Inchoative Present.			
Dal-lagid-ok̓-kan-a-e, He is about to strike.	*Dal-lagidok̓-kan*, Who is about to strike.	*Dal-lagidok̓-kan-khan*, Being (now) about to strike.	*Dal-lagidok̓-kan-reak̓*, *te*, *re*, *etc.*, Of, by, in (etc.) being about to strike now.
Inchoative Past.			
Dal-lagid-ok̓-kan-ta-hĕkan-a-e, He was about to strike.	*Dal-lagidok̓-kan-ta-hĕkan*, Who was about to strike.	*Dal-lagidok̓-kan-ta-hĕkan-khan*, Being (then) about to strike.	*Dal-lagidok̓-kan-tahĕkan-reak̓*, *te*, *re*, *(etc.,)* Of, by in (etc.) being about to strike then.

Tenses.	Adjective Participles.	Adverbial Participles.	Gerunds.
Optative.			
Dal-ke-a-e, He would strike.	*Dal-ke*, Who would (like to) strike or have struck.	*Dal-ke-khan*, Wishing to strike.	*Dal-ke-reak̆-te, re, etc.* Of, by, in wishing (or the possibility) to strike.
Conditional.			
(Oho̱) Dal-le-a-e, He would (not) strike.	*Dal-le*, Who may have struck.	*Dal-le-khan*, In case of striking or having struck.	*Dal-le-reak̆-te-re, etc.* Of, by, in (etc.) striking.
Contingent.			
Dal-ket̕-gi-e, He strikes, will, or would strike.			
Preliminary Future.			
Dal-le-gi-e, He will first strike.			
Preliminary Expostulative.			
Dal-le-nahĩ-e, He must first strike.		*Dal-le-nahĩ*, First striking, or having first struck.	
Preliminary Persuasive.			
Dal-le-ba-e, He must first strike.		*Dal-le-bañ*, First striking or having first struck.	

Tenses.	Adjective Participles.	Adverbial Participles.	Gerunds.
Preliminary Admissive.			
Dal-le-en-a-e, He must first strike.		*Dal-le-ena,* First striking, or having first struck.	
Preliminary Benedictive.			
Dal-le-ma-m! Mayest thou first strike!			
Preliminary Imperative.			
Dal-le-m! Strike first!			
Benedictive.			
Dal-ma-m! Mayest thou strike!			
Imperative.			
Dal-me! Strike thou!			
Infinitive.			
Dal, To strike.			

TABLES OF THE FORMATION OF THE TENSES.

THE REFLEXIVE VOICE.

NOM. WITH ACC.

(INANIMATE.)

TENSES.	ADJECTIVE PARTICIPLES.	ADVERBIAL PARTICIPLES.	GERUNDS.
FUTURE.			
Dal-ok-a, It will be struck.	*Dal-ok*, Which will be struck.	*Dal-ok-khan*, If to be struck.	*Dal-ok-reak*, *te*, *re etc.*, Of, by, in being struck.
SPECIAL INCOMPLETE PRESENT.			
Dal-ok-kan-a, It is being struck.	*Dal-ok-kan*, Which is being struck.	*Dal-ok-kan-khan*, Being struck (now.)	*Dal-ok-kan-reak*, *te*, *re etc.*, Of, by, in being struck (now.)
RECENT PAST.			
Dal-en-a, It was struck.	*Dal-en*, Which was* struck.	*Dal-en-khan*, Having been struck.	*Dal-en-reak*, *te*, *re etc.*, Of, by, in having been struck.
ANTERIOR PAST.			
Dal-len-a, It was struck.	*Dal-len*, Which was† struck.	*Dal-len-khan*, Having been struck.	*Dal-len-reak*, *te*, *re etc.*, Of, by, in having been struck.
SPECIAL INCOMPLETE PAST.			
Dal-ok-kan-tahēkan-a, It was being struck.	*Dal-ok-kan-tahēkan*, Which was being struck.	*Dal-ok-kan-tahēkan-khan*, Being struck (then.)	*Dal-ok-kan-tahēkan-reak*, *te*, *re etc.*, Of, by, in being struck (then.)

* Or has been. † Or had been.

Tenses.	Adjective Participles.	Adverbial Participles.	Gerunds.
Indicisive Pluperfect.			
Dal-len-tahĕkan-a, It had been struck.	*Dal-len-tahĕkan,* Which had been struck.	*Dal-len-tahĕkan-khan,* Having been struck.	*Dal-len-tahĕkan-reak̓, te, re,* Of, by, in having been struck.
Inchoative Future.			
Dal-ok̓-lagit̓, It will be about to be struck.	*Dal-ok-lagit̓,* About to be struck.	*Dal-ok-lagit̓-khan,* Being about to be struck.	*Dal-ok̓-lagit̓-reak̓, te, re etc.* Of, by, in being about to be struck,
Inchoative Present.			
Dal-ok̓-lagidok̓-kan-a, It is about to be struck.	*Dal-ok̓-lagidok̓-kan,* About being struck (now.)	*Dal-ok̓-lagidok̓-kan-khan,* Being about to be struck (now).	*Dal-ok̓-lagidok̓-kan-reak̓, te, re etc.,* Of, by, in being about to be struck (now.)
Inchoative Past.			
Dal-ok̓-lagidok̓-kan-tahĕkan-a, It was about to be struck.	*Dal-ok̓-lagidok̓-kan-tahĕkan,* About being struck (then.)	*Dal-ok̓-lagidok̓-kan-tahĕkan-khan,* Being about to be struck (then.)	*Dal-ok̓-lagidok̓-kan-tahĕkan-reak̓, te, re etc.,* Of, by, in being about to be struck (then.)
Optative.			
Dal-kok̓-a, It will, may, would, might be struck.	*Dal-kok̓,* Which would, might be struck.	*Dal-kok̓-khan,* If it only would be struck.	*Dal-kok̓-reak, te, re etc.,* Of by, in the possibility of being struck.

Tenses.	Adjective Participles.	Adverbial Participles.	Gerunds.
Conditional.			
(Oho) *Dal-len-a*, It will, can, would could not be struck.	*Dal-len*, Being struck or in case of being struck.	*Dal-len-khan*, Being or having been struck.	*Dal-len-reak', te, re etc.*, Of, by, in being struck.
Contingent.			
Dal-en-gi, It will or would be struck.			
Preliminary Future.			
Dal-len-gi, It will (must) first be struck.			
Preliminary Expostulative.			
Dal-len-nahī, It must first be struck.		*Dal-len-ṅahī*, Being first struck.	
Preliminary Persuasive.			
Dal-len-baṅ, It must first be struck.		*Dal-len-baṅ*, Being first struck.	
Preliminary Admissive.			
Dal-len-en-a, It must first be struck.		*Dal-len-ena*, Being first struck.	

Tenses.	Adjective Participles.	Adverbial Participles.	Gerunds.
Preliminary Benedictive.			
Dal-len-ma! May it first be struck!			
Preliminary Imperative.			
Dal-len-ma! Let it first be struck.			
Benedictive.			
Dal-ok̇-ma! May it be struck!			
Imperative.			
Dal-ok̇-ma! Let it be struck.			
Infinitive.			
Dal-ok̇, To be struck.			

TABLES OF THE FORMATION OF THE VERBS.

ACTIVE.

ACCUSATIVE.

(ANIMATE.)

THE TENSES.	ADJECTIVE PARTICIPLES.	ADVERBIAL PARTICIPLES.	GERUNDS.
FUTURE.			
Dal-ko-a-e, He will strike them.	*Dal-ko*,* (the) struck (ones.)	*Dal-ko-khan*, Striking them.	*Dal-ko-reaḱ, te, re*, Of, by, in striking them.
GENERAL INOCMPLETE PRESENT.			
Dal-et'-ko-a-e, He strikes them.	*Dal-et'-ko*, They whom they strike.	*Dal-et'-ko-khan*, Striking them.	*Dal-et'-ko-reaḱ, te, re*, Of, by, in striking them.
SPECIAL INCOMPLETE PRESENT.			
Dal-et'-ko-† *kan-a-e*, He is striking them.	*Dal-et'-ko-kan*, They whom they are stricking.	*Dal-et'-ko-kan-khan* Striking them (now.)	*Dal-et'-ko-kan-reaḱ, te, re*, Of, by, in striking them now.
RECENT PAST.			
Dal-ket'-ko-a-e, He struck, or, has struck them.	*Dal-ket'-ko*, They whom they struck.	*Dal-ket'-ko-khan*, Having struck them.	*Dal-ket'-ko-reaḱ, te, re*, Of, by, in having struck them.

* Any of the pronominal suffixes may be affixed or infixed to show the nominative and accusative respectively; as *Dal-e-a-ko*, they will strike him; *Dal-ben-a-kin*, they two will strike you two.

† In 1st and 3rd person singular *et'* is generally dropped; as *Dal-eǹ-kanae*, *Dal-e-kanae*.

Tenses.	Adjective Participles.	Adverbial Participles.	Gerunds.
Anterior Past.			
*Dal-let'-ko-a-e,** He struck or had struck them.	*Dal-let'-ko,* They whom they struck.	*Dal-let'-ko-khan,* Having struck them.	*Dal-let'-ko-reak', te, re,* Of, by, in having struck them.
General Incomplete Past.			
Dal-et'-ko-tahēkan-a-e, He used to strike them.	*Dal-et'-ko-takē-kan,* They whom they used to strike.	*Dal-et'-ko-tahēnkan-khan,* Using to strike them.	*Dal-et'-ko-tahēkan-reak', te, re,* Of, by, in using to strike them.
Special Incomplete Past.			
Dal-et'-ko-kan-tahē-kan-a-e, He was striking them.	*Dal-et'-ko-kan-tahē-kan,* They whom they were striking.	*Dal-et'-ko-kan-tahē-kan-khan,* Striking them then.	*Dal-et'-ko-kan-tahēkan-reak', te, re,* Of, by, in striking them then.
Indicisive Pluperfect.			
Dal-let'-ko-tahēkan-a-e,† He had struck them.	*Dal-let'-ko-tahēkan,* They whom they had struck.	*Dal-let'-ko-tahēkan-khan,* Having struck them.	*Dal-let'-ko-tahēkan-reak', te, re,* Of, by, in having struck them.
Inchoative Future.			
Dal-ko-lagit'-e, He will be about to strike them.	*Dal-ko-lagit',* They whom they will be about to strike.	*Dal-ko-lagit-khan,* Being about to strike them.	*Dal-ko-lagit'-reak', te, re,* Of, by, in being about to strike them.

* There is yet another form for this tense : *Dal-lak'-ko-a-e.* † Also for this tense is another form, *Dal-lak'-ko-takē-kanae.*

Tenses.	Adjective Participles.	Adverbial Participles.	Gerunds.
Inchoative Present.			
Dal-ko-lagid-ok̆-kan-a-e, He is about to strike them.	*Dal-ko-lagidok̆-kan*, They whom they are about to strike.	*Dal-ko-lagidok̆-kan-khan*, Being now about to strike them.	*Dal-ko-lagidok̆-kan-reak̆, re*, Of, by, in being about to strike them now.
Inchoative Past.			
Dal-ko-lagid-ok̆-kan tahēkan-a-e, He was about to strike them.	*Dal-ko-lagidok̆-kan-tahēkan*, They whom they were about to strike.	*Dal-ko-lagidok̆-kan-tahēkan-khan*, Being then about to strike them.	*Dal-ko-lagidok̆-kan-tahēkan-reak̆, te, re*, Of, by, in being about to strike them then.
Optative.			
Dal-ke-ko-a-e, He would strike them.	*Dal-keko*, They whom they would strike or have struck.	* *Dal-ke-ko-khan*, Wishing to strike them.	*Dal-ke-ko-reak̆, te, re*, Of, by, in wishing or having opportunity to strike them.
Conditional.			
(Oho) Dal-le-ko-a-e, He would (not) strike them.	*Dal-le-ko*, They whom they may have struck.	* *Dal-le-ko-khan*, In case of striking them.	*Dal-le-ko-reak̆, te, re*, Of, by, in striking them.
Contingent.			
Dal-ket'-ko-gi-e, He strikes, will or would strike, them.			

* The difference between *lekhan* and *kekhan* is that the former shows only the condition, whereas the latter also expresses the wish; as *onam emliǹ-khan iǹ hataokea*, If you gave it to me I would take it; *onam emkiǹkhan adiǹ raskakok'a*, If you only would give it etc.

TENSES.	ADJECTIVE PARTICIPLES.	ADVERBIAL PARTICIPLES.	GERUNDS.
PRELIMINARY FUTURE.			
Dal-le-ko-gi-e, He will first strike them.			
PRELIMINARY EXPOSTULATIVE.			
Dal-le-ko-nahī-e, He must first strike them.		*Dal-le-ko-nohī,* First striking them.	
PRELIMINARY PERSUASIVE.			
Dal-le-ko-ba-e, He must first strike them.		*Dal-le-ko-bań,* First striking then.	
PRELIMINARY ADMISSIVE.			
Dal-le-ko-en-a-e, He must first strike them.		*Dal-le-ko-ena,* First striking them.	
PRELIMINARY BENEDICTIVE.			
Dal-le-ko-ma-m! Mayest thou first strike them!			
PRELIMINARY IMPERATIVE.			
Dal-le-ko-m! (or ko me), Strike thou them first!			

Tenses.	Adjective Participles.	Adverbial Participles.	Gerunds.
Benedictive. *Dal-ko-ma-m!* Mayest thou strike them!			
Imperative. *Dal-ko-m*, (or *ko me*) Strike thou them!			
Infinitive. *Dalko*, To strike them.			

Remark. Any of the accusative suffixes may be inserted instead of *ko*; as *dal-iñ*, *dal-me*, *dal-e*, *dal-liñ*, *dal-ben*, *dal-kin*, *dal-le*, *dal-pe*, to strike me, thee, him, us two etc.

TABLES OF THE FORMATION OF THE TENSES.

THE REFLEXIVE VOICE.

(ANIMATE.) *ACC. WITH NOM.*

TENSES.	ADJECTIVE PARTICIPLES.	ADVERBIAL PARTICIPLES	GERUNDS.
FUTURE.			
Dal-oḱ-a-e, He will strike himself.*	*Dal-oḱ*† Who will strike himself.	*Dal-oḱ-khan,* Willing to strike himself.	*Dal-oḱ-reaḱ, te, re, etc.,* Of, by, in (etc.) striking himself.
SPECIAL INCOMPLETE PRESENT.			
Dal-oḱ-kan-a-e, He is striking himself.	*Dal-oḱ-kan,* Who is striking himself.	*Dal-oḱ-kan-khan* Striking himself (now.)	*Dal-oḱ-kan-reaḱ, te, re, etc.* Of, by, in (etc.) striking himself (now.)
RECENT PAST.			
Dal-en-a-e, He struck, or has struck himself.	*Dal-en,* Who struck or has struck himself.	*Dal-en-khan,* Having struck himself.	*Dal-en-reaḱ te, re, etc.,* Of, by, in (etc.) having struck himself.
ANTERIOR PAST.			
Dal-len-a-e, He struck or had struck himself.	*Dal-len,* Who struck or had struck himself.	*Dal-len-khan,* Having struck himself.	*Dal-len-reaḱ, te, re, etc.* Of, by, in (etc.) having struck himself.

* Or *Dal-ok'-a-m,* thou wilt strike theyself etc.

† Any of the pronominal suffixes may be affixed, to show the nominative; as *Dalok'-ko,* they who will strike themselves, *Dalok'-ben,* you two, who will strike yourwselves.

Tenses.	Adjective Participles.	Adverbial Participles.	Gerunds.
Special Incomplete Past.			
Dal-oǩ-kan-tahēkan-a-e, He was striking himself.	*Dal-oǩ-kan-tahēkan,* Who was striking himself.	*Dal-oǩ-kan-tahēkan-khan,* Striking himself (then.)	*Dal-oǩ-kan-tahēkan-reaǩ, te, re, re etc.,* Of, by, in (etc.) striking himself, (then.)
Indecisive Pluperfect.			
Dal-len-tahēkan-a-e, He had struck himself.	*Dal-len-tahēkan,* Who had struck himself.	*Dal-len-tahēkhan-khan,* Having struck himself (before.)	*Dal-len-tahēkan-reaǩ, te, re etc.,* Of, by, in (etc.) having struck himself (before.)
Inchoative Future.			
Dal-oǩ-lagit'-e, He will be about to strike himself.	*Dal-oǩ-lagit',* Who will be about to strike himself.	*Dal-oǩ-lagit'-khan,* Being about to strike himself.	*Dal-oǩ-lagit'-reaǩ, te, re etc.,* Of, by, in (etc.) being about to strike himself.
Inchoative Present.			
Dal-oǩ-lagidoǩ-kan-a-e, He is about to strike himself.	*Dal-oǩ-lagidoǩ-kan,* Who is about to strike himself.	*Dal-oǩ-lagidoǩ-kan-khan,* Being about to strike himself (now.)	*Dal-oǩ-lagidoǩ-kan-reaǩ, te, re, etc.,* Of, by, in (etc.) being about to strike himself (now.)
Inchoative Past.			
Dal-oǩ-lagidoǩ-kan-tahēkan-a-e He was about to strike himself.	*Dal-oǩ-lagidoǩ-kan-tahēkan,* Who was about to strike himself.	*Dal-oǩ-lagidoǩ-kan-tahēkan-khan,* Being about to strike himself (then.)	*Dal-oǩ-lagidoǩ-kan-tahēkan-reaǩ te, re etc.,* Of, by, in (etc.) being about to strike himself (then.)

TENSES.	ADJECTIVE PARTICIPLES.	ADVERBIAL PARTICIPLES.	GERUNDS.
OPTATIVE. *Dal-koḱ-a-e*, He will or would strike himself.	*Dal-koḱ*, Who will or would strike himself.	*Dal-koḱ-khan*, Wishing to strike himself.	*Dal-koḱ-reaḱ, te, re, etc.*, Of, by, in (etc.) wishing to strike himself.
CONDITIONAL. *(Oho) Dal-len-a-e*, He will or would (not) strike himself.	*Dal-len*, Who may have struck himself.	*Dal-len-khan*, In case of striking or, having struck himself.	*Dal-len-reaḱ, te, re etc.*, Of, by, in (etc.) striking himself.
CONTINGENT. *Dal-en-gi-e*, He strikes, will or would strike himself.			
PRELIMINARY FUTURE. *Dal-len-gi-e*, He will first strike himself.			
PRELIMINARY EXPOSTULATIVE. *Dal-len-nahĩ-e*, He must first strike himself.		*Dal-len-nahĩ*, Having first struck himself.	
PRELIMINARY PERSUASIVE. *Dal-len-ba-e*, He must first strike himself.		*Dal-len-baṅ*, Having first struck himself.	

TENSES.	ADJECTIVE PARTICIPLES.	ADVERBIAL PARTICIPLES.	GERUNDS.
PRELIMINARY ADMISSIVE.			
Dal-len-en-a-e, He must first strike himself.		*Dal-len-ena,* Having first struck himself.	
PRELIMINARY BENEDECTIVE.			
Dal-len-ma-m! Mayest thou first strike thyself!			
PRELIMINARY IMPERATIVE.			
Dal-len-me! First strike thyself!			
BENEDICTIVE.			
Dal-ok-ma-m! Mayest thou strike thyself!			
IMPERATIVE.			
Dal-ok-me! Strike thyself!			
INFINITIVE.			
Dal-ok, To strike oneself.			

TABLES OF THE FORMATION OF THE TENSES.

ACTIVE.

(INANIMATE.) *DAT. WITH NOM.*

TENSES.	ADJECTIVE PARTICIPLES.	ADVERBIAL PARTICIPLES.	GERUNDS.
FUTURE.			
Dal-a-k̇-a-e, He will strike at or on it.	*Dal-ak̇*,* That at or on which one will strike.	*Dal-a-k̇-khan*, Striking at or on it.	*Dal-a-k̇-reak̇, te, re*, Of, by, in striking at it.
SPECIAL INCOMPLETE PRESENT.			
Dal-a-k̇-kan-a-e, He is striking at it.	*Dal-ak̇-kan*, That at which one is striking.	*Dal-a-k̇-kan-khan*, Striking now at it.	*Dal-a-k̇-kan-reak̇, te, re*, Of, by, in striking at it now.
RECENT PAST.			
Dal-at'-a-e, He struck at it.	*Dal-at'*, That at which one struck.	*Dal-at'-khan*, Having struck at it.	*Dal-at'-reak̇, te, re*, Of, by, in having struck at it.
PERFECT.			
Dal-akao-at'-a-e, He has struck at it.	*Dal-akao-at'*, That at which one has struck.	*Dal-akao-at'-khan*, Having struck at it.	*Dal-akao-at'-reak̇, te, re*, Of, by, in having struck at it.
SPECIAL INCOMPLETE PAST			
Dal-a-k̇-kan-tahē-kan-a-e, He was striking at it.	*Dal-ak̇-kan-tahē-kan*, That at which one was striking.	*Dal-ak̇-kan-tahē-kan-khan*, Striking at it then.	*Dal-ak̇-kan-tahēkan-reak̇, te, re*, Of, by, in striking at it then.

* Any of the pronominal suffixes may be affixed to show the nominative.

Tenses.	Adjective Participles.	Adverbial Participles.	Gerunds.
Indecisive Pluperfect.			
Dal-at'-tuhēkan-a-e, He had struck at it.	*Dal-at'-tahĕkan*, That at hich one had struck.	*Dal-at'-tahĕkan-khan*, Having struck at it.	*Dal-at'-tahĕkan-reak̓, te, re*, Of, by, in having struck at it.
Decisive Pluperfect.			
Dal-akao-at'-tahē-kan-a-e, He had struck at it.	*D.l-akao-at'-hahĕ-kan*, That at which one had struck.	*Dal-akao-at'-tahĕka-khan*, Having struck at it.	*Dal-akaoat'-tahĕkan-reak̓, te, re*, Of, by, in having struck at it.
Inchoative Future.			
Dal-a-k̓-lagit'-e, He will be about to strike at it.	*Dal-a-k̓-lagit'*, That at which one will be about to strike.	*Dal-a-k̓-lagit'-khan*, Being about to strike at it.	*Dal-ak̓-lagit'-reak̓, te, re*, Of, by, in being about to strike at it.
Inchoative Present.			
Dal a-k̓-lagid-ok̓-kun-a-e, He is about to strike at it.	*Dal-a-k̓-lagidok̓-kan*, That at which one is about to strike.	*Dal-a-k̓-lagidok̓-kan-khan*, Being now about to strike at it.	*Dal-ak̓-lagidok̓-kan-reak̓, te, re*, Of, by, in being now about to strike at it.
Inchoative Past.			
Dal-a-k̓-lagidok̓-kan-tahĕkan-a-e, He was about to strike at it.	*Dal-a-k̓-lagi 'ok̓-kan-tahĕkan*, That at which one was about to strike.	*Dal-a-k̓-lagidok̓-kan-tahĕkan-khan*, Being then about to strike at it.	*Dal-a-k̓-lagidok̓-kan-tahĕ,kan-reak̓, te, re*, Of, by, in being then about to strike at it.
Conditional Is wanting.	*Dal-akao-ak̓*, That at which one may have struck.	*Dal-akao-ak̓-khan*, Having struck at it.	*Dal-akao-ak̓-reak̓, te, re*, Of, by, in having struck at it.

TENSES.	ADJECTIVE PARTICIPLES.	ADVERBIAL PARTICIPLES.	GERUNDS.
CONTINGENT.			
Dal-at'-gi-e, He strikes, will or would strike at it.			
PRELIMINARY EXPOSTULATIVE.			
Dal-akao-a-k̇-nahī-e, He must first strike at it.		*Dal-akao-ak-nahī*, First striking at it.	
PRELIMINARY PERSUASIVE.			
Dal-akao-a-k̇-ba-e, He must first strike at it.		*Dal-akao-ak̇-baṅ*, First striking at it.	
PRELIMINARY ADMISSIVE.			
Dal-akao-a-k̇-ena-e, He must first strike at it.		*Dal-akao-ak̇-ena*, First striking at it.	
BENEDICTIVE.			
Dal-a-k̇-ma-m! May-est thou strike at it.			

Remark. By leaving out the nominative Suffixes, the dative case Neuter may be used as a passive; as *dare mak'-at'-a*. the tree was cut a little.

TENSES.	ADJECTIVE PARTICIPLES.	ADVERBIAL PARTICIPLES.	GERUNDS.
IMPERATIVE. *Dal-ak-me!* Strike thou at it! INFINITIVE. *Dal-ak*, To strike at it.			

Remark. The Preliminary Benedictive and Imperative are sometimes used, but very seldom; as *Sap'-akao-ak'-me.* be holding it!

TABLES OF THE FORMATION OF THE TENSES.

ACTIVE VOICE.

(ANIMATE.) *DAT. WITH NOM.*

TENSES.	ADJECTIVE PARTICIPLES.	ADVERBIAL PARTICIPLES.	GERUNDS.
FUTURE.			
Dal-a-ko-a-e, He will strike for them.	*Dal-a-ko*, They, for whom they,* or one will strike.	*Dal-a-ko-khan*, Striking for them.	*Dal-a-ko-reak', te, re etc.*, Of, by, in striking for them.
SPECIAL INCOMPLETE PRESENT.			
Dal-a-ko-kan-a-e, He is striking for them.	*Dal-a-ko-kan*, They, for whom, they are striking.	*Dal-a-ko-kan-khan*, Striking for them now.	*Dal-a-ko-kan-reak', te, re etc.*, Of, by, in striking for them now.
RECENT PAST.			
Dal-at'-ko-a-e, He struck or has struck for them.	*Dal-at'-ko*, They for whom they struck.	*Dal-at'-ko-khan*, Having struck for them.	*Dal-at'-ko-reak', te, re etc.*, Of, by, in having struck for them.
PERFECT.			
Dal-akao-at'-ko-a-e, He has struck for them.	*Dal-akao-at'-ko*, They for whom they have struck.	*Dal-a-kao-at'-ko-khan*, Having struck for them.	*Dal-akao-at'-ko-reak', te, re etc.*, Of by, in having struck for them.

* Impersonal. (*Germ. fur welche* man schlagen wird.)

Tenses.	Adverbial Participles.	Adjective Participles.	Gerunds.
Special incomplete Past.			
Dal-a-ko-kan-tahē-kan-a-e, He was striking for them.	*Dal-a-ko-kan-tahē-kan,* They, for whom they were striking.	*Dal-ako-kan-tahē-kan-khan,* Striking for them then.	*Dal-ako-kan-tahē an-reaķ, te, re etc.,* Of, by, in striking for them then.
Indicisive Pluperfect.			
Dal-at'-ko-tahē kan-a-e, He had struck for them.	*Dal-at'-ko-tahēkan,* They, for whom they had struck.	*Dal-at'-ko-tahēkhan khan,* Having struck for them.	*Dal-at'-ko-tahēkan-reaķ, te, re etc.,* Of, by, in having struck for them.
Decisive Pluperfect.			
Dal-akao-at'-ko-tahē-kan-a-e, He had struck for them.	*Dal-akao-at'-ko-tahē-kan,* They, for whom they had struck.	*Dal-akao-at'-ko-tahē-kan-khan,* Having struck for them.	*Dal-akao-at'-ko-tahē kan-reaķ, te, re etc.,* Of, by, in having struck for them.
Inchoative Future.			
Dal-ako-lagit'-e, He will be about to strike for them.	*Dal-ako-lagit',* They, for whom they will be about to strike.	*Dal-ako-lagit'-khan,* Being about to strike for them.	*Dal-ako-lagit'-reaķ, te, re etc.* Of by, in being about to strike for them.
Inchoative Present.			
Dal-a-ko-lagidoķ-kan-a-e, He is about to strike for them.	*Dal-ako-lagidoķ-kan,* They, for whom they are about to strike.	*Dal-ako-lagidoķ-kan-khan,* Being now about to strike for them.	*Dal-ako-lagidoķ-kan-reaķ, te, re etc.* Of, by, in being about to strike for them.

Tenses.	Adjective Participles.	Adverbial Participles.	Gerunds.
Inchoative Past.			
Dal-a-ko-lagidoḱ-kan tahēkan-a-e, He was about to strike for them.	*Dal-ako-lagidoḱ-kan tahēkan,* They, for whom they were about to strike.	*Dal-ako-lagidoḱ-kan -tahēkan-khan,* Being then about to strike for them.	*Dal-ako-lagidoḱ-kan-tahē-kan-reaḱ, te, re etc.,* Of, by, in being about to strike for them then.
Conditional.			
Is Wanting.	*Dal-akao-a-ko,* They for whom they may have struck.	*Dal-akao-a-ko-khan,* In case of having struck for them.	*Dal-akao-ako-reaḱ, te, re,* Of, by, in having struck for them.
Contingent.			
Dal-at'-ko-gi-e, He strikes, will or would strike, for them.			
Preliminary Expostulative.			
Dal-akao-a-ko-nahĩ-e, He must first strike for them.		*Dal-akao-ako-nahĩ,* First striking for them.	
Preliminary Persuasive.			
Dal-akao-a-ko-ba-e, He must first strike for them.		*Dal-akao-ako-baṅ,* First striking for them.	
Preliminary Admissive.			
Dal-akao-a-ko-en-a-e, He must first strike for them.		*Dal-akao-a-ko-ena,* First striking for them.	

TENSES.	ADJECTIVE PARTICIPLES.	ADVERBIAL PARTICIPLES.	GERUNDS.
BENEDICTIVE.			
Dal-a-ko-ma-m, Mayest thou strike for them!			
IMPERATIVE.			
Dal-a-ko-m! (or a-ko-me!) Strike thou for them!			
INFINITIVE.			
Dal-a-ko To strike for them.			

TABLES OF THE FORMATION OF THE TENSES.

THE REFLEXIVE VOICE.

(ANIMATE.)

DATIVE WITH NOMINATIVE.

TENSES.	ADJECTIVE PARTICIPLES.	ADVERBIAL PARTICIPLES	GERUNDS.
FUTURE.			
Dal-joiṅ-a-e, He will strike for himself.	*Dal-joṅ*,* Who will strike for himself.	*Da-joṅ-khan*, Striking for himself.	*Dal-joṅ-reak̇, te, re*, Of, by, in striking for himself.
SPECIAL INCOMPLETE PRESENT.			
Dal-joṅ-kan-a-e, He is striking for himself.	*Dal-joṅ-kan*, Who is striking for himself.	*Dal-joṅ-kan-khan*, Striking now for himself.	*Dal-joṅ-kan-reak̇, te, re*, Of, by, in striking for himself now.
RECENT PAST.			
Dal-an-a-e, He struck or has struck for himself.	*Dal-an*, Who struck for himself.	*Dal-an-khan*, Having struck for himself.	*Dal-an-reak̇, te, re*, Of, by, in having struck for himself.
PERFECT.			
Dal-akao-an-a-e, He has struck for himself.	*Dal-akao-an*, Who has struck for himself.	*Dal-akao-an-khan*, Having struck for himself.	*Dal-akao-an-reak̇, te, re*, Of, by, having struck for himself.

* Any of the pronominal suffixes may be affixed to show *who* will strike for himself; *Dal-joṅ-ko, Dal-joṅ-ben, Dal-joṅ-kin.*

Tenses.	Adjective Participles.	Adverbial Participles.	Gerunds.
Special incomplete Past.			
Dal-joṅ-kan-tahē-kan-a-e, He was striking for himself.	*Dal-joṅ-kan-tahē-kan,* Who was striking for himself.	*Dal-joṅ-kan-tahēkan-khan,* Striking then for himself.	*Dal-joṅ-kan-tahēkan-reaḱ, te, re,* Of, by, in striking then for himself.
Indecisive Pluperfect.			
Dal-an-tahēkan-a-e, He had struck for himself.	*Dal-an-tahēkan,* Who had struck for himself.	*Dal-an-tahēkan-khan* Having struck for himself.	*Dal-an-tahēkan-reaḱ, te, re,* Of, by, in having struck for himself.
Decisive Pluperfect.			
Dal-akao-an-tahēkan a-e, He had struck for himself.	*Dal-akao-an-tahēkan,* Who had struck for himself.	*Dal-akao-an-tahēkan-khan,* Having struck for himself.	*Dal-akao-an-tahēkan-reaḱ, te, re,* Of, by, in having struck for himself.
Inchoative Future.			
Dal-joṅ-lagit'-e, He will be about to strike for himself.	*Dal-joṅ-lagit',* Who will be about to strike for himself.	*Dal-joṅ-lagit'-khan,* Being about to strike for himself.	*Dal-joṅ-lagit'-reaḱ, te, re,* Of, by, in being about to strike for himself.
Inchoative Present.			
Dal-joṅ-lagidoḱ-kan-a-e, He is about to strike for himself.	*Dal-joṅ-lagidoḱ-kan,* Who is about to strike for himself.	*Dal-joṅ-lagidoḱ-kan-khan,* Being now about to strike for himself.	*Dal-joṅ-lagidoḱ-kan-reaḱ, te, re,* Of, by, in being about to strike for himself now.
Inchoative Past.			
Dal-joṅ-lagidoḱ-kan-tahēkan-a-e, He was about to strike for himself.	*Dal-joṅ-lagidoḱ-kan-tahēkan,* Who was about to strike for himself.	*Dal-joṅ-lagidoḱ-kan-tahēkan-khan* Being then about to strike for himself.	*Dal-joṅ-lagidoḱ-kan-tahē-kan-reaḱ, te, re,* Of by, in being about to strike for himself then.

Tenses.	Adjective Participles.	Adverbial Participles.	Gerunds.
Conditional.			
Is Wanting.	*Dal-an*, Who may have struck for himself.	*Dal-an-khan*, In case of striking for himself.	*Dal-an-reaḱ, te, ṛe*, Of, by, in striking for himself.
Conditional Perfect.			
Is wanting	*Dal-akao-an*, Who may have struck for himself.	*Dal-akao-an-khan*, Having struck for oneself.	*Dal-akao-an-reaḱ, te, ṛe*, Of by, in having struck for oneself.
Preliminary Future.			
Dal-an-gi-e, He will first strike for himself.			
Contingent.			
Dal-an-gi-e, He will or would strike, or strikes, for himself.			
Preliminary Expostultive.			
Dal-an-nahĩe, He must first strike for himself.		*Dal-an-nahĩ*, First striking for himself.	
Preliminary Persuasive.			
Dal-an-ba-e, He must first strike for himself.		*Dal-an-baṅ*, First striking for himself.	

Tenses.	Adjective Participles.	Adverbial Participles.	Gerunds.
Preliminary Admissive.			
Dal-an-en-a-e, He must first strike for himself.		*Dal-an-ena,* First striking for himself.	
Preliminary Perfect Expostulative.			
Dal-akao-an-nahĩ-e, He must first have struck for himself.		*Dal-akao-an-nahĩ,* Having first struck for himself.	
Preliminary Perfect Persuasive.			
Dal-akao-an-ba-e, He must first have struck for himself.		*Dal-akao-an-baṅ,* Having first struck for himself.	
Preliminary Perfect Admissive.			
Dal-akao-an-en-a-e, He must first have struck for himself.		*Dal-akao-an-ena,* Having first struck for himself.	
Preliminary Benedictive.			
Dal-an-ma-m! Mayest thou first strike for thyself.			
Preliminary Imperative.			
Dal-an-me, Strike thou first for thyself!			

TENSES.	ADJECTIVE PARTICIPLES.	ADVERBIAL PARTICIPLES.	GERUNDS.
BENEDICTIVE. *Dal-joṅ-ma-m!* Mayest thou strike for thyself! IMPERATIVE. *Dal-joṅ-me!* Strike thou for thyself! INFINITIVE. *Dal-joṅ,* To strike for oneself.			

TABLES OF THE FORMATION OF THE TENSES.

THE RESERVATIVE FORM.

(ANIMATE.)

ACC. WITH NOM. ACTIVE.

TENSES.	ADJECTIVE PARTICIPLES.	ADVERBIAL PARTICIPLES.	GERUNDS.
FUTURE.			
Dal-kak̇-a-e, He will strike it (and leave it.)	*Dal-kak̇,* * Which one wills trike (and leave.)	*Dal-kak̇-khan,* Striking it (and leaving it.)	*Dal-kak̇-reak̇, te, re,* Of, by, in striking it.
SPECIAL INCOMPLETE PRESENT.			
Dal-kak̇-kan-a-e, He is striking it.	*Dal-kak̇-kan,* Which one is striking.	*Dal-kak̇-kan-khan,* Striking it now.	*Dal-kak̇-kan-rĕak̇, te, re.* Of, by, in striking it now.
RECENT PAST.			
Dal-kat'-a-e, He struck it.	*Dal-kat',* Which one struck.	*Dal-kat'-khan,* Having struck it.	*Dal-kat'-reak̇, te, re,* Of, by in having struck it.
PERFECT.			
Dal-akat'-a-e, He has struck it.	*Dal-akat',* Which one has struck.	*Dal-akat'-khan,* Having struck it.	*Dal-akat'-reak̇, te, re,* Of, by, in having struck it.
SPECIAL INCOMPLETE PAST.			
Dal-kak̇-kan-tahē-kan-a-e, He was striking it.	*Dal-kak̇-kan-tahē-kan,* Which one was striking.	*Dal-kak̇-kan-tahē-kan-khan,* Striking it then.	*Dal-kak̇-kan-tahĕkan-reak̇-te, re,* Of, by, in striking it then.

* Any of the Pronominal suffixes may be affixed to show the nominative case.

TENSES	ADJECTIVE PARTICIPLES.	ADVERBIAL PARTICIPLES.	GERUNDS.
INDECISIVE PLUPERFECT.			
Dal-kat'-tahēkan-a-e, He had struck it.	*Dal-kat'-tahēkan*, Which one had struck.	*Dal-kat'-tahēkan-khan*, Having struck it.	*Dal-kat'-tahēkan-reaḱ, te, re*, Of by, in having struck it.
DECISIVE PLUPERFECT.			
Dal-akat'-tahēkan-a-e, He had struck it.	*Dal-akat'-tahēkan*, Which one had struck.	*Dal-akat'-tahēkan-khan*, Having struck it.	*Dal-akat'-tahēkan-reaḱ, te, re*, Of, by, in having struck it.
INCHOATIVE FUTURE.			
Dal-kaḱ-lagit'-e, He will be about to strike it.	*Dal-kaḱ-lagit'*, Which one will be about to strike.	*Dal-kaḱ-lagit'-khan*, Being about to strike it.	*Dal-kaḱ-lagit'-reaḱ, te, re*, Of, by, in being about to strike it.
INCHOATIVE PRESENT.			
Dal-kaḱ-lagidoḱ-kan-a-e, He is about to strike it.	*Dal-kaḱ-lagidoḱ-kan*, Which one is about to strike.	*Dal-kaḱ-lagidoḱ-kan-khan*, Being now about to strike it.	*Dal-kaḱ-lagidoḱ-kan-reaḱ te, re*, Of, by, in being, now about to strike it.
INCHOATIVE PAST.			
Dal-kaḱ-lagidoḱ-kan-tahēkan-a-e, He was about to strike it.	*Dal-kaḱ-lagidoḱ-kan-tahēkan*, Which one was about to strike.	*Dal-kaḱ-lagidoḱ-kan-tahēkan-khan*, Being then about to strike it.	*Dal-kaḱ-lagidoḱ-kan-tahēkan-reaḱ, te, re*, Of, by, in being then about to strike it.
CONDITIONAL.			
Is wanting.	*Dal-akae*, Which they may have struck.	*Dal-akae-khan*, (In case) of having struck it.	*Dal-akae-reaḱ, te, re, etc.* Of by in (etc.) having struck.

TENSES.	ADJECTIVE PARTICIPLES.	ADVERBIAL PARTICIPLES.	GERUNDS.
CONTINGNT.			
Dal-kat'-gi-e, He strikes, will or would strike it.			
PRELIMINARY EXPOSTULATIVE.			
Dal-akae-nahī-e, He must first have struck it.		*Dal-akae-nahī*, Having struck it.	
PRELIMINARY PERSUASIVE.			
Dal-akae-ba-e, He must first have struck it.		*Dal-akae-baṅ*, Having struck it.	
PRELIMINARY ADMISSIVE.			
Dal-akae-en-a-e, He must first have struck it.		*Dal-akae-ena*, Having struck it.	
PRELIMINARY BENEDICTIVE.			
Dal-akae-ma-m! Mayest thou be striking (it.)			
PRELIMINARY IMPERATIVE.			
Dal-akae-me! Be thou striking!			

TENSES.	ADJECTIVE PARTICIPLES.	ADVERBIAL PARTICIPLES.	GERUNDS.
BENEDICTIVE. *Dal-ka-k̓-ma-m!* Mayest thou strike it! IMPERATIVE. *Dal-ka-k̓-me!* Strike it! INFINITIVE. *Dal-kak̓*, To strike it.			

Remarks. The preliminary future is formed in an irregular way : *dal-kak̓-ge-re-e*, he will first strike.

TABLES OF THE FORMATION OF THE TENSES.

THE RESERVATIVE FORM. ACTIVE.

ACC. WITH NOM.

(ANIMATE.)

TENSES.	ADJECTIVE PARTICIPLES.	ADVERBIAL PARTICIPLES.	GERUNDS.
FUTURE. *Dal-ka-ko-a-e*, He will strike them (and leave them till further.)	*Dal-ka-ko,** They whom they will strike (and leave.)	*Dal-ka-ko-khan*, striking them.	*Dal-ka-ko-reak*, *te*, *re*, Of, by, in striking them.
SPECIAL INCOMPLETE PRESENT. *Dal-ka-ko-kan-a-e*, He is striking them.	*Dal-ka-ko-kan*, They whom thy are striking.	*Dal-ka-ko-kan-khan*, Striking them now.	*Dal-ka-ko-kan-reak*, *te*, *re*, Of, by, in striking them now.
RECENT PAST. *Dal-kat'-ko-a-e*, He struck them.	*Dal-kat'-ko*, They whom they struck.	*Dal-kat'-ko-khan*, Having struck them.	*Dal-kat'-ko-reak*, *te*, *re*, Of, by, in having struck them.
PERFECT. *Dal-akat'-ko-a-e*, He has struck them.	*Dal-akat'-ko*, They whom they have struck.	*Dal-akat'-ko-khan*, Having struck them.	*Dal-akat'-ko-reak*, *te*, *re*, Of, by, in having struck them.

* Any of the pronomninal suffixes may be affixed to show the nominativeor case.

Tenses.	Adjective Participles.	Adverbial Participles.	Gerunds.
Special Incomplete Past.			
Dal-ka-ko-kan-tahĕkan-a-e, He was striking them.	*Dal-ka-ko-kan-tahĕkan,* They whom they were striking.	*Dal-ka-ko-kan-tahĕkan-khan,* striking them then.	*Dal-ka-ko-kan-tahĕkan-reaḱ, te, re,* Of, by, in striking them then.
Indecisive Pluperfect.			
Dal-kat'-ko-tahĕkan-a-e, He had struck them.	*Dal-kat'-ko-tahĕkan,* They whom they had struck.	*Dal-kat'-ko-tahĕkan-khan,* Having struck them.	*Dal-kat'-ko-tahĕkan-reaḱ, te, re,* Of, by, in having struck them.
Decisive Pluperfect.			
Dal-akat'-ko-tahĕkan-a-e, He had struck them.	*Dal-akat'-ko-tahĕkan,* They, whom they had struck.	*Dal-akat'-ko-tahĕkan-khan,* Having struck them.	*Dal-akat'-ko-tahĕkan-reaḱ, te, re,* Of, by, in having struck them.
Inchoative Future.			
Dal-ka-ko-lagit'-e, He will be about to strike them.	*Dal-ka-ko-lagit'* They whom they will be about to strike.	*Dal-ka-ko-lagit'-khan,* Being about to strike them.	*Dal-ka-ko-lagit'-reaḱ, te, re,* Of, by, in being about to strike them.
Inchoative Present.			
Dal-ka-ko-lagidoḱ-kan-a-e, He is about to strike them.	*Dal-ka-ko-lagidoḱ-kan,* They whom they are now about to strike.	*Dal-ka-ko-lagidoḱ-kan-khan,* Being now about to strike them.	*Dal-ka-ko-lagidoḱ-kan-reaḱ, te, re,* Of, by, in being now about to strike them.

TENSES.	ADJECTIVE PARTICIPLES.	ADVERBIAL PARTICIPLES.	GERUNDS.
INCHOATIVE PAST.			
Dal-ka-ko-lagi dok̇-kan-tahĕkan-a-e, He was about to strike them.	*Dal-ka-ko-lagi dok̇-kan-tahĕkan*, They whom they were about to strike.	*Dal-ka-ko-lagi dok̇-kan-tahĕkan-khan*, Being then about to strike them.	*Dal-ka-ko-lagidok̇, -kan-tahĕkan-reak̇,-te,re*, Of, by, in being then about to strike them.
CONDITIONAL. Is wanting.	*Dal-aka-ko*, They whom they may have struck.	*Dal-aka-ko-khan*, Having struck them.	*Dal-aka-ko-reak̇, te, re*, Of, by, in having struck them.
CONTINGENT.			
Dal-kat'-ko-gi-e, He strikes, will or would strike them.			
PRELIMINARY EXPOSTULATIVE.			
Dal-aka-ko-nahĩ-e, He must first have struck them.		*Dal-aka-ko-nahĩ*, Having first struck them.	
PRELIMINARY PERSUASIVE.			
Dal-aka-ko-ba-e, He must first have struck them.		*Dal-aka-ko-baṅ*, Having first struck them.	

TENSES.	ADJECTIVE PARTICIPLES.	ADVERBIAL PARTICIPLES.	GERUNDS.
PRELIMINARY ADMISSIVE.			
Dal-aka-ko-en-a-e, He must first have struck them.		*Dal-aka-ko-ena*, Having first struck them.	
PRELIMINARY BENEDICTIVE.			
Dal-aka-ko-ma-m! Mayest thou be striking them!			
PRELIMINARY IMPERATIVE.			
Dal-aka-ko-m! Be thou striking them!			
BENEDICTIVE.			
Dal-ka-ko-ma-m! Mayest thou strike them!			
IMPERATIVE.			
Dal-ka-ko-m! (*or-ko-me!*) Strike thou them!			
INFINITIVE.			
Dal-ka-ko, To strike them.			

TABLES OF THE FORMATION OF THE TENSES.

RESERVATIVE FORM.

(ANIMATE.)

REFLEXIVE VOICE.

TENSES.	ADJECTIVE PARTICIPLES.	ADVERBIAL PARTICIPLES.	GERUNDS.
FUTURE.			
Dal-kok-a-e, He will strike himself.	*Dal-kok,** Who will strike himself.	*Dal-kok-khan,* Striking himself.	***Dal-kok-reak, te, re,*** Of, by, in striking himself.
SPECIAL INCOMPLETE PRESENT.			
Dal-kok-kan-a-e. He is striking himself.	*Dal-kok-kan,* Who is striking himself.	*Dal-kok-kan-khan,* Striking himself now.	***Dal-kok-kan-reak, te, re,*** Of, by, in striking himself now.
SPECIAL INCOMPLETE PAST.			
Dal-kok-kan-tahēkan-a-e, He was striking himself.	*Dal-kok-kan-tahēkan,* Who was striking himself.	*Dal-kok-kan-tahēkan-khan,* Striking himself then.	*Dal-kok-kan-tahēkan-reak, te, re,* Of, by, in striking himself then.
PERFECT.			
Dal-akan-a-e, He has struck himself.	*Dal-akan,* Who has struck himself.	*Dal-akan-khan,* Having struck himself.	*Dal-akan-reak, te, re,* Of, by, in having struck himself.
DECISIVE PLUPERFECT.			
Dal-akan-tahēkan-a-e, He had struck himself.	*Dal-akan-tahēkan,* Who had struck himself.	*Dal-akan-tahēkan-khan,* Having struck himself.	*Dal-akan-tahēkan-reak, te, re,* Of, by, in having struck himself.

* Any of the pronominal suffixes may be affixed to show the Nominative case.

Remark.—The Preliminary Future is formed irregularly; as *dal-kok-ge-re,* I will first strike myself.

TENSES.	ADJECTIVE PARTICIPLES.	ADVERBIAL PARTICIPLES.	GERUNDS.
INCHOATIVE FUTURE.			
Dal-koǩ-lagit'-e, He will be about to strike himself.	*Dal-koǩ-lagit'*, Who will be about to strike himself.	*Dal-koǩ-lagit'-khan*, Being about to strike himself.	*Dal-koǩ*, *lagit' reaǩ*, *te*, *re*, Of, by, in being about to strike himself.
INCHOATIVE PRESENT.			
Dal-koǩ-lagidoǩ-kan-a-e, He is about to strike himself.	*Dal-koǩ-lagidoǩ-kan*, Who is about to strike himself.	*Dal-koǩ-lagidoǩ-kan-khan*, Being now about to strike himself.	*Dal-koǩ-lagidoǩ-kan-reaǩ*, *te*, *re*, Of, by, in being now about to strike himself.
INCHOATIVE PAST.			
Dal-koǩ-lagidoǩ-kan-tahēkan-a-e, He was about to strike himself.	*Dal-koǩ-lagidoǩ-kan-tahēkan*, Who was about to strike himself.	*Dal-koǩ-lagidoǩ-kan-tahēkan-khan*, Being then about to strike himself.	*Dal-koǩ-lagidok-kan-tahē-kan-reaǩ*, *te*, *re*, Of, by, in being then about to strike himself.
PRELIMINARY EXPOSTULATIVE.			
Dal-akan-nahī-e, He must first have struck himself.		*Dal-akan-nahī*, Having first struk himself.	
PRELIMINARY PERSUASIVE.			
Dal-akan-ba-e, He must first have struck himself.		*Dal-akan-baṅ*, Having first struk himself.	

Tenses.	Adjective Participles.	Adverbial Participles.	Gerunds.
PRELIMINARY ADMISSIVE.			
Dal-akan-en-a-e, He must first have struck himself.		*Dal-akan-ena*, Striking first himself.	
BENEDICTIVE.			
Dal-koḱ-ma-m! Mayest thou strike thyself!			
IMPERATIVE.			
Dal-koḱ-me! Strike thou thyself!			
INFINITIVE.			
Dal-koḱ, To strike oneself.			

TABLES OF THE FORMATION OF THE TENSES.

INTENSIVE FORM.

NOM. CASE. ACTIVE.

(ANIMATE.)

TENSES.	ADJECTIVE PARTICIPLES.	ADVEBIAL PARTICIPLES.	GERUNDS.
FUTURE.			
Da-dal-a-e, He will strike.	*Da-dal*, Striking, strikes.	*Da-dal-khan*, Striking.	*Da-dal-reak̃*, *te*, *re*, Of, by, in striking.
SPECIAL INCOMPLETE PRESENT.			
Da-dal-kan-a-e, He is striking.	*Da-dal-kan*, Who is striking.	*Da-dal-kan-khan*, Being striking now.	*Da-dal-kan-reak̃*, *te*, *re*, Of, by, in striking now.
SPECIAL INCOMPLETE PAST.			
Da-dal-kan-tahē-kan-a-e, He was striking.	*Da-dal-kan-tahēkan*, Who was striking.	*Da-dal-kan-tahēkan-khan*, Being striking then.	*Da-dal-kan-tahēkan-reak̃*, *te*, *re*, Of, by, in striking then.
INCHOATIVE FUTURE.			
Da-dal-lagit'-e, He will be about to strike.	*Da-dal-lagit'*, Who will be about to strike.	*Da-dal-lagit'-khan*, Being about to strike.	*Da-dal-lagit'-reak̃*, *te*, *re*, Of, by, in being about to strike.
INCHOATIVE PRESENT.			
Da-dal-lagidok̃-kan-a-e, He is about to strike.	*Da-dal-lagidok̃-kan*, Who is about to strike.	*Da-dal-lagidok̃-kan-khan*, Being about to strike now.	*Da-dal-lagidok̃-kan-reak̃*, *te*, *re*. Of, by, in being now about to strike.

TENSES.	ADJECTIVE PARTICIPLES.	ADVERBIAL PARTICIPLES.	GERUNDS.
INCHOATIVE PAST. *Da-dal-lagidok̇-kan-tahēkan-a-e*, He was about to strike.	*Da-dal-lagidok̇-kan-thaēkan*, Who was about to strike.	*Da-dal-lagidok̇-kan-tahēkan-khan*, Being about to strike then.	*Da-dal-lagidok̇-kan-tahē-kan-reak̇*, *te*, *re*, Of, by, in being then about to strike.
INFINITIVE. *Da-dal*, To strike.			

Remark.—The Repetitive Form *d̀al-dal* has also an intensive form; as *Dak'-dal-a-e*, he will go on to strike (till he is ready). The full form would be *da-da-dal-a-e*, but the repetition is effected by the *k'*; as *Bek'-naoich'*, instead of *Be-be-naoich'*.

TABLES OF THE FORMATION OF THE TENSES.

THE INTENSIVE FORM.

(ANIMATE). *REFLEXIVE VOICE.*

TENSES.	ADJECTIVE PARTICIPLES.	ADVERBIAL PARTICIPLES.	GERUNDS.
FUTURE.			
Dal-og-oǩ-a-e, He will strike himself.	*Dal-og-oǩ*, Who will strike himself.	*Dal-og-oǩ-khan*, Striking himself.	*Dal-og-oǩ-reaǩ-te, re*, Of, by, in striking himself.
SPECIAL INCOMPLETE PRESENT.			
Dal-og-oǩ-kan-a-e, He is striking himself.	*Dal-og-oǩ-kan*, Who is striking himself.	*Dal-og-oǩ-kan-khan*, Striking now himself.	*Dal-og-oǩ-kan-reaǩ, te, re* Of, by, in striking himself now.
SPECIAL INCOMPLETE PAST.			
Dal-og-oǩ-kan-tahē-kan-a-e, He was striking himself.	*Dal-og-oǩ-kan-tahē-kan*, Who was striking himself.	*Dal-og-oǩ-kan-tahē-kan-khan*, Striking then himself.	*Dal-og-oǩ-kan-tah ē kan-reaǩ' te, re*, Of, by, in striking himself then.
INCHOATIVE FUTURE.			
Dal-og-oǩ-lagit'-e, He will be about to strike himself.	*Dal-og-oǩ-lagit'*, Who will be about to strike himself.	*Dal-og-oǩ-logit'-khan*, Being about to strike himself.	*Dal-og-oǩ-lagit'-reaǩ, te, re*, Of, by, in being about to strike himself.
INCHOATIVE PRESENT.			
Dal-og-oǩ-lagidoǩ-kan-a-e, He is about to strike himself.	*Dal-og-oǩ-lagidoǩ-kan*, Who is about to strike himself.	*Dal-og-oǩ-lagidoǩ-kan-khan*, Being now about to strike himself.	*Dal-og-oǩ-lagidoǩ-kan-reaǩ, te, re*, Of, by, in being now about to strike himself.

TENSES.	ADJECTIVE PARTICIPLES.	ADVERBIAL PARTICIPLES.	GERUNDS.
INCHOATIVE PAST. *Dal-og-ok̓-lagidok̓-kan-tahēkan-a-e*, He was about to strike himself.	*Dal-og-ok̓-lagi dok̓-kan-tahēkan*, Who was about to strike himself.	*Dal-og-ok̓-lagi dok̓-kan-tahēkan-khan*, Being then about to strike himself.	*Dal-og-ok̓-lagidok̓-kan-ta-hēkan-reak̓*, *te*, *re*, Of, by, in then being about to strike himself.
BENEDICTIVE. *Dal-og-ok̓-mam*, Mayest thou strike thyself!			
IMPERATIVE. *Dal-og-ok̓-me*, Strike thou thyself!			
INFINITIVE. *Dal-og-ok̓*, To strike oneself.			

Remark.—By ommitting the nominative suffix "e" the subject will be inanimate, and is used passively; as ***dal-og-ok'-a***, it will be struck.

TABLES OF THE FORMATION OF THE TENSES.

THE CONTINUATIVE FORM.

(OBJECT INANIMATE.) *NOMINATIVE. ACTIVE.*

TENSES.	ADJECTIVE PARTICIPLES.	ADVERBIAL PARTICIPLES.	GERUNDS.
FUTURE.			
Dal-akae-tahen-a-e, He will continue to strike.	*Dal-akae-tahen,* Who will continue to strike.	*Dal-akae-tahen-khan,* Continuing to strike.	*Dal-akae-tahen-reaḱ, te, re,* Of, by, in continuing to strike.
SPECIAL INCOMPLETE PRESENT.			
Dal-akae-tahen-kan-a-e, He is continuing to strike.	*Dal-akae-tahen-kan,* Who is continuing to strike.	*Dal-akae-tahen-kan-khan,* Continuing now to strike.	*Dal-akae-tahen-kan-reaḱ, te, re,* Of, by, in continuing to strike now.
SPECIAL INCOMPLETE PAST.			
Dal-akae-tahĕkan-a-e, He was continuing to strike.	*Dal-akae-tahĕkan,* Who was continuing to strike.	*Dal-akae-tahĕkan-khan,* Continuing then to strike.	*Dal-akae-tahĕkan-reaḱ, te, re,* Of, by, in continuing to strike then.
INCHOATIVE FUTURE.			
Dal-akae-tahen-lagit'-e, He will be about to continue to strike.	*Dal-akae-tahen-lagit'* Who will be about to continue to strike.	*Dal-akae-tahen-lagit'-khan,* Being about to continue to strike.	*Dal-akae-tahen-lagit'-reaḱ, te, re,* Of, by, in being about to continue to strike.

Tenses.	Adjective Participles.	Adverbial Participles.	Gerunds.
Inchoative Present. *Dal-akae-tahen-lagi-dok̓-kan-a-e,* He is about to continue to strike.	*Dal-akae-tahen-lagi-dok̓-kan,* Who is about to continue to strike.	*Dal-akae-tahen-lagi-dok̓-kan-khan,* Being now about to continue to strike.	*Dal-akae-tahen-lagidok̓-kan-reak̓, te, re,* Of by, in being about to continue to strike now.
Inchoative Past. *Dal-akae-tahen-la-gidok̓-kan-tahēkan-a-e,* He was about to continue to strike.	*Dal-akae-tahen-lagi-dok̓-kan-tahēkan,* Who was about to continue to strike.	*Dal-akae-tahen-lagi-dok̓-kan-tahēkan-khan,* Being then about to continue to strike.	*Dal-akae-tahen-lagidok̓-kan-tahēkan-reak̓, te, re,* Of, by, in being then about to continue to strike.
Optative. *Dal-akae-tahē-ke-a-e,* He would continue to strike.	*Dal-akae-tahēke,* Who would continue to strike.	*Dal-akae-tahē-ke-khan,* (If one) willing to continue to strike.	*Dal-akae-tahēkan-reak̓, te, re,* Of, by, in wishing to continue to strike.
Conditional. *(Ohọ) Dal-akae-tahē-le-a-e,* He would (not) continue to strike.	*Dal-akae-tahē-le,* Who may have continued to strike.	*Dal-akae-tahē-le-khan* In case of continuing striking.	*Dal-akae-tahē,-le-reak̓, te. re,* Of, by, in continuing striking.
Contingent. *Dal-akae-tahē-ket'-gi-e* He continues, will or would continue to strike.			

TENSES.	ADJECTIVE PARTICIPLES.	ADVERBIAL PARTICIPLES.	GERUNDS.
PRELIMINARY FUTURE.			
Dal-akae-tahē-legi-e, He will first continue to strike.			
PRELIMINARY EXPOSTULATIVE.			
Dal-akae-tahē-le-nahī-e, He must first continue to strike.		*Dal-akae-tahē-le-nahī*, First continuing to strike.	
PRELIMINARY PERSUASIVE.			
Dal-akae-tahē-le-ba-e, He must first continue to strike.		*Dal-akae-tahē-le-baṅ*, First continuing to strike.	
PRELIMINARY ADMISSIVE.			
Dal-akae-tahē-le-éna-e, He must first continue to strike.		*Dal-akae-tahē-le-ena*, First continuing to strike.	
PRELIMINARY BENEDICTIVE.			
Dal-akae-tahē-le-mam! Mayest thou first continue to strike.			
PRELIMINARY IMPERATIVE.			
Dal-akae-tahē-le-m! Continue thou first to strike.			

TENSES.	ADJECTIVE PARTICIPLES.	ADVERBIAL PARTICIPLES.	GERUNDS.
BENEDICTIVE. *Dal-akae-tahen-mam!* Mayest thou continue to strike.			
IMPERATIVE. *Dal-akae-tahen-me!* Continue thou to strike.			
INFINITIVE. *Dal-akae-tahen,* To continue to strike.			

TABLES OF THE FORMATION OF THE TENSES.

THE CONTINUATIVE FORM.

(ANIMATE.) *ACC. WITH NOM. ACTIVE.*

TENSES.	ADJECTIVE PARTICIPLES.	ADVERBIAL PARTICIPLES.	GERUNDS.
FUTURE.			
Dal-aka-ko-tahen-a-e, He will continue to strike them.	*Dal-aka-ko-tahen,* They whom they will continue to strike.	*Dal-aka-ko-tahen-khan,* Continuing to strike them.	*Dal-aka-ko-tahen-reak̕, te, re,* Of, by, in continuing to strike them.
SPECIAL INCOMPLETE PRESENT.			
Dal-aka-ko-tahen-kan-a-e, He is continuing to strike them.	*Dal-aka-ko-tahen-kan,* They, whom they are continuing to strike.	*Dal-aka-ko-tahen-kan-khan,* Continuing now to strike them.	*Dal-aka-ko-tahen-kan-reak̕ to, re,* Of, by, in continuing to strike them now.
SPECIAL INCOMPLETE PAST.			
Dal-aka-ko-tahēkan-a-e, He was continuing to strike them.	*Dal-aka-ko-tahēkan,* They, whom they were continuing to strike.	*Dal-aka-ko-tahēkan-khan,* Continuing then to strike them.	*Dal-aka-ko-tahēkan-reak̕-te, re,* Of by, in continuing to strike them.
INCHOATIVE FUTURE.			
Dal-aka-ko-tahen-lagit̕-e, He will be about to continue to strike them.	*Dal-aka-ko-tahen-lagit̕,* They whom they will be about to continue to strike.	*Dal-akā-ko-tahen-lagit̕-khan,* Being about to continue to strike them.	*Dal-aka-ko-tahen-lagit̕-reak̕, te, re,* Of, by, in being about to continue to strike them.

TENSES.	ADJECTIVE PARTICIPLES.	ADVERBIAL PARTICIPLES.	GERUNDS.
INCHOATIVE PRESENT.			
Dal-aka-ko-tahen-lagidoḱ-kan-a-e, He is about to continue to strike them.	*Dal-aka-ko-tahen-lagidoḱ-kan,* They whom they are about to continue etc.	*Dal-aka-ko-tahen-lagidoḱ-kan-khan,* Being now about to continue to strike them.	*Dal-aka-ko-tahen-lagidoḱ-kan-reaḱ, te, re,* Of, by, in being now about to continue to strike them.
INCHOATIVE PAST.			
Dal-aka-ko-tahen-lagidoḱ-kan-tahēkan-a-e, He was about to continue to strike them.	*Dal-aka-ko-tahen-lagidoḱ-kan-tahīkan,* They, whom they were about to continue to strike.	*Dal-akako-tahen-lagidoḱ-kan-khan,* Being then about to continue to strike them.	*Dal-aka-ko-tahen-lagidoḱ-kan-tahēkan-reaḱ te, re,* Of, by, in being then about to continue to strike them.
OPTATIVE.			
Dal-aka-ko-tahē-ke-a-e He would continue to strike them.	*Dal-aka-ko-tahē-ke,* They, whom they would continue to strike.	*Dal-aka-ko-tahē-ke-khan,* Wishing to continue to strike them.	*Dal-aka-ko-tahē-ke-reaḱ, te, re,* Of, by, in wishing to continue to strike them.
CONDITIONAL.			
(Qhọ) Dal-aka-ko-tahē-le-a-e, He would (not) continue to strike them.	*Dal-aka-ko-tahē-le,* They whom they may have continued to strike.	*Dal-aka-ko-tahē-le-khan,* In case of having continued to strike them.	*Dal-aka-ko-tahē-le-reaḱ, te, re,* Of, by, in having continued to strike them.

Tenses.	Adjective Participles.	Adverbial Participles.	Gerunds.
Contingent.			
Dal-aka-ko-tahĕ-ket'-gi-e, He continues, will or would continue to strike them.			
Preliminary Future.			
Dal-aka-ko-tahĕ-le-gi-e, He will first continue to strike them.			
Preliminary Expostulative.			
Dal-aka-ko-tahĕ-le-nahĭ-e, He must first continue to strike them.		*Dal-aka-ko-tahĕ-le-nahĭ,* Having first continued to strike them.	
Preliminary Persuasive.			
Dal-aka-ko-tahĕ-le-ba-e, He must first continue to strike them.		*Dal-aka-ko-tahĕ-le-baṅ,* Having first continued to strike them.	
Preliminary Admissive.			
Dal-aka-ko-tahĕ-le-ena-e, He must first continue to strike them.		*Dal-aka-ko-tahĕ-le-ena,* Having first continued to strike them.	

Tenses.	Adjective Participles.	Adverbial Participles.	Gerunds.
Preliminary Benedictive.			
Dal-aka-ko-tahē-le-mam! Mayest thou first continue to strike them!			
Preliminary Imperative.			
Dal-aka-ko-tahē-le-m! Continue thou first to strike them!			
Benedictive.			
Dal-aka-ko-tahen-mam! Mayest thou continue to strike them!			
Imperative.			
Dal-aka-ko-tahen-me! Continue thou to strike them!			
Infinitive.			
Dal-aka-ko-tahen, To continue to strike them.			

TABLES OF THE FORMATION OF THE TENSES.

REFLEXIVE.

(ANIMATE.) *ACC. WITH NOMINATIVE.*

TENSES.	ADJECTIVE PARTICIPLES.	ADVERBIAL PARTICIPLES.	GERUNDS.
FUTURE.			
Dal-akan-tahen-a-e, He will continue to strike himself.	*Dal-akan-tahen*, Who will continue to strike himself.	*Dal-akan-tahen-khan*, Continuing to strike himself.	*Dal-akan-tahen-reak', te, re*, Of, by, in continuing to strike himself.
SPECIAL INCOMPLETE PRESENT.			
Dal-akan-tahen-kan-a-e, He is continuing to strike himself.	*Dal-akan-tahen-kan*, Who is continuing to strike himself.	*Dal-akan-tahen-kan-khan*, Continuing to strike himself now.	*Dal-akan-tahen-kan-reak', te, re*, Of, by, in continuing to strike himself now.
SPECIAL INCOMPLETE PAST.			
Dal-akan-tahēkan-a-e, He was continuing to strike himself.	*Dal-akan-tahēkan*, Who was continuing to strike himself.	*Dal-akan-tahē-kan-khan*, Continuing to strike himself then.	*Dal-akan-tahēkan-reak', te, re*, Of, by, in continuing to strike himself then.
INCHOATIVE FUTURE.			
Dal-akan-tahen-lagit'-e, He will be about to continue to strike himself.	*Dal-akan-tahen-lagit'*, Who will be about to continue to strike himself.	*Dal-akan-tahen-lagit'-khan*, Being about to continue to strike himself.	*Dal-akan-tahen-lagit'-reak', te, re*, Of, by, in being about to continue to strike himself.

Tenses.	Adjective Participles.	Adverbial Participles.	Gerunds.
Inchoative Present.			
Dal-akan-tahen-lagid-ok̀-kan-a-e, He is about to continue to strike himself.	*Dal-akan-tahen-lagid-ok̀-kan,* Who is about to continue to strike himself.	*Dal-akan-tahen-lagid-ok̀-kan-khan,* Being now about to continue to strike himself.	*Dal-akan-tahen-lagidok̀-kan-reak̀, te, re,* Of, by, in being now about to continue to strike himself.
Inchoative Past.			
Dal-akan-tahen-lagid-ok̀-kan-tahēkan-a-e, He was about to continue to strike himself.	*Dal-akan-tahen-lagid-ok̀-kun-tahēkan,* Who was about to continue to strike himself.	*Dal-akan-tahen-lagid-ok̀-kan-tahēkan-khan,* Being then about to continue to strike himself.	*Dal-akan-tahen-lagidok̀-kan-tahēkan-reak̀, te, re,* Of, by, in being then about to continue to strike himself.
Optative.			
Dal-akan-tahē-kok̀-a-e, He would continue to strike himself.	*Dal-akan-tahē-kok̀,* Who would continue to strike himself.	*Dal-akan-tahē-kok̀-khan,* Willing to continue striking himself.	*Dal-akan-tahē-kok̀-reak̀, te, re,* Of, by, in wishing to continue to strike himself.
Conditional.			
(Qho) Dal-akan-tahē-len-a-e, He would (not) continue to strike himself.	*Dal-akan-tahē-len,* Who may have continued to strike himself.	*Dal-akan-tahē-len-khan,* In case of having continued striking himself.	*Dal-akan-tahē-len-reak̀, te, re,* Of, by, in continuing to strike himself.

Tenses.	Adjective Participles.	Adverbial Participles.	Gerunds.
Contingent.			
Dal-akan-tahē-en-gi-e, He continues or would continue to strike himself.			
Preliminary Future.			
Dal-akan-tahē-len-gi-e, He will first continue to strike himself.			
Preliminary Expostulative.			
Dal-akan-tahē-len-nahī-e, He must first continue to strike himself.		*Dal-akan-tahē-len-nahī,* First having continued to strike himself.	
Preliminary Persuasive.			
Dal-akan-tahē-len-ba-e, He must first continue to strike himself.		*Dal-akan-tahē-len-ban,* First having continued to strike himself.	
Preliminary Admissive.			
Dal-akan-tahē-len-en-a-e, He must first continue to strike himself.		*Dal-akan-tahē-len-ena,* First having continued to strike himself.	

I

Tenses.	Adjective Participles.	Adverbial Participles.	Gerunds.
PRELIMINARY BENEDICTIVE.			
Dal-akan-tahē-len-ma-m! Mayest thou first continue to strike thyself!			
PRELIMINARY IMPERATIVE.			
Dal-akan-tahē-len-me! Continue thou first to strike thyself!			
BENEDICTIVE.			
Dal-akan-tahen-ma-m! Mayest thou continue to strike thyself!			
IMPERATIVE.			
Dal-akan-tahen-me! Continue thou to strike thyself!			
INFINITIVE.			
Dal-akan-tahen, To continue to strike oneself.			

Remark. The neuter is conjugated in the same manner as the common gender, the nominative suffixes being of course excluded; as *Dalakantahena*, it will continually be struck.

TABLES OF THE FORMATION OF THE TENSES.

ACTIVE.

DAT. WITH NOM.

(INANIMATE)

TENSES.	ADJECTIVE PARTICIPLES.	ADVERBIAL PARTICIPLES.	GERUNDS.
FUTURE.			
Dal-akao-a-k̇-tahen-a-e, He will continue to strike at or on it.	*Dal-akao-a-k̇-tahen*, At, or on which they will continue to strike.	*Dal-akao-a-k̇-tahen-khan*, Continuing to strike at it.	*Dal-akao-a-k̇-tahen-reak̇, te, re*, Of, by, in continuing to strike at it.
SPECIAL INCOMPLETE. PRESENT.			
Dal-akao-a-k̇-tahen-kan-a-e, He is continuing to strike at, or on it.	*Dal-akao-a-k̇-tahen-kan*, At which they are continuing to strike.	*Dal-akao-a-k̇-tahen-kan-khan*, Continuing to strike at it now.	*Dal-akao-a-k̇-tahen-kan-reak̇, te, re*, Of, by, in now continuing to strike at it.
SPECIAL INCOMPLETE. PAST.			
Dal-akao-a-k̇-tahē-kan-a-e, He was continuing to strike at, or on it.	*Dal-akao-a-k̇-tahē-kan*, At which they were continuing to strike.	*Dal-akao-a-k̇-tahē-kan-khan*, Continuing to strike at it then.	*Dal-akao-a-k̇-tahēkan-reak̇ te, re*, Of, by, in then continuing to strike at it.
INCHOATIVE FUTURE.			
Dal-akao-a-k̇-tahen-lagit'-e, He will be about to continue to strike at it.	*Dal-akao-a-k̇-tahen-lagit'*. At which they will be about to continue to strike.	*Dal-akao-a-k̇-tahen-lagit'-khan*, Being about to continue to strike at it.	*Dal-akao-a-k̇-tahen-lagit'-reak̇, te, re*, Of, by, in being about to continue to strike at it.

TENSES.	ADJECTIVE PARTICIPLES.	ADVERBIAL PARTICIPLES.	GERUNDS.
INCHOATIVE PRESENT.			
Dal-akao-a-k̓-tahen-lagidok̓-kan-a-e, He is about to continue to strike at it.	*Dal-akao-a-k̓-tahen-lagidok̓-kan,* At which they are about to continue to strike.	*Dal-akao-a-k̓-tahen-lagidok̓-kan-khan,* Being now about to continue to strike at it.	*Dal-akao-a-k̓-tahen-lagi-dok̓-kan-reak̓, te, re,* Of, by, in now being about to continue etc.
INCHOATIVE PAST.			
Dal-akao-a-k̓-tahen-lagidok̓-kan-tahē kan-a-é, He was about to continue to strike at it.	*Dal-akao-a-k̓-tahēn lagidok̓-kan-tahēn-kan,* At which they were about to continue to strike.	*Dal-akao-a-k̓-tahen-lagidok̓-kan-tahē kan-khan,* Being then about to continue to strike at it.	*Dal-akao-a-k̓-tahen-lagi-dok̓-kan-tahēkan-reak̓, te, re,* Of, by, in then being about to continue etc.
OPTATIVE.			
Dal-akao-a-k̓-tahē-ke-a-e, He would continue to strike at it.	*Dal-akao-a-k̓-tahē-ke,* At which they would continue to strike.	*Dal-akao-a-k̓-tahē-ke-khan,* Wishing to continue to strike at it.	*Dal-akao-a-k̓-tahē-ke-reak̓, te, re,* Of, by, in wishing to continue etc.
CONDITIONAL.			
(Qho) Dal-akao-a-k̓-tahē-le-a-e, He would (not) continue to strike at it.	*Dal-akao-a-k̓-tahē-le.* At which they may have continued to strike.	*Dal-akao-a-k̓-tahē-le-khan,* Having continued to strike at it.	*Dal-akao-a-k̓-tahē-le-reak̓, te, re,* Having continued to strike at it.

Tenses.	Adjective Participles.	Adverbial Participles.	Gerunds.
Contingent.			
Dal-akao-a-k̓-tahē-ket'-gi-e, He will or would continue or continues to strike at it.			
Preliminary Future.			
Dal-akao-a-k̓-tahē-le-gi-e, He will first continue to strike at it.			
Preliminary Expostulative.			
Dal-akao-a-k̓-tahē-le-nahī-e, He must first continue to strike at it.		*Dal-akao-a-k̓-tahē-le-nahī*, First continuing to strike at it.	
Preliminary Persuasive.			
Dal-akao-a-k̓-tahē-le-ba-e, He must first continue to strike at it.		*Dal-akao-a-k̓-tahē-le-bań*, First continuing to strike at it.	
Preliminary Admissive.			
Dal-akao-a-k̓-tahē-le-en-a-e, He must first continue to strike at it.		*Dal-akao-a-k̓-tahē-le-ena*, First continuing to strike at it.	

Tenses.	Adjective Participles.	Adverbial Participles.	Gerunds.
Preliminary Benedictive.			
Dal-akao-a-k̇-tahĕ-le-ma-m! Mayest thou first continue to strike at it!			
Preliminary Imperative.			
Dal-akao-a-k̇-tahĕ-le-m! Continue thou first to strike at it.			
Benedictive.			
Dal-akao-a-k̇-tahen-ma-m! Mayest thou continue to strike at it.			
Imperative.			
Dal-akao-a-k̇-tahen-me! Continue thou to strike at it.			
Infinitive.			
Dal-akao-a-k̇-tahen, To continue to strike at it.			

TABLES OF THE FORMATION OF THE TENSES.

ACTIVE.

(ANIMATE.) *DATIVE WITH NOMINATIVE.*

TENSES.	ADJECTIVE PARTICIPLES.	ADVERBIAL PARTICIPLES.	GERUNDS.
FUTURE.			
Dal-akao-a-ko-tahen-a-e, He will continue to strike for them.	*Dal-akao-a-ko-tahen,* They for whom they will continue to strike.	*Dal-akao-a-ko-tahen-khan,* Continuing to strike for them.	*Dal-akao-ako-tahen-reak,te, re,* Of, by, in continuing to strike for them.
SPECIAL INCOMPLETE PRESENT.			
Dal-akao-a-ko-tahen-kan-a-e, He is continuing to strike for them.	*Dal-akao-a-ko-tahen-kan,* They, for whom they are continuing to strike.	*Dal-akao-a-ko-tahen-kan-khan,* Continuing now to strike for them.	*Dal-akao-a-ko-tahen-kan-reak, te, re,* Of, by, in now continuing to strike for them.
SPECIAL INCOMPLETE PAST.			
Dal-akao-a-ko-tahē-kan-a-e, He was continuing to strike for them.	*Dal-akao-a-ko-tahē-kan,* They, for whom they were continuing to strike.	*Dal-akao-a-ko-tahē-kan-khan,* Continuing then to strike for them.	*Dal-akao-a-ko-tahēkan-reak, te, re,* Of, by, in then continuing to strike for them.

TENSES.	ADJECTIVE PARTICIPLES.	ADVERBIAL PARTICIPLES.	GERUNDS.
INCHOATIVE FUTURE.			
Dal-akao-a-ko-tahen-lagit'-e, He will be about to continue to strike for them.	*Dal-akao-a-ko-tahen-lagit',* They, for whom they will be about to continue etc.	*Dal-akao-a-ko-tahen-lagit'-khan,* Being about to continue to strike for them.	*Dal-akao-a-ko-tahen-lagit'-reaḱ, te, re,* Of, by, in being about to continue to strike for them.
INCHOATIVE PRESENT.			
Dal-akao-a-ko-tahen-logidoḱ-kan-a-e, He is about to continue to strike for them.	*Dal-akao-a-ko-tahen-logidoḱ-kan,* They, for whom they are about to continue to strike.	*Dal-akao-a-ko-tahen-lagidoḱ-kan-khan,* Being now about to continue to strike for them.	*Dal-akao-a-ko-tahen-lagid-oḱ-kan-reaḱ, te, re,* Of, by, in now being about to continue etc.
INCHOATIVE PAST.			
Dal-akao-a-ko-tahen-logidoḱ-kan-tahē-kan-a-e, He was about to continue to strike for them.	*Dal-akao-a-ko-tahen-logidoḱ-kan-tahē-kan,* They, for whom they were about to continue to strike.	*Dal-akao-a-ko-tahen-lagidoḱ-kan-tahē-kan-khan,* Being then about to continue to strike for them.	*Dal-akao-a-ko-tahen-lagid-oḱ-kan-tahēkan-reaḱ, te, re,* Of, by, in then being about to continue etc.
OPTATIVE.			
Dal-akao-a-ko-tahē-ke-a-e, He would continue to strike for them.	*Dal-akao-a-ko-tahēn-ke,* They, for whom they would continue to strike.	*Dal-akao-a-ko-tahē-ke-khan,* Wishing to continue to strike for them.	*Dal-akao-a-ko-tahē-ke-reaḱ, te, re,* Of, by, in wishing to continue to strike for them.

Tenses.	Adjective Participles.	Adverbial Participles.	Gerunds.
Conditional. (*Oho̱*) *Dal-akao-a-ko-tahē-le-a-e*, He would (not) continue to strike for them.	*Dal-akao-a-ko-tahē-le*, They, for whom they may have continued to strike.	*Dal-akao-a-ko-tahē-le-khan*, In case of having continued to strike for them.	*Dal-akao-a-ko-tahē-le-reak̓, te, re*, Of, by, in having continued to strike for them.
Contingent. *Dal-akao-a-ko-tahē-ket'-gi-e*, He will or would continue to strike for them.			
Preliminary Future. *Dal-akao-a-ko-tahē-le-gi-e*, He will first continue to strike for them.			
Preliminary Expostulative. *Dal-akao-a-ko-tahē-le-nahī-e*, He must first continue to strike for them.		*Dal-akao-a-ko-tahē-le-nahī*, Having first continued to strike for them.	

Tenses.	Adjective Participles.	Adverbial Participles.	Gerunds.
Preliminary Persuasive.			
Dal-akao-a-ko-tahē-le-ba-e, He must first continue to strike for them.		*Dal-akao-a-ko-tahē-le-baṅ,* Having first continued to strike for them.	
Preliminary Admissive.			
Dal-akao-a-ko-tahē-le-en-a-e, He must first continue to strike for them.		*Dal-akao-a-ko-tahē-le-ena,* Having first continued to strike for them.	
Preliminary Benedictive.			
Dal-akao-a-ko-tahē-le-ma-m! Mayest thou first continue to strike for them!			
Preliminary Imperative.			
Dal-akao-a-ko-tahē-le-m! Continue thou first to strike for them!			
Benedictive.			
Dal-akao-a-ko-tahen-ma-m! Mayest thou continue to strike for them!			

Tenses.	Adjective Participles.	Adverbial Participles.	Gerunds.
Imperative. *Dal-akao-a-ko-tahen-me !* Continue thou to strike for them ! **Infinitive.** *Dal-akao-a-ko-tahen,* To continue to strike for them.			

Remark :—The nominative case may also be added here to the Adjective Participles ; as *Dalakaoakotahenko,* they who will continue to strike for them.

TABLES OF THE FORMATION OF THE TENSES.

REFLEXIVE.

(ANIMATE.)

DAT. WITH NOM.

TENSES.	ADJECTIVE PARTICIPLES.	ADVERBIAL PARTICIPLES.	GERUNDS.
FUTURE.			
Dal-akao-an-tahen-a-e, He will continue to strike for himself.	*Dal-akao-an-tahen,* Who will continue to strike for himself.	*Dal-akao-an-tahen-khan,* Continuing to strike for himself.	*Dal-akao-an-tahen-reak̓, te, re,* Of, by, in continuing to strike for himself.
SPECIAL INCOMPLETE PRESENT.			
Dal-akao-an-tahen-kan-a-e, He is continuing to strike for himself.	*Dal-akao-an-tahen-kan,* Who is continuing to strike for himself.	*Dal-akao-an-tahen-kan-khan,* Continuing to strike for himself now.	*Dal-akao-an-tahen-kan-reak̓, te, re,* Of, by, in now continuing to strike etc.
SPECIAL INCOMPLETE PAST.			
Dal-akao-an-tahēkan-a-e, He was continuing to strike for himself.	*Dal-akao-an-tahē-kan,* Who was continuing to strike for himself.	*Dal-akao-an-tahē-kan-khan,* Continuing to strike for himself then.	*Dal-akao-an-tahēkan-reak̓, te, re,* Of by, in then continuing to strike etc.

TENSES.	ADJECTIVE PARTICIPLES.	ADVERBIAL PARTICIPLES.	GERUNDS.
INCHOATIVE FUTURE.			
Dal-akao-an-tahen-lagit'-e, He will be about to continue to strike for himself.	*Dal-akao-an-tahen-lagit',* Who will be about to continue to strike for himself.	*Dal-okao-an-tahen-lagit'-khan,* Being about to continue etc.	*Dal-akao-an-tahen-lagit'-reak', te, re,* Of, by, in being about to continue to strike etc.
INCHOATIVE PRESENT.			
Dal-akao-an-tahen-lagidok'-kan-a-e, He is about to continue to strike for himself.	*Dal-akao-an-tahen-lagidok'-kan,* Who is about to continue to strike for himself.	*Dal-akao-an-tahen-lagidok'-kan-khan,* Being now about to continue etc.	*Dal-akao-an-tahen-lagid-ok'-kan-reak', te, re,* Of, by, in now being about to continue etc.
INCHOATIVE PAST.			
Dal-akao-an-tahen-lagidok'-kan-tahē-kan-a-e, He was about to continue to strike for himself.	*Dal-akao-an-tahen-lagidok'-kan-tahē-kan,* Who was about to continue to strike for himself.	*Dal-akao-an-tahen-lagidok'-khan-tahē-kan-khan,* Being then about to continue etc.	*Dal-akao-an-tahen-lagidok' -kan tahēkan-reak, te, re,* Of, by, in then being about to continue etc.
OPTATIVE.			
Dal-akao-an-tahē-kok'-a-e, He would continue to strike for himself.	*Dal-akao-an-tahē-kok',* Who would continue to strike for himself.	*Dal-akao-an-tahēkok'-khan,* Wishing to continue to strike for oneself.	*Dal-akao-an-tahē-kok'-reak', te, re,* Of, by, in wishing to continue to strike etc.

Tenses.	Adjective Participles	Adverbial Participles.	Gerunds.
Conditional.			*Dal-akao-an-tahē-len-reak, te, re,* Of, by, in having continued to strike for oneself.
(Qho) Dal-akao-an-tahē-len-a-e, He would (not) continue to strike for himself.	*Dal-akao-an-tahē-len,* Who may have continued to strike for himself.	*Dal-akao-an tahē-len-khan,* In case of having continued to strike etc.	
Contingent.			
Dal-akao-an-tahē-en-gi-e, He continues or would continue to strike, for himself.			
Preliminary Future.			
Dal-akao-an-tahē-len-gi-e, He will first continue to strike for himself.			
Preliminary Expostulative.			
Dal-akao-an-tahē-len-nahī-e, He must first continue to strike etc.		*Dal-akao-an-tahē-len nahī,* First having continued to strike for himself.	

TENSES.	ADJECTIVE PARTICIPLES.	ADVERBIAL PARTICIPLES.	GERUNDS.
PRELIMINARY PERSUASIVE.			
Dal-akao-an-tahē-len-ba-e, He must first continue to strike etc.		*Dal-akao-an-tahē-len-baṅ,* First having continued to strike for himself.	
PRELIMINARY ADMISSIVE.			
Dal-akao-an-tahē-len-en-a-e, He must first continue to strike etc.		*Dal-akao-an-tahē-len-ena,* First having continued to strike for himself.	
PRELIMINARY BENEDICTIVE.			
Dal-akao-an-tahē-len-ma-m !, Mayest thou first continue to strike etc.			
PRELIMINARY IMPERATIVE.			
Dal-akao-an-tahē-len-me !, Continue thou first to strike etc.			
BENEDICTIVE.			
Dal-akao-an-tahen-ma-m !, Mayest thou continue to strike etc.			

TENSES.	ADJECTIVE PARTICIPLES.	ADVERBIAL PARTICIPLES.	GERUNDS.
IMPERATIVE. *Dal-akao-an-tahen-me!*, Continue thou to strike etc. INFINITIVE. *Dal-akao-an-tahen*, To continue to strike for oneself.			

THE SIGNS OF THE TENSES STRIPPED OF ALL INFLEXIONS.

	ACTIVE.			REFLEXIVE.		
	NOM. AND ACC.	*DATIVE.*	*ACC. RESERVATIVE FORM.*	*ACCUSATIVE.*	*DATIVE.*	*ACC. RESERVATIVE FORM.*
Future.	*Root.*	*a-.*	*ka-.*	*ok̆.*	*joĭ.*	*kok̆.*
General incomplete Present.	*et',* or *ed.*	—	—	—	—	—
Special incomplete Present.	*et'-kan,* or *ed-kan.*	*a-kan.*	*ka-kan.*	*ok̆kan.*	*joĭkan.*	*kok̆kan.*
Recent Past.	*ket',* or *ked.*	*at',*or *ad.*	*kat',* or *kad.*	*en.*	*an.*	—
Anterior Past.	*let',* or *led.*	—	—	*len.*	—	—
Perfect.	—	*akaoat',* or *akaoad.*	*akat',* or *akad.*	—	*akaoan.*	*akan.*
General incomplete Past.	*et'-*or *ed-tahĕkan.*	—	—	—	—	—
Special incomplete Past.	*et'-,* or *ed- kantahĕkan.*	*a-kan-tahĕkan.*	*ka-kan-tahĕkan.*	*ok̆kantahĕkan.*	*joĭkantahĕkan.*	*kok̆kantahĕkan.*
Indecisive Pluperfect.	*let'-,*or *led-tahĕkan.*	*at'-,*or *ad-tahĕkan.*	*kat'-,*or *kad-tahĕkan.*	*lentahĕkan.*	*antahĕkan.*	—
Decisive Pluperfect.	—	*akaoat'-*or *akaoad-tahĕkan*	*akat'-,*or *akad-tahĕkan.*	—	*akaoantahĕkan.*	*akantahĕkan.*
Inchoative Future.	*-lagit'.*	*a-lagit'.*	*ka-lagit'.*	*ok̆lagit'.*	*joĭlagit'.*	*kok̆lagit'.*
Inchoative Present.	*-lagidok̆kan.*	*a-lagidok̆kan.*	*ka-lagidok̆kan.*	*ok̆lagidok̆kan.*	*joĭlagidok̆kan.*	*kok̆lagidok̆kan.*
Inchoative Past.	*-lagidok̆kantahĕkan.*	*a-lagidok̆kantahĕkan*	*ka-lagidok̆kantahĕkan.*	*ok̆lagidok̆kantahĕkan.*	*joĭlagidok̆kantahĕkan.*	*kok̆lagidok̆kantahĕkan.*
Optative.	*ke.*	—	—	*kok̆.*	—	—
Conditional.	*le.*	—	—	*len.*	—	—
Contingent.	*ket'-*or *ked-gi.*	*at'-,*or *ad-gi.*	*kat'-,*or *kad-gi.*	*engi.*	*angi.*	—
Preliminary Future.	*le-gi.*	*a-gere.*	*ka-gere.*	*lengi.*	*angi.*	*kok̆gere.*
Preliminary Expostulative.	*le-nahĭ*	—	—	*len nahĭ.*	*an nahĭ.*	—
Preliminary Persuasive.	*le-ba.*	—	—	*len ba.*	*an ba.*	—
Preliminary Admissive.	*le-ena.*	—	—	*len ena.*	*an ena.*	—
Preliminary perfect Expostulative	—	*akaoa-nahĭ.*	*aka-nahĭ.*	—	*akaoan nahĭ.*	*akan nahĭ.*
Preliminary perfect Persuasive.	—	*akaoa-ba.*	*aka-ba.*	—	*akaoan ba.*	*akan ba.*
Preliminary perfect Admissive.	—	*akaoa-ena.*	*aka-ena.*	—	*akaoan ena.*	*akan ena.*
Preliminary Benedictive.	*le-ma-m, ben, pe!*	—	—	*len ma-m, ben, pe.*	*an ma-m, ben, pe!*	—
Preliminary Imperative.	*le- m, ben, pe!*	—	—	*len me, ben, pe.*	*an me, ben, pe!*	—
Benedictive.	*- ma-m, ben, pe!*	*a- ma-m. ben, pe!*	*ka-ma-m, ben, pe!*	*ok̆ ma m, ben, pe.*	*joĭ ma-m, ben, pe!*	*kok̆ ma-m, ben, pe!*
Imperative.	*- me, ben, pe!*	*a- me, ben, pe!*	*ka-me, ben, pe!*	*ok̆ me, ben, pe.*	*joĭ me, ben, pe!*	*kok̆ me, ben, pe!*

Remark. 1 The stroke " — " denotes, that the accusative or dative infixes shall be put there: as "*a-kan*" may become *aokan, akokan, ak'kan etc.*

Remark. 2 It is only necessary to affix the causative sign *ocko* to the root, in order to form the causative.

Remark. For a table of the abridged pronouns vide page 29-30.

J

CONJUGATION

I.—Of the defective impersonal verb MENA *to*

PRESENT

Indicative.	Subjunctive with "*Khan.*"	Subjunctive with "*Paset'.*"
Singular.	Singular.	Singular.
1 *Mena-ń-a*, I exist, or I am.	*Mena-ń-khan*, If I am.	*Paset' mena-ń*, Perhaps I am.
2 *Mena-m-a*, Thou art.	*Mena-m-khan*, If thou art.	*Paset' mena-m*, Perhaps thou art.
3 *Mena-e-a*, He or she is.	*Mena-e-khan*, If he is.	*Paset' mena-e*, Perhaps he is.
Dual.	Dual.	Dual.
1 *Mena-liń-a*, We two are.	*Mena-liń-khan*, If we two are.	*Paset' mena-liń*, Perhaps we two are.
2 *Mena-ben-a*, You two are.	*Mena-ben-khan*, If you two are.	*Paset' mena-ben*, Perhaps you two are,
3 *Mena-kin-a*, They two are.	*Mena-kin-khan*, If they two are.	*Paset' mena-kin*, Perhaps they two are.
Plural.	Plural.	Plural.
1 *Mena-le-a*, We are.	*Mena-le-khan*, If we are.	*Paset' mena-le*, Perhaps we are.
2 *Mena-pe-a*, You are.	*Mena-pe-khan*, If you are.	*Paset' mena-pe*, Perhaps you are.
3 *Mena-ko-a*, They are.	*Mena-ko-khan*, If they are.	*Paset' mena-ko*, Perhaps they are.
Neture. *Menak'-a*, It is, they are.	*Menak'-khan*, If it is.	*Paset' menak'*, Perhaps it is.

Remark. The other Tenses are wanting. For the Past of this tense vide "*Tahĕkana.*"

OF VERBS.

exist, to be.

TENSE.

Adjective Participles.	Gerunds.
1 *Mena-ń,* I who am.	*Menań-reak', te, re, khon etc.* Of, by, in from my being.
2 *Mena-m,* Thou, who art.	*Menam-reak', te, re, khon,* Of, by, in thy being.
3 *Mena-e,* He or she, who is.	*Menae-reak', te, re, khon,* Of, by, in his being.
1 *Mena-liń,* We two, who are.	*Menaliń-reak', te, re, khon,* Of, by, in our (two) being.
2 *Mena-ben,* You two, who are.	*Menaben-reak', te, re, khon* Of, by, in your (two) being.
3 *Mena-kin,* They two, who are.	*Menakin-reak', te, re, khon,* Of, by, in their (two) being,
1 *Mena-le,* We, who are.	*Menale-reak', te, re khon,* Of, by, in from our being.
2 *Mena-pe,* You, who are.	*Menape-reak', te, re, khon,* Of, by, in from your being.
3 *Mena-ko,* They, who are.	*Menako-reak', te, re, khon,* Of, by, in, from their being,
Neuter. *Mena-k',* It, which is.	*Menak'-reak', te, re, khon,* Of by, in from its being.

Remark. This verb means to *exist,* and is not used as a *copula* to form a predicate: hence it is wrong to say *Herel menama, sem baña?* for that means, you man, are you (here for instance) or not? and not, are you a man or not. (Vide *kana*).

II—Of the copula KAN, *to be*.

Indicative.	Subjunctive with "*Khnn*"	Subjunctive with "*Paset'*."
Singular.	Singular.	Singular.
1 *Kan-a-ń*, I am.	*Kan-hkan-lń*, If I am.	*Paset'-i ń*—**kan*, Perhaps I am.—
2 *Kan-a-m*, Thou art.	*Kan-khan-em*, If thou art.	*Paset'-em*—*kan*, Perhaps thou art.—
3 *Kan-a-e*, He or she is.	*Kan-khan-e*, If he is.	*Paset'-e*—*kan*, Perhaps he is.—
Dual.	Dual.	Dual.
1 *Kan-a-liń*, We two are.	*Kan-khan-liń*, If we two are.	*Paset'-liń*—*kan*, Perhaps we two are.—
2 *Kan-a-ben*, You two are.	*Kan-khan-ben*, If you two are.	*Paset'-ben*—*kan*, Perhaps you two are.
3 *Kan-a-kin*, They two are.	*Kan-khan-kin*, If they two are.	*Paset'-kin*—*kan*, Perhaps they two are.—
Plural.	Plural.	Plural.
1 *Kan-a-le*, We are.	*Kan-khan-le*, If we are.	*Paset'-le*—*kan*, Perhaps we are.—
2 *Kan-a-pe*, You are.	*Kan-khan-pe*, If you are.	*Paset'-pe*—*kan*, Perhaps they are.—
3 *Kan-a-ko*, They are.	*Kan-khan-ko*, If they are.	*Paset'-ko*—*kan*, Perhaps they are.—
Neuter. *Kan-a*, It is.	*Kan-khan*, If it is.	*Paset'*—*kan*, Perhaps it is.—

Remark. This verb is always used as a Copula to form predicates; as *Marań-kanae*, he is great, *Bugi-kanae*, he is good.

* This stroke (—) denotes, that the adjective or noun shall be in serted.

III.—Of the past tense TAHĔKAN.

Indicative.	Subjunctive with "*Khan.*"	Subjuctive with "*Paset'.*"
Singular.	Singular.	Singulaar.
1 *Tahĕkan-a-ń,* I was.	*Tahĕkan-khan-iń,* If I was.	*Paset'-iń-tahĕkan,* Perhaps I was.
2 *Tahĕkan-a-m,* Thou wast.	*Tahĕkan-khan-em,* If thou wast.	*Paset'-em-tahĕkan,* Perhaps thou wast.
3 *Tahĕkan-a-e,* He or she was.	*Tahĕkan-khan-e,* If he was.	*Paset'-e-tahĕkan,* Perhaps he was.
Dual.	Dual.	Dual.
1 *Tahĕkan-a-liń,* We two were.	*Tahĕkan-khan-liń,* If we two were.	*Paset'-liń-tahĕkan,* Perhaps we two were
2 *Tahĕkan-a-ben,* You two were.	*Tahĕkan-khan-ben,* If you two were.	*Paset'-ben-tahĕkan,* Perhaps you two were.
3 *Tahĕkan-a-kin,* They two were.	*Tahĕkan-khan-kin* If they two were.	*Paset'-kin-tahĕkan,* Perhaps they two were
Plurar.	Plural.	Plural.
1 *Tahĕkan-a-le,* We were.	*Tahĕkan-khan-le,* If we were.	*Paset'-le-tahĕkan,* Perhaps we were.
2 *Tahĕkan-a-pe,* You were.	*Tahĕkan-khan-pe,* If you were.	*Paset'-pe-tahĕkan,* Perhaps you were.
3 *Tahĕkan-a-ko,* They were.	*Tahĕkan-khan-ko,* If they were.	*Paset'-ko-tahĕkan,* Perhaps they were.
Neuter. *Tahĕkan-a,* It was.	*Tahĕkan-khan,* If it was.	*Paset'-tahĕkan,* Perhaps it was.

Paticiple: *Tahĕkan, Tahĕkankin, Tahĕkanko,* he they two, they, who were, Gerund: *Tahĕkan-reak', te re etc.,* Of, by, in being then.

Remark. This tense is used as past tense both for *Mena,* and for *Kana.*

IV.—Of the negative impersonal verb

Indicative.	Subjunctive with *Khan*.	Subjuctive with *Paset'*.
Singular.	**Singular.**	**Singular.**
1 *Banu-gi-ń-a*, I am not.	*Banu-giń khan*, If I am not.	*Paset', banu-gi-ń* Perhaps I am not.
2 *Banuk'-me-a*, Thou art not.	*Banuk'-me-khan*, If thou art not.	*Paset' banuk'-me*, Perhaps thou art not.
3 *Banu-gi-ch'-a*, He is not.	*Banu-gi-ch'-khan*, If he is not.	*Paset' banu-gi-ch'*, Perhaps he is not.
Dual.	**Dual.**	**Dual.**
1 *Banuk'-liń-a*, We two are not.	*Banuk'-liń-khan*, If we two are not.	*Paset' banuk'-liń*, Perhaps we two are not.
2 *Banuk'-ben-a*, You two are not.	*Banuk'-ben-khan*, If you two are not.	*Paset' banuk'-ben*, Perhaps you two are not.
3 *Banuk'-kin-a*, They two are not.	*Banuk'-kin-khan*, If they two are not.	*Paset' banuk'-kin*, Perhaps they two are not.
Plural.	**Plural.**	**Plural.**
1 *Banuk'-le-a*, We are not.	*Banuk'-le-khan*, If we are not.	*Paset' banuk'-le*, Perhaps we are not.
2 *Banuk'-pe-a*, You are not,	*Banuk'-pe-khan*, If you are not.	*Paset' banuk'-pe*, Perhaps you are not.
3 *Banuk'-ko-a*, They are not.	*Banuk'-ko-khan*, If they are not.	*Paset' banuk'-ko*, Perhaps they are not.
Neuter. *Banuk'-a*, It is not.	*Banuk'-khan*, If it is not.	*Paset' banuk'*, Perhaps it is not.

Remark. This verb is the negative of *Mena*, not of *Kan*, consequently it can not be used like the English Copula.

BANU, *not to be.*

Adverbial Participles.	Gerunds.
1 *Banugiń,* I who am not.	*Banugiń-reak', te, re,* Of, by, in my not being.
2 *Banuk'-me,* Thou who art not.	*Banuk'-me-reak', te, re,* Of, by, in thy not being.
3 *Banugick',* He or she is not.	*Banugick'-reak', te, re,* Of, by, in his not being.
1 *Banuk'-liń,* We two who are not.	*Banuk'-liń-reak', te, re,* Of, by, in our (two) not being.
2 *Banuk'-ben,* You two who are not.	*Banuk'-ben-reak', te, re,* Of, by, in your (two) not being.
3 *Banuk'-kin,* They two who are not.	*Banuk'-kin-reak', te, re,* Of, by, in their (two) not being.
1 *Banuk'-le,* We who are not.	*Banuk'-le-reak', te, re,* Of, by, in our not being.
2 *Banuk'-pe,* You who are not.	*Banuk'-pe-reak', te, re,* Of, by, in your not being.
3 *Banuk'-ko,* They who are not.	*Banuk'-ko-reak' te, re,* Of, by, in their not being.
Neuter. *Banuk',* That, which is not.	*Banuk'-reak', te, re,* Of, by, in it not being.

Remark. There are several terminations to this negative verb, as, *banuk' anań, banuk'-anak', banuk'-anech', banugick'an,* the three first being Neuter and the last 3rd person common gender.

V.—Of the genitive of MENA.

A. Object inanimate.

Indicative.	Subjunctive with "*Khan.*"	Subjunctive with "*Paset'.*"
Singular.	**Singular.**	**Singular.**
1 *Mena-k'-tiń-a*, I have (lit. mine is.)	*Mena-k'-tiń-khan*, If I have.	*Paset' mena-k'-tiń*, Perhaps I have.
2 *Mena-k'-tam-a*, Thou hast.	*Mena-k'-tam-khan*, If thou hast.	*Paset' mena-k'-tam*, Perhaps thou hast.
3 *Mena-k'-tae-a*, He or she has.	*Mena-k'-tae-khan*, If he has.	*Paset' mena-k'-tae*, Perhaps he has.
Dual.	**Dual.**	**Dual.**
1 *Mena-k'-taliń-a*, We two have.	*Mena k'-taliń-khan*, If we two have.	*Paset' mena-k'-taliń*, Perhaps we two have.
2 *Mena-k'-taben-a*, You two have.	*Mena-k'-taben-khan*, If you two have.	*Paset' mena-k'-taben*, Perhaps you two have.
3 *Mena-k'-takin-a*, They two have.	*Mena-k'-takin-khan*, If they two have.	*Paset' mena-k'-takin*, Perhaps they two have.
Plural.	**Plural.**	**Plural.**
1 *Mena-k'-tale-a*, We have.	*Mena-k'-tale-khan*, If we have.	*Paset' mena-k'-tale*, Perhaps we have.
2 *Mena-k'-tape-a*, You have.	*Mena-k'-tape-khan*, If you have.	*Paset' mena-k'-tape*, Perhaps you have.
3 *Mena-k'-tako-a*, They have. Neuter.	*Mena-k'-tako-khan*, If they have.	*Paset' mena-k'-tako*, Perhaps they have.

Remark. 1. *Banuk'tiña*, I have not, is conjugated in the same manner as *menak'tiña*.

Remark. 2. The Intensive form Reflexive, *Mena-g-ok'-tae-a*, with its negative, *Banu-g-ok'-tae-a*, he makes as if he has, he makes as if he has not, is used ironically.

ADJECTIVE PARTICIPLES.	GERUNDS.
1 *Menaktiń,* Which I have.	*Menak-tiń-reak, te, re,* Of, by, in my having,
2 *Menaktam,* Which thou hast.	*Menak tam-reak, te, re,* Of, by, in thy having.
3 *Menaktae,* Which he has.	*Menak tae-reak, te, re,* Of, by, in his having.
1 *Menaktaliń,* Which we two have.	*Menak taliń-reak, te, re,* Of, by, in our (two) having.
2 *Menaktaben,* Which you two have.	*Menak taben-reak, te, re,* Of, by, in your (two) having.
3 *Menaktakin,* Which they two have.	*Menak takin-reak, te, re,* Of, by, in their (two) having.
1 *Menaktale,* Which we have.	*Menak tale-reak, te, re,* Of, by, in our having.
2 *Menaktape,* Which you have.	*Menak tape reak, te, re,* Of, by, in your having.
3 *Menaktako,* Which they have.	*Menak tako-reak, te, re,* Of, by, in their having.

Remark. The Neuter has no Genetive Suffix, hence the Genetive case of the nouns must be used in order to convey the idea of "*it has*"; as *dare-reak', aḍi ḍar menak'a,* the tree has many branches.

B. OBJECT ANIMATE.

	INDICATIVE.	SUBJUNCTIVE with "*Khan*."	SUBJUNCTIVE with "*Paset'*."
	SINGULAR.	SINGULAR.	SINGULAR.
1	*Mena-ń-tae-a*, He has me. *	*Menańtae-khan*, If he has me.	*Paset' menańtae*, Perhaps he has me.,
2	*Mena-m-tae-a*, He has thee.	*Menamtae-khan*, If he has thee.	*Paset' menamtae* Perhaps he has thee.
3	*Mena-e-tae-a*, He has him, or her.	*Menae tae-khan*, If he has him or her.	*Paset' menaetae*, Perhaps he has him, or her.
	DUAL.	DUAL.	DUAL.
1	*Mena-liń-tae-a*, He has us two.	*Menaliń tae-khan*, If he has us two.	*Paset' menaliń tae*, Perhaps he has us two.
2	*Mena-ben tae-a*, He has you two.	*Menaben-tae-khan*, If he has you two.	*Paset' mena-ben-tae* Perhaps he has you two.
3	*Mena-kin-tae-a*, He has them two.	*Mena kin tae-khan*, If he has them two.	*Past' mena kin tae* Perhaps he has them two.
	PLURAL.	PLURAL.	PLURAL.
1	*Mena-le-tae-a*, He has us.	*Menale tae-khan*, If he has us.	*Paset' menaletae*, Perhaps he has us.
2	*Mena-pe-tae-a*, He has you.	*Menape tae-khan*, If he has you.	*Paset' menapetae*, Perhaps he has you.
3	*Mena-ko-tae-a*, He has them.	*Menako tae-khan*, If he has them.	*Paset' menakotae*, Perhaps he has them.

* Or I, who am his (still) exist or am (here or there); as *hopon menaetaea, se goch'enae?* Is his son still alive, or is he dead? *gidra menako taea, se orak'te ko chalaoena?* Are his children here (or there,) or have they gone home.

Remark. Any of the nominative suffixes may be substituted for *tae*; as *enańtakoa, menakotińa* etc.

	Adjective Participles.	Gerunds.
1	*Menańtae,* I, whom he has.*	*Menańtae-reak', te, re.* Of, by, in his having me.
2	*Menamtae,* Thou whom he has.	*Menamtae-reak', te, re,* Of, by, in his having thee.
3	*Menaetae,* He, or her, whom he has.	*Menaetae-reak', te, re,* Of, by, in his having him or her.
1	*Menalińtae,* We two, whom he has.	*Menalińtae-reak', te, re,* Of, by, in his having us two.
2	*Menabentae,* You two, whom he has.	*Menabentae-reak', te, re,* Of, by, in his having you two.
3	*Menakintae,* They two, whom he has.	*Menakintae-reak', te re,* Of, by, in his having them two.
1	*Menaletae,* We, whom he has.	*Menaletae,-reak', te re,* Of, by, in his having us.
2	*Menapetae,* You, whom he has.	*Menapetae-reak', te re,* Of, by, in his having you.
3	*Menakotae,* They, whom he has.	*Menakotae-reak' te, re,* Of, by, in his having them.

* Or, I (who am his), who am alive or am here.

Remark. *Banuk'kotae,* he has none, is conjugated in the same manner; as *Menańtae.*

ACTIVE VOICE.

1. Paradigm of a regular transitive verb.

A. with the nominative case. *FUTURE TENSE.*

Indicative.	Subjuctive with "*Khan.*"	Subjunctive with "*Paset'.*"
Singular.	Singular.	Singular.
1 *Dal-a-ń,* I shall strike.	*Dal-khan-iń,* If I shall strike.	*Paset'-iń-dal,* Perhaps* I shall strike.
2 *Dal-a-m,* Thou wilt strike.	*Dal-khan-em,* If thou wilt strike.	*Paset'-em-dal,* Perhaps thou wilt strike.
3 *Dal-a-e,* He or she will strike.	*Dal-khan-e,* If he or she will strike.	*Paset'-e-dal,* Perhaps he or she will strike.
Dual.	Dual.	Dual.
1 *Dal-a-liń,* We two shall strike.	*Dal-khan-liń,* If we two shall strike.	*Paset'-liń-dal,* Perhaps we two shall strike.
2 *Dal-a-ben,* You two will strike.	*Dal-khan ben,* If you two will strike.	*Paset'-ben-dal,* Perhaps you two will strike.
3 *Dal-a-kin,* They two will strike.	*Dal-khan-kin,* If they two will strike.	*Paset'-kin-dal,* Perhaps they two will strike.
Plural.	Plural.	Plural.
1 *Dal-a-le,* We shall strike.	*Dal-khan-le,* If we shall strike.	*Paset'-le-dal,* Perhaps we shall strike.
2 *Dal-a-pe,* You will strike.	*Dal-khan-pe,* If you will strike.	*Paset'-pe-dal,* Perhaps you will strike.
3 *Dal-a-ko,* They will strike.	*Dal-khan-ko,* If they will strike.	*Paset'-ko-dal,* Perhaps they will strike.

Note.—This tense is rather non-descript than exclusively future; it may be used to express future present and past tense. It is always used when a general statement has to be made; as, for hunting, we *go* to the hill, *offer* a sacrifice, and then ascend.

GENERAL INCOMPLETE PRESENT.

INDICATIVE.	SUBJUNCTIVE with "*Khan.*"	SUBJUNCTIVE with "*Khan.*"
SINGULAR.	SINGULAR.	SINGULAR.
1 *Dal-et'-a-ń,* I strike.*	*Dal-et'-khan-iń,* If I strike.*	*Paset'-iń-dal-et',* Perhaps I strike.*
2 *Dal-et'-a-m,* Thou strikest.	*Dal-et'-khan-em* If thou strikest.	*Paset'-em-dal-et',* Perhaps thou strickest.
3 *Dal-et'-a-liń,* He or she strikes.	*Dal-et'-khan-e,* If he or she strikes.	*Paset'-e-dal-et',* Perhaps he or she strikes.
DUAL.	DUAL.	DUAL
1 *Dal-et'-a-liń* We two strike.	*Dal-et'-khan-liń,* If we two strike.	*Paset'-liń-dal-et',* Perhaps we two strike.
2 *Dal-et'-a-ben,* You two strike.	*Dal-et'-khan-ben,* If you two strike.	*Paset'-ben-dal-et',* Perhaps you two strike.
3 *Dal-et'-a-kin,* They two strike.	*Dal-et'-khan-kin,* If they two strike.	*Paset'-kin-dal-et',* Perhaps they two strike.
PLURAL.	PLURAL.	PLURAL.
1 *Dal-et'-a-le,* We strike.	*Dal-et'-khan-le,* If we strike.	*Paset'-le-dal-et',* Perhaps we strike.
2 *Dal-et'-a-pe,* You strike.	*Dal-et'-khan-pe,* If you strike.	*Paset'-pe-dal-et',* Perhaps you strike.
Dal-et'-a-ko, They strike.	*Dal-et' khan-ko,* If they strike.	*Paset'-ko-dal-et',* Perhaps they strike.

* Or am striking. *Note.*—This tense is not the English present indefinite, but is an incomplete present *e. i.* it can not be used without regard to time to express general truths etc., but is confined to an action going on (not necessarily just now) but not finished. (See remarks on this tense).

SPECIAL INCOMPLETE PRESENT.

INDICATIVE.	SUBJUNCTIVE with "*Khan*."	SUBJUNCTIVE with "*Paset'*."
SINGULAR.	SINGULAR.	SINGULAR.
1 *Dal-et'-kan-a-ń,* I am striking.	*Dal-et'kan-khan-iń,* If I am striking.	*Paset'-iń-dal-et'kan,* Perhaps I am striking.
2 *Dal-et'-kan-a-m,* Thou art striking.	*Dal-et'kan-khan-em,* If thou art striking.	*Paset'-em-dal-et'kan,* Perhaps thou art striking.
3 *Dal-et'-kan-a-e,* He or she is striking.	*Dal-et'kan-khan-e,* If he or she is striking.	*Paset'-e-dal-et'kan,* Perhaps he or she is striking.
DUAL.	DUAL.	DUAL.
1 *Dal-et'-kan-a-liń* We two are striking.	*Dal-et'kan-khan-liń,* If we two are striking.	*Paset'-liń-dal-et'kan,* Perhaps we two are striking.
2 *Dal-et'-kan-a-ben,* You two are striking.	*Dal-et'kan-khan-ben,* If you two are striking.	*Paset'-ben-dal-et'kan,* Perhaps you two are striking.
3 *Dal-et'-kan-a-kin,* They two are striking.	*Dal-et'kan-khan-kin,* If they two are striking.	*Paset'-kin-dal-et'kan,* Perhaps they two are striking.
PLURAL.	PLURAL.	PLURAL.
1 *Dal-et'-kan-a-le,* We are striking.	*Dal-et'kan-khan-le,* If we are striking.	*Paset'-le-dal-et'kan,* Perhaps we are striking.
2 *Dal-et'kan-a-pe,* You are striking.	*Dal-et'kan-khan-pe,* If you are striking.	*Paset'-pe-dal-et'kan,* Perhaps you are striking.
3 *Dal-et'kan-a-ko,* They are striking.	*Dal-et'kan-khan-ko,* If they are striking.	*Paset'-ko-dal-et'kan,* Perhaps they are striking.

Note.—This tense is more confined to the present moment, than the general incomplete present.

RECENT PAST.

INDICATIVE.	SUBJUNCTIVE with "*Khan.*"	SUBJUNCTIVE with "*Paset'.*"
SINGULAR.	SINGULAR.	SINGULAR.
1 *Dal-ket'-a-ń*, I struck.*	*Dal-ket'-khan-iń*, If I struck.†	*Paset'-iń-dal-ket'*, Perhaps I struck.
2 *Dal-ket'-a-m*, thou struck'st.	*Dal-ket'-khan-em*, If thou struck'st.	*Paset'-em-dal-ket'*, Perhaps thou struck'st.
3 *Dal-ket'-a-e*, He or she struck.	*Dal-ket'-khan-e*, If he or she struck.	*Paset'-e-dal-ket'*, Perhaps he or she struck.
DUAL.	DUAL.	DUAL.
1 *Dal-ket'-a-liń*, We two struck.	*Dal-ket'-khan-liń*, If we two struck.	*Paset'-liń-dal-ket'*, Perhaps we two struck.
2 *Dal-ket'-a-ben*, You two struck.	*Dal-ket'-khan-beń*, If you two struck.	*Paset'-ben-dal-ket'*, Perhaps you two struck.
3 *Dal-ket'-a-kin*, They two struck.	*Dal-ket'-khan-kin*, If they two struck.	*Paset'-kin-dal-ket'*, Perhaps they two struck.
PLURAL.	PLURAL.	PLURAL.
1 *Dal-ket'-a-le*, We struck.	*Dal-ket'-khan-le*, If we struck.	*Paset'-le-dal-ket'*, Perhaps we struck.
2 *Dal-ket'-a-pe*, You struck.	*Dal-ket'-khan-pe*, If you struck.	*Paset'-pe-dal-ket'*, Perhaps you struck.
3 *Dal-ket'-a-ko*, They struck.	*Dal-ket'-khan-ko*, If they struck.	*Paset'ko-dal-ket'*, Perhaps they struck.

* Or have struck just now.† This is never used as a Conditional.

Note.—This tense always expresses something momentary, a point, not a line. It has great similarity with the Greek Aorist and the Latin perfectum historicum, and still greater with the Bengalee past tense in lam, la, lo.

ANTERIOR PAST.

	INDICATIVE.	SUBJUNCTIVE with "*Khan.*"	SUBJUNCTIVE with "*Paset'.*"
	SINGULAR.	SINGULAR.	SINGULAR.
1	*Dal-let'-a-ń*, I struck.*	*Dal-let'-khan-iń*, If I struck.†	*Paset'-iń-dal-let'*, Perhaps I struck.‡
2	*Dal-let'-a-m*, Thou struck'st.	*Dal-let'-khan-em*, If thou struck'st.	*Paset'-em-dal-let'*, Perhaps thou struck'st.
3	*Dal-let'-a-e*, He or she struck.	*Dal-let'-khan-e*, If he or she struck.	*Paset'-e-dal-let'*, Perhaps he or she struck.
	DUAL.	DUAL.	DUAL.
1	*Dal-let'-a-liń*, We two struck.	*Dal-let-khan-liń*, If we two struck.	*Paset'-liń-dal-let'*, Perhaps we two struck.
2	*Dal-let'-a-ben*, You two struck.	*Dal-let'-khan-ben*, If you two struck.	*Paset'-len-dal-let'*, Perhaps you two struck.
3	*Dal-let'-a-kin*, They two struck.	*Dal-let'-khan-kin*, If they two struck.	*Past'-kin-dal-let'*, Perhaps they two struck.
	PLURAL.	PLURAL.	PLURAL.
1	*Dal-let'-a-le*, We struck.	*Dal-let'-khan-le*, If we struck.	*Paset'-le-dal-let'* Perhaps we struck.
2	*Dal-let'-a-pe*, You struck.	*Dal-let'-khan-pe*, If you struck.	*Paset'-pe-dal-let'* Perhaps you struck.
3	*Dal-let'-a-ko*, They struck.	*Dal-let'-khan-ko*, If they struck.	*Paset'-ko-dal-let'* Perhaps they struck.

* Or had struck.

† This tense is never used as a Conditional.

‡ Another form *Dal-lak'-ań* is also used.

Note.—This tense, like the Recent Past, always expresses something momentary. It denotes, *let* something was done, but has lost its effect either by its not remaining in that state, or that something has afterwards taken place, and that it is of no more importance. The reason why it has been called Anterior Past is, that it precides the Recent Past in time.

GENERAL INCOMPLETE PAST.

INDICATIVE.	SUBJUNCTIVE with "*Khan.*"	SUBJUNCTIVE with "*Paset'.*"
SINGULAR.	SINGULAR.	SINGULAR.
1 *Dal-et'-tahēkan-a-ń*, I used to strike.	*Dal-et'-tahēkan-khan-iń*, If I used to strike.	*Paset'-iń-dal-et'-tahēkan*, Perhaps I used to strike.
2 *Dal-et'-tahēkan-a-m*, Thou used'st to strike.	*Dal-et'-tahēkan-khan-em*, If thou used'st to strike.	*Paset'-em-dal-et'-tahēkan*, Perhaps thou used'st to strike.
3 *Dal-et'-tahēkan-a-e*, He used to strike.	*Dal-et'-tahēkan-khan-e*, If he used to strike.	*Paset'-e-dal-et'-tahēkan*, Perhaps he used to strike.
DUAL.	DUAL.	DUAL.
1 *Dal-et'-tahēkan-a-liń*, We two used to strike.	*Dal-et'-tahēkan-khan-liń*, If we two used to strike.	*Paset'-liń-dal-et'-tahēkan*, Perhaps we two used to strike.
2 *Dal-et'-tahēkan-a-ben*, You two used to strike.	*Dal-et'-tahēkan-khan-ben*, If you two used to strike.	*Paset'-ben-dal-et'-tahēkan*, Perhaps you two used to strike.
3 *Dal-et'-tahēkan-a-kin*, They two used to strike.	*Dal-et'-tahēkan-khan-kin*, If they two used to strike.	*Paset'-kin-dal et'-tahēkan*, Perhaps they two used to strike.
PLURAL.	PLURAL.	PLURAL.
1 *Dal-et'-tahēkan-a-le*, We used to strike.	*Dal-et'-tahēkan-khan-le*, If we used to strike.	*Paset'-le-dal-et'-tahēkan*, Perhaps we used to strike.
2 *Dal-et'-tahēkan-a-pe*, You used to strike.	*Dal-et'-tahēkan-khan-pe*, If you used to strike.	*Paset'-pe-dal-et'-tahēkan*, Perhaps you used to strike.
3 *Dal-et'-tahēkan-a-ko*, They used to strike.	*Dal-et'-tahēkau khan-ko*f they, I used to strike.	*Paset'-ko-dal-et'-tahēkan*, Perhaps they used to strike.

Or was striking or also sometimes, I struck.

Remark. This tense denotes that something was going on at *those times*. not neccessarily *then*.

SPECIAL INCOMPLETE PAST.

	INDICATIVE.	SUBJUNCTIVE, with "*Khan*"	SUBJUNCTIVE, with "*Paset'*."
	SINGULAR.	SINGULAR.	SINGULAR.
1	*Dal-et'kan-tahe-kan-a-ń*, I was striking*	*Dal-et'kan-tahē-kan-khan-iń*, If I was striking.	*Paset'-iń-dal-et'kan-tahēkan*, Perhaps I was striking.
2	*Dal-et'kan-takē-kan-a-m*, Thou wast striking.	*Dal-et'kan-tahē-kan-khan-em*, If thou wast striking.	*Paset'-em-dal-et'kan-tahēkan*, Perhaps thou wast striking.
3	*Dal-et'kan-tahē-kan-a-e*, He or she was striking.	*Dal-et'kan-tahē-kan-khan-e*, If he or she was striking.	*Paset'-e-dal-et'kan-tahēkan*, Perhaps he or she was striking.
	DUAL.	DUAL.	DUAL.
1	*Dal-et'kan-tahē-kan-a-liń*, We two were striking.	*Dal-et'kan-tahē-kan-khan-liń*, If we two were striking.	*Paset'-liń-dal-et' kan-tahēkan*, Perhaps we two were striking.
2	*Dal-et'kan-tahē-kan-a-ben*, You two were striking.	*Dal-et'kan-tahē-kan-khan-ben*, If you two were striking.	*Paset'-ben-dal-et'kan-tahēkan*, Perhaps you two were striking.
3	*Da -et'kan-tahē-kan-a-kin*, They two were striking.	*Dal-et'kan-tahē-kan-khan-kin*, If they two were striking.	*Paset'-kin-dal-et'kan-tahēkan*, Perhaps they two were striking.
	PLURAL.	PLURAL.	PLURAL.
1	*Dal-et'kan-tahē-kan-a-le*, We were striking.	*Dal-et'kan-tahē-kan-khan-le*, If we were striking.	*Paset'-le-dal-et'kan-tahēkan*, Perhaps we were striking.
2	*Dal-et'kan-tahē-kan-a-pe*, You were striking.	*Dal-et'kan-tahē-kan-khan-pe*, If you were striking.	*Paset'-pe-dal-et'kan-tahēkan*, Perhaps you were striking.
3	*Dal-et'kan-tahē-kan-a-ko*, They were striking.	*Dal-et'kan-tahē-kan-khan-ko*, If they were striking.	*Paset'-ko-dal-et'kan-tahēkan*, Perhaps they were striking.

* Or was trying to strike.

Note.—This tense denotes that something was going on, (incomplete) when another action took place. This tense is also used to denote, that the Agent was attempting to do something, but failed.

INDECISIVE PLUPERFECT.

	INDICATIVE.	SUBJUNCTIVE with "*Khan.*"	SUBJUNCTIVE with "*Paset.*"
	SINGULAR.	SINGULAR.	SINGULAR.
1	*Dal-let'-tahĕkan-a-ń*, I had struck.*	*Dal-let'-tahĕkan-khan-iń*, If I had struck.	*Paset'-iń-dal-let'-tahĕkan*, Perhaps I had struck.
2	*Dal-let'-tahĕkan-a-m*, Thou hadst struck.	*Dal-let'-tahĕkan-khan-em*, If thou hadst struck.	*Paset'-em-dal-let'-tahĕkan*, Perhaps thou hadst struck.
3	*Dal-let'-tahĕkan-a-e*, He or she had struck.	*Dal-let'-tahĕkan-khan-e*, If he or she had struck.	*Paset'-e-dal-let'-tahĕkan*, Perhaps he or she had struck.
	DUAL.	DUAL.	DUAL.
1	*Dal-let'-tahĕkan-a-liń*, We two had struck.	*Dal-let'-tahĕkan-khan-liń*, If we two had struck.	*Paset'-liń-dal-let'-tahĕkan*, Perhaps we two had struck.
2	*Dal-let'-tahĕkan-a-ben*, You two had struck.	*Dal-let-tahĕkan-khan-ben*, If you two had struck.	*Paset'-ben-dal-let'-tahĕkan*, Perhaps you two had struck.
3	*Dal-let'-tahĕkan-a-kin*, They two had struck.	*Dal-let'-tahĕkan-khan-kin*, If they two had struck.	*Paset'-kin-dal-let'-tahĕkan*, Perhaps they two had struck.
	PLURAL.	PLURAL.	PLURAL.
1	*Dal-let'-tahĕkan-a-le*, We had struck.	*Dal-let'-tahĕkan-khan-le*, If we had struck.	*Paset'-le-dal-let'-tahĕkan*, Perhaps we had struck.
2	*Dal-let'-tahĕkan-a-pe*, You had struck.	*Dal-let'-tahĕkan-khan-pe*, If you had struck.	*Paset'-pe-dal-let'-tahĕkan*, Perhaps you had struck.
3	*Dal-let'-tahĕkan-a-ko*, They had struck.	*Dal-let'-tahĕkan-khan-ko*, If they had struck.	*Paset'-ko-dal-let'-tahĕkan*, Perhaps they had struck.

* Or would have struck.

Note.—This tense denotes that a certain action was already over, and *had lost its importance*, or *had again been altered*, when another took place in the past. It is also used to denote that something had been attempted, but had failed. (See remarks on this tense.)

INCHOATIVE FUTURE.

INDICATIVE.	SUBJUNCTIVE with "*Khan.*"	SUBJUNCTIVE with "*Paset*"
SINGULAR.	SINGULAR.	SINGULAR.
1 *Dal-lagit'-iń*, * I shall be about to strike.	*Dal-lagit'-khan-iń*, If I shall be about to strike.	*Paset'-iń-dal-lagit'*, Perhaps I shall be about to strike.
2 *Dal-lagit'-em*, Thou wilt be about to strike.	*Dal-lagit'-khan-em*, If thou wilt be about to strike.	*Paset'-em-dal-lagit'*, Perhaps thou wilt be about to strike.
3 *Dal-lagit'-e*, He or she will be about to strike.	*Dal-lagit'-khan-e*, If he or she will be about to strike.	*Paset'-e-dal-lagit'*, Perhaps he or she will be about to strike.
DUAL.	DUAL.	DUAL.
1 *Dal-lagit'-liń*, We two shall be about to strike.	*Dal-lagit'-khan-liń*, If we two shall be about to strike.	*Paset'-liń-dal-lagit'*, Perhaps we two shall be about to strike.
2 *Dal-lagit'-ben*, You two will be about to strike.	*Dal-lagit'-khan-ben* If you two will be about to strike.	*Paset'-ben-dal-lagit'*, Perhaps you two will be about to strike.
3 *Dal-lagit'-kin*, They two will be about to strike.	*Dal-lagit'-khan-kin* If they two will be about to strike.	*Paset'-kin-dal-lagit'*, Perhaps they two will be about to strike.
PLURAL.	PLURAL.	PLURAL.
1 *Dal-lagit'-le*, We shall be about to strike.	*Dal-lagit'-khan-le*, If we shall be about to strike.	*Past'-le-dal-lagit'*, Perhaps we shall be about to strike.
2 *Dal-lagit'-pe*, You will be about to strike.	*Dal-lagit'-khan-pe*, If you will be about to strike.	*Paset'-pe-dal-lagit'*, Perhaps you will be about to strike.
3 *Dal-lagit'-ko*, They will be about to strike.	*Dal-lagit'-khan-ko*, If they will be about to strike.	*Paset'-ko-dal-lagit'*, Perhaps they will be about to strike.

Note.— What has been said about the simple future, holds also good in this, namely that it is used to express general statements and must in such cases be rendered in English, by the Present Indefinite. (See remarks on this tense.)

* Or *Lagat'*.

INCHOATIVE PRESENT.

INDICATIVE.	SUBJUNCTIVE with "*Khan*."	SUBJUNCTIVE with "*Paset'*"
SINGULAR.	SINGULAR.	SINGULAR.
1 *Dal-lagidoḱkan-a-ń*, I am about to strike.	*Dal-lagidoḱ-kan-khan-iń*, If am about to strike.	*Paset'-iń-dal-lagidoḱ kan*, Perpaps I am about to strike.
2 *Dal-lagidoḱ-kan-a-m*, Thou art about to strike.	*Dal-lagidoḱ-kan-khan-em*, If thou art about to strike.	*Paset'-em-dal-lagidoḱ kan*, Perhaps thou art about to strike.
3 *Dal-lagidoḱ-kan a-e*, He or she is about to strike.	*Dal-lagidoḱkan-khan-e*. If he or she is about to strike.	*Paset'-e-dal-lagidoḱ-kan*, Perhaps he or she is about to strike.
DUAL.	DUAL.	DUAL.
1 *Dal-lagidoḱ-kan-a-liń*, We two are about to strike.	*Dal-lagidoḱ-kan-khan-liń*, If we two are about to strike.	*Paset'-liń-dal-lagidoḱ kan*, Perhaps we two are about to strike.
Dal-lagidoḱ-kan-a-ben, You two are about to strike.	*Dal-lagidoḱ-kan-khan-ben*, If you two are about to strike.	*Paset'-ben-dal-lagid-oḱ-kan*, Perhaps you two are about to strike.
3 *Dal-lagidoḱ-kan-a-kin*, They two are about to strike.	*Dal-lagido-ḱkan-khan-kin*, If they two are about to strike.	*Paset'-kin-dal-lagid-oḱ-kan*, Perhaps they two are about to strike.
PLURAL.	PLURAL.	PLURAL.
1 *Dal-lagidoḱ-kan-a-le*, We are about to strike.	*Dal-lagidoḱ-kan-khan-le*, If we are about to strike.	*Paset'-le-dal-lagidoḱ-kan*, Perhaps we are about to strike.
2 *Dal-lagidoḱ-kan-a-pe*, You are about to strike.	*Dal-lagidoḱ-kan-khan-pe*, If you are about to strike.	*Paset'-pe-dal-lagid-oḱ-kan*, Perhaps you are about to strike.
3 *Dal-lagidoḱkan-a-ko*, They are about to strike.	*Dal-lagidoḱkan-khan-ko*, If they about to strike.	*Pase-t'-ko-dal-lagid-oḱ-kan*, Perhaps they are about to strike.

INCHOATIVE PAST.

	Indicative.	Subjunctive with "*Khan*"	Subjunctive with "*Paset'*."
	Singular.	Singular.	Singular.
1	*Dal-lagidok'kan-tahĕkan-a-ń*, I was about to strike.	*Dal-lagidok'kan-tahĕkan-khan-iń*, If I was about to strike.	*Paset'iń-dal-lagidok'-kan-tahĕkan*, Perhaps I was about to strike.
2	*Dal-lagidok'kan-tahĕkan-a-m*, Thou wast about to strike.	*Dal-lagidok'kan-tahĕkan-khan-em*, thou wast about to strike.	*Paset'em-dal-lagidok'-kan-tahĕkan*, Perhaps thou wast about to strike.
3	*Dal-lagidok'kan-tahĕkan-a-e*, He or she was about to strike.	*Dal-lagidok'kan-tahĕkan-khan-e*, If he or she was about to strike.	*Paset'-e-dal-lagidok'-kan-tahĕkan*, Perhaps he or she was was about to strike.
	Dual.	Dual.	Dual.
1	*Dal-lagidok'kan-tahĕkan-a-liń*, We two were about to strike.	*Dal-lagidok'kan-tahĕkan-khan-liń*, If we two were about to strike.	*Paset'-liń-dal-lagid-ok'-kan-tahĕkan*, Perhaps we two were about to strike.
2	*Dal-lagidok'an-tahĕkan-a-ben*, You two were about to strike.	*Dal-lagidok'kan-tahĕkan-khan-ben*, If you two were about to strike.	*Paset'-ben-dal-lagid-ok'-kan-tahĕkan*, Perhaps you two were about to strike.
3	*Dal-lagidok'kan-tahĕkan-a-kin*, They two were about to strike.	*Dal-lagidok'-kan-tahĕkan-khan-kin*, If they two were about to strike.	*Paset'-kin-dal-lagid-ok'-kan-tahĕkan*, Perhaps they two were about to strike.

INCHOATIVE PAST *(Continued).*

	INDICATIVE.	SUBJUNCTIVE with "*Khan.*"	SUBJUNCTIVE with "*Paset'.*"
	PLURAL.	PLURAL.	PLURAL.
1	*Dal-lagidok'kan-tahēkan-a-le,* We were about to strike.	*Dal-lagidok'kan-tahēkan-khan-le,* If we were about to strike.	*Paset'-le-dal-lagidok'kan-tahēkan,* Perhaps we were about to strike.
2	*Dal-lagidok'kan-tahēkan-a-pe,* You were about to strike.	*Dal-lagidok'kan-tahēkan-khan-pe,* If you were about to strike.	*Paset'-pe-dal-lagidok'kan-tahēkan,* Perhaps you were about to strike.
3	*Dal-lagidok'kan-tahēkan-a-ko,* They were about to strike.	*Dal-lagidok'kan-tahēkan-khan-ko* If they were about to strike.	*Paset'-ko-dal-lagidok'kan-tahēkan,* Perhaps they were about to strike.

OPTATIVE.

	Singular.	Singular.	Singular.
1	*Dal-ke-a-ń*, I would * strike.	*Dal-ke-khan-iń*, If I would strike.	*Paset'-iń-dal-ke*, Perhaps I would strike.*
2	*Dal-ke-a-m*, Thou would'st strike.	*Dal-ke-khan-em*, If thou would'st strike.	*Paset'-em-dal-ke*, Perhaps thou would'st strike.
3	*Dal-ke-a-e*, He would strike.	*Dal-ke-khan-e*, If he would strike.	*Paset'-e-dal-ke*, Perhaps he would strike.
	Dual.	**Dual.**	**Dual.**
1	*Dal-ke-a-liń*, We two would strike.	*Dal-ke-khan-liń*, If we two would strike.	*Paset'-liń-dal-ke*, Perhaps we two would strike.
2	*Dal-ke-a-ben*, You two would strike.	*Dal-ke-khan-ben*, If you two would strike.	*Paset'-ben-dal-ke*, Perhaps you two would strike.
3	*Dal-ke-a-kin*, They two would strike.	*Dal-ke-khan-kin* If they two would strike.	*Paset'-kin-dal-ke*, Perhaps they two would strike.
	Plural.	**Plural.**	**Plural.**
1	*Dal-ke-a-le*, We would strike.	*Dal-ke-khan-le*, If we would strike.	*Paset'-le-dal-ke*, Perhaps we would strike.
2	*Dal-ke-a-pe*, You would strike.	*Dal-ke-khan-pe*, If you would strike.	*Paset'-pe-dal-ke*, Perhaps you would strike.
3	*Dal-ke-a-ko*, They would strike.	*Dal-ke-khan-ko*, If they would strike.	*Paset'-ko-dal-ke*, Perhaps they would strike.

* Or will strike, or would have struck.

Note.—The difference between *Dal-ke-khan*, and *dal-le-khan*, is that the first is only used when the thing is wished for, whereas the latter is used both when wished for and when not; *Apaṛi-m em-kiń-khan, adi-ń raskakok'a*. If you (only) would give me the arrow-head, how glad should I be! (Vide remarks on this mood).

CONDITIONAL.

	SINGULAR.	SINGULAR.	SINGULAR.
1	(*Ohọ*) *Dal-le-a-ń*, I should (not) strike.*	*Dal-le-khan-iń*, If I should strike.†	*Paset'-iń-dal-le*, Perhaps I should strike.‡
2	(*Ohọ*) *Dal-le-a-m*, Thou would'st (not) strike.*	*Dal-le-khan-em*, If thou would'st strike.†	*Paset'-em-dal-le*, Perhaps thou would'st strike.‡
3	(*Ohọ*) *Dal-le-a-e*, He would (not) strike.*	*Dal-le-khan-e*, If he would strike.†	*Paset'-e-dal-le*, Perhaps he would strike.‡
	DUAL.	DUAL.	DUAL.
1	(*Ohọ*) *Dal-le-a-liń*, We two should (not) strike.*	*Dal-le-khan-liń*, If we two should strike.†	*Paset'-liń-dal-le*, Perhaps we two should strike.‡
2	(*Ohọ*) *Dal-le-a-ben*, You two would (not) strike.*	*Dal-le-khan-ben*, If you two would strike.†	*Paset'-ben-dal-le*, Perhaps you two would strike.‡
3	(*Ohọ*) *Dal-le-a-kin*, They two would (not) strike.*	*Dal-le-khan-kin*, If they two would strike.†	*Paset'-kin-dal-le*, Perhaps they two would strike.‡
	PLURAL.	PLURAL.	PLURAL.
1	(*Ohọ*) *Dal-le-a-le*, We should (not) strike.*	*Dal-le-khan-le*, If we should strike.†	*Paset'-le-dal-le*, Perhaps we should strike.‡
2	(*Ohọ*) *Dal-le-a-pe*, You would (not) strike.*	*Dal-le-khan-pe*, If you would strike.†	*Paset'-pe-dal-le*, Perhaps you would strike.‡
3	(*Ohọ*) *Dal-le-a-ko*, They would (not) strike.	*Dal-le-khan-ko*, If they would strike.†	*Paset'-ko-dal-le*, Per- they would strike.‡

* Or will or should (not) strike, or would (not) have struck.

† Or if I struck, or had struck, or will strike, or if I strike.

‡ Or will strike, or had struck.

Note.—(Vide *dal-ke-n-khan*) *Dal-le-khan* is used both when the thing is wished and not wished for; as *Onie ere-liń-khan, adi baṛich' iń dal-ke-a.* If he had cheated me, I should have struck him severely.

Remark. This is only used negatively.

CONTINGENT.

Singular.	Singular.	Singular.
1 *Dal-ket'-gi-ń*,* I will strike.		*Paset'-iń-dal-ket'-gi*, Perhaps I will strike.
2 *Dal-ket'-gi-m*, Thou wilt strike.		*Paset'-em-dal-ket'-gi*, Perhaps thou wilt strike.
3 *Dal-ket'-gi-e*, He will strike.		*Paset'-e-dal-ket'-gi*, Perhaps he will strike.
Dual.	Dual.	Dual.
1 *Dal-ket'-gi-liń*, We two will strike.		*Paset'-liń-dal-ket'-gi*, Perhaps we two will strike.
2 *Dal-ket'-gi-ben*, You two will strike.		*Paset'-ben-dal-ket'-gi*, Perhaps you two will strike.
3 *Dal-ket'-gi-kin*, They two will strike.		*Paset'-kin-dal-ket'-gi*, Perhaps they two will strike.
Plural.	Plural.	Plural.
1 *Dal-ket'-gi-le*, We will strike.		*Paset'-le-dal-ket'-gi*, Perhaps we will strike.
2 *Dal-ket'-gi-pe*, You will strike.		*Paset'-pe-dal-ket'-gi*, Perhaps you will strike.
3 *Dal-ket' gi-ko*, They will strike.		*Paset'-ko-dal-ket'-gi*, Perhaps they will strike.

* Or would strike, or would have struck, or I strike; as *bae doho liń-khan adoń hech' ruar̨ engi.* If he does not keep me then I will come back; *Hola-m dal-le-khan, adoe dar̨ ket' gi, ado-m chika-ke-a?* If you had struck her yesterday and *she had ran away*, what would you then do or have done; *hor iń ba, tao ama ho! Suluṅga kulhi talatem chalak'a, Gadiolem parom ket'gi, ado Damra-m tioket'gi.* You go through *Salungah, pass Gaḍiol*, and you are in *Damra.*

PRELIMINARY FUTURE.

SINGULAR.	SINGULAR.	SINGULAR.
1 *Dal-le-gi-ń*, I will first strike.		*Paset'-iń-dal-le-gi*, Perhaps I will first strike.
2 *Dal-le-gi-m*, Thou wilt first strike.		*Paset'-em-dal-le-gi*, Perhaps thou wilt first strike.
3 *Dal-le-gi-e*, He will first strike.		*Paset'-e-pal-le-gi*, Perhaps he will first strike.
DUAL.	DUAL.	DUAL.
1 *Dal-le-gi-liń*, We two will first strike.		*Paset'-liń-dal-le-gi*, Perhaps we two will first strike.
2 *Dal-le-gi-ben*, You two will first strike.		*Paset'-ben-dal-le-gi*, Perhaps you two will first strike.
3 *Dal-le-gi-kin*, They two will first strike.		*Paset'-kin-dal-le-gi*, Perhaps they two will first strike.
PLURAL.	PLURAL.	PLURAL.
1 *Dal-le-gi-le*, We will first strike.		*Paset'-le-dal-le-gi*, Perhaps we will first strike.
2 *Dal-le-gi-pe*, You will first strike.		*Paset'-dal-le-gi*, Perhaps you will first strike.
3 *Dal-legi-ko*, They will first strike.		*Paset'-ko-dal-le-gi*, Perhaps they will first strike.

PRELIMINARY EXPOSTULATIVE.

	SINGULAR.	DUAL.	PLURAL.
1	*Dal-le-nahī-ń*, I must first strike.	*Dal-le-nahī-liń*, We two must first strike.	*Dal-le-nahī-le*, We must first strike.
2	*Dal-le-nahī-m*, Thou must first strike.	*Dale-le-nahī-ben*, You two must first strike.	*Dal-le-nahī-pe*, You must first strike.
3	*Dal-le-nahī-e*, He must first strike.	*Dal-le-nahī-kin*, They two must first strike.	*Dal-le-nahī-ko*, They must first strike.

PRELIMINARY PERSUASIVE.

	SINGULAR.	DUAL.	PLURAL.
1	*Dal-le-ba-ń*, I must first strike.	*Dal-le-ba-liń*, We two must first strike.	*Dal-le-ba-le*, We must first strike.
2	*Dal-le-ba-m*, Thou must first strike.	*Dal-le-ba-ben*, You two must first strike.	*Dal-le-ba-pe*, You must first strike.
3	*Dal-le-ba-e*, He must first strike.	*Dal-le-ba-kin*; They two must first strike.	*Dal-le-ba-ko*, They must first strike.

PRELIMINARY ADMISSIVE.

	SINGULAR.	DUAL.	PLURAL.
1	*Dal-le-en-a-ń*, I must first strike.	*Dal-le-en-a-liń*, We two must first strike.	*Dal-le-en-a-le*, We must first strike.
2	*Dal-le-en-a-m*, Thou must first strike.	*Dal-le-en-a-ben*, You two must first strike.	*Dal-le-en-a-pe*, You must first strike.
3	*Dal-le-en-a-e*, He must first strike.	*Dal-le-en-a-kin*, They two must first strike.	*Dal-le-en-a-ko*. They must first strike.

Note.—The difference between these three tenses (or rather moods) is as follows: The first is used in remonstrating or retorting; as *Chak' bam agu-lak'*, *a? ńamlenahiń endenahiń aguea*, Why did you not bring it? I must first get it and then I will bring it. The second is used *consideratively* as *adiń dalea*, I will strike him very much. *Sap'le bam*, you must first *catch* him (remember:) and the third is used admissingly; as *hẽ, sap'le enań*, yes (it is true) I must first *catch* him.

PRELIMINARY BENEDICTIVE OR PRECATIVE.

	SINGULAR.	DUAL.	PLURAL.
1	*Dal-le-ma-ń!* May I first strike!	*Dal-le-ma-liń!* May we two first strike!	*Dal-le-ma-le!* May we first strike!
2	*Dal-le-ma-m!* Mayest thou first strike!	*Dal-le-ma-ben!* May you two first strike!	*Dal-le-ma-pe!* May you first strike!
3	*Dal-le-ma-e!* May he first strike!	*Dal-le-ma-kin!* May they two first strike!	*Dal-le-ma-ko!* May they first strike!

PRELIMINARY IMPERATIVE.

2	*Dal-le-m!* Strike thou first.	*Dal-le-ben!* Strike you two first!	*Dal-le-pe!* Strike you first.

BENEDICTIVE OR PRECATIVE.

1	*Dal-ma-ń!* May I strike!	*Dal-ma-liń!* May we two strike!	*Dal-ma-le!* May we strike!
2	*Dal-ma-m!* Mayest thou strike!	*Dal-ma-ben!* May you two strike!	*Dal-ma-pe!* May you strike!
3	*Dal-ma-e!* May he strike!	*Dal-ma-kin!* May they two strike!	*Dal-ma-ko!* May they strike!

IMPERATIVE.

2	*Dal-me!* Strike thou! or that.	*Dal-ben!* Strike you two!	*Dal-pe!* Strike you!

Note.—The 1st and 3rd person in all three numbers are the same in Benedictive and Imperative—thus *dal-mań* may both mean, *May I strike,* and let me strike!

PARTICIPLES.

ADJECTIVE PARTICIPLES.	ADVERBIAL PARTICIPLES.	GERUNDS.
FUTURE.		
Dal (kin, ko), Struck.	*Dal-khan*, Striking.	*Dal-reaḱ, te,re,* Of, by, in striking.
GENERAL INCOMPLETE PRESENT.		
Dal-et', Who strikes.	*Dal-et'-khan*, Striking.	*Dal-et'-reaḱ, te, re,* Of, by, in striking.
SPECIAL INCOMPLETE PRESENT.		
Dal-et'-kan, Who is striking.	*Dal-et'-kan-khun*, Striking now.	*Dal-et'-kan-reaḱ, te, re,* Of, by, in striking now.
RECENT PAST.		
Dal-ket', Who struck or has struck.	*Dal-ket'-khan*, Having struck.	*Dal-ket'-reaḱ, te, re,* Of, by, in having struck.
ANTERIOR PAST.		
Dal-let', Who struck or had struck.	*Dal-let'-khan*, Having struck.	*Dal-let'-reaḱ, te, re,* Of, by, in having struck.
GENERAL INCOMPLETE PAST.		
Dal-et'-tahēkan, Who used to strike or was striking.	*Dal-et'-tahēkan-khan*. Using to strike then.	*Dal-et'-tahēkan-reaḱ, te, re,* Of, by, in using to strike then.
SPECIAL INCOMPLETE PAST.		
Dal-et'-kan-tahēkan, Who was striking.	*Dal-et'-kan-tahēhan-khan*, Striking then.	*Dal-et'-kan-takēḱan-reaḱ, te, re,* Of, by, in striking then.
INDICISIVE PLUPERFECT.		
Dal-let'-tahēkan, Who had struck.	*Dal-let'-tahēkhan-khan*, Having struck.	*Dal-let'-tahēkan-reaḱ, te, re,* Of, by, in having struck.

Inchoative Future. *Dal-lagit'*, Who will be about to strike.	*Dal-lagit'-khan*, Being about to strike.	*Dal-lagit'-reaḱ, te, re*, Of, by, in being about to strike.
Inchoative Present. *Dal-lagidoḱ-kan*, Who is about to strike.	*Dal-lagidoḱ-kan-khan*, Being now about to strike.	*Dal-lagidoḱ-kan-reaḱ, te, re*, Of, by, in being about to strike now.
Inchoative Past. *Dal-lagidoḱ-kan-tahēkan*, Who was about to strike.	*Dal-lagidoḱ-kan-tahē-han-khan*, Being then about to strike.	*Dal-lagidoḱ-kan-tahēkan-reaḱ, te, re*, Of, by, in being about to strike then.
Optative. *Dal-ke*, Who would strike, or have struck.	*Dal-ke-khan*, Willing to strike.	*Dal-ke-reaḱ, te, re*, Of, by, in that one would strike.
Conditional. *Dal-le*, Who may have struck.	*Dal-le-khan*, In case of striking.	*Dal-le-reaḱ, te, re*, Of, by, in striking.
Preliminary Expostulative.	*Dal-le-nahĩ*, First striking.	
Preliminary Persuasive.	*Dal-le-baṅ*, First striking.	
Preliminary Admissive.	*Dal-le-ena*, First striking.	
Infinitive.	*Dal*, To strike.	

Remark. Any of the nominative Suffixes may be affixed to the adjective participles; as *dal-et'-ko*, they who strike; *dal-ket'-pe*, you who struck etc.

GENITIVE WITH NOMINATIVE.

INDICATIVE.	SUBJUNCTIVE with "*Khan.*" *FUTURE TENSE.*	SUBJUNCTIVE with "*Paset.*"
SINGULAR.	SINGULAR.	SINGULAR.
1 *Dal-tiń-a-e,* He will strike my.	*Dal-tiń-khan-e,* If he will strike my.	*Paset'-e-dal-tiń,* Perhaps he will strike my.
2 *Dal-tam-a-e,* He will strike thy.	*Dal-tam-khan-e,* If he will strike thy.	*Paset'-e-dal-tam,* Perhaps he will strike thy.
3 *Dal-tae-a-e,* He will strike his.	*Dal-tae-khan-e,* If he will strike his.	*Paset'-e-dal-tae,* Perhaps he will strike his.
DUAL.	DUAL.	DUAL.
1 *Dal-taliń-a-e,* He will strike our. (two).	*Dal-taliń-khan-e,* If he will strike our (two).	*Paset'-e-dal-taliń,* Perhaps he will strike our (two).
2 *Dal-taben-a-e,* He will strike your (two).	*Dal-taben-khan-e,* If he will strike your (two).	*Paset'-e-dal-taben,* Perhaps he will strike your (two).
3 *Dal-takin-a-e,* He will strike their (two).	*Dal-takin-khan-e,* If he will strike their (two).	*Paset'-e-dal-takin,* Perhaps he will strike their (two).
PLURAL.	PLURAL.	PLURAL.
1 *Dal-tale-a-e,* He will strike our.	*Dal-tale-khan-e,* If he will strike our.	*Paset'-e-dal-tale,* Perhaps he will strike our.
2 *Dal-tape-a-e,* He will strike your.	*Dal-tape-khan-e,* If he will strike your.	*Paset'-e-dal-tape,* Perhaps he will strike your.
3 *Dal-tako-a-e,* He will strike their.	*Dal-tako-khan-e,* If he will strike their.	*Paset'-e-dal-tako,* Perhaps he will strike their.

Note.—The 3rd person Singular of the Nominative suffixes "e" has been affixed to the final "a" to show how any of those suffixes may be added to form the required subject of the sentence; as *Dal-tam-a-ko,* They will strike thy. *Dal-tako-a-m.* Thou wilt strike their etc.

GENERAL INCOMPLETE PRESENT.

INDICATIVE.	SUBJUNCTIVE with "*Khan.*"	SUBJUNCTIVE with "*Paset.*"
Dal-et'-tiń-a-e, He strikes my.	*Dal-et'-tin-khan-e,* If he strikes my.	*Paset'-e-dal-et'-tiń,* Perhaps he strikes my.
SPECIAL INCOMPLETE PRESENT.		
Dal-et'-kan-tiń-a-e, He is striking my.	*Dal-et'kan-tiń-khan-e,* If he is striking my.	*Paset'-e-dal-et'-kan-tiń,* Perhaps he is striking my.
RECENT PAST.		
Dal-ket'-tiń-a-e, He struck or has struck my.	*Dal-ket'-tiń-khan-e,* If he struck my.	*Paset'-e-dal-ket'-tiń,* Perhaps he struck my.
ANTERIOR PAST.		
Dal-let'-tiń-a-e, He struck or had struck my.	*Dal-let'-tiń-khan-e,* If he struck my.	*Paset'-e-dal-let'-tiń,* Perhaps he struck my.
GENERAL INCOMPLETE PAST.		
Dal-et'-tahēkan-tiń-a-e, He used to strike my.	*Dal-et'-tahēkan-tiń-khan-e,* If he used to strike my.	*Paset'-e-dal-et'-tahēkan tiń,* Perhaps he used to strike my.
SPECIAL INCOMPLETE PAST.		
Dal-et'-kan-tahē-kan-tiń-a-e, He was striking my.	*Dal-et'-kan-tahē-kan-tiń-khan-e,* If he was striking my.	*Paset'-e-dal-et'-kan-tahē-kan-tiń,* Perhaps he was striking my.
INDECISIVE PLUPERFECT.		
Dal-let'-tahēkan-tiń-a-e, He had struck my.	*Dal-let'-tahēkan-tiń-khan-e,* If he had struck my.	*Paset'-e-dal-let'-tahē-kan-tiń,* Perhaps he had struck my.

INCHOATIVE FUTURE.

Dal-tiń-lagit'-e, He will be about to strike my.	*Dal-tiń-lagit'-khan-e*, If he will be about to strike my.	*Paset'-e-dal-tiń-lagit'*, Perhaps he will be about to strike my.

INCHOATIVE PRESENT.

Dal-tiń-lagidok'-kan-a-e, He is about to strike my.	*Dal-tiń-lagidok'-kan-khan-e*, If he is about to strike my.	*Paset'-e-dal-tiń-lagi-dok'-kan*, Perhaps he is about to strike my.

INCHOATIVE PAST,

Dal-tiń-lagidok'-kan-tahēkan-a-e, He was about to strike my.	*Dal-tiń-lugidok'-kan-takēkan-khan-e*, If he was about to strike my.	*Paset'-e-dal-tiń-lagi-dok'-kan tahēk'an*, Perhaps he was about to strike my.

OPTATIVE.

Dal-ke-tiń-a-e, He will or would strike my.	*Dal-ke-tiń-khan-e*, If he would strike my.	*Past'-e-dal-ke-tiń*, Perhaps he would strike my.

CONDITIONAL.

(Qho) Dal-le-tińa-e, He will r would (not) strike my.	*Dal-le-tiń-khan-e*, If he will or would strike my.	*Paset'-e-dal-le-tiń*, Perhaps he will or would strike my.

CONTINGENT.

Dal-ket'-tiń-gi-e, He strikes, or will or would strike my.		*Paset'-e-dal-ket'-tiń-gi-e*, Perhaps he will or would strike my.

PRELIMINARY FUTURE.

Dal-le-tiń-gi-e, He will first strike my.		*Paset'-e-dal-le-tiń-gi-e*, Perhaps he will first strike my.

SINGULAR.	DUAL.	PLURAL.

PRELIMINARY EXPOSTULATIVE.

Dal-le-tiń-nahī-e, He must first strike my.	*Dal-le-taliń-nahī-e*, He must first strike our (two.)	*Dal-le-tale-nahī-e*, He must first strike our.

SINGULAR.	DUAL.	PLURAL.
PRE	LIMINARY PERSUAS	IVE.
Dal-le-tiṅ-ba-e, He must first strike my.	*Dal-le-taliṅ-ba-e*, He must first strike our (two).	*Dal-le-tale-ba-e*, He must first strike our.
PRE	LIMINARY ADMISSI	VE.
Dal-le-tiṅ-en-a-e, He must first strike my.	*Dal-le-taliṅ-en-a-e*, He must first strike our (two).	*Dal-le-tale-en-a-e*, He must first strike our.
PRE	LIMINARY BENEDIC	TIVE.
Dal-letiṅ-ma-e! * May he first strike my!	*Dal-le-taliṅ-ma-e!* May he first strike our (two).	*Dal-le-tal e-ma-e!* May he first strike our!
PRE	LIMINARY IMPERAT	IVE.
2 *Dal-le-tiṅ me!* Strike thou first my!	*Dal-le-taliṅ-me!* Strike thou first our (two).	*Dal-le-tale-me!* Strike thou first our!
	BENEDICTIVE.	
Dal-tiṅ-ma-e! * May he strike my!	*Dal-taliṅ-ma-e!* May he strike our (two)!	*Dal-tale-ma-e!* May he strike our!
	IMPERATIVE.	
2 *Dal-tiṅ-me!* Strike thou my!	*Dal-taliṅ-me!* Strike thou our (two)!	*Dal-tale-me!* Strike thou our!

* Or that he may or might etc.

* *Note.*—It will be observed, that besides in the Future tense, only the Synopsis of the Genitive case has been given, as the student will easily be able to insert any required Genitive Suffix between the tense-sign and the final "*a*."

This form is used when the object is Neuter.

ADJECTIVE PARTICIPLES.	ADVERBIAL PARTICIPLES.	GERUNDS.
FUTURE.		
Dal-tin * *(tum talc.)* Who will strike my (thy, our etc.)	*Dal-tiń-khan,* Striking my.	*Dal-tiń, tam, tape-reak̉, te, re, etc,* Of, by, in striking my, thy, your.
GENERAL INCOMPLETE PRESENT.		
Dal-et'-tiń, Who strikes my.	*Dal-et'-tin-khan,* Striking my.	*Dal-et'-tiń-reak̉, te, re, etc.* Of, by, in striking my.
SPECIAL INCOMPLETE PRESENT.		
Dal-et'-kan-tiń, Who is striking my.	*Dal-et'-kan-tin-khan,* Striking my *now.*	*Dal-et'-kan-tiń-reak̉, te, etc.* Of, by, in striking my *now.*
RECENT PAST.		
Dal-ket'-tiń, Who struck my.	*Dal-ket'-tiń-khan,* Having struck my.	*Dal-ket'-tiń-reak̉, te, etc.* Of, by, in having struck my.
ANTERIOR PAST.		
al-let'-tiń. Who struck my.	*Dal-let'-tiń-khan,* Having struck my.	*Dal-let'-tiń-reak̉, te, etc.* Of, by, in having struck my.
GENERAL INCOMPLETE PAST.		
Dal et'-tahēkan-tiń, Who used to strike my.	*Dal-et'-tahēkan-tiń-khan,* Used to strike my.	*Dal-et'-tahēkan-tiń-reak̉, te, etc.* Of, by, in using to strike my.
SPECIAL INCOMPLETE PAST.		
Dal-et'-kan tahēkan-tiń, Who was striking my then.	*Dal-et'-kan tahēkan tiń-khan,* Striking my *then.*	*Dal-et'-kan-tahēkan-tiń-reak̉, te, etc,* Of, by, in striking my then.
INDECISIVE PLUPERFECT.		
Dal-let'-tahēkan-tiń, Who had struck my.	*Dal-let'-tahēkan-tiń-khan,* Having struck my.	*Dal-let'-tahēkan-tiń-reak̉, te, etc,* Of, by, in having struck my.

* Any of the Genitive suffixes may of course be affixed; as *Dal-ket'-tam hor,* the person who struck thy, *Dal-et'-taben iń ńel let'koa.* I saw them striking your (two.)

INCHOATIVE FUTURE. *Dal-tiń-lagit'*, Who will be about to strike my.	*Dal-tiń-lagit'-khan*, Being about to strike my.	*Dal-tiń-lagit'-reaḱ, te, etc*, Of, by, in being about to strike my.
INCHOATIVE PRESENT. *Dal-tiń-lagidoḱ-kan*, Who is about to strike my.	*Dal-tiń-lagidoḱ-kan-khan*, Being now about to strike my.	*Dal-tiń-lagidoḱ-kan-reaḱ, re, te*, Of, by, in being about to strike my.
INCHOATIVE PAST. *Dal-tiń-lagidoḱ kan-tahēkan*, Who was about to strike my.	*Dal-tiń-lagidoḱ-kan-ta-hē-kan khan*, Being then about to strike my.	*Dal-tiń-lagidoḱ-kan-ta hē kan-reaḱ, te, etc*, Of, by, in being then about to strike my.
OPTATIVE. *Dal-ke-tiń*, Who would strike my.	*Dal-ke-tiń-khan*, Wishing to strike my.	*Dal-ke-tiń-reaḱ, te, etc*, Of, by, in wishing to strike my.
CONDITIONAL. *Dal le tiń*, Who may have struck my.	*Dal-le-tiń-khan*, Having first struck my.	*Dal-le-tiń-reaḱ, te, re, etc*, In case of or having struck my.
INFINITIVE. *Dal-tiń-tam-tae-etc.*, To strike my etc.		

Remark **—The Preliminary Expostulative, Persuasive and Admissive *Dal-le-tiń-nahi, Dal-le-tiń-bań, Dal-le-tiń-ena*, being first obliged to strike my, are not unfrequently heard.**

FUTURE.

WITH THE ACCUSATIVE CASE.

	INDICATIVE.	SUBJUNCTIVE with "*Khan.*"	SUBJUNCTIVE with "*Paset'.*"
	SINGULAR.	SINGULAR.	SINGULAR.
1	*Dal-iń-a-e*, He will strike me.	*Dal-iń-khan-e*, If he will strike me.	*Paset'-e-dal-iń*,* Perhaps he will strike me.
2	*Dal-me-a-e*, He will strike thee.	*Dal-me-khan-e*, If he will strike thee.	*Paset'-e-dal-me*, Perhaps he will strike thee.
3	*Dal-e-a-e*, He will strike him or her.	*Dal-e-khan-e*, If he will strike him or her.	*Paset'-e-dal-e*, Perhaps he will strike him or her.
	DUAL.	DUAL.	DUAL.
1	*Dal-liń-a-e*, He will strike us two.	*Dal-liń-khan-e*, If he will strike us two.	*Paset'-e-dal-liń*, Perhaps he will strike us two.
2	*Dal-ben-a-e*, He will strike you two.	*Dal-ben-khan-e*, If he will strike you two.	*Paset'-e-dal-ben*, Perhaps he will strike you two.
3	*Dal-kin-a-e*, He will strike them two.	*Dal-kin-khan-e*, If he will strike them two.	*Paset'-e-dal-kin*, Perhaps he will strike them two.
	PLURAL.	PLURAL.	PLURAL.
1	*Dal-le-a-e*, He will strike us.	*Dal-le-khan-e*, If he will strike us.	*Paset'-e-dal-le*, Perhaps he will strike us
2	*Dal-pe-a-e*, He will strike you.	*Dal-pe-khan-e*, If he will strike you.	*Paset'-e-dal-pe*, Perhaps he will strike you.
3	*Dal-ko-a-e*, He will strike them.	*Dal-ko-khan-e*, If he will strike them.	*Paset'-e-dal-ko*, Perhaps he will strike them.

* Or may strike.

Note.—In this case all forms are made to agree with a Nominative of the third person singular common Gender. The student will easily be able to affix any required nominative suffix to the final "a."

GENERAL INCOMPLETE PRESENT.

	INDICATIVE.	SUBJUNCTIVE with "*Khan.*"	SUBJUNCTIVE with "*Paset'.*"
	SINGULAR.	SINGULAR.	SINGULAR.
1	*Dal-ed-iń-a-e*, He strikes me.*	*Dal-ed-iń-khan-e*, If he strikes me.*	*Paset'-e-dal-ed-iń*, Perhaps he strikes me.*
2	*Dal-et'-me-a-e*, He strikes thee.	*Dal-et'-me-khan-e*, If he strikes thee.	*Paset'-e-dal-et'-me*, Perhaps he strikes thee.
3	*Dal-ed-e-a-e*, He strikes him or her.	*Dal-ed-e-khan-e*, If he strikes him or her.	*Paset'-e-dal-ed-e*, Perhaps he strikes him or her.
	DUAL.	DUAL.	DUAL.
1	*Dal-et'-liń-a-e*, He strikes us two.	*Dal-et'-liń-khan-e*, If he strikes us two.	*Paset'-e-dal-et'-liń* Perhaps he strikes, us two.
2	*Dal-et'-ben-a-e*, He strikes you two.	*Dal-et'-ben-khan-e*, If he strikes you two.	*Paset'-e-dal-et'-ben*, Perhaps he strikes you two.
3	*Dal-et'-kin-a-e*, He strikes them two.	*Dal-et'-kin-khan-e*, If he strikes them two.	*Paset'-e-dal-et'-kin*, Perhaps he strikes, them two.
	PLURAL.	PLURAL.	PLURAL.
1	*Dal-et'-le-a-e*, He strikes us	*Dal-et'-le-khan-e*, If he strikes us.	*Paset'-e-dal-et'-le*, Perhaps he strikes us.
2	*Dal-et'-pe-a-e*, He strikes you.	*Dal-et'-pe-khan-e*, If he strikes you.	*Paset'-e-dal-et'-pe*, Perhaps he strikes you.
3	*Dal-et'-ko-a-e*, He strikes them.	*Dal-et'-ko-khan-e*, If he strikes them.	*Paset'-e-dal-et'-ko*, Perhaps he strikes them.

* Or is striking.

SPECIAL INCOMPLETE PRESENT.

Indicative.	Subjunctive with "*Khan.*"	Subjunctive with "*Paset'.*"
Singular.	**Singular.**	**Singular.**
1 * *Dal-ed-iṅ-kan--a-e,* He is striking me.	* *Dal-ed-iṅ-kan-khan-e,* If he is striking me.	* *Paset'-e-dal-ed-iṅ-kan,* Perhaps he is striking me.
2 *Dal-et'-me-kan-a-e,* He is striking thee.	*Dal-et'-me-kan khan-e,* If he is striking thee.	*Paset'-e-dal et'-me-kan,* Perhaps he is striking thee.
3 † *Dal-ed e-kan-a-e,* He is striking him or her.	† *Dal-ed-e-kan-khan-e,* If he is striking him. &c.	† *Paset'-e-dal-ed-e-kan,* Perhaps he is striking him. &c.
Dual.	**Dual.**	**Dual.**
1 *Dal-et'-liṅ-kan-a-e,* He is striking us two.	*Dal-et'-liṅ-kan-khan-e,* If he is striking us two.	*Paset'-e-dal-et'-liṅ-kan,* Perhaps he is striking us two.
2 *Dal-et'-ben-kan-a-e,* He is striking you two.	*Dal-et'-ben-kan-khan-e,* If he is striking you two.	*Paset'-e-dal-et'-ben-kan,* Perhaps he is striking you two.
3 *Dal-et'-kin-kan-a-e,* He is striking them two.	*Dal-et'-kin-kan-khan-e,* If he is striking them two.	*Paset'-e-dal-et'-kin-kan,* Perhaps he is striking them two.
Plural.	**Plural.**	**Plural.**
1 *Dal-et'-le-kan-a-e,* He is striking us.	*Dal et'-le-kan-khan-e,* If he is striking us.	*Paset'-e-dal-et'-le-kan,* Perhaps he is striking us.
2 *Dal-et'-pe-kan-a-e,* He is striking you.	*Dal-et'-pe-kan-khan-e,* If he is striking you.	*Paset'-e-dal-et'-pe-kan,* Perhaps he is striking you.
3 *Dal-et'-ko-kan-a-e,* He is striking them.	*Dal-et'-ko-kan-khan-e,* If he is striking them.	*Paset'-e-dal-et'-ko-kan,* Perhaps he is striking them.

* Or usually *dal-iṅ-kan-a-e.*

† Or usually *dal-e-kan-a-e.*

RECENT PAST.

	INDICATIVE.	SUBJUNCTIVE with "*Khan.*"	SUBJUNCTIVE with "*Paset.*"
	SINGULAR.	SINGULAR.	SINGULAR.
1	*Dal-ked-iń-a-e*, He struck me.	*Dal-ked-iń-kan-e*, If he struck me.	*Paset'-e-dal-ked-iń*, Perhaps he struck me.
2	*Dal-ket'-me-a-e*, He struck thee.	*Dal-ket'-me-khan-e*, If he struck thee.	*Paset'-e-dal-ket'-me*, Perhaps he struck thee.
3	*Dal-ked-e-a-e*, He struck him or her.	*Dal-ked-e-khan-e*, If he struck him or her.	*Paset'-e-dal-ked-e* Perhaps he struck him or her.
	DUAL.	DUAL.	DUAL.
1	*Dal-ket'-liń-a-e*, He struck us two.	*Dal-ket'-liń-khan-e*, If he struck us two.	*Paset'-e-dal-ket'-liń*, Perhaps he struck us two.
2	*Dal-ket'-ben-a-e*, He struck you two.	*Dal-ket'-ben-khan-e*, If he struck you two.	*Paset'-e-dal-ket'-ben*, Perhaps he struck you two.
3	*Dal-ket'-kin-a-e*, He struck them two.	*Dal-ket'-kin-khan-e*. If he struck them two.	*Paset'-e-dal-ket'-kin*, Perhaps he struck them two.
	PLURAL.	PLURAL.	PLURAL.
1	*Dal-ket'-le-a-e*, He struck us.	*Dal-ket'-le-khan-e*, If he struck us.	*Paset'-e-dal-ket'-le*, Perhaps he struck us.
2	*Dal-ket'-pe-a-e*, He struck you.	*Dal-ket'-pe-khan-e*, If he struck you.	*Paset'-e-dal-ket'-pe*, Perhaphs he struck you.
3	*Dal-ket'-ko-a-e*, He struck them.	*Dal-ket'-ko-khan-e*, If he struck them.	*Paset'-e-dal-ket'-ko*, Perhaps he struck them.

ANTERIOR PAST.

INDICATIVE.	SUBJUNCTIVE with "*Khan.*"	SUBJUNCTIVE with "*Poset'.*"
SINGULAR.	SINGULAR.	SINGULAR.
1 *Dal-led-iń-a-e,* He struck* me.	*Dal-led-iń-khan-e,* If he struck* me.	*Past'-e-dal-led-iń,* Perhaps he struck* me.
2 *Dal-let'-me-a-e,* He struck thee.	*Dal-let'-me-khan-e,* If he struck thee.	*Past'-e-dal-let'-me,* Perhaps he struck thee.
3 *Dal-led-e-a-e,* He struck him or her.	*Dal-led-e-khan-e,* If he struck him or her.	*Paset'e-dal-led-e,* Perhaps he struck him or her.
DUAL.	DUAL.	DUAL.
1 *Dal-let'-liń-a e,* He struck us two.	*Dal-let'-liń-khan-é,* If he struck us two.	*Paset'-e-dal-let'-liń* Perhaps he struck us two.
2 *Dal-let'-ben-a-e,* He struck you two.	*Dal-let'-ben-khan-e,* If he struck you two.	*Paset'-e-dal-let'-ben,* Perhaps he struck you two.
3 *Dal-let'-kin-a-e,* He struck them two.	*Dal-let'-kin-khan-e,* If he struck them two.	*Paset'-e-dal-let'-kin,* Perhaps he struck them two.
PLURAL.	PLURAL.	PLURAL
1 *Dal-let'-le-a-e,* He struck us.	*Dal-let'-le-khan-e,* If he struck us.	*Paset'-e-dal-let'-le,* Perhaps he struck us.
2 *Dal-let'-pe-a-e,* He struck you.	*Dal-let'-pe-khan-e,* If he struck you.	*Paset'-e-dal-let'-pe,* Perhaps he struck you.
3 *Dal-let-ko-a-e,* He struck them.	*Dal-let'-ko-khan-e,* If he struck them.	*Paset'-e-dal-let'-ko,* Perhaps he struck them.

* Or had struck.

Note.—The other form mentioned in the Nominative case Anterior Past is not used in the 1st and 3rd person Singular, and even seldom in the other persons; as *Dal-lak'-ko-a-e,* He struck them.

GENERAL INCOMPLETE PAST.

	INDICATIVE.	SUBJUNCTIVE with "*Khan*."	SUBJUNCTIVE with "*Paset'*."
	SINGULAR.	SINGULAR.	SINGULAL'
1	*Dal-ed-iń-tahēkan-a-e*, He * struck or used to strike me.	*Dal-ed-iń-tahēkan-khan-e*, If he struck or used to strike me.	*Paset'-e-dal-ed-iń-tahēkan*, Perhaps he struck or used to strike me.
2	*Dal-et'-me-tahēkan-a-e*, He struck or used to strike thee.	*Dal-et'-me-tahēkan-khan-e*, If he struck or used to strike thee.	*Paset'-e-dal-et'-me-tahēkan*, Perhaps he struck or used to strike thee.
3	*Dal-ed-e-tahēkan-a-e*, He struck or used to strike him.	*Dal-ed-e-tahēkan-khan-e*, If he struck or used to strike him.	*Paset'-e-dal-ed-e-tahēkan*, Perhaps he struck or used to strike him.
	DUAL.	DUAL.	DUAL.
1	*Dal-et'-liń-tahēkan-a-e*, He struck or used to strike us two.	*Dal-et'-liń-tahēkan-khan-e*, If he struck or used to strike us two.	*Paset'-e-dal-et'-liń-tahēkan*, Perhaps he struck or used to strike us two.
2	*Dal-et'-ben-tahēkan-a-e*, He struck or used to strike you two.	*Dal-et'-ben-tahēkankhan-e*, If he struck or used to strike you two.	*Paset'-e-dal-et'-ben-tahēkan*, Perhaps he struck or used to strike you two.
3	*Dal-et'-kin-tahēkan-a-e*, He struck or used to strike them two.	*Dal-et'-kin-tahēkan-khan-e*, If he struck or used to strike them two.	*Paset'-e-dal-et'-kin-tahēkan*, Perhaps he struck or used to strike them two.
	PLURAL.	PLURAL.	PLURAL.
1	*Dal-et'-le-tahēkan-a-e*, He struck or used to strike us.	*Dal-et'-le-tahēkan-khan-e*, If he struck or used to strike us.	*Paset'-e-dal-et'-le-tahēkan*, Perhaps he struck or used to strike us.
2	*Dal-et'-pe-tahēkan-a-e*, He struck or used to strike you.	*Dal-et'-pe-tahēkan-khan-e*, If he struck or used to strike you.	*Paset'-e-dal-et'-pe-tahēkan*, Perhaps he struck or used to strike you.
3	*Dal-et'-ko-tahēkan-a-e*, He struck or used to strike them.	*Dal-et'-ko-tahēkan-khan-e*, If he struck or used to strike them.	*Paset'-e-dal-et'-ko-tahēkan*, Perhaps he struck or used to strike them.

* Or was striking. (*Vide Nom. case*).

SPECIAL INCOMPLETE PAST.

	INDICATIVE.	SUBJUNCTIVE with "*Khan.*"	SUBJUNCTIVE with "*Paset'.*"
	SINGULAR.	SINGULAR.	SINGULAR.
1	*Dal-ed-iń-kan-tahēkan-a-e*, He was striking me.*	*Dal-ed-iń-kan, takēkan-khan-e*, If he was strikingme.	*Paset'-e-dal-ed-iń-kan-tahēkan*, Perhaps he was striking me.
2	*Dal-et'-me-kan-tahēkan-a-e*, He was striking thee.	*Dal-et'-me-kan-tahēkan-khan-e*, If he was striking thee.	*Paset'-e-dal-et'-me-kan-tahēkan*, Perhaps he was striking thee.
3	*Dal-ed-e-kan-tahēkan-a-e*, He was striking him.*	*Dal-ed-e-kan-tahēkan-khan-e*, If he wasstrikinghim.	*Paset'-e-dal-ed-e-kan-tahēkan*, Perhaps he was striking him.
	DUAL.	DUAL.	DUAL.
	Dal-et'-liń-kan-tahēkan-a-e, He as striking us two.	*Dal-et'-liń kan-tahēkan-khan-e*, If he was striking us two.	*Paset'-e-dal-et'-liń-kan-tahēkan*, Perhaps he was striking us two.
2	*Dal-et'-ben-kan-tahēkan-a-e*, He was striking you two.	*Dal-et'-ben-kan-tahēkan-khan-e*, If he was striking you two.	*Paset'-e-dal-et'-ben-kan-tahēkan*, Perhaps he was striking you two.
3	*Dal-et'-kin-kan-tahēkan-a-e*, He was striking them two.	*Dal-et'-kin-kan-, tahēkan khan-e.* If he was striking them two.	*Paset'-e-dal-et'-kin-kan-tahēkan*, Perhaps he was striking them two.
	PLURAL.	PLURAL.	PLURAL.
1	*Dal-et'-le-kan-tahēkan-a-e*, He was striking us.	*Dal-et'-le-kan-tahēkan-khan-e*, If he was striking us.	*Paset'-e-dal-et'-le-kan-tahēkan*, Perhaps he was striking us.
2	*Dal-et'-pe-kan-tahēkan-a-e*, He was striking you.	*Dal-et'-pe-kan-tahēkan-khan-e*, If he was striking you.	*Paset'-e-dal-et'-pe-kan-tahēkan*, Perhaps he was striking you.
3	*Dal-et'-ko-kan-tahēkan-a-e*, He was striking them.	*Dal-et'-ko-kan-tahēkan-khan-e*, If he was striking them.	*Paset'-e-dal-et'-ko-kan-tahēkan*, Perhaps he was strikthem.

* Or *Dal-iń-kan-tahēkan-a-e.*

† Or *Dal-e-kan-takēkan-a-e.*

INDICISIVE PLUPERFECT.

	INDICATIVE.	SUBJUNCTIVE with "*Khan.*"	SUBJUNCTIVE with "*Paset'.*"
	SINGULAR.	SINGULAR.	SINGULAR.
1	*Dal-led-iń-tahē-kan-a-e*, He had struck me.	*Dal-led-iń-tahē-kan-khan-e*, If he had struck me.	*Paset'-e-dal-led-iń-tahēkan*, Perhaps he had struck me.
2	*Dal-let'-me-tahēkan-a-e*, He had struck thee.	*Dal-let'-me-tahē-kan-khan-e*, If he had struck thee.	*Paset'-e-dal-let'-me-tahēkan*, Perhaps he had struck thee.
3	*Dal-led-e-tahē-kan-a-e*, He had struck him.	*Dal-led-e-tahē-kan-khan-e*, If he had struck him.	*Paset'-e-dal-led-e-tahē-kan*, Perhaps he had struck him.
	DUAL.	DUAL.	DUAL.
1	*Dal-let'-liń-tahēkan-a-e*, He had struck us two.	*Dal-let'-liń-tahē-kan-khan-e*, If he had struck us two.	*Paset'-e-dal-let'-liń-tahēkan*, Perhaps he had struck us two.
2	*Dal-let'-ben-tahēkan-a-e*, He had struck you two.	*Dal-let'-ben-tahē-kan-khan-e*, If he had struck you two.	*Paset'-e-dal-let'-ben-tahēkan*, Perhaps he had struck you two.
3	*Dal-let'-kin-tahēkan-a-e*, He had struck them two.	*Dal-let'-kin-tahē-kan-khan-e*, If he had struck them two.	*Paset'-e-dal-let'-kin-tahēkan*, Perhaps he had struck them two.
	PLURAL.	PLURAL.	PLURAL.
1	*Dal-let'-le-tahē-kan-a-e*, He had struck us.	*Dal-let'-le-tahē-kan-khan-e*, If he had struck us.	*Paset'-e-dal-let'-le-tahēkan*, Perhaps he had struck us.
2	*Dal-let'-pe-tahē-kan-a-e*, He had struck you.	*Dal-let'-pe-tahē-kan khan-e*, If he had struck you.	*Paset'-e-dal-let'-pe-tahēkan*, Perhaps he had struck you.
3	*Dal-let'-ko-tahē-kan-a-e*, He had struck them.	*Dal-let'-ko-tahē-kan-khan-e*, If he had struck them.	*Paset'-e-dal-let'-ko-tahēkan*, Perhaps he had struck them.

INCHOATIVE FUTURE.

	Indicative.	Subjunctive with "*Khan.*"	Subjunctive with "*Paset'.*"
	Singular.	**Singular.**	**Singular.**
1	*Dal-iń-lagit'-e*, He will be about to strike me.	*Dal-iń-lagit'-khan-e*, If he will be about to strike to me.	*Paset'-e-dal-iń-lagit'*, Perhaps he will be about to strike me.
2	*Dal-me-lagit'-e*, He will be about to strike thee.	*Dal-me-lagit'-khan-e*, If he will about tostrike thee.	*Paset'-e-dal-me-lagit'*, Perhaps he will be about to strike thee.
3	*Dal-e-lagit'-e*, He will be about to strike him.	*Dal-e-lagit'-khan-e*, If he will be about to strike him.	*Paset'-e-dal-e-lagit'*, Perhaps he will be about to strike him.
	Dual.	**Dual.**	**Dual.**
1	*Dal-liń-lagit'-e*, He will be about to strike us two.	*Dal-liń-lagit'-khan-e*, If he will be about to strike us two.	*Paset'-e-dal-liń-lagit'*, Perhaps he will be about to strike us two.
2	*Dal-ben-lagit-e*, He will be about to strike you two.	*Dal-ben-lagit'-khan-e*, If he will be about to strike you two.	*Paset'-e-dal-ben-lagit'*, Perhaps he will be about to strike you two.
3	*Dal-kin-lagit'-e*, He will be about to strike them two.	*Dal-kin-lagit'-khan-e*, If he will be about to strike them two.	*Paset'-e-dal-kin-lagit'*, Perhaps he will be about to strike them two.
	Plural.	**Plural.**	**Plural.**
1	*Dal-le-lagit'-e*, He will be about to strike us.	*Dal-le-lagit'-khan-e*, If he will be about to strike us.	*Paset'-e-dal-le-lagit'*, Perhaps he will be about to strike us.
2	*Dal-pe-lagit'-e*, He will be about to strike you.	*Dal-pe-lagit'-khan-e*, If he will be about to strike you.	*Paset'-e-dal-pe-lagit'*, Perhaps he will be about to strike you.
3	*Dal-ko-lagit'-e*, He will be about to strike them.	*Dal-ko-lagit'-khan-e*, If he will be about tostrike them.	*Paset'-e-dal-ko-lagit'*, Perhaps he will be about to strike them.

INCHOATIVE PRESENT.

	Indicative.	Subjunctive with "*Khan.*"	Subjunctive with "*Paset'.*"
	Singular.	**Singular.**	**Singular.**
1	*Dal-iń-lagid-oḱ-kan-a-e,* He is about to strike me.	*Dal-iń-lagid-oḱ-kan-khan-e,* If he is about to strike me.	*Paset'-e-dal-in-lagid-oḱ-kan,* Perhaps he is about to strike me.
2	*Dal-me-lagid-oḱ-kan-a-e,* He is about to strike thee.	*Dal-me-lagid-oḱ-kan-khan-e,* If he is about to strike thee.	*Paset'-e-dal-me-lagid-oḱ-kan,* Perhaps he is about to strike thee.
3	*Dal-e-lagid-oḱ-kan-a-e,* He is about to strike him.	*Dal-e-lagid-oḱ-kan-khan-e,* If he is about to strike him.	*Paset'-e-dal-e-lagid-oḱ-kan,* Perhaps he is about to strike him.
	Dual.	**Dual.**	**Dual.**
1	*Dal-liń lagid-oḱ-kan-a-e,* He is about to strike us two.	*Dal-liń-lagid-oḱ-kan-khan-e,* If he is about to strike us two.	*Paset'-e-dal-liń-lagid-oḱ-kan,* Perhaps he is about to strike us two.
2	*Dal-ben-lagid-oḱ-kan-a-e,* He is about to strike you two.	*Dal-ben-lagid-oḱ-kan-khan-e* If he is about to strike you two.	*Paset'-e-dal-ben-lagid-oḱ-kan,* Perhaps is about to strike you two.
3	*Dal-kin-lagid-oḱ-kan-a-e,* He is about to strike them two.	*Dal-kin-lagid-oḱ-kan-khan-e,* If he is about to strike them two.	*Paset'-e-dal-kin-lagid-oḱ-kan,* Perhaps he is about to strike them two.
	Plural.	**Plural.**	**Plural.**
1	*Dal-le-lagid-oḱ-kan-a-e,* He is about to strike us.	*Dal-le-lagid-oḱ-kan-khan-e,* If he is about to strike us.	*Paset'-e-dal-le-lagid-oḱ-kan,* Perhaps he is about to strike us.
2	*Dal-pe-lagid-oḱ-kan-a-e,* He is about to strike you.	*Dal-pe-lagid-oḱ-kan-khan-e,* If he is about to strike you.	*Paset'-e-dal-pe-lagid-oḱ-kan,* Perhaps he is about to strike you.
3	*Dal-ko-lagid-oḱ-kan-a-e,* He is about to strike them.	*Dal-ko-lagid-oḱ-kan-khan-e,* If he is about to strike them.	*Paset'-e-dal-ko-lagid-oḱ-kan,* Perhaps he is about to strike them.

INCHOATIVE PAST.

	Indicative.	Subjunctive with "*Khan.*"	Subjunctive with "*Paset'.*"
	Singular.	**Singular.**	**Singular.**
1	*Dal-iń-lagid-oḱ-kan-tahēkan-a-e,* He was about to to strike me.	*Dal-iń-lagid-oḱ-kan-tahēkan-khan-e,* If he was about to strike me.	*Paset'-e-dal-iń-lagid-oḱ-kan-tahēkan,* Perhaps he was about to strike me.
2	*Dal-me-lagidoḱ-kan-tahēkan-a-e,* He was about to strike thee.	*Dal-me-lagid-oḱ-kan-tahēkan-khan-e,* If he was about to strike thee.	*Paset'-e-dal-me-lagid-o-ḱ-kan-tahēkan,* Perhaps he was about to strike thee.
3	*Dal-e-lagid-oḱ-kan-tahēhan-a-e,* He was about to strike him.	*Dal-e-lagid-oḱ-kan-tahēhan-khan-e,* If he was about to strike him.	*Paset'-e-dal-e-lagid-oḱ-kan-tahēkan,* Perhaps he was about to strike him.
	Dual.	**Dual.**	**Dual.**
1	*Dal-liń-lagid-oḱ-kan-tahēkan-a-e,* He was about to strike us two.	*Dal-liń-lagid-oḱ-kan-tahēkan-khan-e,* If he was about to strike us two.	*Paset'-e-dal-liń-lagid-oḱ-kan-tahēkan,* Perhaps he was about to strike us two.
2	*Dal-ben-lagid-oḱ-kan-tahē-kan-a-e,* He was about to strike you two.	*Dal-ben-lagid-oḱ-kan-tahēkan-khan-e,* If he was about to strike you two.	*Paset'-e-dal-ben-lagid-oḱ-kan-tahēkan,* Perhaps he was about to strike you two.
3	*Dal-kin-lagid-oḱ-kan-tahē-kan-a-e,* He was about to strike them two.	*Dal-kin-lagid-oḱ-kan-tahēkan-khan-e,* If he was about to strike them two.	*Paset'-e-dal-kin-lagid-oḱ-kan-tahēkan,* Perhaps he was about to strike them two.

	PLURAL.	PLURAL.	PLURAL.
1	*Dal-le-lagid-ok-kan-tahēkan-a-e*, He was about to strike us.	*Dal-le-lagid-ok-kan-tahēkan-khan-e*, If he was about to strike us.	*Paset'-e-dal-le-lagid-ok-kan-tahēkan*, Perhaps he was about to strike us.
2	*Dal-pe-lagid-ok-kan-tahēkan-a-e*, He was about to strike you.	*Dal-pe-lagid-ok-kan-tahē-kan-khan-e*, If he was about to strike you.	*Paset'-e-dal-pe-lagid-ok-kan-tahēkan*, Perhaps he was about to strike you.
3	*Dal-ko-lagid-ok-kan-tahēkan-a-e*, He was about to strike them.	*Dal-ko-lagid-ok-kan-tahēkan-khan-e*, If he was about to strike them.	*Paset'-e-dal-ko-lagid-ok-kan-tahēkan*, Perhaps he was about to strike them.

OPTATIVE.

	SINGULAR.	SINGULAR.	SINGULAR.
1	*Dal-ke-ń-a-e*, * He will or would strike me.	*Dal-ke-ń-khan-e*, * If he will or would strike me.	*Paset'-e-dal-ke-ń*, * Perhaps he will or would strike me.
2	*Dal-ke-m-a-e*, He will or would strike thee.	*Dal-ke-m-khan-e*, If he will or would strike thee.	*Paset'-e-dal-ke-m*, Perhaps he will or would strike thee.
3	*Dal-ke-a-e*, He will or would strike him.	*Dal-ke-khan-e*, If he will or would strike him.	*Paset'-e-dal-ke*, Perhaps he will or would strike him.
	DUAL.	DUAL.	DUAL.
1	*Dal-ke-liń-a-e*, He will or would strike us two.	*Dal-ke-liń-khan-e*, If he will or would strike us two.	*Paset'-e-dal-ke-liń*, Perhaps he will or would strike us two,
2	*Dal-ke-ben-a-e*, He will or would strike you two.	*Dal-ke-ben-khan-e*, If he will or would strike you two.	*Paset'-e-dal-ke-ben*, Perhaps he will or would strike you two.
3	*Dal-ke-kin-a-e*, He will or would strike them two.	*Dal-ke-kin-khan-e*, If he will or would strike them two.	*Paset'-e-dal-ke-kin*, Perhaps he will or would strike them two.
	PLURAL.	PLURAL.	PLURAL.
1	*Dal-ke-le-a-e*, He will or would strike us.	*Dal-ke-le-khan-e*, If he will or would strike us.	*Paset'-e-dal-ke-le*, Perhaps he will or would strike us.
2	*Dal-ke-pe-a-e*, He will or would strike you.	*Dal-ke-pe-khan-e*, If he will or would strike you.	*Paset'-e-dal-ke-pe*, Perhaps he will or would strike you.
3	*Dal-ke-ko-a-e*, He will or would strike them.	*Dal-ke-ko-khan-e*, If he will or would strike them.	*Paset'-e-dal-ke-ko*, Perhaps he will or would strike them.

* Or have struck.

CONDITIONAL.

	SINGULAR.	SINGULAR.	SINGULAR.
1	*(Qhọ) Dal-le-ń-a-e,* He will or would (not) strike* me.	*Dal-le-ń-khan-e,* If he will or would strike* me.	*Paset'-e-dal-le-ń,* Perhaps he will or would strike* me.
2	*(Qhọ) Dal-le-m-a-e,* He will or would (not) strike thee.	*Dal-le-m-khan-e,* If he will or would strike thee.	*Paset'-e-dal-le-m,* Perhaps he will or would strike thee.
3	*(Qhọ) Dal-le-ae,* He will or would (not) strike him.	*Dal-le-khan-e,* If he will or would strike him.	*Paset'-e-dal-le,* Perhaps he will or would strike him.
	DUAL.	DUAL.	DUAL.
1	*(Qhọ) Dal-le-liń-a-e,* He will or would (not) strike us two.	*Dal-le-liń-khan-e,* If he will or would strike us two.	*Paset'-e-dal-le-liń,* Perhaps he will or would strike us two.
2	*(Qhọ) Dal-le-ben-a-e,* He will or would (not) strike you two.	*Dal-le-ben-khan-e,* If he will or would strike you two.	*Paset'-e-dal-le-ben,* Perhaps he will or would strike you two.
3	*(Qhọ) Dal-le kin-a-e,* He will or would (not) strike them two.	*Dal-le-kin-khan-e,* If he will or would strike them two.	*Paset'-e-dal-le-kin,* Perhaps he will or would strike them two.
	PLURAL.	PLURAL.	PLURAL.
1	*(Qhọ) Dal-le-le-a-e,* He will or would (not) strike us.	*Dal-le-le-khan-e,* If he will or would strike us.	*Paset'-e-dal-le-le,* Perhaps he will or would strike us.
2	*(Qhọ) Dal-le-pe-a-e,* He will or would (not) strike you.	*Dal-le-pe-khan-e,* If he will or would strike you.	*Paset'-e-dal-le-pe,* Perhaps he will or would strike you.
3	*(Qhọ) Dal-le-ko-a-e,* He will or would (not) strike them.	*Dal-le-ko-khan-e,* If he will or would strike them.	*Paset'-e-dal-le-ko,* Perhaps he will or would strike them.

* Or have struck.

CONTINGENT.

SINGULAR.	SINGULAR.	SINGULAR.
1 *Dal-ked-iń-gi-e*, He strikes, will or would strike* me.		*Paset'-e-dal-ked-iń-gi*, Perhaps he will or would strike* me.
2 *Dal-ked-me-gi-e*, He will or would strike thee.		*Paset'-e-dal-ket'-me-gi*, Perhaps he will or would strike thee.
3 *Dal-ked-e-gi-e*, He will or would strike him.		*Paset'-e-dal-ked-e-gi*, Perhaps he will or would strike him.
DUAL.		DUAL.
1 *Dal-ket'-liń-gi-e*, He will or would strike us two.		*Paset'-e-dal-ket'-liń-gi*, Perhaps he will or would strike us two.
2 *Dal-ket'-ben-gi-e*, He will or would strike you two.		*Paset'-e-dal-ket'-ben-gi*, Perhaps he will or would strike you two.
3 *Dal-ket'-kin gi-e, e*, He will or would strike them two.		*Paset'-e-dal-ket'-kin-gi*, Perhaps he will or would strike them two.
PLRUAL.		DUAL.
1 *Dal-ket'-le-gi-e*, He will or would strike us.		*Paset'-e-dal-ket'-le-gi*, Perhaps he will or would strike us.
2 *Dal-ket'-pe-gi-e*, He will or would strike you.		*Paset'-e-dal-ket'-pe-gi*, Perhaps he will or would strike you.
3 *Dal-ket'-ko-gi-e*, He will or would strike them.		*Paset'-e-dal-ket'-ko-gi*, Perhaps he will or would strike them.

* Or have struck, or he strikes me.

PRELIMINARY FUTURE.

SINGULAR.	SINGULAR.	SINGULAR.
1 *Dal-le-ń-gi-e*, He will first strike me.		*Paset'-e-dal-le-ń-gi*, Perhaps he will first strike me.
2 *Dal-le-m-gi-e*, He will first strike thee.		*Paset'-e-dal-le-m-gi* Perhaps he will first strike thee.
3 *Dal-le-gi-e*. He will first strike him.		*Paset'-e-dal-le-gi*, Perhaps he will first strike him.
DUAL.		DUAL.
1 *Dal-le-liń-gi-e*, He will first strike us two.		*Paset'-e-dal-le-liń-gi*, Perhaps he will first strike us two.
2 *Dal-le-ben-gi-e*, He will first strike you two.		*Paset'-e-dal-le-ben, gi*, Perhaps he will first strike you two.
3 *Dal-le-kin-gi-e*, He will first strike them two.		*Paset'-e-dal-le-kin-gi*, Perhaps he will first strike them two.
PLURAL.		PLURAL.
1 *Dal-le-le-gi-e*, He will first strike us.		*Paset'-e-dal-le-le-gi*, Perhaps he will first strike us.
2 *Dal-le-pe-gi-e*, He will first strike you.		*Paset-e-dal-le-pe-gi*, Perhaps he will first strike you.
3 *Dal-le-ko-gi-e*, He will first strike them.		*Paset'-e-dal-le-ko-gi*, Perhaps he will first strike them.

PRELIMINARY EXPOSTULATIVE.

	SINGULAR.	DUAL.	PLURAL.
1	*Dal-le-ń-nahī-e,* He must first strike me.	*Dal-le-liń-nahī-e,* He must first strike us two.	*Dal-le-le-nahī-e,* He must first strike us.
2	*Dal-le-m-nahī-e,* He must first strike thee.	*Dal-le-ben-nahī-e,* He must first strike you two.	*Dal-le-pe-nahī-e,* He must first strike you.
3	*Dal-le-nahī-,* He must first strike him.	*Dal-le-kin-nahī-e,* He must first strike them two.	*Dal-le-ko-nahī-e,* He must first strike them.

PRELIMINARY PERSUASIVE.

	SINGULAR.	DUAL.	PLURAL.
1	*Dal-le-ń-ba-e,* He must first strike me.	*Dal-le-liń-ba-e,* He must first strike us two.	*Dal-le-le-ba-e,* He must first strike us.
2	*Dal-le-m-ba-e,* He must first strike thee!	*Dal-le-ben-ba-e,* He must first strike you two.	*Dal-le-pe-ba-e,* He must first strike you.
3	*Dal-le-ba-e,* He must first strike him.	*Dal-le-kin-ba-e,* He must first strike them two.	*Dal-le-ko-ba-e,* He must first strike them.

PRELIMINARY ADMISSIVE.

	SINGULAR.	DUAL.	PLURAL.
1	*Dal-le-ń-en-a-e,* He must first strike me.	*Dal-le-kiń-en-a-e,* He must first strike us two.	*Dal-le-le-en-a-e,* He must first strike us.
2	*Dal-le-m-en-a-e,* He must first strike thee.	*Dal-le-ben-en-a-e,* He must first strike you two.	*Dal-le-pe-en-a-e,* He must first strike you.
3	*Dal-le-en-a-e,* He must first strike him.	*Dal-le-kin-en-a-e,* He must first strike them two.	*Dal-le-ko-en-a-e,* He must first strike them.

PRELIMINARY BENEDICTIVE.

	SINGULAR.	DUAL.	PLURAL.
1	*Dal-le-ń-ma-m!* Mayest thou first strike me!	*Dal-le-liń-ma-ben!* May you two first strike us two!	*Dal-le-le-ma-pe!* May you first strike us!
2	*Dal-le-m-ma-e!* May he first strike thee!	*Dal-le-ben-ma-ko!* May they first strike you two!	*Dal-le-pe-ma-kin!* May they two first strike you!
3	*Dal-le-ma-ń* May I first strike him!	*Dal-le-kin-ma-liń* May we two first strike them two!	*Dal-le-ko-ma-m!* Mayest thou first strike them!

PRELIMINARY IMPERATIVE.

1	*Dal-liń-me!* Strike thou first me!	*Dal-le-liń-me!* Strike thou first us two!	*Dal-le-le-pe!* Strike you first us!
3	*Dal-le-m!* strike thou first him!	*Dal le-kin-ben!* Strike you two first them two!	*Dal-le-ko-m!* Strike thou first them!

BENEDICTIVE.

1	*Dal-iń-ma-m!* Mayest thou strike me!	*Dal-liń-ma ben!* May you two strike us two!	*Dal-le-ma-ko!* May they strike us!
2	*Dal-me-ma-e!* May he strike thee!	*Dal-ben-ma-kin!* May they two strike you two!	*Dal-pe-ma-le!* May we strike you!
3	*Dal-e-ma-ń!* May I strike him!	*Dal-kin-ma-liń!* May we two strike them two!	*Dal-ko-ma-pe,* May you strike them!

IMPERATIVE.

1	*Dal-iń-me!* Strike thou me!	*Dal-liń-ben!* Strike you two us two!	*Dal-le-pe-!* Strike you us!
3	*Dal-e-me!* Strike thou him!	*Dal-kin-ben!* Strike you two them two!	*Dal-ko-pe!* Strike you them!

Note. The 2nd person in Preliminary Imperative is the same as the 2nd person Preliminary Benedictive, and the 2nd person Imperative is the same as 2nd person Benedictive.

ADJECTIVE PARTICIPLES.	GERUNDS.
FUTURE.	
Dal-iń (kin or ko) (hor) who will strike me.	*Dal-ko-reaḱ. te, re, khon,* Of, by, in striking them.
GENERAL INCOMPLETE PRESENT.	
Dal-et'-me, Who strikes thee.	*Dal-et'-ko-reaḱ, te, re,* Of, by, in striking them.
SPECIAL INCOMPLETE PRESENT.	
Dal-ed-e-kan, He, whom they are striking.	*Dal-et'-ko-kan-reaḱ, te, re,* Of, by, in striking them now.
RECENT PAST.	
Dal-ket'-liń, Who struck us two.	*Dal-ket'-ko-reaḱ, te, re,* Of, by, in having struck them.
ANTERIOR PAST.	
Dal-let'-ben, Who struck you two.	*Dal-let'-ko-reaḱ, te, re,* Of, by, in having struck them.
GENERAL INCOMPLETE PAST.	
Dal-et'-kin-tahēkan, They two, whom they used to strike.	*Dal-et'-ko-tahēkan-reaḱ, te, re,* Of, by, in using to strike them then.
SPECIAL INCOMPLETE PAST.	
Dal-et'-le-kan-tahēkan, Who was striking us.	*Dal-et'-ko-kan-tahēkan-reaḱ te, re,* Of, by, in striking them then.
INDECISIVE PLUPERFECT.	
Dal-let'-pe-tahēkan, Who was striking you.	*Dal-let'-ko-tahēkan-reaḱ, te, re,* Of, by, in having struck them.
INCHOATIVE FUTURE.	
Dal-ko-lagit', They, whom they will be about to strike.	*Dal-ko-lagit'-reaḱ, te, re,* Of, by, in being about to strike them.

ADJECTIVE PARTICIPLES.	GERUNDS.
INCHOATIVE PRESENT.	
Dal-ko-lagidoḱ-kan, They, whom they are about to strike.	*Dal-ko-lagidoḱ-kan-reaḱ, te, re,* Of, by, in being about to strike them now.
INCHOATIVE PAST.	
Dal-ko-lagidoḱ-kan-tahēkan, They whom they were about to strike.	*Dal-ko-lagidoḱ-kan-tahēkan-reaḱ, te re,* Of, by, in being about to strike them then.
OPTATIVE.	
Dal-ke-ko, They, whom they would strike, or have struck.	*Dal-ke-ko-reaḱ, te, re,* Of, by, in wishing to strike them.
CONDITIONAL.	
Dal-le-ko, They, whom they may have struck.	*Dal-le-ko-reaḱ, te, re,* Of, by, in having struck them.

Note—It will be observed, that the noun, which succeeds the participle is *the Nominative*, when the accusative suffix or infix is either 1*st* or 2*nd* person, whereas it is the *Accusative*, when the Suffix is 3*rd* person; as *Dal-le-hoṛ Dal-pe hoṛ* the man, who will strike us, or you; but *Dal-ko hoṛ* is the men whom somebody has struck.

ADVERBIAL PARTICIPLES.

FUTURE.	*Dal-me-khan,* Striking thee.
GENERAL INCOMPLETE PRESENT.	*Dal-ed-iṅ-khan,* Striking me.
SPICIAL INCOMPLETE PRESENT.	*Dal-ed-e-kan-hkan,* Striking him now.
RECENT PAST.	*Dal-ket'-liṅ-khan,* Having struck us two.
ANTERIOR PAST.	*Dal-let'-ben-khan,* Having struck you two.
GENERAL INCOMPLETE PAST.	*Dal-et'-kin-tahēkan-khan,* Using to strike them two *then.*
SPECIAL INCOMPLETE PAST.	*Dal-et'-le-kan-tahēkan-khan,* Striking us *then.*
INDICISIVE PLUPERFECT.	*Dal-let- pe-tahēkan-khan,* Having struck you.
INCHOATIVE FUTURE.	*Dal-ko-lagit'-khan,* Being about to strike them.
INCHOATIVE PRESENT.	*Dal-ko-lagidok-kan-khan,* Being now about to strike them.
INCHOATIVE PAST.	*Dal-ko-lagid-ok-kan-tahēkan-khan,* Being *then* about to strike them.
OPTATIVE.	*Dal-ke-ko-khan,* Willing to strike them.
CONDITIONAL.	*Dal-le-ko-khan,* Striking or having struck (i. e. in case of) them.
PRELIMINARY EXPOSTULATIVE.	*Dal-le-ko-nahī,* Striking them first.
PRELIMINARY PERSUASIVE.	*Dal-le-ko-baṅ,* Striking them first.
PRELIMINARY ADMISSIVE.	*Dal-le-ko-ena,* Striking them first.
INFINITIVE.	*Dal-ko, kin, pe &c.* to strike them, them two, you &c.

Note.—Any of the Nominative Suffixes may be affixed to the Adjective Participles in the Accusative case, so that both Accusative and Nominative may be represented in the same participles; as *Dal-ked-e-ṅ,* I, who struck him; *Dal-ket'-ko-pe,* you, who struck them; *Dal-ked-iṅ-kin,* they two, who struck me; *Dal-ket'-pe-le,* we who struck you; *Dal-ket'- le-pe,* you, who struck us.

Any of the Accusative Suffixes can of course be infixed in the Gerunds; as *Dal-ko-re, Dal-pe-re, Dal-liṅ-re, &c.*

REFLEXIVE (AND PASSIVE.)

C. WITH THE NOMINATIVE AND ACCUSATIVE.

INDICATIVE.	SUBJUNCTIVE with "*Khan.*" *FUTURE TENSE*	SUBJUNCTIVE with "*Paset'.*"
SINGULAR.	SINGULAR.	SINGULAR.
1 *Dal-ok'-a-ń*, I shall strike myself.	*Dal-ok'-khan-iń*, If I shall strike myself.	*Paset'-iń-dal-ok'*, Perhaps I shall strike myself.
2 *Dal-ok'-a-m*, Thou wilt strike thyself.	*Dal-ok'-khan-em*, If thou wilt strike thyself.	*Paset'-em-dal-ok'*, Perhaps thou wilt strike thyself.
3 *Dal-ok'-a-e*, He will strike himself.	*Dal-ok'-khan-e*, If he will strike himself.	*Paset'-e-dal-ok'*, Perhaps he will strike himself.
DUAL.	DUAL.	DUAL.
1 *Dal-ok'-a-liń*, We two will strike ourselves.	*Dal-ok'-khan-liń*, If we two shall strike ourselves.	*Paset'-liń-dal-ok'*, Perhaps we two shall strike ourselves
2 *Dal-ok'-a-ben*, You two will strike yourselves.	*Dal-ok'-khan-ben*, If you two will strike yourselves.	*Paset'-ben-dal-ok'*, Perhaps you two will strike yourselves
3 *Dal-ok'-a-kin*, They two will strike themselves.	*Dal-ok'-khan-kin*, If they two will strike themselves.	*Paset'-kin-dal-ok'*; Perhaps they two will strike themselves.
PLURAL.	PLURAL.	PLURAL.
1 *Dal-ok'-a-le*, We shall strike ourselves.	*Dal-ok'-khan-le*, If we shall strike ourselves.	*Paset'-le-dal-ok'*, Perhaps we shall strike ourselves.
2 *Dal-ok'-a-pe*, You will strike yourselves.	*Dal-ok'-khan-pe*, If you will strike yourselves.	*Past'-pe-dal-ok'*, Perhaps you will strike yourselves.
3 *Dal-ok'-a-ko*, They will strike themselves.	*Dal-ok'-khan-ko*, If they will strike themselves.	*Paset'-ko-dal-ok'*, Perhaps they will strike themselves.
Neuter. *Dal-ok'-a*, It will be struck.	*Dal-ok'-khan*, If it will be struck.	*Paset'-dal-ok'*, Perhaps it will be struck.

SPECIAL INCOMPLETE PRESENT.

	INDICATIVE.	SUBJUNCTIVE with "*Khan.*"	SUBJUNCTIVE with "*Paset'.*"
	SINGULAR.	SINGULAR	SINGULAR.
1	*Dal-ok'-kan-a-ń*, I am striking myself.	*Dal-ok'-kan-khan-iń*, If I am striking myself.	*Paset'-iń-dal-ok'-kan*, Perhaps I am striking myself.
2	*Dal-ok'-kan-a-m*, Thou art striking, thyself.	*Dal-ok'-kan-khan-em*, If thou art striking thyself.	*Past'-em-dal-ok'-kan*, Perhaps thou art striking thyself.
3	*Dal-ok'-kan-a-e*, He is striking himself.	*Dal-ok'-kan-khan-e*, If he is striking himself.	*Past'-e-dal-ok'-kan*, Perhaps he is striking himself.
	DAUL.	DAUL.	DUAL.
1	*Dal-ok'-kan-a-liń*, We two are striking ourselves.	*Dal-ok'-kan-khan-liń*, If we two are striking ourselves.	*Paset'-liń-dal-ok'-kan*, Perhaps we two are striking ourselves.
2	*Dal-ok'-kan-a-ben*, You two are striking yourselves.	*Dal-ok'-kan-khan-ben*, If you two are striking yourselves.	*Paset'-ben-dal-ok'-kan*, Perhaps you two are striking yourselves.
3	*Dal-ok'-kan-a-kin*, They two are striking themselves.	*Dal-ok'-kan-khan-kin*, If they two are striking themselves.	*Paset'-kin-dal-ok'-kan*, Perhaps they two are striking themselves.
	PLURAL.	PLURAL.	PLURAL.
1	*Dal-ok'-kan-a-le*, We are striking ourselves.	*Dal-ok'-kan-khan-le*, If we are striking ourselves.	*Paset'-le-dal-ok'-kan*, Perhaps we are striking ourselves.
2	*Dal-ok'-kan-a-pe*, You are striking yourselves.	*Dal-ok'-kan-khan-pe*, If you are striking yourselves.	*Paset'-pe-dal-ok'-kan*, Perhaps you are striking yourselves.
3	*Dal-ok'-kan-ako*, They are striking themselves.	*Dal-ok'-kan-khan-ko*, If they are striking themselves.	*Paset'-ko-dal-ok'-kan*, Perhaps they are striking themselves.
Neuter	*Dal-ok'-kan-a*, It is being struck.	*Dal-ok'-kan-khan*, If it is being struck.	*Paset' dal-ok'-kan*. Perhaps it is being struck

RECENT PAST.

INDICATIVE.	SUBJUNCTIVE with "*Khan.*"	SUBJUNCTIVE with "*Paset'.*"
SINGULAR.	SINGULAR.	SINGULAR.
1 *Dal-en-a-ń*, I struck myself. *	*Dal-en-khan-iń*, If I struck myself.	*Paset'-iń-dal-en*, Perhaps I struck myself.
2 *Dal-en-a-m*, Thou struckest thyself.	*Dal-en-khan-em*, If thou struckest thyself.	*Paset'-em-dal-en* Perhaps thou struckest thyself.
3 *Dal-en-a-e*, He struck himself.	*Dal-en-khan-e*, If he struck himself.	*Paset-e-dal-en*, Perhaps he struck himself.
DAUL.	DUAL.	DUAL.
1 *Dal-en-a-liń*, We two struck ourselves.	*Dal-en-khan-liń*, If we two struck ourselves.	*Paset'-liń-dal-en*, Perhaps we two struck ourselves.
2 *Dal-en-a-ben*, You two struck yourselves.	*Dal-en-khan-ben*, If you two struck yourselves.	*Paset'-ben-dal-en*, Perhaps you two struck yourselves.
3 *Dal-en-a-kin*, They two struck themselves.	*Dal-en-khan-kin*, If they two struck themselves.	*Paset'-kin-dal-en*, Perhaps they two struck themselves.
PLURAL.	PLURAL.	PLURAL,
1 *Dal-en-a-le*, We struck ourselves.	*Dal-en-khan-le*, If we struck ourselves.	*Paset'-le-dal-en*, Perhaps we struck ourselves.
2 *Dal-en-a-pe*, You struck yourselves.	*Dal-en-khan-pe*, If you struck yourselves.	*Paset'-pe-dal-en*, Perhaps you struck yourselves.
3 *Dal-en-a-ko*, They struck themselves.	*Dal-en-khan-ko*, If they struck themselves.	*Paset'-ko-dal-en*, Perhaps they struck themselves.
Neuter. *Dal-en a*, It was struck.	*Dal-en-khan*, If it was struck.	*Paset'-dal-en*, Perhaps it was struck.

* Or have struck myself.

ANTERIOR PAST.

	Indicative.	Subjunctive with "*Khan*"	Subjunctive with "*Paset'*."
	Singular.	**Singular.**	**Singular.**
1	*Dal-len-a-ń*, I struck myself. *	*Dal-len-khan-iń*, If I struck myself.	*Paset'-iń-dal-len*, Perhaps I struck myself.
2	*Dal-len-a-m*, Thou struckst thyself.	*Dal-len-khan-em*, If thou struckst thyself.	*Paset'-em-dal-len*, Perhaps thou struckst thyself.
3	*Dal-len-a-e*, He struck himself.	*Dal-len-khan-e*, If he struck himself.	*Paset'-e-dal-len*, Perhaps he struck, himself.
	Daul.	**Daul.**	**Daul.**
1	*Dal-len-a-liń*, We two struck ourselves.	*Dal len-khan-liń*, If we two struck ourselves.	*Paset'-liń-dal-len*, Perhaps we two struck ourselves.
2	*Dal-len-a-ben*, You two struck yourselves.	*Dal-len-khan-ben*, If you two struck yourselves.	*Paset'-ben-dal-len*, Perhaps you two struck yourselves.
3	*Dal-len-a-kin*, They two struck themselves.	*Dal-len-khan-kin*,- If they two struck themselves.	*Paset'-kin-dal-len*, Perhaps they two struck themselves.
	Plural.	**Plural.**	**Plural.**
1	*Dal-len-a-le*, We struck ourselves.	*Dal-len-khan-le*, If we struck ourselves.	*Paset'-le-dal-len*, Perhaps we struck ourselves.
2	*Dal-len-a-pe*, You struck yourselves.	*Dal-len-khan-pe*, If you struck yourselves.	*Paset'-pe-dal-len* Perhaps you struck yourselves.
3	*Dal-len-a-ko*, They struck themselves.	*Dal-len-khan-ko*, If they struck themselves.	*Paset'-ko-dal-len*, Perhaps they struck themselves.
	Neuter. *Dal-len-a*, It was, or had been struck.	*Dal-len-khan*, If it was struck.	*Paset'-dal-len*, Perhaps it was struck.

* Or had struck myself.

SPECIAL INCOMPLETE PAST.

INDICATIVE.	SUBJUNCTIVE with "*Khan*"	SUBJUNCTIVE with "*Paset'*."
SINGULAR.	SINGULAR.	SINGULAR.
1 *Dal-ok'-kan-ta-hē-kan-a-ń*, I was striking myself.	*Dal-ok'-kan-tahē-kan-khan-iń*, If I was striking myself.	*Paset'-iń-dal-ok'-kan-tahēkan*, Perhaps I was striking myself.
2 *Dal-ok'-kan-ta-hēkan-a-m*, Thou wast striking thyself.	*Dal-ok'-kan-tahē-kan-khan-e-m*, If thou wast striking thyself.	*Paset'-em-dal-ok'-kan-tahēkan*, Perhaps thou wast striking thyself.
3 *Dal-ok'-kan-ta-hē-kan-a-e*, He was striking himself.	*Dal-ok'-kan-tahē-kan-khan-e*, If he was striking himself.	*Paset'-e-dal-ok'-kan-tahēkan*, Perhaps he was striking himself.
DAUL.	DAUL.	DUAL.
1 *Dal-ok'-kan-ta-hē-kan-a-liń*, We two were striking ourselves.	*Dal-ok'-kan-tahē-kan-khan-liń*, If we two were striking ourselves.	*Paset'-liń dal-ok'-kan tahēkan*, Perhaps we two were striking ourselves.
2 *Dal-ok'-kan-ta-hēkan-a-ben*, You two were striking yourselves.	*Dal-ok'-kan-tahē-kan-khan-ben*, If you two were striking yourselves.	*Paset'-ben-dal-ok'-kan-tahēkan*, Perhaps you two were striking yourselves.
3 *Dal-ok'-kan-ta-hēkan-a-kin*, They two were striking themselves.	*Dal-ok'-kan-tahē-kan-khan-kin*, If they two were striking themselves.	*Paset'-kin-dal-ok'-kan-tahēkan*, Perhaps they two were striking themselves.

PLURAL.	PLURAL.	PLURAL.
1 *Dal-ok'-kan-ta-hĕkan-a-le,* We were striking ourselves.	*Dal-ok'-kan-tahĕ-kan-khan-le,* If we were striking ourselves.	*Paset'-le-dal-ok'-kan-tahĕkan,* Perhaps we were striking ourselves.
2 *Dal-ok'-k'an-ta-hĕ-kan-a-pe,* You were striking yourselves.	*Dal-ok'-kan-tahĕ-kan-khan-pe,* If you were striking yourselves.	*Paset'-pe-dal-ok'-kan-tahĕkan,* Perhaps you were striking yourselves.
3 *Dal-ok'-kan-ta-hĕkan-a-ko,* They were striking themselves.	*Dal-ok'-kan-tahĕ-kan-khan-ko,* If they were striking themselves.	*Paset'-ko-dal-ok'-kan-tahĕkan,* Perhaps they were striking themselves.
Neuter. *Dal-ok'-kan-tahĕkan-a,* It was being struck.	*Dal-ok'-kan-tahĕ-kan-khan,* If it was being struck.	*Paset'-dal-ok'-kan-ta-hĕkan,* Perhaps it was being struck.

Note.—This tense is used both for special and general incomplete *Past.*

INDECISIVE PLUPERFECT.

	INDICATIVE.	SUBJUNCTIVE with "*Khan.*"	SUBJUNCTIVE with "*Paset'.*"
	SINGULAR.	**SINGULAR.**	**SINGULAR.**
1	*Dal--len-tahē-kan-a-ń,* I had struck myself.	*Dal-len-tahēkan-khan-iń,* If I had struck myself.	*Paset'-iń-dal-len-ta-hēkan,* Perhaps I had struck myself.
2	*Dal-len-tahē-kan-a-m,* Thou hadst struck thyself.	*Dal-len-tahēkan-khan-em,* If thou hadst struck thyself.	*Paset'-em-dal-len-ta-hēkan,* Perhaps thou hadst struck thyself.
3	*Dal-len-tahē-kan-a-e,* He had struck himself.	*Dal-en-tahēkan-khan-e,* If he had struck himself.	*Paset'-e-dal-len-tahē kan,* Perhaps he had struck himself.
	DUAL.	**DUAL.**	**DUAL.**
1	*Dal-len-tahēkan a-liń,* We two had struck ourselves.	*Dal-len-tahēkan-khan-liń,* If we two had struck ourselves.	*Paset'-liń-dal-len-ta-hēkan,* Perhaps we to had struck ourselves.
	Dal-len-tahēkan-a-ben, You two had struck yourselves.	*Dal-len-tahēkan-khan-ben,* If you two had struck yourselves.	*Paset'-ben-dal-len-ta-hēkan,* Perhaps you two had struck yourselves.
3	*Dal-len-tahē-kan-a-kin,* They two had struck themselves.	*Dal-len-tahēkan-khan-kin,* If they two had struck themselves.	*Paset'-kin-dal-len-ta-hēkan,* Perhaps they two had struck themselves.
	PLURAL.	**PLURAL.**	**PLURAL.**
1	*Dal-len-tahēkan-a-le,* We had struck ourselves.	*Dal-len-tahēkan-khan-le,* If we had struck ourselves.	*Paset'-le-dal-len-ta-hē-kan,* Perhaps we had struck ourselves.

2 *Dal-len-tahēkan-a-pe,* You had struck yourselves.	*Dal-len-tahēkan-khan-pe,* If you had struck yourselves.	*Paset'-pe-dal-len-ta-hēkan,* Perhaps you had struck yourselves.
3 *Dal-len-tahēkan-a-ko,* They had struck themselves.	*Dal-len-tahēhan-khan-ko,* If they had struck themselves.	*Paset'-ko-dal-len-ta-hēkan,* Perhaps they had struck themselves.
Neuter. *Dal-len-ta-hēkan-a,* It had been struck.	*Dal-len-tahēkan-khan,* If it had been struck.	*Paset'-dal-len-ta-hēkan,* Perhaps it had been struck.

INCHOATIVE FUTURE.

	Indicative.	Subjunctive with "*Khan.*"	Subjunctive with "*Paset'.*"
	Singular.	**Singular.**	**Singular.**
1	*Dal-ok'-lagit'-iń,* I shall be about to strike myself.	*Dal-ok'-lagit'-khan-iń,* If I shall be about to strike myself.	*Paset'-iń-dal-ok'-lagit',* Perhaps I shall be about to strike myself.
2	*Dal-ok'-lagit'-em,* Thou wilt be about to strike thyself.	*Dal-ok'-lagit'-khan-em,* If thou wilt be about to strike thyself.	*Paset'-em-dal-ok'-lagit',* Perhaps thou wilt be about to strike thyself.
3	*Dal-ok'-lagit'-e,* He will be about to strike himself.	*Dal-ok'-lagit'-khan-e,* If he will be about to strike himself.	*Paset'-e-dal-ok'-lagit',* Perhaps he will be about to strike himself.
	Dual.	**Dual.**	**Dual.**
1	*Dal-ok'-lagit'-liń,* We two shall be about to strike ourselves.	*Dal-ok'-lagit'-khan-liń,* If we two shall be about to strike ourselves.	*Paset'-liń-dal-ok'-lagit',* Perhaps we two shall be about to strike ourselves.
2	*Dal-ok'-lagit'-ben,* You two will be about to strike yourselves.	*Dal-ok'-lagit'-khan-ben,* If you two will be about to strike yourselves.	*Paset'-ben-dal-ok'-lagit',* Perhaps you two will be about to strike yourselves.
3	*Dal-ok'-lagit'-kin,* They two will be about to strike themselves.	*Dal-ok'-lagit'-khan-kin,* If they two will be about to strike themselves.	*Paset'-kin-dal-ok'-lagit',* Perhaps they two will be about to strike themselves.

	PLURAL.	PLURAL.	PLURAL.
1	*Dal-ok-lagit'-le*, We shall be about to strike ourselves.	*Dal-ok-lagit'-khan-le*, If we shall be about to strike ourselves.	*Paset'-le-dal-ok-lagit'*, Perhaps we shall be about to strike ourselves.
2	*Dal-ok-lagit' pe*, You will be about to strike yourselves.	*Dal ok-lagit'-khan-pe*, If you will be about to strike yourselves.	*Paset'-pe-dal-ok-lagit'*, Perhaps you will be about to strike yourselves.
3	*Dal-ok-lagit'-ko*, They will be about to strike themselves.	*Dal-ok-lagit'-khan ko*, If they will be about to strike themselves.	*Paset'-ko-dal-ok-lagit'*, Perhaps they will be about to strike themselves.
Neuter.	*Dal-ok-lagit'*, It will be about to be struck.	*Dal-ok-lagit'-khan*, If it will be about to be struck.	*Paset'-dal-ok-lagit'*, Perhaps it will be about to be struck.

INCHOATIVE PRESENT.

	INDICATIVE.	SUBJUNCTIVE with "*Khan.*"	SUBJUNCTIVE with "*Paset'.*"
	SINGULAR.	SINGULAR.	SINGULAR.
1	*Dal-ok̇-lagid-ok̇-kan-a-ń*, I am about to strike myself.	*Dal-ok̇-lagid-ok̇-kan-khan-iń*, If I am about to strike myself.	*Paset'-iń-dal-ok̇-lagid-ok̇-kan*, Perhaps I am about to strike myself.
2	*Dal-ok̇-lagid-ok̇-kan-a-m*, Thou art about to strike thyself.	*Dal-ok̇-lagid-ok̇-kan-khan-em*, If thou art about to strike thyself.	*Paset'-em-dal-ok̇-lagid-ok̇-kan*, Perhaps thou art about to strike thyself.
3	*Dal-ok̇-lagid-ok̇-kan-a-e*, He is about to strike himself.	*Dal-ok̇-lagid-ok̇-kan-khan-e*, If he is about to strike himself.	*Paset'-e-dal-ok̇-lagid-ok̇-kan*, Perhaps he is about to strike himself.
	DUAL.	DUAL.	DUAL.
1	*Dal-ok̇-lagid-ok̇-kan-liń*, We two are about to strike ourselves.	*Dal-ok̇-lagid-ok̇-kan-khan-liń*, If we two are about to strike ourselves.	*Paset'-liń-dal-ok̇-lagid-ok̇-kan*, Perhaps we two are about to strike ourselves.
2	*Dal-ok̇-lagid-ok̇-kan-a-ben*, You two are about to strike yourselves.	*Dal-ok̇-lagid-ok̇-kan-khan-ben*, If you two are about to strike yourselves.	*Paset'-ben-dal-ok̇-lagid-ok̇-kan*, Perhaps you two are about to strike yourselves.
3	*Dal-ok̇-lagid-ok̇-kan-a-kin*, They two are about to strike themselves.	*Dal-ok̇-lagid-ok̇-kan-khan-kin*, If they two are about to strike themselves.	*Paset'-kin-dal-ok̇-lagid-ok̇-kan*, Perhaps they two are about to strike themselves.

PLURAL.	PLURAL.	PLURAL.
1 *Dal-ok̇-lagid-ok̇-kan-a-le*, We are about to strike ourselves.	*Dal-ok̇-lagid-ok̇-kan-khan-le*, If we are about to strike ourselves.	*Paset'-le-dal-ok̇-lagid-ok̇-kan*, Perhaps we are about to strike ourselves.
2 *Dal-ok̇-lagid-ok̇-kan-a-pe*, You are about to strike yourselves.	*Dal-ok̇-lagid-ok̇-kan-khan-pe*, If you are about to strike yourselves.	*Paset'-pe dal-ok̇-lagid-ok̇-kan*, Perhaps you are about to strike yourselves.
3 *Dal-ok̇-lagid-ok̇-kan-a-ko*, They are about to strike themselves.	*Dal-ok̇-lagid-ok̇-kan-khan-ko*, If they are about to strike themselves.	*Paset'-ko-dal-ok̇-lagid-ok̇-kan*, Perhaps they are about to strike themselves.
Neuter. *Dal-ok̇-lagid-ok̇-kan-a*, It is about to be struck.	*Dal-ok̇-lagid-ok̇-kan-khan*, If it is about to be struck.	*Paset'-dal-ok̇-lagid-ok̇-kan*, Perhaps it is about to be struck.

INCHOATIVE PAST.

	Indicative.	Subjunctive with "*Khan.*"	Subjunctive with "*Paset'.*"
	Singular.	**Singular.**	**Singular.**
1	*Dal-oḱ-lagid-oḱ-kan-tahēkan-a-ń,* I was about to strike myself.	*Dal-oḱ-lagid-oḱ-kan-tahēkan-khan-iń,* If I was about to strike myself.	*Paset'-iń-dal-oḱ-lagid-oḱ-kan-tahēkan,* Perhaps I was about to strike myself.
2	*Dal-oḱ-lagid-oḱ kan-tahēkan-a-m,* Thou wast about to strike thyself.	*Dal-oḱ-lagid-oḱ-kan-tahēkan-khan-em,* If thou wast about to strike thyself.	*Paset'-em-dal-oḱ-lagid-oḱ-kan-tahēkan* Perhaps thou wast about to strike thyself.
3	*Dal-oḱ-lagid-oḱ-kan-tahēkan-a-e,* He was about to strike himself.	*Dal-oḱ-lagid-oḱ-kan-tahēkan-khan-e,* If he was about to strike himself.	*Paset'-e-dal-oḱ-lagid-oḱ-kan-tahēkan,* Perhaps he was about to strike himself.
	Dual.	**Dual.**	**Dual.**
1	*Dal-oḱ-lagid-oḱ kan-tahēkan-a-liń,* We two were about to strike ourselves.	*Dal-oḱ-lagid-oḱ-kan-tahēkan-khan-liń,* If we two were about to strike ourselves.	*Paset'-liń-dal-oḱ-lagid-oḱ-kan-tahēhan,* Perhaps we two were about to strike ourselves.
2	*Dal-oḱ-lagidoḱ-kan-tahēkan-a-ben,* You two were about to strike yourselves.	*Dal-oḱ-lagid-oḱ-kan-tahēkan-khan-ben,* If you two were about to strike yourselves.	*Paset'-ben-dal-oḱ-lagid-oḱ-kan-tahēkan,* Perhaps you two were about to strike yourselves.
3	*Dal-oḱ-lagid-oḱ-kan-tahēhan-a-kin,* They two were about to strike themselves.	*Dal-oḱ-lagid oḱ-kan-tahēkan-hkan-kin,* If they two were about to strike themselves.	*Paset'-kin-dal-oḱ-lagid-oḱ-kan-tahēkan,* Perphaps they two were about to strike themselves.

PLURAL.	PLURAL.	PLURAL.
1 *Dal-ok'-lagid-ok'-kan-tahĕkan-a-le,* We were about to strike ourselves.	*Dal-ok'-lagid-ok'-kan-tahēkan-khan-le,* If we were about to strike ourselves.	*Paset'-le-dal-ok'-lagid-ok'-kan-tahēkan,* Perhaps we were about to strike ourselves.
2 *Dal-ok'-lagid-ok'-kan-tahĕkan-a-pe,* You were about to strike yourselves.	*Dal-ok'-lagid-ok'-kan-tahēkan-khan-pe,* If you were about to strike yourselves.	*Paset'-pe-dal-ok'-lagid-ok'-kan-tahēkan,* Perhaps you were about to strike yourselves.
3 *Dal-ok'-lagid-ok'-kan-tahĕkan-a-ko,* They were about to strike themselves.	*Dal-ok'-lagid-ok'-kan-tahēkan-khan-ko,* If they were about to strike themselves.	*Paset'-ko-dal--ok'-lagid-ok'-kan-tahēkan,* Perhaps they were about to strike themselves.
Neuter. *Dal-ok'-lagidok'-kan-tahē-kan-a,* It was about to be struck.	*Dal-ok'-lagid-ok'-kan-tahēkan-khan,* If it was about to be struck.	*Paset'-dal-ok'-lagid-ok'-kan-tahēkan,* Perhaps it was about to be struck.

OPTATIVE.

INDICATIVE.	SUBJUNCTIVE with "*Khan.*"	SUBJUNCTIVE with "*Paset'.*"
SINGULAR.	SINGULAR.	SINGULAR.
1 *Dal-kok'-a-ń*, I will or would strike myself.	*Dal-kok'-khan-iń*, If I would strike myself.	*Paset'-iń-dal-kok'*, Perhaps I would strike myself.
2 *Dal-kok'-a-m*, Thou wilt or would'st strike thyself.	*Dal-kok'-khan-em*, If thou would'st strike thyself.	*Paset'-em-dal-kok'*, Perhaps thou would'st strike thyself.
3 *Dal-kok'-a-e*, He will or would strike himself.	*Dal-kok'-khan-e*, If he would strike himself.	*Paset'-e-dal-kok'*, Perhaps he would strike himself.
DUAL.	DUAL.	DUAL.
1 *Dal-kok'-a-liń*, We two* would strike ourselves.	*Dal-kok'-khan-liń*, If we two would strike ourselves.	*Paset'-liń-dal-kok'*, Perhaps we two would strike ourselves.
2 *Dal-kok'-a-ben*, You two would strike yourselves.*	*Dal-kok'-khan-ben*, If you two would strike yourselves.	*Paset'-ben-dal-kok'*, Perhaps you two would strike yourselves.
3 *Dal-kok'-a-kin*, They two* would strike themselves.	*Dal-kok'-khan-kin*, If they two would strike themselves.	*Paset'-kin-dal-kok'*, Perhaps they two will strike themselves.
PLURAL.	PLURAL.	PLURAL.
1 *Dal-kok'-a-le*, We* would strike ourselves.	*Dal-kok'-khan-le*, If we would strike ourselves.	*Paset'-le-dal-kok'*, Perhaps we will strike ourselves.
2 *Dal-kok'-a-pe*, You *would strike yourselves.	*Dal-kok'-khan-pe*, If you would strike yourselves.	*Paset'-pe-dal-kok'*, Perhaps you will strike yourselves.
3 *Dal-kok'-a-ko*, They *would strike themselves.	*Dal-kok'-khan-ko*, If they would strike themselves.	*Paset'-ko-dal-kok'*, Perhaps they will strike themselves.
Neuter. *Dal-kok'a*, It would be struck.*	*Dal-kok'-khan*, If it would be struck.	*Paset'-dal-kok'*, Per- it would be struck.

* Or will.

CONDITIONAL.

	INDICATIVE.	SUBJUNCTIVE with "*Khan.*"	SUBJUNCTIVE with *Paset'.*"
	SINGULAR.	SINGULAR..	SINGULAR.
1	*(Qhǫ) Dal-len-a-ń,* Iwould will or should (not) strike myself.	*Dal-len-khan-iń,* If I would strike or have struck myself.	*Paset'-iń-dal-len,* Perhaps I would strike myself.
2	*(Qhǫ) Dal-len-a-m,* Thou would'st (not) strike thyself.	*Dal-len-khan-em,* If thou wouldst strike thyself.	*Paset'-em-dal-len,* Perhaps thou wouldst strike thyself.
3	*(Qhǫ) Dal-len-a-e,* He would (not) strike himself.	*Dal-len-khan-e,* If he wouldstrike himself.	*Paset'-e-dal-len,* Perhaps he would strike himself.
	DUAL.	DUAL.	DUAL.
1	*(Qhǫ) Dal-len-a-liń,* We two would (not) strike ourselves.	*Dal-len-khan-liń,* If we two would strike ourselves.	*Paset'-liń-dal-len,* Perhaps we two would strike ourselves.
2	*(Qhǫ) Dal--len-a-ben,* You two would (not) strike yourselves.	*Dal-len-khan-ben,* If you two would strike yourselves.	*Paset'-ben-dal-len,* Perhaps you two would strike yourselves.
3	*(Qhǫ) Dal-len-a-kin,* They two would (not) strike themselves.	*Dal-len-khan-kin,* If they two would strike themselves.	*Paset'-kin-dal-len,* Perhaps they two would strike themselves.
	PLURAL.	PLURAL.	PLURAL.
1	*(Qhǫ) Dal-len-a-le,* We would not strike ourselves.	*Dal-len-khan-le* If we would strike ourselves.	*Paset'-le-dal-len,* Perhaps we would strike ourselves.
2	*(Qhǫ) Dal-len-a-pe,* You would not strike yourselves.	*Del-len-khan-pe,* If you would strike yourselves.	*Paset'-pe-dal-len,* Perhaps you would strike yourselves.
3	*(Qho) Dal-len-a-ko,* They would not strike themselves.	*Dal-len-khan-ko,* If they would strike themselves.	*Paset'-ko-dal-len,* Perhaps they would strike themselves.
Neuter.	*(Qhǫ) Dal-len-a,* It would not be struck.	*Dal-len-khan,* If it would be struck.	*Paset'-dal-len,* Perhaps it would be struck.

CONTINGENT.

SINGULAR.	SINGULAR.	SINGULAR.
1 *Dal-en-gi-ń*, I strike,* will or would strike, myself.		*Paset'-iń-dal-en-gi*, Perhaps I might strike myself.
2 *Dal-en-gi-m*, Thou strikest or wilt strike thyself.		*Paset'-em-dal-en-gi*, Perhaps thou mightest strike thyself.
3 *Dal-en-gi-e*, He strikes, or will strike himself.		*Paset'-e-dal-en-gi*, Perhaps he might strike himself.
DUAL.	DUAL.	DUAL.
1 *Dal-en-gi-liń*, We two strike, or will strike ourselves.		*Paset'-liń-dal-en-gi*, Perhaps we two might strike ourselves.
2 *Dal-en-gi-ben*, You two strike, or will strike yourselves.		*Paset'-ben-dal-en-gi*, Perhaps you two might strike yourselves.
3 *Dal-en-gi-kin*, They two strike or will strike themselves.		*Paset'-kin-dal-en-gi*, Perhaps they two might strike themselves.
PLURAL.	PLURAL.	PLURAL.
1 *Dal-en-gi-le*, We strike or will strike ourselves.		*Paset'-le-dal-en-gi*, Perhaps we might strike ourselves.
2 *Dal-en-gi-pe*, You strike, or will strike yourselves.		*Paset'-pe-dal-en-gi*, Perhaps you might strike yourselves.
3 *Dal-en-gi-ko*, They strike or will strike themselves.		*Paset'-ko-dal-en-gi*, Perhaps they might strike themselves.
Neuter. *Dal-en-gi*, It will be struck.		*Paset'-dal-en-gi*, Perhaps it might be struck.

* The Contingent must sometimes be rendered into English by the Future, at other times by the Present, and very frequently by the Subjunctive Past.

PRELIMINARY FUTURE.

SINGULAR.	SINGULAR.	SINGULAR.
1 *Dal-len-gi-ṅ,* I will first strike myself.		*Paset'-iṅ-dal-len-gi,* Perhaps I first will strike myself.
2 *Dal-len-gi-m,* Thou wilt first strike thyself.		*Paset'-em-dal-len-gi,* Perhaps thou first wilt strike thyself.
3 *Dal-len-gi-e,* He will first strike himself.		*Paset'-e-dal-len-gi,* Perhaps he first will strike himself.
DUAL.	DUAL.	DUAL.
1 *Dal-len-gi-liṅ,* We two will first strike ourselves.		*Paset'-liṅ-dal-len-gi,* Perhaps we two will first strike ourselves.
2 *Dal-len-gi-ben,* You two will first strike yourselves.		*Paset'-ben-dal-len-gi,* Perhaps you two will first strike yourselves.
3 *Dal-len-gi-kin,* They two will first strike themselves.		*Paeset'-kin-dal-len-gi,* Perhaps they two will first strike themselves.
PLURAL.	PLURAL.	PLURAL.
1 *Dal-len-gi-le,* We will first strike ourselves.		*Paset'-le-dal-len-gi,* Perhaps we will first strike ourselves.
2 *Dal-len-gi-pe,* You will first strike yourselves.		*Paset'-pe-dal-len-gi,* Perhaps you will first strike yourselves.
3 *Dal-len-gi-ko,* They will first strike themselves.		*Paset'-ko-dal-len-gi,* Perhaps they will first strike themselves.
Neuter. *Dal-len-gi,* It will first be struck.		*Paset'-dal-len-gi-* Perhaps it will first be struck.

PRELIMINARY EXPOSTULATIVE.

	Singular.	Daul.	Plural.
1	*Dal-len-nahī-ń*, I must first strike myself.	*Dal-len-nahī-liń*, We two must first strike ourselves.	*Dal-len-nahī-le*, We must first strike ourselves.
2	*Dal-len-nahī-m*, Thou must first strike thyself.	*Dal-len-nahī-ben*, You two must first strike yourselves.	*Dal-len-nahī-pe*, You must first strike yourselves.
3	*Dal-len-nahī-e*, He must first strike himself.	*Dal-len-nahī-kin*, They two must first strike themselves.	*Dal-len-nahī-ko*, They must first strike themselves.
	Neuter. *Dal-len-nahī*. It must first be struck.		

PRELIMINARY PERSUASIVE.

	Singular.	Daul.	Plural.
1	*Dal-len-ba-ń*, I must first strike myself.	*Dal-len-ba-liń* We two must first strike ourselves.	*Dal-len-ba-le*, We must first strike ourselves.
2	*Dal-len-ba-m*, Thou must first strike thyself.	*Dal-len-ba-ben*, You two must first strike yourselves.	*Dal-len-ba-pe*, You must first strike yourselves.
3	*Dal-len-ba-e*, He must first strike himself.	*Dal-len-ba-kin*, They two must first strike themselves.	*Dal-len-ba-ko*, They must first strike themselves.
	Neuter. *Dal-len-bań*, It must first be struck.		

PRELIMINARY ADMISSIVE.

1 *Dal-len-en-a-ń* I must first strike myself.	*Dal-len-en-a-liń,* We two must, first strike ourselves.	*Dal-len-en-a-le,* We must first strike ourselves.
2 *Dal-len-en-a-m,* Thou must first strike thyself.	*Dal-len-en-a-ben,* You two must first strike yourselves.	*Dal-len-en-a-pe,* You must first strike yourselves.
3 *Dal-len-en-a-e,* He must first strike himself. Neuter. *Dal-len-en-a,* It must first be struck.	*Dal-len-en-a-kin,* They two must first strike themselves.	*Dal-len-en-a-ko,* They must first strike themselves.

Remark. Regarding the difference between these three tenses or moods, vide remark on the same in the active nominative case.

PRELIMINARY BENEDICTIVE.

	SINGULAR.	DUAL.	PLURAL.
1	*Dal-len-ma-ń,* May I first strike myself!	*Dal-len-ma-lin!* May we two first strike ourselves.	*Dal-len-ma-le!* May we first strike ourselves!
2	*Dal-len-ma-m!* Mayest thou first strike thyself!	*Dal-len-ma-ben!* May you two first strike yourselves.	*Dal-len-ma-pe!* May you first strike yourselves!
3	*Dal-len-ma-e!* May he first strike himself!	*Dal-len-ma-kin!* May they two first strike themselves.	*Dal-len-ma-ko!* May they first strike themselves!
Neuter.	*Dal-len-ma!* May it first be struck!		

PRELIMINARY IMPERATIVE.

	SINGULAR.	DUAL.	PLURAL.
2	*Dal-len-me!* Strike thou first thyself!	*Dal-len-ben!* Strike you two first yourselves!	*Dal-len-pe!* Strike first yourselves!

BENEDICTIVE.

	SINGULAR.	DUAL.	PLURAL.
1	*Dal-ok-ma-ń!* May I strike myself!	*Dal-ok-ma-liń!* May we two strike ourselves!	*Dal-ok-ma-le!* May we strike ourselves!
2	*Dal-ok-ma-m!* Mayest thou strike thyself!	*Dal-ok-ma-ben!* May you two strike yourselves!	*Dal ok-ma-pe!* May you strike yourselves!
3	*Dal-ok-ma-e!* May he strike himself!	*Dal-ok-ma-kin!* May they two strike themselves!	*Dal-ok-ma-ko!* May they strike themselves!

IMPARATIVE.

	SINGULAR.	DUAL.	PLURAL.
2	*Dal-ok-me!* Strike thou thyself!	*Dal-ok-ben!* Strike you two yourselves!	*Dal-ok-pe!* Strike you yourself!

ADJECTIVE PARTICIPLES.	GERUNDS.
FUTURE.	
*Dal-ok' (kin, * ben pe,) etc.* Who will strike himself.	*Dal-ok'-reak', te, re,* Of, by, in striking oneself.
SPECIAL INCOMPLETE PRESENT.	
Dal-ok'-kan, Who is striking himself.	*Dal-ok'-kan-reak', te, re,* Of, by, in striking oneself now.
RECENT PAST.	
Dal-en, Who struck himself.	*Dal-en-reak', te, re,* Of, by, in having struck oneself.
ANTERIOR PAST.	
Dal-len, Who struck himself.	*Dal-len-reak', te, re,* Of, by, in having struck oneself.
SPECIAL INCOMPLETE PAST.	
Dal-ok'-kan-tahēkan, Who was striking himself.	*Dal-ok'-kan-tahēkan-reak', te, re.* Of, by, in striking oneself then.
INDICISIVE PLUPERFECT.	
Dal-len-tahēkan, Who had struck himself.	*Dal-len-tahēkan-reak', te, re,* Of, by, in, having struck oneself.
INCHOATIVE FUTURE.	
Dal-ok'-lagit', Who will be about to strike himself.	*Dal-ok'-lagit'-reak', te, re,* Of, by, in being about to strike oneself.
INCHOATIVE PRESENT.	
Dal-ok'-lagidok'-kan, Who is about to strike himself.	*Dal-ok'-lagidok'-kan reak', te, re,* Of, by, in being about to strike oneself now.
INCHOATIVE PAST.	
Dal-ok'-lagidok'-kan-tahēkan, Who was about to strike himself.	*Dal-ok'-lagidok'-kan-tahēkan-reak', te, re,* Of, by, in being about to strike oneself then.
OPTATIVE.	
Dal-kok', Who will or would strike himself.	*Dal-kok'-reak', te, re,* Of, by, in wishing to strike oneself.
CONDITIONAL.	
Dal-len, Who may have struck himself.	*Dal-len-reak', te, re,* Of, by, in striking or having struck oneself.

* Any of the Nominative Suffixes may be affixed to show who will strike him or themselves.

Note.—The neuter Participles and Gerunds are like those belonging to the common gender, only with a passive meaning; as *Dal-ok' Janhe, the Janhe* which will be struck *(Der-züschlagende Janhe).*

ADVERBIAL PARTICIPLES.

FUTURE.	
Dal-oǩ-khan,	Striking * oneself.
SPECIAL INCOMPLETE PRESENT.	
Dal-oǩ-kan-khan,	Striking oneself now.
RECENT PAST.	
Dal-en-khan,	Having struck oneself.
ANTERIOR PAST.	
Dal-len-khan,	Having struck oneself.
SPECIAL INCOMPLETE PAST.	
Dal-oǩ-kan-tahĕhan-khan,	Striking oneself then.
INDICISIVE PLUPERFECT.	
Dal-lẹn-tahĕkan-khan,	Having struck oneself.
INCHOATIVE FUTURE.	
Dal-oǩ-lagidoǩ-khan,	Being about to strike oneself.
INCHOATIVE PRESENT.	
Dal-oǩ-lagidoǩ-kan-khan,	Being now about to strike oneself.
INCHOATIVE PAST.	
Dal-oǩ-lagidoǩ-kan-tahĕkan-khan,	Being then about to strike oneself.
OPTATIVE.	
Dal-koǩ-khan,	Wishing to strike oneself.
CONDITIONAL.	
Dal-len-khan,	Striking or having struck oneself.
PRELIMINARY EXPOSTULATIVE	
Dal-len-nahĩ,	First striking oneself.
PRELIMINARY PERSUASIVE.	
Dal-len-bañ,	First striking oneself.
PRELIMINARY ADMISSIVE.	
Dal-len-ena,	Firt striking oneself.
INFINITIVE.	*Dal-oǩ,* To strike oneself.

* Or being Neuter : being struck.

REFLEXIVE CAUSATIVE (and PASSIVE.)

FUTURE.

Dal-ochoḱ-a-ń, I shall allow myself to be struck.*

SPECIAL INCOMPLETE PRESENT.

Dal-ochoḱ-kan-a-ń, I am allowing myself to be struck.

RECENT PAST.

Dal-ocho-en-a-ń, I allowed myself to be struck.

ANTERIOR PAST.

Dal-ocho-len-a-ń, I allowed myself to be struck.

SPECIAL INCOMPLETE PAST.

Dal-ochoḱ-kan-tahĕkan-a-ń, I was allowing myself to be struck.

INDECISIVE PLUPERFECT.

Dal-ocho-len-tahĕkan-a-ń, I had allowed myself to be struck.

INCHOATIVE FUTURE.

Dal-ochoḱ-lagiť-iń, I shall be about to allow myself to be struck.

INCHOATIVE PRESENT.

Dal-ochoḱ-lagidoḱ-kan-a-ń, I am about to allow myself to be struck.

INCHOATIVE PAST.

Dal-ochoḱ-lagidoḱ-kan-tahĕkan-a-ń, I was about to allow myself to be struck.

OPTATIVE.

Dal-ocho-koḱ-a-ń, I will or would allow myself to be struck.

CONDITIONAL.

(Qhọ) Dal-ocho-len-a-ń, I shall or should (not) allow myself to be struck.

---

* Or I shall be struck. Although this Causative is extensively used as a Passive, it does not lose its causative signification, and can not therefore always be an equivalent for our Passive; as *tọpa-ocho-en-a-e,* does not mean, "he was burried; but either that he allowed himself to be burried alive, or that he was caused to be burried (dead or alive) by a third party.

Remark.—As this Causative follows "the Reflexive" the other tenses need not be written.

FUTURE.

D. WITH THE DATIVE CASE.

INDICATIVE.	SUBJUNCTIVE with "*Khan.*"	SUBJUNCTIVE with "*Paset'.*"
SINGULAR.	SINGULAR.	SINGULAR.
1 *Dal-añ-a-e*, He will strike * for me.	*Dal-a-ñ-khan-e*, If he will strike for me.	*Paset'-e-dal-a-ñ*, Perhaps he will strike for me.
2 *Dal-a-m-a-e*, He will strike for thee.	*Dal-a-m-khan-e*, If he will strike for thee.	*Paset'-e-dal-a-m*, Perhaps he will strike for thee.
3 *Dal-a-e-a-e*, He will strike for him.	*Dal-a-e-khan-e*, If he will strike for him.	*Paset'-e-dal-a-e*, Perhaps he will strike for him.
DUAL.	DUAL.	DUAL.
1 *Dal-a-liñ-a-e*, He will strike for us two.	*Dal-a-liñ-khan-e*, If he will strike for us two.	*Paset'-e-dal-a-liñ*, Perhaps he will strike for us two.
2 *Dal-a ben-a-e*, He will strike for you two.	*Dal-a-ben-khan-e*, If he will strike for you two.	*Paset'-e-dal-a-ben*, Perhaps he will strike for you two.
3 *Dal-a-kin-a-e*, He will strike for them two.	*Dal-a-kin-khan-e*, If he will strike for them two.	*Paset'-e-dal-a-kin*, Perhaps he will strike for them two.
PLURAL.	PLURAL.	PLURAL.
1 *Dal-a-le-a-e*, He will strike for us.	*Dal-a-le-khan-e*, If he will strike for us.	*Paset'-e-dal-a-le*, Perhaps he will strike for us.
2 *Dal-a-pe-a-e*, He will strike for you.	*Dal-a-pe-khan-e*, If he will strike for you.	*Paset'-e-dal-a pe*, Pehaps he will strike for you.
3 *Dal-a-ko-a-e*, He will strike for them.	*Dal-a-ko-khan-e*, If he will strike for them.	*Paset' e-dal-a-ko*, Perhaps he will strike for them.
Neuter. *Dal-a-k-a-e*, He will strike at, on to it or them.	*Dal a-k-khan-e*, If he will strike at (etc). it, or them.	*Paset'-e-dal-a-k*, Perhaps he will strike at it (etc.) or them.

Note.—Neuter makes no distinction between singular, dual or plural.

* Dative is used in Santali when we in English would use *for, at, to, on*, etc.

SPECIAL INCOMPLETE PRESENT.

INDICATIVE.	SUBJUNCTIVE with "*Khan.*"	SUBJUNCTIVE with "*Paset'.*"
SINGULAR.	SINGULAR.	SINGULAR.
1 *Dal-a-ń-kan-a-e,* He is striking for me.	*Dal-a-ń-kan-khan-e,* If he is striking for me.	*Paset'-e-dal-a-ń-kan,* Perhaps he is striking for me.
2 *Dal-a-m-kan-a-e,* He is striking for thee.	*Dal-a-m-kan-khan-e,* If he is striking for thee.	*Paset'-e-dal-a-m-kan,* Perhaps he is striking for thee.
3 *Dal-a-e-kan-a-e,* He is striking for him.	*Dal-a-e-kan-khan-e,* If he is striking for him.	*Paset'-e-dal-a-e-kan,* Perhaps he is striking for him.
DUAL.	DUAL.	DUAL.
1 *Dal-a-liń-kan-a-e,* He is striking for us two.	*Dal-a-liń-kan-khan-e,* If he is striking for us two.	*Paset'-e-dal-a-liń-kan,* Perhaps he is striking for us two.
2 *Dal-a-ben-kan-a-e,* He is striking for you two.	*Dal-a-ben-kan-khan-e,* If he is striking for you two.	*Paset'-e-dal-a-ben-kan,* Perhaps he is striking for you two.
3 *Dal-a-kin-kan-a-e,* He is striking for them two.	*Dal-a-kin-kan-khan-e,* If he is striking for them two.	*Paset'-e-dal-a-kin-kan,* Perhaps he is striking for them two.
PLURAL.	PLURAL.	PLURAL.
1 *Dal-a-le-kan-a-e,* He is striking for us.	*Dal-a-le-kan-khan-e,* If he is striking for us.	*Paset'-e-dal-a-le-kan,* Perhaps he is striking for us.
2 *Dal-a-pe-kan-a-e,* He is striking for you.	*Dal-a-pe-kan-khan-e,* If he is striking for you.	*Paset'-e-dal-a-pe-kan,* Perhaps he is striking for you.
3 *Dal-a-ko-kan-a-e,* He is striking for them.	*Dal-a-ko-kan-khan-e,* If he is striking for them.	*Paset'-e-dal-a-ko-kan,* Perhaps he is striking for them.
Neuter. *Dal-a-k'-kan-a-e,* He is striking at it.	*Dal-a-k'-kan-khan-e,* If he is striking at it.	*Paset'-e-dal-a-k'-kan,* Perhaps he is striking at it.

Note.—Dative has no general incomplete Present. This tense is used for both.

RECENT PAST.

INDICATIVE.	SUBJUNCTIVE with "*Khan.*"	SUBJUNCTIVE with "*Paset'.*"
SINGULAR.	SINGULAR.	SINGULAR.
1 *Dal-ad-iń-a-e*, He struck for me.	*Dal-ad-iń-khan-e*, If he struck for me.	*Paset'-e-dal-ad-iń*, Perhaps he struck for me.
2 *Dal-at'-me-a-e*, He struck for thee.	*Dal-at'-me-khan-e*, If he struck for thee.	*Paset'-e-dal-at'-me*, Perhaps he struck for thee.
3 *Dal-ad-e-a-e*, He struck for him.	*Dal-ad-e-khan-e*, If he struck for him.	*Paset'-e-dal-ad-e*, Perhaps he struck for him.
DUAL.	DUAL.	DUAL.
1 *Dal-at'-liń-a-e*, He struck for us two.	*Dal-at'-liń-khan-e*, If he struck for us two.	*Paset'-e-dal-at'-liń*, Perhaps he struck for us two.
2 *Dal-at'-ben-ben-a-e*, He struck for you two.	*Dal-at'-ben-khan-e*, If he struck for you two.	*Paset'-e-dal-at'-ben*, Perhaps he struck for you two.
3 *Dal-at'-kin-a-e*, He struck for them two.	*Dal-at'-kin-khan-e*, If he struck for them two.	*Paset'-e-dal-at'-kin*, Perhaps he struck for them two.
PLURAL.	PLURAL.	PLURAL.
1 *Dal-at'-le-a-e*, He struck for us.	*Dal-at'-le-khan-e*, If he struck for us.	*Paset'-e-dal-at'-le*, Perhaps he struck for us.
2 *Dal-at'-pe-a-e*, He struck for you.	*Dal-at'-pe-khan-e*, If he struck for you.	*Paset'-e-dal-at'-pe*, Perhaps he struck for you.
3 *Dal-at'-ko-a-e*, He struck for them.	*Dal-at'-ko-khan-e*, If he struck for them.	*Paset'-e-dal-at'-ko*, Perhaps he struck for them.
Neuter. *Dal-a-t'-a-e*, He struck at it.	*Dal-a-t'-khan-e*, If he struck at it.	*Paset'-e-dal-at'*, Perhaps he struck at it.

Note. Dative has no Anterior Past. This tense is used both as *recent* and *anterior* Past.

PERFECT.

Indicative.	Subjunctive with "*Khan*."	Subjunctive with "*Paset'*."
Singular.	**Singular.**	**Singular.**
1 *Dal-akao-ad-iń-a-e*, He has struck for me.	*Dal-akao-ad-iń-khan-e*, If he has struck for me.	*Paset'-e-dal-akao-ad-iń*, Perhaps he has struck for me.
2 *Dal-akao-at'-me-a-e*, He has struck for thee.	*Dal-akao-at'-me-khan-e*, If he has struck for thee.	*Paset'-e-dal-akao-at'-me*, Perhaps he has struck for thee.
3 *Dal-akao-ad-e-a-e*, He has struck for him.	*Dal-akao-ad-e-khan-e*, If he has struck for him.	*Paset'-e-dal-akao-ad-e*, Perhaps he has struck for him.
Dual.	**Dual.**	**Dual.**
1 *Dal-akao-at'-liń-a-e*, He has struck for us two.	*Dal-akao-at'-liń-khan-e*, If he has struck for us two.	*Paset'-e-dal-akao-at'-liń*, Perhaps he has struck for us two.
2 *Dal-akao-at'-ben-a-e*, He has struck for you two.	*Dal-akao-at'-ben-khan-e*, If he has struck for you two.	*Paset'-e-dal-akao-at'-ben*, Perhaps he has struck for you two.
3 *Dal-akao-at'-kin-a-e*, He has struck for them two.	*Dal-akao-at'-kin-khan-e*, If he has struck for them two.	*Paset'-e-dal-akao-at'-kin*, Perhaps he has struck for them two.
Plural.	**Plural.**	**Plural.**
1 *Dal-akao-at'-le-a-e*, He has struck for us.	*Dal-akao-at'-le-khan-e*, If he has struck for us.	*Paset'-e-dal-akao-at'-le*, Perhaps he has struck for us.
2 *Dal-akao-at'-pe-a-e*, He has struck for you.	*Dal-akao-at'-pe-khan-e*, If he has struck for you.	*Paset'-e-dal-akao-at'-pe*, Perhaps he has struck for you.
3 *Dal-akao-at'-ko-a-e*, He has struck for them.	*Dal-akao-at'-ko-khan-e*, If he has struck for them.	*Paset'-e-dal-akao-at'-ko*, Perhaps he has struck for them.
Neuter. *Dal-akao-at'-a-e*, He has struck at it.	*Dal-akao-at'-khan-e*, If he has struck at it.	*Paset'-e-dal-akao-at'*,* Perhaps he has struck at it.

SPECIAL INCOMPLETE PAST.

INDICATIVE.	SUBJUNCTIVE with "*Khan.*"	SUBJUNCTIVE with "*Paset'.*"
SINGULAR.	SINGULAR.	SINGULAR.
1 *Dal-a-ń-kan-tahēkan-a-e*, He was * striking for me.	*Dal-a-ń-kan-tahēkan-khan-e*, If he was striking for me.	*Paset'-e-dal-a-ń-kan-tahēkan*, Perhaps he was striking for me.
2 *Dal-a-m-kan-tahē-kan-a-e*, He was striking for thee.	*Dal-a-m-kan-tahēkan-khan-e*, If he was striking for thee.	*Paset'-e-dal-a-m-kan-tahēkan*, Perhaps he was striking for thee.
3 *Dal-a-e-kan-tahēkan-a-e*, He was striking for him.	*Dal-a-e-kan-tahē-kan-khan-e*, If he was striking for him.	*Paset'-e-dal-a-e-kan-tahēkan*, Perhaps he was striking for him.
DUAL.	DUAL.	DUAL.
1 *Dal-a-liń-kan-tahēkan-a-e*, He was striking for us two.	*Dal-a-liń-kan-ta-hē-kan-khan-e*, If he was striking for us two.	*Paset'-e-dal-a-liń-kan-tahēkan*, Perhaps he was striking for us two.
2 *Dal-a-ben-kan tahēkan-a-e*, He was striking for you two.	*Dal-a-ben-kan-tahēkan-khan-e*, If he was striking for you two.	*Paset'-e-dal-a-ben-kan-tahēkan*, Perhaps he was striking for you two.
3 *Dal-a-kin-kan-tahēkan-a-e*, He was striking for them two.	*Dal-a-kin-kan-tahē-kan-khan-e*, If he was striking for them two.	*Paset'-e-dal-a-kin-kan-tahēkan*, Perhaps he was striking for them two.
PLURAL.	PLURAL.	PLURAL.
1 *Dal-a-le-kan-tahēkan-a-e*, He was striking for us.	*Dal-a-le-kan-tahēkan-khan-e*, If he was striking for us.	*Paset'--e-dal-a-le-kan-tahēkan*, Perhaps he was striking for us.

Note.—Dative has no general incomplete Past. This tense is used for both.

* Or used to strike for me, or also simply, struck for me.

2 *Dal-a-pe-kan-tahēkan-a-e*, He was striking for you.	*Dal-a-pe-kan-tahēkan-khan-e*, If he was striking for you.	*Paset'-e-dal-a-pe-kan-tahēkan*, Perhaps he was striking for you.
3 *Dal-a-ko-kan-tahēkan-a-e*, He was striking for them.	*Dal-a-ko-kan-tahēkan-khan-e*, If he was striking for them.	*Paset'-e-dal-a-ko-kan-tahēkan*, Perhaps he was striking for them.
Neuter. *Dal-ak-kan-tahēkan-a-e*, He was striking at it.	*Dal-ak-kan-tahēkan-khan-e*, If he was striking at it.	*Paset'-e-dal-ak-kan-tahēkan*, Perhaps he was striking at it.

INDECISIVE PLUPERFECT.

INDICATIVE.	SUBJUNCTIVE with "*Khan.*"	SUBJUNCTIVE with "*Paset'.*"
SINGULAR.	SINGULAR.	SINGULAR.
1 *Dal-ad-iń-tahēkan-a-e*, He had struck * for me.	*Dal-ad-iń-tahēkan-khan-e*, If he had struck * for me.	*Paset'-e-dal-ad-iń-tahēkan*, Perhaps he had struck for me.
2 *Dal-at'-me-tahēkan-a-e*, He had struck for thee.	*Dal-at'-me-tahēkan-khan-e*, If he had struck for thee.	*Paset'-e-dal-at'-me-tahēkan*, Perhaps he had struck for thee.
3 *Dal-ad-e-tahēkan-a-e*, He had struck for him.	*Dal-ad-e-tahēkan--khan-e*, If he had struck for him.	*Paset'-e-dal-ad-e-tahēkan*, Perhaps he had struck for him.
DUAL.	DUAL.	DUAL.
1 *Dal-at'-liń-tahēkan-a-e*, He had struck for us two.	*Dal-at'-liń-tahēkan-khan-e*, If he had struck for us two.	*Paset'-e-dal-at'-liń-tahēkan*, Perhaps he had struck for us two.

* And it had been altered or was no longer of any importance; as *tōl-ad-e-tahēkan-a-ń.* I had put (it) on him, but it was not on him (when another act took place.)

2 *Dal-at'-ben-tahĕkan-a-e*, He had struck for you two.	*Dal-at'-ben-tahĕkan-khan-e*, If he had struck for you two.	*Paset'-e-dal-at'-ben-tahĕkan*, Perhaps he had struck for you two.
3 *Dal-at'-kin-tahĕkan-a-e*, He had struck for them two.	*Dal-at'-kin-tahĕkan-khan-e*, If he had struck for them two.	*Paset'-e-dal-at'-kin-tahĕkan*, Perhaps he had struck for them two.
PLURAL.	PLURAL.	PLURAL.
1 *Dal-at'-le-tahĕkan-a-e*, He had struck for us.	*Dal-at'-le-tahĕkan-khan-e*, If he had struck for us.	*Paset'-e-dal-at'-le-tahĕkan*, Perhaps he had struck for us.
2 *Dal-at'-pe-tahĕkan-a-e*, He had struck for you.	*Dal-at'-pe-tahĕkan-khan-e*, If he had struck for you.	*Paset'-e-dal-at'-pe-tahĕkan*, Perhaps he had struck for you
3 *Dal-at'-ko-tahĕkan-a-e*, He had struck for them.	*Dal-at'-ko-tahĕkan-khan-e*, If he had struck for them.	*Paset'-e-dal-at'-ko-tahĕkan*, Perhaps he had struck for them.
Neuter. *Dal-at'-tahĕkan-a-e*, He had struck at it.	*Dal-at'-tahĕkan-khan-e*, If he had struck at it.	*Paset'-e-dal-at'-tahĕkan*, Perhaps he had struck at it.

DECISIVE PLUPERFECT.

INDICATIVE.	SUBJUNCTIVE with "*Khan.*"	SUBJUNCTIVE with "*Paset'.*"
SINGULAR.	SINGULAR.	SINGULAR.
1 *Dal-akao-ad-iń-tahĕkan-a-e*, He had struck * for me.	*Dal-akao-ad-iń-tahĕkan-khan-e*, If he had struck for me.	*Paset'-e-dal-akao-ad-iń-tahĕkan*, Perhaps he had struck for me.

* And it remained in its affects when another act took place; as *tgl-akao-ad-e-tahekan-a-ń*. I had tied (it) on him and it was on him, when another act took place).

2 *Dal-akao-at'-me-tahēkan-a-e,* He had struck for thee.	*Dal-akao-at'-me-tahēkan-khan-e,* If he had struck for thee.	*Paset'-e dal-akao-at'-me-tahēkan,* Perhaps he had struck for thee.
3 *Dal-akao-ad-e-tahēkan-a-e,* He had struck for him.	*Dal-akao-ad-e-tahēkan-khan-e,* If he had struck for him.	*Paset'-e-dal-akao-ad-e-tahēkan,* Perhaps he had struck for him.
DUAL.	DUAL.	DUAL.
1 *Dal-akao-at'-liṅ-tahēkan-a-e,* He had struck for us two.	*Dal-akao-at'-liṅ-tahēkan-khan-e,* If he had struck for us two.	*Paset'-e-dal-akao-at'-liṅ-tahēkan,* Perhaps he had struck for us two.
2 *Dal-akao-at'-ben-tahēkan-a-e,* He had struck for you two.	*Dal-akao-at'-ben-tahēkan-khan-e,* If he had struck for you two.	*Paset'-e-dal-akao-at'-ben-tahēkan,* Perhaps he had struck for you two.
3 *Dal-akao-at'-kin-tahēkan-a-e,* He had struck for them two.	*Dal-akao-at'-kin-tahēkan-khan-e,* If he had struck for them two.	*Paset'-e-dal-akao-at'-kin-tahēkan,* Perhaps he had struck for them two.
PLURAL.	PLURAL.	PLURAL.
1 *Dal-akao-at'-le-tahēkan-a-e,* He had struck for us.	*Dal-akao-at'-le-tahēkan-khan-e,* If he had struck for us.	*Paset'-e-dal-akao-at'-le-tahēkan,* Perhaps he had struck for us.
2 *Dal-akao-at'-pe-tahēkan-a-e,* He had struck for you.	*Dal-akao-at'-pe-tahēkan-khan-e,* If he had struck for you.	*Paset'-e-dal-akao-at'-pe-tahēkan,* Perhaps he had struck for you.
3 *Dal-akao-at'-pe-tahēkan-a-e,* He had struck for them.	*Dal-akao-at'-ko-tahēkan-khan-e,* If he had struck for them.	*Paset'-e-dal-akao-at'-ko-tahēkan,* Perhaps he had struck for them.
Neuter. *Dal-akao-at'-tahēkan-a-e,* He had struck at it.	*Dal-akao-at'-tahēkan-khan-e,* If he had struck at it.	*Paset'-e-dal-akao-at'-tahēkan,* Perhaps he had struck at it.

INCHOATIVE FUTURE.

	INDICATIVE.	SUBJUNCTIVE with "*Khan.*"	SUBJUNCTIVE with "*Paset'.*"
	SINGULAR.	SINGULAR.	SINGULAR.
1	*Dal-a-ń-lagit'-e*, He will be about to strike for me.	*Dal-a-ń-lagit'-khan-e*, If he will be about to strike for me.	*Paset'-e-dal-a-ń-lagit'*, Perhaps he will be about to strike for me.
2	*Dal-a-m-lagit'-e*, He will be about to strike for thee.	*Dal-a-m-lagit'-khan-e*, If he will be about to strike for thee.	*Paset'-e-dal-a-m-lagit'*, Perhaps he will be about to strike for thee.
3	*Dal-a-e-lagit'-e*, He will be about to strike for him.	*Dal-a-e-lagit'-khan-e*, If he will be about to strike for him.	*Paset'-e-dal-a-e-lagit'*, Perhaps he will be about to strike for him.
	DUAL.	DUAL.	DUAL.
1	*Dal-a-liń-lagit'-e* He will be about to strike for us two.	*Dal-a-liń-lagit'-khan-e*, If he will be about to strike for us two.	*Paset'-e-dal-a-liń-lagit'*, Perhaps he will be about to strike for us two.
2	*Dal-a-ben-lagit'-e*, He will be about to strike for you two.	*Dal-a-ben-lagit'-khan-e*, If he will be about to strike for you two.	*Paset'-e-dal-a-ben-lagit'*, Perhaps he will be about to strike for you two.
3	*Dal-a-kin-lagit'-e* He will be about to strike for them two.	*Dal-a-kin-lagit'-khan-e*, If he will be about to strike for them two.	*Paset'-e-dal-a-kin-lagit'*, Perhaps he will be about to strike for them two.
	PLURAL.	PLURAL.	PLURAL.
1	*Dal-a-le-lagit'-e*, He will be about to strike for us.	*Dal-a-le-lagit'-khan-e*, If he will be about to strike for us.	*Paset'-e-dal-a-le-lagit'*, Perhaps he will be about to strike for us.

2 *Dal-a-pe-lagit'-e,* He will be about to strike for you.	*Dal-a-pe-lagit'-khan-e,* If he will be about to strike for you.	*Paset'-e-dal-a-pe-lagit',* Perhaps he will be about to strike for you.
3 *Dal-a-ko-lagit'-e,* He will be about to strike for them	*Dal-a-ko-lagit'-khan-e,* If he will be about to strike for them.	*Paset'-e-dal-a-ko-lagit',* Perhaps he will be about to strike for them.
Neuter. *Dal-ak-lagit'-e,* He will be about to strike at it.	*Dal-ak-lagit'-khan-e,* If he will be about to strike at it.	*Paset'-e-dal-ak-lagit',* Perhaps he will be about to strike at it.

INCHOATIVE PRESENT.

INDICATIVE.	SUBJUNCTIVE with "*Khan.*"	SUBJUNCTIVE with "*Paset'.*"
SINGULAR.	SINGULAR.	SINGULAR.
1 *Dal-a-ń-lagid-ok-kan-a-e,* He is about to strike for me.	*Dal-a-ń-lagid-ok-kan-khan-e,* If he is about to strike for me.	*Paset'-e-dal-a-ń-lagid-ok-kan,* Perhaps he is about to strike for me.
2 *Dal-a-m-lagid-ok-kan-a-e,* He is about to strike for thee.	*Dal-a-m-lagid-ok-kan-khan-e,* If he is about to strike for thee.	*Paset'-e-dal-a-m-lagid-ok-kan,* Perhaps he is about to strike for thee.
3 *Dal-a-e-lagid-ok-kan-a-e,* He is about to strike for him.	*Dal-a-e-lagid-ok-kan-khan-e,* If he is about to strike for him.	*Paset'-e-dal-a-e-lagid-ok-kan,* Perhaps he is about to strike for him.
DAUL.	DUAL.	DUAL.
1 *Dal-a-liń-lagid-ok-kan-a-e,* He is about to strike for us two.	*Dal-a-liń-lagid-ok-kan-khan-e,* If he is about to strike for us two.	*Paset'-e-dal-a-liń-lagid-ok-kan,* Perhaps he is about to strike for us two.

2	*Dal-a-ben-lagid-oḱ-kan-a-e,* He is about to strike for you two.	*Dal-a-ben-lagid-oḱ-kan-khan-e,* If he is about to strike for you two.	*Paset'-e-dal-a-ben-lagid-oḱ-kan,* Perhaps he is about to strike for you two.
3	*Dal-a-kin-lagid-oḱ-kan-a-e,* He is about to strike for them two.	*Dal-a-kin-lagid-oḱ-kan-khan-e,* If he is about to strike for them two.	*Paset'-e-dal-a-kin-lagid-oḱ-kan,* Perhaps he is about to strike for them two.
	PLURAL.	PLURAL.	PLURAL.
1	*Dal-a-le-lagid-oḱ-kan-a-e,* He is about to strike for us.	*Dal-a-le-lagid-oḱ-kan-khan-e,* If he is about to strike for us.	*Paset'-e-dal-a-le-lagid-oḱ-kan,* Perhaps he is about to strike for us.
2	*Dal-a-pe-lagid-oḱ-kan-a-e,* He is about to strike for you.	*Dal-a-pe-lagid-oḱ-kan-khan-e,* If he is about to strike for you.	*Paset'-e-dal-a-pe-lagid-oḱ-kan,* Perhaps he is about to strike for you.
3	*Dal-a-ko-lagid-oḱ-kan-a-e,* He is about to strike for them.	*Dal-a-ko-lagid-oḱ-kan-khan-e,* If he is about to strike for them.	*Paset'-e-dal-a-ko-lagid-oḱ-kan,* Perhaps he is about to strike for them.
Neuter.	*Dal-aḱ-lagid-oḱ-kan-a-e,* He is about to strike at it.	*Dal-aḱ-lagid-oḱ-kan-khan-e,* If he is about to strike at it.	*Paset'-e-dal-aḱ-lagid-oḱ-kan,* Perhaps he is about to strike at it.

INCHOATIVE PAST.

	INDICATIVE.	SUBJUNCTIVE with "*Khan.*"	SUBJUNCTIVE with "*Paset'.*"
	SINGULAR.	SINGULAR.	SINGULAR.
1	*Dal-a-ń-lagid-oḱ-kan-tahēkan-a-e,* He was about to strike for me.	*Dal-a-ń-lagid-oḱ-kan-tahēkan-khan-e,* If he was about to strike for me.	*Paset'-e-dal-a-ń-lagid-oḱ-kan-tahēkan,* Perhaps he was about to strike for me.

2	*Dal-a-m-lagid-oḱ-kan-tahēkan-e*, He was about to strike for thee.	*Dal-a-m-lagid-oḱ-kan-tahēkan-khan-e*, If he was about to strike for thee.	*Paset'-e-dal-a-m-lagi-doḱ-kan-tahēkan*, Perhaps he was about to strike for thee.
3	*Dal-a-e-lagid-oḱ-kan-tahēkan-a-e*, He was about to strike for him.	*Dal-a-e-lagid-oḱ-kan-tahēkan-khan-e*, If he was about to strike for him.	*Paset'-e-dal-a-e-lagid-oḱ-kan-tahēkan*, Perhaps he was about to strike for him.
	DUAL.	DUAL.	DUAL.
1	*Dal-a-liń-lagid-oḱ-kan-tahēkan-a-e*, He was about to strike for us two.	*Dal-a-liń-lagid-oḱ-kan-tahēkan-khan-e*, If he was about to strike for us two.	*Paset'-e-dal-a-liń-lagid-oḱ-kan-tahē-kan*, Perhaps he was about to strike for us two.
2	*Dal-a-ben-lagid-oḱ-kan-tahēkan-a-e*, He was about to strike for you two.	*Dal-a-ben-lagid-oḱ-kan-tahēkan-khan-e*, If he was about to strike for you two.	*Paset'-e-dal-a-ben-lagid-oḱ-kan-tahē-kan*, Perhaps he was about to strike for you two.
3	*Dal-a-kin-lagid-oḱ-kan-tahēkan-a-e*, He was about to strike for them two.	*Dal-a-kin-lagid-oḱ-kan-tahēkan-khan-e*, If he wasabouttostrike for them two.	*Paset'-e-dal-a-kin-lagid-oḱ-kan-tahē-kan*, Perhaps he was about to strike for them two.
	PLURAL.	PLURAL.	PLURAL.
1	*Dal-a-le-lagid-oḱ-kan-tahēkan-a-e*, He was about to strike for us.	*Dal-a-le-lagid-oḱ-kan-tahēkan-khan-e*, If he was about to strike for us.	*Paset'-e-dal-a-le-lagid-oḱ-kan-tahē-kan*, Perhaps he was about to strike for us.
2	*Dal-a-pe-lagid-oḱ-kan-tahēkan-a-e*, He was about to strike for you.	*Dal-a-pe-lagid-oḱ-kan-tahēkan-khan-e*, If he was about to strike for you.	*Paset'-e-dal-a-pe-lagid-oḱ-kan-tahē-kan*, Perhaps he was about to strike for you.

3 *Dal-a-ko-lagid-ok'-kan-tahēkan-a-e,* He was about to strike for them.	*Dal-a-pe-lagid-ok'-kan-tahēkan-khan-e,* If he was about to strike for them.	*Paset'-e-dal-a-ko-lagid ok'-kan-tahē-kan,* Perhaps he was about to strike for them.
Neuter. *Dal-ak'-lagid-ok'-kan-tahē-kan-a-e,* He was about to strike at it.	*Dal-ak'-lagid-ok'-kan-tahēkan-khan-e,* If he was about to strike at it.	*Paset'-e-dal-ak'-lagid-ok'-kan-tahēkan,* Perhaps he was about to strike at it.

CONDITIONAL.

	Indicative.	Subjunctive with "*Khan.*"	Subjunctive with "*Paset'.*"
	Singular.	Singular.	Singular.
1	Is wanting.	*Dal-akao-a-ń-khan-e,* If he has struck for me.	*Paset'-e-dal-akao-a-ń,* Perhaps he has struck for me.
2		*Dal-akao-a-m-khan-e,* If he has struck for thee.	*Paset'-e-dal-akao-a-m,* Perhaps he has struck for thee.
3		*Dal-akao-a-e-khan e,* If he has struck for him.	*Paset'-e-dal-akao-a-e,* Perhaps he has struck for him.
	Dual.	Dual.	Dual.
1		*Dal-akao-a-liń-khan-e,* If he has struck for us two.	*Paset'-e-dal-akao-a-liń,* Perhaps he has struck for us two.
2		*Dal-akao-a-ben-khan-e,* If he has struck for you two.	*Paset'-e-dal-akao-a-ben,* Perhaps he has struck for you two.
3		*Dal-akao-a-kin-khan-e,* If he has struck for them two.	*Paset'-e-dal-akao-a-kin,* Perhaps he has struck for them two.

	PLURAL.	PLURAL.	PLURAL.
1		*Dal-akao-a-le-khan-e,* If he has struck for us.	*Paset'-e-dal-akao-a-le,* Perhaps he has struck for us.
2		*Dal-akao-a-pe-khan-e,* If he has struck for you.	*Paset'-e-dal-akao-a-pe* Perhaps he has struck for you.
3		*Dal-akao-a-ko-khan-e,* If he has struck for them.	*Paset'-e-dal akao-a-ko,* Perhaps he has struck for them.
		Neuter. *Dal-akao-ak'-khan-e,* If he has struck at it.	*Paset'-e-dal-akao-a-k'* Perhaps he has struck at it.

CONTINGENT.

	SINGULAR.	SINGULAR.	SINGULAR.
1	*Dal-ad-iṅ-gi-e,* He strikes, will † strike for me.		*Paset'-e-dal-ad-iṅ-gi,* Perhaps he will † strike for me.
2	*Dal-at'-me-gi-e,* He strikes* for thee.		*Paset'-e-dal-at'-me-gi,* Perhaps he will † strike for thee.
3	*Dal-ad-e-gi-e,* He strikes* for him.		*Paset'-e-dal-ad-e-gi,* Perhaps he will † strike for him.
	DUAL.	DUAL.	DUAL.
1	*Dal-at'-liṅ-gi-e,* He strikes* for us two.		*Paset'-e-dal-at'-liṅ-gi,* Perhaps he will † strike for us two.
2	*Dal-at'-ben-gi-e,* He strikes* for you two.		*Paset'-e-dal-at'-ben-gi,* Perhaps he will † strike for you two.
3	*Dal-at'-kin-gi-e,* He strikes* for them two.		*Paset'-e-dal-at'-kin-gi,* Perhaps he will † strike for them two.

* Or will or would strike. for (etc) † or would, may or might.

PLURAL.	PLURAL.	PLURAL.
1 *Dal-at'-le-gi-e*, He strikes* for us.		*Paset'-e-dal-at'-le-gi*, Perhaps he will † strike for us.
2 *Dal-at'-pe-gi-e*, He strikes* for you.		*Paset'-e-dal-at'-pe-gi*, Perhaps he will † strike for you.
3 *Dal-at'-ko-gi-e*, He strikes* for them.		*Paset'-e-dal-at'-ko-gi*, Perhaps he will † strike for them.
Neuter. *Dal-at'-gi-e*, He strikes at it.		*Paset'-e-dal-at'-gi*, Perhaps he will † strike at it.

PRELIMINARY EXPOSTULATIVE.

SINGULAR.	DUAL.	PLURAL.
1 *Dal-akao-a-ń-nahī-e*, He must first have struck for me.	*Dal-akao-a-liń-nahī-e*, He must first have struck for us two.	*Dal-akao-a-le-nahī-e*, He must first have struck for us.
2 *Dal-akao-a-m-nahī-e*, He must first have struck for thee.	*Dal-akao-a-ben-nahī-e*, He must first have struck for you two.	*Dal-akao-a-pe-nahī-e*, He must first have struck for you.
3 *Dal-akao-a-e-nahī-e*, He must first have struck for him.	*Dal-akao-a-kin-nahī-e*, He must first have struck for them two.	*Dal-akao-a-ko-nahī-e*, He must first have struck for them.
Neuter. *Dal-akao-ak-nahē-e*, He must first have struck at it.		

* Or will or would strike, for (etc.) † Or would, may or might.

PRELIMINARY PERSUASIVE.

1 *Dal-akao-a-ń-ba-e,* He must first have struck for me.	*Dal-akao-a-liń-ba-e,* He must first have struck for us two.	*Dal-akao-a-le-ba-e,* He must first have struck for us.
2 *Dal-akao-a-m-ba-e,* He must first have struck for them.	*Dal-akao-a-ben-ba-e,* He must first have struck for you two.	*Dal-akao-a-pe-ba-e,* He must first have struck for you.
3 *Dal-akao-a-e-ba-e,* He must first have struck for him.	*Dal-akao-a-kin-ba-e,* He must first have struck for them two.	*Dal-akao-a-ko-ba-e,* He must first have struck for them.
Neuter. *Dal-akao-aḱ-ba-e.* He must first have struck at or on it.		

PRELIMINARY ADMISSIVE.

1 *Dal-akao-a-ń-en-a-e,* He must first have struck for me.	*Dal-akao-a-liń-en-a-e,* He must first have struck for us two.	*Dal-akao-a-le-en-a-e,* He must first have struck for us.
2 *Dal-akao-a-m-en-a-e,* He must first have struck for thee.	*Dal-akao-a-ben--n-a-e,* He must first have struck for you two.	*Dal-akao-a-pe-en-a-e,* He must first have struck for you.
3 *Dal-akao-a-e-en-a-e,* He must first have struck for him.	*Dal-akao-a-kin-en-a-e,* He must first have struck for them two.	*Dal-akao-a-ko-en-a-e,* He must first have struck for them.
Neuter *Dal-akao-aḱ-en-a-e,* He must first have struck at it.		

BENEDICTIVE OR PRECATIVE.

	Singular.	Dual.	Plural.
1	*Dal-a-ń-ma-m!* Mayest thou strike for me!	*Dal-a liń-ma-ko!* May they strike for us two!	*Dal-a-le-ma-pe!* May you strike for us.
2	*Dal-a-m-ma-e!* May he strike for thee!	*Dal-a-ben-ma-liń!* May we two strike for you two!	*Dal-a-pe-ma-ko!* May they strike for you!
3	*Dal-a-e-ma-ń!* May I strike for him!	*Dal-a-kin-ma-ben!* May you two strike for them two!	*Dal-a-ko-ma-le!* May we strike for them!
Neuter.	*Dal-ak̇ ma-e.* May he strike at or on it!		

IMPERATIVE.

1	*Dal-a-ń-me!* Strike thou for me!	*Dal-a-liń-ben!* Strike you two for us two.	*Dal-a-le-pe!* Strike you for us.
2	*Dal-a-e-me!* Strike thou for him!	*Dal-a-kin-ben!* Strike you two for them two.	*Dal-a-ko-pe!* Strike you for them.
Neuter.	*Dal-ak̇-me!* Strike thou at or on it!		

ADJECTIVE PARTICIPLES. (Animate.)	GERUNDS.
Future.	
Dal-a-ń (ko, kin, ben, pe em,) Who will strike for me.	*Dal-a-ko-reak̇, te, re, khon,* Of, by, in, from striking for them.
Special Incomplete Present.	
Dal-a-m-kan, Who is striking for thee.	*Dal-a-ko-kan-reak̇, te, re,* Of, by, in striking for them now.

RECENT PAST.	
Dal-ad-e (ko, kin, pele,) He for whom they struck.	*Dal-at'-ko-reak̕, te, re,* Of, by, in having struck for them.
PERFECT.	
Dal-akao-at'-liń, Who has struck for us two.	*Dal-akao-at'-ko-reak̕, te, re,* Of, by, in having struck for them.
SPECIAL INCOMPLETE PAST.	
Dal-a-ben-kan-tahēkan, Who was striking for you two.	*Dal-a-ko-kan-tahēkan-reak̕, te, re,* Of, by, in striking for them then.
INDECISIVE PLUPERFECT.	
Dal-at'-kin-tahēkan, They two for whom they had struck.	*Dal-at'-ko-tahēkan-reak̕, te, re,* Of, by, in having struck for them.
DECISIVE PLUPERFECT.	
Dal-akao-at'-le-tahēkan, Who had struck for us.	*Dal-akao-at'-ko-tahēkan-reak̕, te, re,* Of, by, in having struck for them.
INCHOATIVE FUTURE.	
Dal-a-pe-lagit', Who will be about to strike for you.	*Dal-a-ko-lagit'-reak̕, te re,* Of, by, in being about to strike for them.
INCHOATIVE PRESENT.	
Dal-a-ko-lagidok̕-kan, They, for whom they are about to strike.	*Dal-a-ko-lagidok̕-kan-reak̕, te, re,* Of, by, in being about to strike for them now.
INCHOATIVE PAST.	
Dal-a-ko-lagidok̕-kan-tahēkan, They, for whom they are about to strike.	*Dal-a-ko-lagidok̕-kan-tahēkan-reak̕, te, re,* Of, by, in being aboutot strike for them then.
CONDITIONAL.	
Dal-akao-a-ko, They, for whom they may have struck.	*Dal-akao-a-ko-reak̕, te, re,* Of, by, in (case) of having struck for them.

Note.—What has already been observed with reference to the participles in the acc. case,. is also the case in the Dative participles, viz. that any of the dative Suffixes may be affixed to the root, and that any of the nominative Suffixes may be added to the Dative Suffixes : as Dal-ako-pe, Dal ape-ko.

ADVERBIAL PARTICIPLES.

FUTURE.	*Dal-ako-khan*, Striking for them.
SPECIAL INCOMPLETE PRESENT.	*Dal-ako-kan-khan*, Striking for them now.
RECENT PAST.	*Dal-at'-ko-khan*, Having struck for them.
PERFECT.	*Dal-akao-at'-ko-khan*, Having struck for them.
SPECIAL INCOMPLETE PAST.	*Dal - ako - kan - tahĕkan - khan*, Striking for them then.
INDECISIVE PLUPERFECT.	*Dal-at'-ko-tahĕkan-khan*, Having struck for them.
DECISIVE PLUPERFECT.	*Dal-akao-at'ko-tahĕkan-khan*, Having struck for them.
INCHOATIVE FUTURE.	*Dal-ako-lagit'-khan*, Being about to strike for them.
INCHOATIVE PRESENT.	*Dal-ako-lagidok̕-kan-khan*, Being now about to strike for them.
INCHOATIVE PAST.	*Dal-ako-lagidok̕-kan-tahĕkan-khan*, Being then about to strike for them.
CONDITIONAL.	*Dal-akao-ako-khan*, (In case of) Having struck for them.
PRELIMINARY EXPOSTULATIVE.	*Dal-akao-ako-nahĭ*, Having first struck for them.
PRELIMINARY PERSUASIVE.	*Dal-akao-ako-bań*, Having first struck for them.
PRELIMINARY ADMISSIVE.	*Dal-akao-ako-ena*, Having first struck for them.
INFINITIVE.	*Dal-ań, am, ae, alin̕, aben, akin, etc.*, To strike for me, thee, etc.

ADJECTIVE PARTICIPLES. (INANIMATE.)	GERUNDS.
FUTURE.	
Dal-ak' (kin, ko, pe, le, ben etc,) At, or on which they (you we etc.) will strike.	*Dal-ak'-reak', te, re,* Of, by, in striking at it.
SPECIAL INCOMPLETE PRESENT.	
Dal-ak'-kan, At which they are striking.	*Dal-ak'-kan-reak', te, re,* Of, by, in striking at it now.
RECENT PAST.	
Dal-at', At which they struck.	*Dal-at'-reak', te, re,* Of, by, in having struck at it.
PERFECT.	
Dal-akao at', At which they have struck.	*Dal akao-at'-reak', te, re,* Of, by, in having struck at it.
SPECIAL INCOMPLETE PAST.	
Dal-ak'-kan-tahēkan, At which they were striking.	*Dal-ak'-kan-tahēkan-reak',te,re,* Of, by, in striking at it then.
INDECISIVE PLUPERFECT.	
Dal-at'-tahēkan, At which they had struck.	*Dal-at'-tahēkan-reak', te, re,* Of, by, in having struck at it.
DECISIVE PLUPERFECT.	
Dal-akao-at'-tahēkan, At which they had struck.	*Dal-akao-at'-tahekan-reak', te, re,* Of, by, in having struck at it.
INCHOATIVE FUTURE.	
Dal-ak'-lagit', At which they will be about to strike.	*Dal-ak'-lagit'-reak', te, re,* Of, by, in being about to strike at it.
INCHOATIVE PRESENT.	
Dal-ak'-lagidok'-kan, At which they are about to strike.	*Dal-ak'-lagidok'-kan-reak', te, re,* Of, by, in being about to strike at it now.
INCHOATIVE PAST.	
Dal-ak'-lagidok'-kan-takēkan, At which they were about to strike.	*Dal ak'-lagidok'-kan-tahēkan-reak', te, re,* Of, by, in being about to strike at it then.
CONDITIONAL.	
Dal-akao-ak', At which they may have struck.	*Dal-akao-ak'-reak', te, re,* Of, by, in having struck at it.

Note.—Any of the Nominative suffixes may be affixed to these dative participles, to show the Agent.

INANIMATE.

ADVERBIAL PARTICIPLES.

FUTURE.	*Dal-ak̇-khan,* Striking at it.
SPECIAL INCOMPLETE PRESENT.	*Dal-ak̇-kan-khan,* Striking at it now.
RECENT PAST.	*Dal-at'-khan,* Having struck at it.
PERFECT.	*Dal-akao-at'-khan,* Having struck at it.
SPECIAL INCOMPLETE PAST.	*Dal-ak̇-kan-tahēkan-khan,* Striking at it then.
INDECISIVE PLUPERFECT.	*Dal-at'-tahēkan-khan,* Having struck at it.
DECISIVE PLUPERFECT.	*Dal-akao-at'-tahēkan-khan,* Having struck at it.
INCHOATIVE FUTURE.	*Dal-ak̇-lagit'-khan,* Being about to strike at it.
INCHOATIVE PRESENT.	*Dal-ak̇-lagidok̇-kan-khan,* Being now about to strike at it.
INCHOATIVE PAST.	*Dal-ak̇-lagidok̇-kan-tahēkan-khan,* Being then about to strike at it.
CONDITIONAL.	*Dal-akao-ak̇-khan,* (in case of) Having struck at it.
PRELIMINARY EXPOSTULATIVE.	*Dal-akao-ak̇-nahī,* Having first struck at it.
PRELIMINARY PERSUASIVE.	*Dal-akao-ak̇-baṅ,* Having first struck at it.
PRELIMINARY ADMISSIVE.	*Dal-akao-ak̇-ena,* Having first struck at it.

INFINITIVE.

Dal-ak̇, To strike at (it.)

REFLEXIVE.

E. WITH THE DATIVE CASE. *FUTURE TENSE.*

INDICATIVE.	SUBJUNCTIVE with "*Khan.*"	SUBJUNCTIVE with "*Paset'.*"
SINGULAR.	SINGULAR.	SINGULAR.
1 *Dal-joṅ-a-ń*, I shall strike for myself.	*Dal-joṅ-khan-i ń*, If I shall strike for myself.	*Paset'-iń-dal-joṅ*, Perhaps I shall strike for myself.
2 *Dal-joṅ-a-m*, Thou wilt strike for thyself.	*Dal-joṅ-khan-em*, If thou wilt strike for thyself.	*Paset'-em-dal-joṅ*, Perhaps thou wilt strike for thyself.
3 *Dal-joṅ-a-e*, He will strike for himself.	*Dal-joṅ-khan-e*, If he will strike for himself.	*Paset'-e-dal-joṅ*, Perhaps he will strike for himself.
DUAL.	DUAL.	DUAL.
1 *Dal-joṅ-a-liń*, We two shall strike for ourselves.	*Dal-joṅ-khan-liń*, If we two shall strike for ourselves.	*Paset'-liń-dal-joṅ*, Perhaps we two shall strike for ourselves.
2 *Dal-joṅ-a-ben*, You two will strike for yourselves.	*Dal-joṅ-khan-ben*, If you two will strike for yourselves.	*Paset'-ben-dal-joṅ*, Perhaps you two will strike for yourselves.
3 *Dal-joṅ-a-kin*, They two will strike for themselves.	*Dal-joṅ-khan-kin*, If they two will strike for themselves.	*Paset'-kin-dal-joṅ*, Perhaps they two will strike for themselves.
PLURAL.	PLURAL.	PLURAL.
1 *Dal-joṅ-a-le*, We shall strike for ourselves.	*Dal-joṅ-khan-le*, If we shall strike for ourselves.	*Paset'-le-dal-joṅ*, Perhaps we shall strike for ourselves.
2 *Dal-joṅ-a-pe*, You will strike for yourselves.	*Dal-joṅ-khan-pe*, If you will strike for yourselves.	*Paset'-pe-dal-joṅ*, Perhaps you will strike for yourselves.
3 *Dal-joṅ-a-ko*, They will strike for themselves.	*Dal-joṅ-khan-ko*, If they will strike for themselves.	*Paset'-ko-dal-joṅ*, Perhaps they will strike for themselves.

SPECIAL INCOMPLETE PRESENT.

	Indicative.	Subjunctive with "*Khan.*"	Subjunctive with "*Paset'.*"
	Singular.	Singular.	Singular.
1	*Dal-jọṅ-kan-a-ń,* I am striking for myself.	*Dal-jọṅ-kan-khan-iń,* If I am striking for myself.	*Pasĕt'-iń-dal-jọṅ-kan,* Perhaps I am striking for myself.
2	*Dal-jọṅ-kan-am,* Thou art striking for thyself.	*Dal-jọṅ-kan-khan-em,* If thou art striking for thyself.	*Paset'-em-dal-jọṅ-kan,* Perhaps thou art striking for thyself.
3	*Dal-jọṅ-kan-a-e,* He is striking for himself.	*Dal-jọṅ-kan-khan-e,* If he is striking for himself.	*Paset'-e-dal-jọṅ-kan,* Perhaps he is striking for himself.
	Dual.	Dual.	Dual.
1	*Dal-jọṅ-kan-a-liń,* We two are striking for ourselves.	*Dal-jọṅ-kan-khan-liń,* If we two are striking for ourselves.	*Paset'-liń-dal-jọṅ-kan,* Perhaps we two are striking for ourselves.
2	*Dal-jọṅ-kan-a-ben,* You two are striking for yourselves.	*Dal-jọṅ-kan-khan-ben,* If you two are striking for yourselves.	*Paset'-ben-dal-jọṅ-kan,* Perhaps you two are striking for yourselves.
3	*Dal-jọṅ-kan-a-kin,* They two are striking for themselves.	*Dal-jọṅ-kan-khan-kin,* If they two are striking for themselves.	*Paset'-kin-dal-jọṅ-kan,* Perhaps they two are striking for themselves.

PLURAL.	**PLURAL.**	**PLURAL.**
1 *Dal-jǫṅ-kan-a-le,* We are striking for ourselves.	*Dal-jǫṅ-kan-khan-le,* If we are striking for ourselves.	*Paset'-le-dal-jǫṅ-kan,* Perhaps we are striking for ourselves.
2 *Dal-jǫṅ-kan-a-pe,* You are striking for yourselves.	*Dal-jǫṅ-kan-khan-pe,* If you are striking for yourselves.	*Paset'-pe-dal-jǫṅ-kan,* Perhaps you are striking for yourselves.
3 *Dal-jǫṅ-kan-a-ko,* They are striking for themselves.	*Dal-jǫṅ-kan-khan-ko,* If they are striking for themselves.	*Paset'-ko-dal-jǫṅ-kan,* Perhaps they are striking for themselves.

RECENT PAST.

INDICATIVE.	SUBJUNCTIVE with "*Khan.*"	SUBJUNCTIVE with "*Paset'.*"
SINGULAR.	**SINGULAR.**	**SINGULAR.**
1 *Dal-an-a-ń,* I struck for myself.	*Dal-an-khan-iń,* If I struck for myself.	*Paset'-iń-dal-an,* Perhaps I struck for myself.
2 *Dal-an-a-m,* Thou struckst for thyself.	*Dal-an-khan-em,* If thou struckst for thyself.	*Paset' em-dal-an,* Perhaps thou struckst for thyself.
3 *Dal-an-a-e,* He struck for himself.	*Dal-an-khan-e,* If he struck for himself.	*Paset'-e-dal-an,* Perhaps he struck for himself.
DUAL.	**DUAL.**	**DUAL.**
1 *Dal-an-a-liń,* We two struck for ourselves.	*Dal-an-khan-liń,* If we two struck for ourselves.	*Paset'-liń-dal-an,* Perhaps we two struck for ourselves.
2 *Dal-an-a-ben,* You two struck for yourselves.	*Dal-an-khan-ben,* If you two struck for yourselves.	*Paset'-ben-dal-an,* Perhaps you two struck for yourselves.
3 *Dal-an-a-kin,* They two struck for themselves.	*Dal-an-khan-kin,* If they two struck for themselves.	*Paset'-kin-dal-an,* Perhaps they two struck for themselves.

Note.—There is no general incomplete present in the Middle voice. This tense is used for both general and special incomplete Present.

PLURAL.	PLURAL.	PLURAL.
1 *Dal-an-a-le,* We struck for ourselves.	*Dal-an-khan-le,* If we struck for ourselves.	*Paset'-le-dal-an,* Perhaps we struck for ourselves.
2 *Dal-an-a-pe,* Your struck for yourselves.	*Dal-an-khan-pe,* If you struck for yourselves.	*Paset'-pe-dal-an,* Perhaps you struck for yourselves.
3 *Dal-an-a-ko,* They struck for themselves.	*Dal-an-khan-ko,* If they struck for themselves.	*Paset'-ko-dal-an,* Perhaps they struck for themselves.

PERFECT.

INDICATIVE.	SUBJUNCTIVE with "*Khan.*"	SUBJUNCTIVE with "*Paset'.*"
SINGULAR.	SINGULAR.	SINGULAR.
1 *Dal-akao-an-a-ń,* I have struck for myself.	*Dal-akao-an-khan-iń,* If I have struck for myself.	*Paset'-iń-dal-akao-an,* Perhaps I have struck for myself.
2 *Dal-akao-an-a-m,* Thou hast struck for thyself.	*Dal-akao-an-khan-em,* If thou hast struck for thyself.	*Paset'-em-dal-akao-an,* Perhaps thou hast struck for thyself.
3 *Dal-akao-an-a-e,* He has struck for himself.	*Dal-akao-an-khan-e,* If he has struck for himself.	*Paset'-e-dal-akao-an,* Perhaps he has struck for himself.
DUAL.	DUAL.	DUAL.
1 *Dal-akao-an-a-liń,* We two have struck for ourselves.	*Dal-akao-an-khan-liń,* If we two have struck for ourselves.	*Paset'-liń-dal-akao-an,* Perhaps we two have struck for ourselves.
2 *Dal-akao-an-a-ben,* You two have struck for yourselves.	*Dal-akao-an-khan-ben,* If you two have struck for yourselves.	*Paset'-ben-dal-akao-an,* Perhaps you two have struck for yourselves.
3 *Dal-akao-an-a-kin,* They two have struck for themselves.	*Dal-akao-an-khan-kin,* If they two have struck for themselves.	*Paset'-kin-dal-akao-an,* Perhaps they two have struck for themselves.

Note.—This term is used both as recent and anterior Past.

PLURAL.	PLURAL.	PLURAL.
1 *Dal-akao-an-a-le,* We have struck for ourselves.	*Dal-akao-an-khan-le,* If we have struck for ourselves.	*Paset'-le-dal-akao-an,* Perhaps we have struck for ourselves.
2 *Dal'akao-an-a-pe,* You have struck for yourselves.	*Dal-akao-an-khan-pe,* If you have struck for yourselves.	*Paset'-pe-dal-akao-an,* Perhaps you have struck for yourselves.
3 *Dal-akao-an-a-ko,* They have struck for themselves.	*Dal-akao-an-khan-ko,* If they have struck for themselves.	*Paset'-ko-dal-akao-an,* Perhaps they have struck for themselves.

SPECIAL INCOMPLETE PAST.

SINGULAR.	SINGULAR.	SINGULAR.
1 *Dal-joṅ-kan-t a-hēkan-aṅ,* I was striking for myself.	*Dal-joṅ-kan-tahē-kan-khan-iṅ,* If I was striking for myself.	*Paset'-iṅ-dal-joṅ-kan-tahēkan,* Perhaps I was striking for myself.
2 *Dal-joṅ-kan-t a-hēkan-a-m,* Thou wast striking for thyself.	*Dal-joṅ-kan-tahē-kan-khan-em,* If thou wast striking for thyself.	*Paset'-em-dal-joṅ-kan-tahēkan,* Perhaps thou wast striking for thyself.
3 *Dal-joṅ-kan-t a-hēkan-a-e,* He was striking for himself.	*Dal-joṅ-kan-tahē-kan-khan-e,* If he was striking for himself.	*Paset'-e-dal-joṅ-kan-tahēkan,* Perhaps he was striking for himself.
DUAL.	**DUAL.**	**DUAL.**
1 *Dal-joṅ-kan-t a-hēkan-a-liṅ,* We two were striking for ourselves.	*Dal-joṅ-kan-tahē-kan-khan-liṅ,* If we two were striking for ourselves.	*Paset'-liṅ-dal-joṅ-kan-tahēkan,* Perhaps we two were striking for ourselves.

2 *Dal-jon-kan-tahēkan-a-ben,* You two were striking for yourselves.	*Dal-jon-kan-tahēkan-khan-ben,* If you two were striking for yourselves.	*Paset'-ben-dal-jon-kan-tahēkan,* Perhaps you two were striking for yourselves.
3 *Dal-jon-kan-tahēkan-a-kin,* They two were striking for themselves.	*Dal-jon-kan-tahēkan-khan-kin,* If they two were striking for themselves.	*Paset'-kin-dal-jon-kan-tahēkan,* Perhaps they two were striking for themselves.
PLURAL.	PLURAL.	PLURAL.
1 *Dal-jon-kan-tahēkan-a-le,* We were striking for ourselves.	*Dal-jon-kan-tahēkan-khan-le,* If we were striking for ourselves.	*Paset'-le-dal-jon-kan-tahēkan,* Perhaps we were striking for ourselves.
2 *Dal-jon-kan-tahēkan-a-pe,* You were striking for yourselves.	*Dal-jon-kan-tahēkan-khan-pe,* If you were striking for yourselves.	*Paset'-pe-dal jon-kan-tahēkan,* Perhaps you were striking for yourselves.
3 *Dal-jon-kan-tahēkan-a-ko,* They were striking for themselves.	*Dal-jon-kan-tahēkan-khan-ko,* If they were striking for themselves.	*Paset'-ko-dal-jon-kan-tahēkan,* Perhaps they were striking for themselves.

INDECISIVE PLUPERFECT.

INDICATIVE.	SUBJUNCTIVE with "*Khan.*"	SUBJUNCTIVE with "*Paset'.*"
SINGULAR.	SINGULAR.	SINGULAR.
1 *Dal-an-tahēkan-a-in,* I had struck for myself.	*Dal-an-tahēkan-khan-in,* If I had struck for myself.	*Paset'-in-dal-an-tahēkan,* Perhaps I had struck for myself.

2	*Dal-an-tahēkan-a-m,* Thou hadst struck for thyself.	*Dal-an-tahēk an-khan-em,* If thou hadst struck for thyself.	*Paset'-em-dal-an-ta-hēkan,* Perhaps thou hadst struck for thyself.
3	*Dal-an-tahēkan-a-e,* He had struck for himself.	*Dal-an-tahēk an-khan-e,* If he had struck for himself.	*Paset'-e-dal-an-tahē-kan,* Perhaps he had struck for himself.
	DUAL.	DUAL.	DUAL.
1	*Dal-an-tahēkan-a-liń,* We two had struck for ourselves.	*Dal-an-tahēk an-khan-liń,* If we two had struck for ourselves.	*Paset'-liń-dal-an-ta-hēkan,* Perhaps we two had struck for ourselves.
2	*Dal-an-tahēkan-a-ben,* You two had struck for yourselves.	*Dal-an-tahēk an-khan-ben,* If you two had struck for yourselves.	*Pasēt'-ben-dal-an-ta-hēkan.* Perhaps you two had struck for yourselves.
3	*Dal-an-tahēkan-a-kin,* They two had struck for themselves.	*Dal-an-tahēk an-khan-kin,* If they two had struck for themselves.	*Paset'-kin-dal-an-ta-hēkan,* Perhaps they two had struck for themselves.
	PLURAL.	PLURAL.	PLURAL.
1	*Dal-an-takēkan-a-le,* We had struck for ourselves.	*Dal-an-takēk an-khan-le,* If we had struck for ourselves.	*Paset'-le-dal-an-tahē-kan,* Perhaps we had struck for ourselves.
2	*Dal-an-tahēkan-a-pe,* You had struck for yourselves.	*Dal-an-tahēk an-khan-pe,* If you had struck for yourselves.	*Paset'-pe-dal-an-tahē-kan,* Perhaps you had struck for yourselves.
3	*Dal-an-tahēkan-a-ko,* They had struck for themselves.	*Dal-an-tahēk an-khan-ko,* If they had struck for themselves.	*Paset'-ko-dal-an-tahē-kan,* Perhaps they had struck for themselves.

DECISIVE PLUPERFECT.

INDICATIVE.	SUBJUNCTIVE with "*Khan.*"	SUBJUNCTIVE with "*Paset'.*"
SINGULAR.	SINGULAR.	SINGULAR.
1 *Dal-akao-an-ta-hēkan-a-ń* I had struck for myself.	*Dal-akao-an-takē-kan-kha n - i ń*, If I had struck for myself.	*Past'-iń-dal-akao-an-tahēka n*, Perhaps I had struck for myself.
2 *Dal-akao-an-ta-hē k a n - a - m*, Thou hadst struck for thyself.	*Dal-akao-an-tahē-kan-khan - e m*, If thou hadst struck for thyself.	*Paset'-em-dal-ak a o-an-tahēkan*, Perhaps thou hadst struck for thyself.
3 *Dal-akao-an-ta-hēkan-a-e*, He had struck for himself.	*Dal-akao-an-tahē-kan-khan-e*, If he had struck for himself.	*Paset'-e-dal-akao-a n-tahēkan*, Perhaps he had struck for himself.
DUAL.	DUAL.	DUAL.
1 *Dal-akao-an-ta-hēkan-a-liń*, We two had struck for ourselves.	*Dal-akao-an-tahē-kan-khan- l i ń*, If we two had struck for ourselves.	*Paset'-liń-dal-ak a o-an-tahēk a n*, Perhaps we two had struck for ourselves.
2 *Dal-akao-an-ta-hēkan- a - b e n*, You two had for yourselves.	*Dal-akao-an-tahē-kan-khan-b e n*, If you two had struck for yourselves.	*Paset'-ben-dal-aka o-an-tahēk a n*, Perhaps you two had struck for yourselves.
3 *Dal-akao - a n-tahēkan-a-k i n*, They two had struck for themselves.	*Dal-akao-an-tahē-kan-khan ki n*, If they two had struck for themselves.	*Paset'-kin-dal-aka o-an-tahēka n*, Perhaps they two had struck for themselves

PLURAL.	PLURAL.	PLURAL.
1 *Dal-akao-an-tahĕkan-a-le*, We had struck for ourselves.	*Dal-akao-an-tahĕkan-khan-le*, If we had struck for ourselves.	*Paset'-le-dal-akao-an tahĕkan*, Perhaps we had struck for ourselves.
2 *Dal-akao-an-tahĕkan-a-pe*, You had struck for yourselves.	*Dal-akao-an-tahĕ kan-khan-pe*, If you had struck for yourselves.	*Paset'-pe-dal-akao-an-tahĕkan*, Perhaps you had struck for yourselves.
3 *Dal-akao-an-tahĕkan-a-ko*, They had struck for themselves.	*Dal-akao-an-tahĕkan-khan-ko*, If they had struck for themselves.	*Paset'-ko-dal-akao-an-tahĕkan*, Perhaps they had struck for themselves.

INCHOATIVE FUTURE.

INDICATIVE.	SUBJUNCTIVE with "*Khan.*"	SUBJUCTIVE with "*Paset'.*"
SINGULAR.	SINGULAR.	SINGULAR.
1 *Dal-jọṅ-lagit'-iṅ*, I shall be about to strike for myself.	*Dal-jọṅ-lagit'-khan-iṅ*, If I shall be about to strike for myself.	*Paset'-iṅ-dal-jọṅ-lagit'*, Perhaps I shall be about to strike for myself.
2 *Dal-jọṅ-lagit'-em*, Thou wilt be about to strike for thyself.	*Dal-jọṅ-lagit'-khan-em*, If thou wilt be about to strike for thyself.	*Paset'-em-dal-jọṅ-lagit'*, Perhaps thou wilt be about to strike for thyself.
3 *Dal-jọṅ-lagit'-e*, He will be about to strike for himself.	*Dal-jọṅ-lagit'-khan-e*, If he will be about to strike for himself.	*Past'-e-dal-jọṅ-lagit'*, Perhaps he will be about to strike for himself.

	DUAL.	DUAL.	DUAL.
1	*Dal-jọṅ-lagit'liṅ*, We two will be about to strike for ourselves.	*Dal-jọṅ-lagit'-khan-liṅ*, If we two shall be about to strike for ourselves.	*Paset'-liṅ-dal-jọṅ-lagit'*, Perhaps we two shall be about to strike for ourselves.
2	*Dal-jọṅ-lagit'-ben*, You two will be about to strike for yourselves.	*Dal-jọṅ-lagit'-khan-ben*, If you two will be about to strike for yourselves.	*Paset'-ben-dal-jọṅ-lagit'*, Perhaps you two will be about to strike for yourselves.
3	*Dal-jọṅ-lagit'-kin*, They two will be about to strike for themselves.	*Dal-jọṅ-lagit'-khan-kin*, If they two will be about to strike for themslves.	*Paset'-kin-dal-jọṅ-lagit'*, Perhaps they two will be about to strike for themselves.
	PLURAL.	PLURAL.	PLURAL.
1	*Dal-jọṅ-lagit'-le*, We shall be about to strike for ourselves.	*Dal-jọṅ-lagit'-khan-le*, If we shall be about to strike for ourselves.	*Paset'-le-dal-jọṅ-lagit'*, Perhaps we shall be about to for strike for ourselves.
2	*Dal-jọṅ-lagit'-pe* You will be about to strike for yourselves.	*Dal-jọṅ-lagit'-khan-pe*, If you will be about to strike for yourselves.	*Paset'-pe-dal-jọṅ-lagit'*, Perhaps you will be about to strike for yourselves.
3	*Dal-jọṅ-lagit'-ko*, They will be about strike for themselves.	*Dal-jọṅ-lagit'-khan-ko*, If they will be about to strike for themselves.	*Paset'-ko-dal-jọṅ-lagit'*, Perhaps they will be about to strike for themselves.

INCHOATIVE PRESENT.

	INDICATIVE.	SUBJUNCTIVE with "*Khan.*"	SUBJUNCTIVE with "*Paset'.*"
	SINGULAR.	**SINGULAR.**	**SINGULAR.**
1	*Dal-jọṅ-lagid-ok'-kan-a-ń*, I am about to strike for myself.	*Dal-jọṅ-lagid-ok'-kan-khan-iń*, If I am about to strike for myself.	*Paset'-iń-dal-jọṅ-la-gid-ok'-kan*, Perhaps I am about to strike for myself.
2	*Dal-jọṅ-lagid-ok'-kan-a-m*, Thou art about to strike for thyself.	*Dal-jọṅ-lagid-ok'-kan-khan-em*, If thou art about to strike for thyself.	*Paset'-em-dal-jọṅ-la-gid-ok'-kan*, Perhaps thou art about to strike for thyself.
3	*Dal-jọṅ-lagid-ok'-kan-a-e*, He is about to strike for himself.	*Dal-jọṅ-lagid-ok'-kan-khan-e*, If he is about to strike for himself.	*Paset'-e-dal-jọṅ-la-gid-ok'-kan*, Perhaps he is about to strike for himself.
	DUAL.	**DUAL.**	**DUAL.**
1	*Dal-jọṅ-lagid-ok'-kan-a-liń*, We two are about to strike for ourselves.	*Dal-jọṅ-lagid-ok'-kan-khan-liń*, If we two are about to strike for ourselves.	*Paset'-liń-dal-jọṅ-la-gid-ok'-kan*, Perhaps we two are about to strike for ourselves.
2	*Dal-jọṅ-lagid-ok'-kan-a-ben*, You two are about to strike for yourselves.	*Dal-jọṅ-lagid-ok'-kan-khan-ben*, If you two are about to strike for yourselves.	*Paset'-ben-dal-jọṅ-la-gid-ok'-kan*, Perhaps you two are about to strike for yourselves.
3	*Dal-jọṅ-lagid-ok'-kan-a-kin*, They two are about to strike for themselves.	*Dal-jọṅ-lagid-ok'-kan-khan-kin*, If they two are about to strike for themselves.	*Paset'-kin-dal-jọṅ-la-gid-ok'-kan*, Perhaps they two are about to strike for themselves.

	Plural.	Plural.	Plural.
1	*Dal-joṅ-lagid-ok̇-kan-a-le,* We are about to strike for ourselves.	*Dal-joṅ-lagid-ok̇-kan-khan-le,* If we are about to strike for ourselves.	*Paset'-le-dal-joṅ-lagid-ok̇-kan,* Perhaps we are about to strike for ourselves.
2	*Dal-joṅ-lagid-ok̇-kan-a-pe,* You are about to strike for yourselves.	*Dal-joṅ-lagid-ok̇-kan-khan-pe,* If your are about to strike for yourselves.	*Paset'-pe-dal-joṅ-lagid-ok̇-kan,* Perhaps you are about to strike for yourselves.
3	*Dal-joṅ-lagid-ok̇-kan-a-ko,* They are about to strike for themselves.	*Dal-joṅ-lagid-ok̇-kan-khan-ko,* If they are about to strike for themselves.	*Paset'-ko-dal-joṅ-lagid-ok̇-kan,* Perhaps they are about to strike for themselves.

INCHOATIVE PAST.

	Indicative.	Subjunctive with "*Khan.*"	Subjunctive with "*Paset'.*"
	Singular.	Singular.	Singular.
1	*Dal-joṅ-lagid-ok̇-kan-tahēkan-a-ń,* I was about to strike for myself.	*Dal-joṅ-lagid-ok̇-kan-tahēkan-khan-iń,* I was about to strike for myself.	*Paset'-iń-dal-joṅ-lagid-ok̇-kan-tahēkan,* Perhaps I was about to strike for myself.
2	*Dal-joṅ-lagid-ok̇-kan-tahēkan-a-m,* Thou wast about to strike for thyself.	*Dal-joṅ-lagid-ok̇-kan-tahēkan-khan-em,* If thou wast about to strike for thyself.	*Paset'-em-dal-joṅ-lagid-ok̇-kan-tahēkan,* Perhaps thou wast about to strike for thyself.
3	*Dal-joṅ-lagid-ok̇-kan-tahēkan-a-e,* He was about to strike for himself.	*Dal-joṅ-lagid-ok̇-kan-tahēkan-khan-e,* If he was about to strike for himself.	*Paset'-e-dal-joṅ-lagid-ok̇-kan-tahēkan,* Perhaps he was about to strike for himself.

	Dual.	**Dual.**	**Dual.**
1	*Dal-jọṅ-lagid-ok'-kan-tahēkan-a-liṅ*, We two were about to strike for ourselves.	*Dal-jọṅ-lagid-ok'-kan-tahēkan-khan-liṅ*, If we two were about to strike for ourselves.	*Paset'-liṅ-dal-jọṅ-lagid-ok'-kan-tahēkan*, Perhaps we two were about to strike for ourselves.
2	*Dal-jọṅ-lagid-ok'-kan-tahēkan-a-ben*, You two were about to strike for yourselves.	*Dal-jọṅ-lagid-ok'-kan-tahēkan-khan-ben*, If you two were about to strike for yourselves.	*Paset'-ben-dal-jọṅ-lagid-ok'-kan-takēkan*, Perhaps you two were about to strike for yourselves.
3	*Dal-jọṅ-lagid-ok'-kan-tahēkan-a-kin*, They two were about to strike for themselves.	*Dal-jọṅ-lagid-ok'-kan-tahēkan-khan-kin*, If they two were about to strike for themselves.	*Paset'-kin-dal-jọṅ-lagid-ok'-kan-tahēkan*, Perhaps they two were about to strike for themselves.
	Plural.	**Plural.**	**Plural.**
1	*Dal-jọṅ-lagid-ok'-kan-tahēkan-a-le*, We were about to strike for ourselves.	*Dal-jọṅ lagid-ok'-kan-tahēkan-khan-le*, If we were about to strike for ourselves.	*Paset'-le-dal-jọṅ-lagid-ok'-kan-tahēkan*, Perhaps we were about to strike for ourselves.
2	*Dal-jọṅ-lagid-ok'-kan-tahēkan-a-pe*, You were about to strike for yourselves.	*Dal-jọṅ-lagid-ok'-kan-tahēkan-khan-pe*, If you were about to strike for yourselves.	*Paset'-pe-dal-jọṅ-lagid-ok'-kan-tahēkan*, Perhaps you were about to strike for yourselves.
3	*Dal-jọṅ-lagid-ok'-kan-tahēkan-a-ko*, They were about to strike for themselves.	*Dal-jọṅ-lagid-ok'-kan-tahēkan-khan-ko*, If they were about to strike for themselves.	*Paset'-ko-dal-jọṅ-lagid-ok'-kan-tahēkan*, Perhaps they were about to strike for themselves.

CONDITIONAL.

	SINGULAR.	SINGULAR.	SINGULAR.
1	Is wanting.	*Dal-an-khan-iń*, If I should strike or have struck for myself.	*Paset'-iń-dal-an*, Perhaps I should strike for myself.
2		*Dal-an-khan-em*, If thou wouldst strike for thyself.	*Paset'-em-dal-an*, Perhaps thou wouldst strike for thyself.
3		*Dal-an-khan-e*, If he would strike for himself,	*Paset'-e-dal-an*, Perhaps he would strike for himself.
	DUAL.	DUAL.	DUAL.
1		*Dal-an-khan-liń*, If we two should strike for ourselves.	*Paset'-liń-dal-an*, Perhaps we two should strike for ourselves.
2		*Dal-an-khan-ben*, If you two would strike for yourselves.	*Paset'-ben-dal-an*, Perhaps you two would strike for yourselves.
3		*Dal-an-khan-kin*, If they two would strike for themselves.	*Paset'-kin-dal-an*, Perhaps they two would strike for themselves.
	PLURAL.	PLURAL.	PLURAL.
1		*Dal-an-khan-le*, If we should strike for ourselves.	*Paset'-le-dal-an*, Perhaps we should strike for ourselves.
2		*Dal-an-khan-pe*, If you would strike for yourselves.	*Paset'-pe-dal-an*, Perhaps you would strike for yourselves.
3		*Dal-an-khan-ko*, If they would strike for themselves.	*Paset'-ko-dal-an*, Perhaps they would strike for themselves.

CONDITIONAL PERFECT.

	Singular.	Singular.	Singular.
1		*Dal-akao-an-khan-iń,* If I have struck for myself.	*Paset'-iń-dal-akao-an,* Perhaps I have struck for myself.
2		*Dal-akao-an-khan-em,* If thou hast struck for thyself.	*Paset'-em-dal-akao-an,* Perhaps thou hast struck for thyself.
3		*Dal-akao-an-khan-e,* If he has struck for himself.	*Paset'-e-dal-akao-an,* Perhaps he has struck for himself.
	Dual.	**Dual.**	**Dual.**
1		*Dal-akao-an-khan-liń,* If we two have struck for ourselves.	*Paset'-liń-dal-akao-an,* Perhaps we two have struck for ourselves.
2		*Dal-akao-an-khan-ben,* If you two have struck for yourselves.	*Paset'-ben-dal-akao-an,* Perhaps you two have struck for yourselves.
3		*Dal-akao-an-khan-kin,* If they two have struck for themselves.	*Paset'-kin-dal-akao-an,* Perhaps they two have struck for themselves,
	Plural.	**Plural.**	**Plural.**
1		*Dl-akao-an-khan-le* If we have struck for ourselves.	*Paset'-le-dal-akao-an,* Perhaps we have struck for ourselves.
2		*Dal-akao-an-khan-pe,* If you have struck for yourselves.	*Paset'-pe-dal-akao-an,* Perhaps you have struck for yourselves.
3		*Dal-akao-an-khan-ko,* If they have struck for themselves.	*Paset'-ko-dal-a-kao-an,* Perhaps they have struck for themselves.

PRELIMINARY FUTURE.

SINGULAR.	SINGULAR.	SINGULAR.
1 *Dal-an-gi-ń*, I will first strike for myself.		*Paset'-iń-dal-an-gi*, Perhaps I will first strike for myself.
2 *Dal-an-gi-m*, Thou wilt first strike for thyself.		*Paset'-em-dal-an-gi*, Perhaps thou wilt first strikefor thyself.
3 *Dal-an-gi-e*, He will first strike for himself.		*Paset'-e-dal-an-gi*, Perhaps he will first strike for himself.
DUAL.	DUAL.	DUAL.
1 *Dal-an-gi-liń*, We two will first strike for ourselves.		*Paset'-liń-dal-an-gi*, Perhaps we two will first strike for ourselves.
2 *Dal-an-gi-ben*, You two will first strike for yourselves.		*Paset'-ben-dal-an-gi*, Perhaps you two will first strike for yourselves-
3 *Dal-an-gi-kin*, They two will first strike for themselves.		*Paset'-kin-dal-an-gi*, Perhaps they two will first strike for themselves.
PLURAL.	PLURAL.	PLURAL.
1 *Dal-an-gi-le*, We will first strike for ourselves.		*Paset'-le-dal-an-gi*, Perhaps we will first strike for ourselves.
2 *Dal-an-gi-pe*, You will first strike for yourselves.		*Paset'-pe-dal-an-gi*, Perhaps you will first strike for yourselves.
3 *Dal-an-gi-ko*, They will first strike for themselves.		*Paset'-ko-dal-an-gi*, Perhaps they will first strike for themselves.

CONTINGENT.

SINGULAR.	SINGULAR.	SINGULAR.
1 *Dal-a-gin-ń.* I strike † for myself.		*Paset'-iń-dal-an-gi*, Perhaps I strike † for myself.
2 *Dal-an-gi-m*, Thou strikest † for thyself.		*Paset'-em-dal-an-gi*, Perhaps thou strikest † for thyself.
3 *Dal-an-gi-e*, He strikes † for himself.		*Paset'-e-dal-an-gi*, Perhaps he strikes † for himself.
DUAL.	DUAL.	DUAL.
1 *Dal-an-gi-liń*, We two strike † for ourselves.		*Paset'-liń-dal-an-gi*, Perhaps we two strike † for ourselves.
2 *Dal-an-gi-ben*, You two strike † for yourselves.		*Paset'-ben-dal-an-gi*, Perhaps you two strike † for yourself.
3 *Dal-an-gi-kin*, They two strike † for themselves.		*Paset'-kin-dal-an-gi*, Perhaps they two strike † for themselves.
PLURAL.	PLURAL.	PLURAL.
1 *Dal-an-gi-le*, We strike † for ourselves.		*Paset'-le-dal-an-gi*, Perhaps we strike † for ourselves.
2 *Dal-an-gi-pe*, You strike † for yourselves.		*Paset'-pe-dal-an-gi*, Perhaps you strike † for yourselves.
3 *Dal-an-gi-ko*, They strike † for themselves.		*Paset'-ko-dal-an-gi*, Perhaps they strike † for themselves.

† Or will or would strike.

Note. It will be observed, that *an* represents both the *en* and *len* of the Accusative Reflexive.

PRELIMINARY EXPOSTULATIVE.

	Singular.	Dual.	Plural.
1	*Dal-an-nahī-ń*, I must first strike for myself.	*Dal-an-nahī-liń*, We two must first strike for ourselves.	*Dal-an-nahī-le*, We must first strike for ourselves.
2	*Dal-an-nahī-m*, Thou must first strike for thyself.	*Dal-an-nahī-ben*, You two must first strike for yourselves.	*Dal-an-nahī-pe*, You must first strike for yourselves.
3	*Dal-an-nahī-e*, He must first strike for himself	*Dal-an-nahī-kin*, They two must first strike for themselves.	*Dal-an-nahī-ko*, They must first strike for themselves.

PRELIMINARY PERSUASIVE.

	Singular.	Dual.	Plural.
1	*Dal-an-ba-ń*, I must first strike for myself.	*Dal-an-ba-liń*, We two must first strike for ourselves.	*Dal-an-ba-le*, We must first strike for ourselves.
2	*Dal-an-ba-m*, Thou must first strike for thyself.	*Dal-an-ba-ben*, You two must first strike for yourselves.	*Dal-an-ba-pe*, You must first strike for yourselves.
3	*Dal-an-ba-e*, He must first strike for himself	*Dal-an-ba-kin*, They two must first strike for themselves.	*Dal-an-ba-ko*, They must first strike for themselves.

PRELIMINARY ADMISSIVE.

1	*Dal-an en-a-ń*, I must first strike for myself.	*Dal-an-en-a-liń* We two must first strike for ourselves.	*Dal-an-en-a-le*, We must first strike for ourselves.
2	*Dal-an-en-a-m*, Thou must first strike for thyself.	*Dal-an-en-a-ben*, You two must first strike for yourselves.	*Dal-an-en-a pe*, You must first strike for yourselves.
3	*Dal-an-en-a-e*, He must first strike for himself.	*Dal-an-en-a-kin*, They two must first strike for themselves.	*Dal-an-en-a-ko*, They must first strike for themselves

PRELIMINARY PERFECT EXPOSTULATIVE.

	SINGULAR.	DUAL.	PLURAL.
1	*Dal-akao-an-nahī-ń*, I must first have struck for myself.	*Dal-akao-an-nahī-liń*, We two must first have struck for ourselves.	*Dal-akao-an-nahī-le*, We must first have struck for ourselves.
2	*Dal-akao-an-nahī-m*, Thou must first have struck for thyself.	*Dal-akao-an-nahī-ben*, You two must first have struck for yourselves.	*Dal-akao-an-nahī-pe* You must first have struck for yourselves.
3	*Dal-akao-an-nahī-e*, He must first have struck for himself.	*Dal-akao-an-nahī-kin*, They two must first have struck for themselves.	*Dal-akao-an-nahī-ko*, They must first have struck for themselves.

PRELIMINARY PERFECT PERSUASIVE.

	Singular	Dual	Plural
1	*Dal-akao-an-ba-ń* I must first have struck for myself.	*Dal-akao-an-ba-liń,* We two must first have struck for ourselves.	*Dal-akao-an-ba-le,* We must first have struck for ourselves.
2	*Dal-akao-an-ba-m,* Thou must first have struck for thyself.	*Dal-akao-an-ba-ben,* You two must first have struck for yourselves.	*Dal-akao-an-ba-pe* You must first have struck for yourselves.
3	*Dal-akao-an-ba-e,* He must first have struck for himself.	*Dal-akao-an-ba-kin,* They two must first have struck for themselves.	*Dal-akao-an-ba-ko,* They must first have struck for themselves.

PRELIMINARY PERFECT ADMISSIVE.

	Singular	Dual	Plural
1	*Dal-akao-an-en-a-ń* I must first have struck for myself.	*Dal-akao-an-en-a-liń,* We two must first have struck for ourselves.	*Dal-akao-an-en-a-le,* We must first have struck for ourselves.
2	*Dal-akao-an-en-a-m,* Thou must first have struck for thyself.	*Dal-akao an-en-a-ben,* You two must first have struck for yourselves.	*Dal-akao-an-en-a-pe,* You must first have struck for yourselves.
3	*Dal-akao-an-en a-e,* He must first have struck for himself.	*Dal-akao-an-en-a-kin,* They two must first have struck for themselves.	*Dal-akao-an-en-a-ko,* They must first have struck for themselves.

PRELIMINARY BENEDICTIVE

	SINGULAR.	DUAL.	PLURAL.
1	*Dal-an-ma-ń!* May I first strike for myself!	*Dal-an-ma-liń!* May we two first strike for ourselves!	*Dal-an-ma-le!* May we first strike for ourselves!
2	*Dal-an-ma-m!* Mayest thou first strike for thyself!	*Dal-an-ma-ben!* May you two first strike for yourselves!	*Dal-an-ma-pe!* May you first strike for yourselves!
3	*Dal-an-ma-e,* May he first strike for himself!	*Dal-an-ma-kin!* May they two first strike for themselves!	*Dal-an-ma-ko!* May they first strike for themselves!

PRELIMINARY IMPERATIVE.

2	*Dal-an-me!* Strike thou first for thyself!	*Dal-an-ben!* Strike you two for yourselves!	*Dal-an-pe!* Strike you first for yourselves!
3			

BENEDICTIVE.

1	*Dal-jọń-ma-ń!* May I strike for myself!	*Dal-jọń-ma-liń!* May we two strike for ourselves!	*Dal-jọń-ma-le!* May we strike for ourselves!
2	*Dal-jọń-ma-m!* Mayest thou strike for thyself!	*Dal-jọń-ma-ben!* May you two strike for your-yourselves!	*Dal-jọń-ma-pe!* May you strike for yourselves!
3	*Dal-jọń-ma-e!* May he strike for himself!	*Dal-jọń-ma-kin!* May they two strike for themselves!	*Dal-jọń-ma-ko!* May they strike for themselves.

IMPERATIVE.

Dal-joṅ-me! Strike thou for thyself!	*Dal-joṅ-ben,* Strike you two for yourselves.	*Dal-joṅ-pe!* Strike you for yourselves!

ADJECTIVE PARTICIPLES.	GERUNDS.
FUTURE.	
Dal-joṅ-(kiṅ, ko, ben, pe, etc,) Who will strike for himself.*	*Dal-joṅ-reak', te, re, khan,* Of, by, in striking for oneself.
SPECIAL INCOMPLETE PRESENT.	
Dal-joṅ kan, Who is striking for himself.	*Dal-joṅ-kan-reak', te, re,* Of, by, in striking for oneself, *now.*
RECENT PAST.	
Dal-an, Who struck for himself.	*Dal-an-reak', te, re,* Of, by, in having struck for oneself.
PERFECT.	
Dal-akao-an, Who has struck for himself.	*Dal-akaao-an-reak', te, re,* Of, by, in having struck for oneself.
SPECIAL INCOMPLETE PAST.	
Dal-joṅ-kan-takĕkan, Who was striking for himself.	*Dal-joṅ-kan-tahĕkaṅ-reak', te, re,* Of, by, in striking for oneself, *then.*
INDECISIVE PLUPERFECT.	
Dal-an-tahĕkan, Who had struck for himself.	*Dal-an-tahĕkan-reak', te, re,* Of, by, in having struck for oneself.
DECISIVE PLUPERFECT.	
Dal-akao-an-tahĕkan, Who had struck for himself.	*Dal-akao-an-tahĕkan-reak', te, re,* Of, by, in having struck for oneself.
INCHOATIVE FUTURE.	
Dal-joṅ lagit', Who will be about to strike for himself.	*Dal-joṅ-lagit'-reak', te, re* Of, by, in being about to strike for oneself.

* Any of the nominative suffixes may be affixed to the participles in order to show *who* is the Agent.

INCHOATIVE PRESENT.	
Dal-jōṅ-lagidoḱ-kan, Who is about to strike for himself.	*Dal-jo̱ṅ-lagidoḱ-kan-reaḱ, te, re,* Of, by, in being now about to strike for oneself.
INCHOATIVE PAST.	
Dal-jo̱ṅ-lagidoḱ-tahēkan, Who was about to strike for himself.	*Dal-jo̱ṅ-lagidoḱ-kan-tahēkan-reaḱ, te, re,* Of, by, in then being about to strike for oneself.
CONDITIONAL.	
Dal-an, Who may have struck for himself.	*Dal-an-reaḱ; te, re,* Of, by, in (case of) striking or having struck for oneself.
CONDITIONAL PERFECT.	
Dal-akao-an, Who may have struck for himself.	*Dal-akao-an-reaḱ, te, re,* Of, by, in (case of) having struck for oneself.

ADVERBIAL PARTICIPLES.

FUTURE.	*Dal-jo̱ṅ-khan,* Striking for oneself.
SPECIAL INCOMPLETE PRESENT.	*Dal-jo̱ṅ-kan-khan,* Striking for oneself now.
RECENT PAST.	*Dal-an-khan,* Having struck for oneself.
PERFECT.	*Dal-akao-an-khan,* Having struck for oneself.
SPECIAL INCOMPLETE PAST.	*Dal-jo̱ṅ-kan-tahēkan-khan*, Striking for oneself then.
INDECISIVE PLUPERFECT.	*Dal-an-tahēkan-khan,* Having struck for oneself.
DECISIVE PLUPERFECT.	*Dal-akao-an-tahēkan-khan*, Having struck for oneself.
INCHOATIVE FUTURE.	*Dal-jo̱ṅ-lagit'-khan*, Being about to strike for oneself.
INCHOATIVE PRESENT.	*Dal-jo̱ṅ lagidoḱ-kan-khan*, Being now about strike for to oneself.

INCHOATINE PAST.	*Dal-jọṅ lagidok-kan-tahēkan-khan.* Being then about to strike for one self.
CONDITIONAL.	*Dal-an-khan,* Striking or having struck for oneself.
CONDITIONAL PERFECT.	*Dal-akao-an-khan,* Having. (in case of) struck for oneself.
PRELIMINARY EXPOSTULATIVE.	*Dal-an-nahī,* Striking first for oneself.
PRELIMINARY PERSUASIVE.	*Dal-an-baṅ,* Striking first for oneself.
PRELIMINARY ADMISSIVE.	*Dal-an-ena,* Striking first for oneself.
PRELIMINARY PERFECT EXPOSTULATIVE.	*Dal-akao-an-nahī,* Having first struck for one self.
PRELIMINARY PERFECT PRESUASIVE.	*Dal-akao-an-baṅ.* Having first struck for oneself.
PRELIMINARY PERFECT ADMISSIVE.	*Dal-akao-an-ena,* Having first struck for oneself.
INFINITIVE.	*Dal-joṅ,* To strike for oneself

F. THE RESERVATIVE FORM.

ACTIVE. *FUTURE TENCE.*

INDICATIVE.	SUDJUNCTIVE with "*Khan*"	SUBJUNCTIVE with "*Paset*."
SINGULAR.	SINGULAR.	SINGULAR.
1 *Dal-ka-ṅ-a-e,* He will strike me (and leave† me.)	*Dal-ka-ṅ-khan-e* If he will strike me.	*Paset'-e dal-ka-ṅ,* Perhaps he will strike me.
2 *Dal-ka-m-a-e,* He will strike thee.	*Dal-ka-m-khan-e,* If he will strike thee.	*Paset'-e-dal-ka-m,* Perhaps he will strike thee.
3 *Dal-ka-e-a-e,* He will strike him.	*Dal-ka-e-khan-e,* If he will strike him.	*Paset'-e-dal-ka-e,* Perhaps he will strike him.

Note. The Neuter has no Reflective Dative.

* *As gọck'-kad-e-a-ṅ,* I killed him and left him, *kiriṅ-kad-e-aṅ,* I bought him and left him (did not take him with me.)

Dual.	**Dual.**	**Dual.**
1 *Dal-ka-liń-a-e*, He will strike us two.	*Dal-ka-liń-khan-e*, If he will strike us two.	*Paset'-e-dal-ka-liń*, Perhaps he will strike us two.
2 *Dal-ka-ben-a-e*, He will strike you two.	*Dal-ka-ben-khan-e*, If he will strike you two.	*Paset'-e-dal-ka-ben*, Perhaps he will strike you two.
3 *Dal-ka-kin-a-e*, He will strike them two.	*Dal-ka-kin-khan-e*, If he will strike them two.	*Paset'-e-dal-ka-kin*, Perhaps he will strike them two.
Plural.	**Plural.**	**Plural.**
1 *Dal-ka-le-a-e*, He will strike us.	*Dal-ka-le-khan-e*, If he will strike us.	*Paset'-e-dal-ka-le*, Perhaps he will strike us.
2 *Dal-ka-pe-a-e*, He will strike you.	*Dal-ka-pe-khan-e*, If he will strike you.	*Paset'-e-dal-ka-pe*, Perhaps he will strike you.
3 *Dal-ka-ko-a-e*, He will strike him.	*Dal-ka-ko-khan-e*, If he will strike them.	*Paset'-e-dal-ka-ko*, Perhaps he will strike them.
Neuter. *Dal-kak'-a-e*, He will strike it.	*Dal-kak'-khan-e*, If he will strike it.	*Paset'-e-dal-kak'*, Perhaps he will strike it.

SPECIAL INCOMPLETE PRESENT.

Singular.	**Singular.**	**Singular.**
1 *Dal-ka-ń-kan-a-e*, He is striking me.	*Dal-ka-ń-kan-khan-e*, If he is striking me.	*Paset'-e-dal-ka-ń-kan*, Perhaps he is striking me.
2 *Dal-m-kan-a-e*, He is striking thee.	*Dal-ka-m-kan-khan-e*, If he is striking thee.	*Paset'-e-dal-ka-m-kan*, Perhaps he is striking thee.
3 *Dal-ka-e-kan-a-e*, He is striking him.	*Dal-ka-e-kan-khan-e*, If he is striking him.	*Past'-e-dal-ka-e-kan*, Perhaps he is striking him.

Dual.	Dual.	Dual.
1 *Dal-ka-liń-kan-a-e,* He is striking us two.	*Dal-ka-liń-kan-khan-e,* If he is striking us two.	*Paset'-e-dal-ka-liń-kan,* Perhaps he is striking us two.
2 *Dal-ka-ben-kan-a-e,* He is striking you two.	*Dal-ka-ben-kan-khan-e,* If he is striking you two.	*Paset'-e-dal-ka-ben-kan,* Perhaps he is striking you two.
3 *Dal-ka-kin-kan-a-e,* He is striking them two.	*Dal-ka-kin-kan-khan-e,* If he is striking them two.	*Paset'-e-dal-ka-kin-kan,* Perhaps he is striking them two.
Plural.	**Plural.**	**Plural.**
1 *Dal-ka-le-kan-a-e,* He is striking us.	*Dal-ka-le-kan-khan-e,* If he is striking us.	*Paset'-e-dal-ka-le-kan,* Perhaps he is striking us.
2 *Dal-ka-pe-kan-a-e,* He is striking you.	*Dal-ka-pe-kan-khan-e,* If he is striking you.	*Paset'-e-dal-ka-pe-kan,* Perhaps he is striking you.
3 *Dal-ka-ko-kan-a-e,* He is striking them.	*Dal-ka-ko-kan-khan-e,* If he is striking them.	*Paset'-e-dal-ka-ko-kan,* Perhaps he is striking them.
Neuter. *Dal-ka-k'-kan-a-e,* He is striking it.	*Dal-ka-k'-kan-khan-e,* If he is striking it.	*Paset'-e-dal-ka-k'-kan,* Perhaps he is striking it.

RECENT PAST.

Singular.	Singular.	Singular.
1 *Dal-ka-d-iń-a-e,* He struck me (and left me).	*Dal-kad-iń-khan-e,* If he struck me.	*Paset'-e-dal-kad--iń,* Perhaps he struck me.
2 *Dal-kat'-me-a-e,* He struck thee.	*Dal-kat'-me-khan-e,* If he struck thee.	*Paset'-e-dal-kat'-me,* Perhaps he struck thee.
3 *Dal-kad-e-a-e,* He struck him.	*Dal-kad-e-khan-e,* If he struck him.	*Paset'-e-dal-kad-e,* Perhaps he struck him.

Dual.	**Dual.**	**Dual.**
1 *Dal-kat'-liń-a-e,* He struck us two.	*Dal-kat'-liń-khan-e,* If he struck us two	*Paset'-e-dal-kat'-liń,* Perhaps he struck us two.
2 *Dal-kat'-ben-a-e,* He struck you two.	*Dal-kat'-ben-khan-e,* If he struck you two.	*Paset'-e-dal-kat'-ben,* Perhaps he struck you two.
3 *Dal-kat'-kin-a-e,* He struck them two.	*Dal-kat'-kin-khan-e,* If he struck them two.	*Paset'-e-dal-kat'-kin,* Perhaps he struck them two.
Plural.	**Plural.**	**Plural.**
1 *Dal-kat'-le-a-e,* He struck us.	*Dal-kat'-le-khan-e,* If he struck us.	*Paset'-e dal-kat'-le,* Perhaps he struck us.
2 *Dal-kat'-pe-a-e,* He struck you.	*Dal-kat'-pe-khan-e,* If he struck you.	*Paset'-e-dal-kat'-pe* Perhaps he struck you.
3 *Dal-kat'-ko-a-e,* He struck them.	*Dal-kat'-ko-khan-e,* If he struck them.	*Paset'-e-dal-kat'-ko,* Perhaps he struck them.
Neuter. *Dal-kat'-a-e,* He struck it.	*Dal-kat'-khan-e,* If he struck it.	*Paset'e-dal-kat',* Perhaps he struck it.

PERFECT.

Singular.	**Singular.**	**Singular.**
1 *Dal-akad-iń-a-e,* He has struck me.	*Dal-akad-iń-khan-e,* If he has struck me.	*Paset'-e-dal-akad-iń,* Perhaps he has struck me.
2 *Dal-akat'-me-a-e,* He has struck thee.	*Dal-akat'-me-khan-e,* If he has struck thee.	*Paset'-e-dal-akat'-me,* Perhaps he has struck thee.
3 *Dal-akad-e-a-e,* He has struck him.	*Dal-akad-e-khan-e,* If he has struck him.	*Paset'-e-dal-akad-e,* Perhaps he has struck him.

DUAL.	**DUAL.**	**DUAL.**
1 *Dal-akat'-liń-a-e*, He has struck us two.	*Dal-akat'-liń-khan-e*. If he has struck us two.	*Paset'-e-dal-akat'-liń*, Perhaps he has struck us two.
2 *Dal-akat'-ben-a-e*, He has struck you two.	*Dal-akat'-ben-khan-e*, If he has struck you two.	*Paset'-e-dal-akat'-ben*, Perhaps he has struck you two.
3 *Dal-akat'-kin-a-e*, He has struck them two.	*Dal-akat'-kin-khan-e*, If he has struck them two.	*Paset'-e-dal-akat'-kin*, Perhaps he has struck them two.
PLURAL.	**PLURAL.**	**PLURAL.**
1 *Dal-akat'-le-a-e*, He has struck us.	*Dal-akat'-le-khan-e*, If he has struck us.	*Paset' e-dal-akat'-le*, Perhaps he has struck us.
2 *Dal-akat'-pe-a-e*, He has struck you.	*Dal-akat'-pe-khan-e*, If he has struck you.	*Paset-e-dal-akat'-pe*, Perhaps he has struck you.
3 *Dal-akat'-ko-a-e*, He has struck them.	*Dal-akat'-ko-khan-e*, If he has struck them.	*Paset'-e-dal-akat'-ko*, Perhaps he has struck them.
Neuter. *Dal-akat'-a-e*, He has struck it.	*Dal-akat'-khan-e*, If he has struck it.	*Paset'-e-dal-akat'*, Perhaps he has struck it.

SPECIAL INCOMPLETE PAST.

SINGULAR.	**SINGULAR.**	**SINGULAR.**
1 *Dal-ka-ń-kan-tahēkan-a-e*, He was striking me.	*Dal-ka-ń-kan-tahē-kan-khan-e*, If he was striking me.	*Paset'-e-dal-kań-kan-tahēkan*, Perhaps he was striking me.
2 *Dal-ka-m-kan-tahēkan-a-e*, He was striking thee.	*Dal-ka-m-kan-ta-hēkan-khan-e*, If he was striking thee.	*Paset'-e-dal-ka-m-kan-tahēkan*, Perhaps he was striking thee.
3 *Dal-ka-e-kan-takēkan-a-e*, He was striking him.	*Dal-ka-e-kan-ta-hēkan-khan-e*, If he was striking him.	*Paset'-e-dal-ka-e-kan-tahēkan*, Perhaps he was striking him.

	DUAL.	DUAL.	DUAL.
1	*Dal-ka-liń-kan-tahēkan-a-e,* He was striking us two.	*Dal-ka-lin-kan-tahēkan-khan-e*, If he was striking us two.	*Paset'-e-dal-ka-liń-kan-tahēkan,* Perhaps he was striking us two.
2	*Dal-ka-ben-kan-tahēkan-a-e,* He was striking you two.	*Dal-ka-ben-kan-tahēkan-khan-e,* If he was striking you two.	*Paset'-e-dal-ka-ben-kan-tahēkan,* Perhaps he was striking you two.
3	*Dal-ka-kin-kan-tahēkan-a-e,* He was striking them two.	*Dal-ka-kin-kan-tahēkan-khan-e,* If he was striking them two.	*Paset'-e-dul-ka-kin-kan-tahēkan,* Perhaps he was striking them two.
	PLURAL.	PLURAL.	PLURAL.
1	*Dal-ka-le-kan-tahēkan-a-e,* He was striking us.	*Dal-ka-le-kan-tahēkan-khan-e,* If he was striking us.	*Paset'-e-dal-ka-le-kan-tahēkan,* Perhaps he was striking us.
2	*Dal-ka-pe-kan-tahēkan-a-e,* He was striking you.	*Dal-ka-pe-kan-tahēkan-khan-e,* If he was striking you.	*Paset'-e-dal-ka-pe-kan-tahēkan,* Perhaps he was striking you.
3	*Dal-ka-ko-kan-tahēkan-a-e,* He was striking them.	*Dal-ka-ko-kan-tahēkan-khan-e,* If he was striking them.	*Paset'-e-dal-ka-ko-kan-tahēkan,* Perhaps he was striking them.
Neuter.	*Dal-kak'-kan-tahēkan-a-e,* He was striking it.	*Dal-ka-k'-kan-tahēkan-khan-e,* If he was striking it.	*Paset'-e-dal-k-kak'-kan-tahēkan,* Perhaps he was striking it.

INDECISIVE PLUPERFECT.

	SINGULAR.	SINGULAR.	SINGULAR.
1	*Dal-kad-iń-tahē kan-a-e,* He had struck me.	*Dal-kad-iń-tah-ē-kan-khan-e,* If he had struck me.	*Paset'-e-dal-kad-iń-tahēkan,* Perhaps he had struck me.
2	*Dal-kat'-me-tahē-kan-a-e,* He had struck thee.	*Dal-kat'-me-tahē-kan-khan-e,* If he had struck thee.	*Paset'-e-dal-kat'-me-tahēkan,* Perhaps he had struck thee.
3	*Dal-kad-e-tahē-kan-a-e,* He had struck him.	*Dal-kad-e-tahē-kan-khan-e,* If he had struck him.	*Paset'-e-dal-kad-e-tahēkan,* Perhaps he had struck him.
	DUAL.	DUAL.	DUAL.
1	*Dal-kat'-liń-tahēkan-a-e,* He had struck us two.	*Dal-kat'-liń-tahē-kan-khan-e,* If he had struck us two.	*Paset'-e-dal-kat'-liń-tahēkan,* Perhaps he had struck us two.
2	*Dal-kat'-ben-tahēkan-a-e,* He had struck you two.	*Dal-kat'-ben-tahē-kan-khan-e,* If he had struck you two.	*Paset'-e-dal-kat'-ben-tahē-kan,* Perhaps he had struck you two.
3	*Dal-kat'-kin-tahēkan-a-e,* He had struck them two.	*Dal-kat'-kin-tahē-kan-khan-e,* If he had struck them two.	*Paset'-e-dal-kat'-kin-tahēhan,* Perhaps he had struck them two.
	PLURAL.	PLURAL.	PLURAL.
1	*Dal-kat'-le-tahē-kan-a-e,* He had struck us.	*Dal-kat'-le-tahē-kan-khan-e,* If he had struck us.	*Paset'-e-dal-kat'-le-tahēkan,* Perhaps he had struck us.
2	*Dal-kat'-pe-tahē-kan-a-e,* He had struck you.	*Dal-kat'-pe-tahē-kan-khan-e,* If he had struck you.	*Paset'-e-dal-kat'-pe-tahēkan,* Perhaps he had struck you.
3	*Dal-kat'-ko-tahēkan-a-e,* He had struck them.	*Dal-kat'-ko-tahē-kan-khan-e,* If he had struck them.	*Paset'-e-dal-kat'-ko-tahē-kan,* Perhaps he had struck them.
Neuter.	*Dal-kat'-tahēkan-a-e,* He had struck it.	*Dal-kat'-tahē-kan, khan-e,* If he had struck it.	*Paset'-e-dal-kat'-tahē-kan,* Perhaps he had struck it.

DECISIVE PLUPERFECT.

	SINGULAR.	SINGULAR.	SINGULAR.
1	*Dal-akad-iń-tahēkan-a-e*, He had struck me.	*Dal-akad-in-tahēkan-khan-e*, If he had struck me.	*Paset'-e-dal-akad-iń-tahēkan*, Perhaps he had struck me.
2	*Dal-a-ka-t'-me-tahēkan-a-e*, He had struck thee.	*Dal-akat'-me-tahēkan-khan-e*, If he had struck thee.	*Paset'-e-dal-akat'-me tahēkan*, Perhaps he had struck thee.
3	*Dal-akad-e-tahēkan-a-e*, He had struck him.	*Dal-akad-e-tahēkan-khan-e*, If he had struck him.	*Paset'-e-dal-akad-e-tahēkan*, Perhaps he had struck him.
	DUAL.	DUAL.	DUAL.
1	*Dal-akat'-liń-tahēkan-a-e*, He had struck us two.	*Dal-akat'-liń-tahēkan-khan-e*, If he had struck us two.	*Paset'-e-dal-akat'-liń-tahēkan*, Perhaps he had struck us two.
2	*Dal-akat'-ben-tahēkan-a-e*, He had struck you two.	*Dal-akat'-ben-tahēkan-khan-e*, If he had struck you two.	*Paset'-e-dal-akat'-ben-tahē-kan*, Perhaps he had struck you two.
3	*Dal-akat'-kin-tahēkan-a-e*, He had struck them two.	*Dal-akat'-kin-tahē-kan-khan-e*, If he had struck them two.	*Paset'-e-dal-akat'-kin-tahēkan*, Perhaps he had struck them two.
	PLURAL.	PLURAL.	PLURAL.
1	*Dal-akat'-le-tahēkan-a-e*, He had struck us.	*Dal-akat'-le-tahēkan-khan-e*, If He had struck us.	*Paset'-e-dal-akat'-le-tahēkan*, Perhaps he had struck us.
2	*Dal-akat'-pe-tahēkan-a-e*, He had struck you.	*Dal-akat'-pe-tahēkan-khan-e*, If he had struck you.	*Paset-e-dal-akat'-pe-tahēkan*, Perhaps he had struck you.
3	*Dal-akat'-ko-tahēkan-a-e*, He had struck them.	*Dal-akat'-ko-tahēkan-khan-e*, If he had struck them.	*Paset'-e-dal-akat'-ko-tahēkan*, Perhaps he had struck them.
Neuter.	*Dal-akat'-tahēkan-a-e*, He had struck it.	*Dal-akat'-tahēkan-khan-e*, If he had struck it.	*Paset'-e-dal-akat'-tahēkan*, Perhaps he had struck it.

INCHOATIVE FUTURE.

SINGULAR.

1 *Dal-ka-ṅ-lagit'-e*, He will be about to strike me.

2 *Dal-ka-m-lagit'-e*, He will be about to strike thee.

3 *Dal-ka-e-lagit'-e*, He will be about to strike him.

DUAL.

1 *Dal-ka-liṅ-lagit'-e*, He will be about to strike us two.

2 *Dal-ka-ben-lagit'-e*, He will be about to strike you two.

3 *Dal-ka-kiṅ-lagit'-e*, He will be about to strike them two.

PLURAL.

1 *Dal-ka-le-lagit'-e*, He will be about to strike us.

2 *Dal-ka-pe-lagit'-e*, He will be about to strike you.

SINGULAR.

Dal-ka-ṅ-lagit'-khan-e, If he will be about to strike me.

Dal-ka-m-lagit'-khan-e, If he will be about to strike thee.

Dal-ka-e-lagit'-khan-e, If he will be about to strike him.

DUAL.

Dal-ka-liṅ-lagit'-khan-e, If he will be about to strike us two.

Dal-ka-ben-lagit'-khan-e, If he will be about to strike you two.

Dal-ka-kin-lagit'-khan-e, If he will be about to strike them two.

PLURAL.

Dal-ka-le-lagit'-khan-e, If he will be about to strike us.

Dal-ka-pe-lagit'-khan-e, If he will be about to strike you.

SINGULAR.

Paset'-e-dal-ka-ṅ-lagit', Perhaps he will be about to strike me.

Paset-e-dal-ka-m-lagit', Perhaps he will be about to strike thee.

Paset'-e-dal-ka-e-lagit', Perhaps he will be about to strike him.

DUAL.

Paset'-e-dal-ka-liṅ,-lagit', Perhaps he will be about to strike us two.

Paset'-e-dal-ka-ben-lagit', Perhaps he will be about to strike you two.

Paset'-e-dal-ka-kin-lagit', Perhaps he will be about to strike them two.

PLURAL.

Paset'-e-dal-ka-le-lagit', Perhaps he will be about to strike us.

Paset'-e-dal-ka-pe-lagit', Perhaps he will be about to strike you.

3 *Dal-ka-ko-lagit'-e*, He will be about to strike them.	*Dal-ka-ko-lagit'-khan-e*, If he will be about to strike them.	*Paset-e-dal-ka-ko-lagit'*, Perhaps he will be about to strike them.
Neuter. *Dal-kak-lagit'-e*, He will be about to strike it.	*Dal-ka-k-lagit'-khan-e*, If he will be about to strike it.	*Paset'-e-dal-kak-lagit'*, Perhaps he will be about to strike it.

INCHOATIVE PRESENT.

SINGULAR.	SINGULAR.	SINGULAR.
1 *Dal-ka-ń-lagidok-kan-a-e*, He is about to strike me.	*Dal-kań-lagidok-kan-khan-e*, If he is about to strike me.	*Paset'-e-dal-ka-ń-lagidok-kan*, Perhaps he is about to strike me.
2 *Dal-ka-m-lagidok-kan-a-e*, He is about to strike thee.	*Dal-ka-m-lagidok-kan-khan-e*, If he is about to strike thee.	*Paset'-e-dal-ka-m-lagidok-kan*, Perhaps he is about to strike thee.
3 *Dal-ka-e-lagidok-kan-a-e*, He is about to strike him.	*Dal-ka-e-lagidok-kan-khan-e*, If he is about to strike him.	*Paset'-e-dal-ka-e-lagidok-kan*, Perhaps he is about to strike him.
DUAL.	DUAL.	DUAL.
1 *Dal-ka-liń-lagidok-kan-a-e*, He is about to strike us two.	*Dal-ka-liń-lagidok-kan-khan-e*, If he is about to strike us two.	*Paset'-e-dal-ka-liń-lagidok-kan*, Perhaps he is about to strike us two.
2 *Dal-ka-ben-lagidok-kan-a-e*, He is about to strike you two.	*Dal-ka-ben-lagidok-kan-khan-e*, If he was about to strike you two.	*Paset'-e-dal-ka-ben-lagidok-kan*, Perhaps he is about to strike you two.
3 *Dal-ka-kin-lagidok-kan-a-e*, He is about to strike them two.	*Dal-ka-kin-lagidok-kan-khan-e*, If he is about to strike them two.	*Paset'-e-dal-ka-kin-lagidok-kan*, Perhaps he is about to strike them two.

Plural.	Plural.	Plural.
1 *Dal-ka-le-lagid-oḱ-kan-a-e,* He is about to strike us.	*Dal-ka-le-lagidoḱ-kan-khan-e,* If he is about to strike us.	*Paset'-e-dal-ka-le-la-gidoḱ-kan,* Perhaps he is about to strike us.
2 *Dal-ka-pe-lagid-oḱ-kan-a-e,* He is about to strike you.	*Dal-ka-pe-lagid-oḱ-kan-khan-e,* If he is about to strike you.	*Paset'-e-dal-ka-pe-la-gidoḱ-kan,* Perhaps he is about to strike you.
3 *Dal-ka-ko-lagid-oḱ-kan-a-e,* He is about to strike them.	*Dal-ka-ko-lagid-oḱ-kan-khan-e,* If he is about to strike them.	*Paset'-e-dal-ka-ko-la-gidoḱ-kan,* Perhaps he is about to strike them.
Neuter. *Dal-ka-ḱ-lagidoḱ-kan-a-e,* He is about to strike it.	*Dal-ka-ḱ-lagidoḱ-kan-khan-e,* If he is about to strike it.	*Paset'-e-dal-ka-ḱ-la-gidoḱ-kan,* Perhaps he is about to strike it.

INCHOATIVE PAST.

Singular.	Singular.	Singular.
1 *Dal-ka-ń-lagid-oḱ-kan-tahēkan-a-e,* He was about to strike me.	*Dal-ka-ń-lagidoḱ-kan-tahēkan-khan-e,* If he was about to strike me.	*Paset'-e-dal-ka-ń-lagidoḱ-kan-tahē-kan,* Perhaps he was about to strike me.
2 *Dal-ka-m-lagid-oḱ-kan-tahēkan-a-e,* He was about to strike thee.	*Dal-ka-m-lagi-doḱ-kan-tahē-kan-khan-e,* If he was about to strike thee.	*Paset'-e-dal-ka-m-lagidoḱ-kan-tahē-kan,* Perhaps he was about to strike thee.
3 *Dal-ka-e-lagid-oḱ-kan-tahēkan-a-e,* He was about to strike him.	*Dal-ka-e-lagidoḱ-kan-tahēkan-khan-e,* If he was about to strike him.	*Paset'-e-dal-ka-e-lagidoḱ-kan-tahē-kan,* Perhaps he was about to strike him.

DUAL..	DUAL.	DUAL.
1 *Dal-ka-liń-la-gidoḱ-kan-tahē-kan-a-e*, He was about to strike us two.	*Dal-ka-liń-la gid-oḱ-kan-tahē-kan-khan-e,* If he was about to strike us two.	*Paset'-e-dal-ka-liń-lagidoḱ-kan-tahē-kan,* Perhaps he was about to strike us two.
2 *Dal-ka-ben-la-gidoḱ-kan tahē-kan-a-e,* He was about to strike you two.	*Dal-ka-ben-lagid-oḱ-kan-tahē-kan-khan-e,* If he was about to strike you two.	*Paset'-e-dal-ka-ben-lagidoḱ-kan-tahē-kan,* Perhaps he was about to strike you two.
3 *Dal-ka-kin-lagidoḱ-kan-ta-hēkan-a-e,* He was about to strike them two.	*Dal-ka-kin-lagid-oḱ-kan-tahē-kan-khan-e,* If he was about to strike them two.	*Paset'-e-dal-ka-kin-lagidoḱ-kan-tahē-kan,* Perhaps he was about to strike them two.
PLURAL.	PLURAL.	PLURAL.
1 *Dal-ka-le-lagid-oḱ-kan-tahē-kan-a-e,* He was about to strike us.	*Dal-ka-le-lagid-oḱ-kan-tahē-kan-khan-e,* If he was about to strike us.	*Paset'-e-dal-ka-le-lagidoḱ-kan-tahē-kan,* Perhaps he was about to strike us.
2 *Dal-ka-pe-lagid-oḱ-kan-tahē-kan-a-e,* He was about to strike you.	*Dal-ka-pe-lagid-oḱ-kan-tahē-kan-khan-e,* If he was about to strike you.	*Paset'-e-dal-ka-pe-lagidoḱ-kan-tahē-kan,* Perhaps he was about to strike you.
3 *Dal-ka-ko-lagid-oḱ-kan-tahē-kan-a-e,* He was about to strike them.	*Dal-ka-ko-lagid-oḱ-kan-tahē-kan-khan-e,* If he was about to strike them.	*Paset'-e-dal-ka-ko-lagidoḱ-kan-tahē-kan,* Perhaps he was about to strike them.
Neuter. *Dal-kaḱ-lagidoḱ-kan-tahēkan-a-e,* He was about to strike it.	*Dal-ka-ḱ-lagidoḱ-kan-tahēkan-khan-e,* If he was about to strike it.	*Paset'-e-dal-ka-ḱ-lagidoḱ-kan-tahē-kan,* Perhaps he was about to strike it.

CONDITIONAL.

SINGULAR.	**SINGULAR.**	**SINGULAR.**
1 Is wanting.	*Dal-aka-ñ-khan-e*, If he has struck me.	*Paset'-e-dal-aka-ñ* Perhaps he has struck me.
2	*Dal-aka-m-khan-e*, If he has struck thee.	*Paset'-e-dal-aka-m*, Perhaps he has struck thee.
3	*Dal-aka-e-khan-e*, If he has struck him.	*Paset'-e-dal-aka-e*, Perhaps he has struck him.
DUAL.	**DUAL.**	**DUAL.**
1	*Dal-aka-liñ-khan-e*, If he has struck us two.	*Paset'-e-dal-aka-liñ*, Perhaps he has struck us two.
2	*Dal-aka-ben-khan-e*, If he has struck you two.	*Paset'-e-dal-aka-ben*, Perhaps he has struck you two.
3	*Dal-aka-kin-khan-e*, If he has struck them two.	*Paset'-dal-aka-kin*, Perhaps he has struck them two.
PLURAL.	**PLURAL.**	**PLURAL.**
1	*Dal-aka-le-khan-e*, If he has struck us.	*Paset'-e-dal-aka-le*, Perhaps he has struck us.
2	*Dal-aka-pe-khan-e*, If he has struck you.	*Paset'-e-dal-aka-pe*, Perhaps he has struck you.
3	*Dal-aka-ko-khan-e*, If he has struck them.	*Paset'-e-dal-aka-ko*, Perhaps he has struck them.
Neuter.	*Dal-akae-khan-e*, If he has struck it.	*Paset'-e-dal-aka-e*, Perhaps he has struck it.

CONTINGENT.

Singular.	Singular.	Singular.
1 *Dal-kad-iń-gi-e,* He strikes, will, or would strike me.		*Paset'-e-dal-kad-iń-gi,* Perhaps he strikes, will or would strike me.
2 *Dal-kat'-me-gi-e,* He strikes thee.		*Paset'-e-dal-kat'-me-gi,* Perhaps he will strike thee.
3 *Dal-kad-e-gi-e,* He strikes him.		*Paset'-e-dal-kad-e-gi,* Perhaps he will strike him.
Dual.	**Dual.**	**Dual.**
1 *Dal-kat'-liń-gi-e,* He strikes us two.		*Paset'-e-dal-kat'-liń-gi,* Perhaps he will strike us two.
2 *Dal-kat'-ben-gi-e,* He strikes you two.		*Paset'-e-dal-kat'-ben-gi,* Perhaps he will strike you two.
3 *Dal-kat'-kin-gi-e,* He strikes them two.		*Paset'-e-dal-kat'-kin-gi,* Perhaps he will strike them two.
Plural.	**Plural.**	**Plural.**
1 *Dal-kat'-le-gi-e,* He strikes us.		*Paset'-e-dal-kat'-le-gi* Perhaps he will strike us.
2 *Dal-kat'-pe-gi-e,* He strikes you.		*Paset'-e-dal-kat'-pe-gi,* Perhaps he will strike you.
3 *Dal-kat'-ko-gi-e,* He strikes them.		*Paset'-e-dal-kat'-ko-gi,* Perhaps he will strike them.
Neuter. *Dal-kat'-gi-e,* He strikes it.		*Paset'-e-dal-kat'-gi,* Perhaps he will strike it.

PRELIMINARY EXPOSTULATIVE

	Singular.	Dual.	Plural.
1	*Dal-aka-ṅ-nahī-e*, He must first strike me.	*Dal-aka-liṅ-nahī-e*, He must first strike us two.	*Dal-aka-le-na hī-e* He must first strike us.
2	*Dal-aka-m-na-hī-e*, He must first strike thee.	*Dal-aka-ben-na-hī-e*, He must first strike you two.	*Dal-aka-pe-nahī-e*., He must first strike you.
3	*Dal-aka-e-nahī-e*, He must first strike him.	*Dal-aka-kin-na-hī-e*, He must first strike them two.	*Dal-aka-ko-na hī-e-* He must first strike them.
	Neuter. *Dal-akae-nahī-e*, He must first strike it.		

PRELIMINARY PERSUASIVE.

	Singular.	Dual.	Plural.
1	*Dal-aka-ṅ-ba-e*, He must first strike me.	*Dal-aka-liṅ-ba-e*, He must first strike us two.	*Dal-aka-le-ba-e*, He must first strike us.
2	*Dal-aka-m-ba-e* He must first strike thee.	*Dal-aka-ben-ba-e*, He must first strike you two.	*Dal-aka-pe-ba-e*, He must first strike you.
3	*Dal-aka-e-ba-e*, He must first strike him.	*Dal-aka-kin-ba-e*, He must first strike them two.	*Dal-aka-ko-ba-e*, He must first strike them.
	Neuter. *Dal-aka-e-ba-e*. He must first strike it.		

PRELIMINARY ADMISSIVE.

	SINGULAR.	DUAL.	PLURAL.
1	*Dal-aka-ń en-a-e*, He must first strike me.	*Dal-aka-liń-en-a-e*, He must first strike us two.	*Dal-aka-le-e n - a - e*, He must first strike us.
2	*Dal-aka-m-en-a-e*, He must first strike thee.	*Dal-aka-ben-e n - a-e*, He must first strike you two.	*Dal-aka-pe-en - a - e* He must first strike you.
3	*Dal-aka-e-en-a - e*, He must first strike him.	*Dal-aka-kin-e n - a-e*, He must first strike them two.	*Dal-aka-ko-en - a - e*, He must first strike them.
	Neuter. *Dal-akae-ena*, He must first strike. it.		

BENEDICTIVE.

	SINGULAR.	DUAL.	PLURAL.
1	*Dal-ka-ń-ma-e!* May he strike me!	*Dal-ka-liń-ma-ko!* May they strike us two!	*Dal-ka-le-ma- k i n!* May they two strike us!
2	*Dal-ka-m-ma-ń!* May I strike thee!	*Dal-ka-ben- m a - le!* May we strike you two.	*Dal-ka-pe-ma- l i ń*, May we two strike you.
3	*Dal-ka-e-ma-m!* Mayest thou strike him.	*Dal-ka-kin- m a - pe!* May you strike them two!	*Dal-ka-ko-ma-b e n!* May you two strike them!
	Neuter. *Dal-kak-ma-e!* May he strike it.		

IMPERATIVE.

	SINGULAR.	DUAL.	PLURAL.
1	*Dal-ka- ń - m e!* Strike thou me!	*Dal-ka-liń-b e n!* Strike you two us two!	*Dal-ka-le-pe!* Strike you us.
3	*Dal-ka- e - m e!* Strike thou him!	*Dal-ka-kin- be n!* Strike you two them two!	*Dal-ka-ko pe!* Strike you them!
	Neuter. *Dal-kak-me!* Strike thou it.		

ADJECTIVE PARTICIPLES. (ANIMATE.)	GERUNDS.
FUTURE.	
Dal-ka-ń (ko, kin, pe, ben etc.,) Who will strike me (and leave me.)	*Dal-ka-ko-reaḱ, te, re,* Of, by, in striking them now.
GENERAL INCOMPLETE PRESENT.	
Dal-ka-liń-kan, Who is striking us two.	*Dal-ka-ko-kan-reaḱ, te, re,* Of, by, in striking them now.
RECENT PAST.	
Dal-kat'-le, Who struck us.	*Dal-kat'-ko-reak, te, re,* Of, by, in having struck them.
PERFECT.	
Dal-akat'-me, Who has struck thee.	*Dal-akat'-ko-reaḱ, te, re,* Of, by, in having struck them.
GENERAL INCOMPLETE PAST.	
Dal-ka-ben-kan tahēkan, Who was striking you two.	*Dal-ka-ko-kan-tahēkan-reaḱ, te, re,* Of, by, in striking them then.
INDECISIVE PLUPERFECT.	
Dal-kat'-kin-tahēkan, They two, whom they had struck.	*Dal-kat'-ko-tahēkan-reaḱ, te, re,* Of, by, in having struck them.
DECISIVE PLUPERFECT.	
Dal-akat'-ko-tahēkan, They, whom they had struck.	*Dal-akat'-ko-tahēkan,-reaḱ, te, re,* Of, by, in having struck them.
INCHOATIVE FUTURE.	
Dal-ka-e lagit', He, whom they will be about to strike.	*Dal-ka-ko-lagit'-reaḱ, te, re,* Of, by, in being about to strike them.
INCHOATIVE PRESENT.	
Dal-ka-ko-lagidoḱ-kan, They, whom they are about to strike.	*Dal-ka-ko-lagidoḱ-kan-reaḱ, te, re,* Of, by, in being *now* about to strike them.
INCHOATIVE PAST.	
Dal-ka-ko-lagidoḱ-kan-tahē-kan, They, whom they were about to strike.	*Dal-ka-ko-lagidoḱ-kan-takē-kan-reaḱ te, re,* Of. by, in being *then* about to strike them.
CONDITIONAL.	
Dal-aka-ko, They, whom they may have struck.	*Dal-aka-ko-reaḱ, te, re,* Of by, in having struck them.

ADVERBIA PARTICIPLES.

(ANIMATE.)

FUTURE.	*Dal-ka-ko- k h a n*, Striking them.
SPECIAL INCOMPLETING PRESENT.	*Dal-ka-kin-kan-khan*, Striking them two now.
RECENT PAST.	*Dal-kad- e - k h a n*, Having struck him.
PERFECT.	*Dal-akat'-me-khan*, Having struck thee.
SPECIAL INCOMPLETE PAST.	*Dal-ka-ń-kan-tahē-kan-khan*, Striking me then.
INDECISIVE PLUPERFECT.	*Dal-kat'-pe-tahēka n - k h a n*, Having struck you.
DECISIVE PLUPERFECT.	*Dal-akat'-le-tahēkan- k h a n*, Having struck us.
INCHOATIVE FUTURE.	*Dal-ka-ko-lagit'-khan*, Being about to strike them.
INCHOATIVE PRESENT.	*Dal-ka-ko-lagidok'-kan-khan*, Being now about to strike them.
INCHOATIVE PAST.	*Dal-ka ko-lagidok'-kan-tah ē-kan-khan*, Being then about to strike them.
CONDITIONAL.	*Dal-aka-ko- k h a n*, Having struck them (i. e. in case of.)
PRELIMINARY EXPOSTULATIVE.	*Dal-aka-ko- n a h ĩ*, Having first struck them.
PRELIMINARY PERSUASIVE.	*Dal-aka- k o - b a ṅ*, Having first struck them.
PRELIMIRARY ADMISSIVE.	*Dal-aka-ko-ena*, Having first struck them.
INFINITIVE.	*Dal-ka-(ko, kin, e e t c.,)* To strike them etc.

ADJECTIVE PARTICIPLES. (INANIMATE.)	GERUNDS.
FUTURE.	
Dal-kaḱ, Which they will Strike.	*Dal-kaḱ-reaḱ, te, re,* Of, by, in striking it.
SPECIAL INCOMPLETE PRESENT.	
Dal-ka-ḱ-kan, Which they are striking.	*Dal-kaḱ-kan-reaḱ, te, re,* Of, by, in striking it now.
RECENT PAST.	
Dal-kat', Which they struck.	*Dal-kat'-reaḱ, te, re,* Of, by, in having struck it.
PERFECT.	
Dal-akat', Which they have struck.	*Dal-akat'-reaḱ, te, re,* Of, by, in having struck it.
SPECIAL INCOMPLETE PAST.	
Dal-ka-ḱ-kan-tahēkan, which they were striking.	*Dal-kaḱ-kan-tahēkan-reaḱ, te, re,* Of, by, in striking it then.
INDECISIVE PLUPERFECT.	
Dal-kat'-tahēkan, Which they had struck.	*Dal-kat'-tahēkan-reaḱ, te, re,* Of, by, in having struck it.
DECISIVE PLUPERFECT.	
Dal-akat'-tahēkan, Which they had struck.	*Dal-akat'-tahēkan-reaḱ, te, re,* Of, by, in having struck it.
INCHOATIVE FUTURE.	
Dal-ka-ḱ-lagit', Which they will be about to strike.	*Dal-kaḱ-lagit'-reaḱ, te, re,* Of, by, in being about to strike it.
INCHOATIVE PRESENT.	
Dal-kaḱ-lagidoḱ-kan, Which they are about to strike.	*Dal-kaḱ, lagidoḱ kan-reaḱ, te, re,* Of, by, in being about to strike it now.
INCHOATIVE PAST.	
Dal-ka-ḱ-lagidoḱ-kan-tahēkan, Which they were about to strike.	*Dal-kaḱ-lagidoḱ-kan-tahēkan-reaḱ, te, re,* Of, by, in being about to strike it then.
CONDITIONAL.	
Dal-aka-e, Which they may have struck.	*Dal-akae-reaḱ, te, re,* Of, by in having struck it.

ADVERBIAL PARTICIPLES.

(INANIMATE.)

FUTURE.	*Dal-kaǩ-khan*, Striking it.
SPECIAL INCOMPLETE PRESENT.	*Dal-kaǩ-kan-khan*, Striking it *now*.
RECENT PAST.	*Dal-kat'-khan*, Having struck it.
PERFECT.	*Dal-akat'-khan*, Having struck it.
SPECIAL INCOMPLETE PAST.	*Dal-kaǩ-kan-tahēkan-khan*, Striking it *then*.
INDECISIVE PLUPERFECT.	*Dal-kat'-tahēkan-khan*, Having struck it.
DECISIVE PLUPERFECT.	*Dal-akat'-tahēkan-khan*, Having struck it.
INCHOATIVE FUTURE.	*Dal-kaǩ-lagit'-khan*, Being about to strike it.
INCHOATIVE PRESENT.	*Dal-kaǩ-lagidoǩ-kan-khan*, Being now about to strike it.
INCHOATIVE PAST.	*Dal-kaǩ-lagidoǩ-kan-tahēkan-khan*, Being then about to strike it.
CONDITIONAL.	*Dal-akae-khan*, Having struck (in case of.)
PRELIMINARY EXPOSTULATIVE.	*Dal-akae-nahī̃*, Having first struck it.
PRELIMINARY PERSUASIVE.	*Dal-akae-baṅ*, Having first struck it.
PRELIMINARY ADMISSIVE.	*Dal-akae-ena*, Having first struck it.
INFINITIVE.	*Dal-kaǩ*, To strike it.

G. RESERVATIVE FORM.

REFLEXIVE.

FUTURE TENSE.

	SINGULAR.	SINGULAR.	SINGULAR.
1	*Dal-koḱ-a-ń,* I will strike myself.	*Dal-koḱ-khan-iń,* If I will strike myself.	*Paset'-iń-dal-koḱ,* Perhaps I will strike myself.
2	*Dal-koḱ-a-m,* Thou wilt strike thyself.	*Dal-koḱ-khan-em,* If thou wilt strike thyself.	*Paset'-em-dal-koḱ,* Perhaps thou wilt strike thyself.
3	*Dal-koḱ-a-e,* He will strike himself.	*Dal-koḱ-khan-e,* If he will strike himself.	*Paset'-e-dal-koḱ,* Perhaps he will strike himself.
	DUAL.	DUAL.	DUAL.
1	*Dal-koḱ-a-liń,* We two will strike ourselves.	*Dal-koḱ-khan-liń,* If we two will strike ourselves.	*Paset'-liń-dal-koḱ,* Perhaps we two will strike ourselves.
2	*Dal-koḱ-a-ben,* You two will strike yourselves.	*Dal-koḱ-khan-ben,* If you two will strike yourselves.	*Paset'-ben-dal-koḱ,* Perhaps you two will strike yourselves.
3	*Dal-koḱ-a-kin,* They two will themselves.	*Dal-koḱ-khan-kin,* If they two will strike themselves.	*Paset'-kin-dal-koḱ,* Perhaps they two will strike themselves.
	PLURAL.	PLURAL.	PLURAL.
1	*Dal-koḱ-a-le,* We will strike ourselves.	*Dal-koḱ-khan-le,* If we will strike ourselves.	*Paset'-le-dal-koḱ,* Perhaps we will strike ourselves.
2	*Dal-koḱ-a-pe,* You will strike yourselves.	*Dal-koḱ-khan-pe,* If you will strike yourselves,	*Paset'-pe-dal-koḱ,* Perhaps you will strike yourselves.
3	*Dal-koḱ-a-ko,* They will strike themselves.	*Dal-koḱ-khan-ko,* If they will strike themselves.	*Paset'-ko-dal-koḱ* Perhaps they will strike themselves.

SPECIAL INCOMPLETE PRESENT.

	Singular.	Singular.	Singular.
1	*Dal-kok̓-kan-a-e,* He is striking himself.	*Dal-kok̓-han-hhan-e,* If he is striking himself.	*Paset'-e-dal-kok̓-kan,* Perhaps he is striking himself.

SPECIAL INCOMPLETE PAST.

1	*Dal-kok̓-kan-tahēkan-a-e,* He was striking himself.	*Dal-kok̓-kan-tahēkan-hhan-e,* If he was striking himself.	*Paset'-e-dal-kok̓-kan-tahēkan,* Perhaps he was striking himself.

PERFECT.

1	*Dal-akan-a-e,* He has struck himself.	*Dal-akan-khan-e,* If he has struck himself.	*Paset'-e-dal-akan,* Perhaps he has struck himself.

DECISIVE PLUPERFECT.

1	*Dal-akan-tahēkan-a-e,* He had struck himself.	*Dal-akan-tahēkan-kkan-e,* If he had struck himself.	*Paset'-e-dal-akan-tahēkan,* Perhaps he had struck himself.

INCHOATIVE FUTURE.

1	*Dal-kok̓-lagit'-e,* He will be about to strike himself.	*Dal-kok̓-lagit'-khan-e,* If he will be about to strike himself.	*Paset'-e-dal-kok̓-lagit',* Perhaps he will be about to strike himself.

INCHOATIVE PRESENT.

1	*Dal-kok̓-lagidok̓-kan-a-e,* He is about to strike himself.	*Dal-kok̓-lagidok̓-kan-khan-e,* If he is about to strike himself.	*Paset'-e-dal-kok̓-lagidok̓-kan,* Perhaps he is about to strike himself.

INCHOATIVE. PAST

1	*Dal-kok-lagid-ok-han-tahē-kan-a-e*, He was about to strike himself.	*Dal-kok-lagidok-kan-tahē kan-khan-e*, If he was about to strike himself.	*Paset'-e-dal-kok-la-gidok-kan-tahēkan*, Perhaps he was about to strike himself.

PRELIMINARY EXPOSTULATIVE.

	SINGULAR.	DUAL.	PLURAL.
1	*Dal-akan-nahī-ń*, I must first have struck myself.	*Dal-akan-na hī-liń*, We two must first have struck ourselves.	*Dal-akan-na hī-le*, We must first have struck ourselves.

PRELIMINARY PERSUASIVE.

1	*Dal-akan-ba-ń*, I must first have struck myself.	*Dal-akan-ba-liń*, We two must first have struck ourselves.	*Dal-akan-ba-le*. We must first have struck ourselves.

BENEDICTIVE.

2	*Dal-kok-ma-m!* Mayest thou strike thyself!	*Dal-kok-ma ben!* May you two strike yourselves!	*Dal-kok-ma-pe*, May you strike yourselves!

IMPERATIVE.

2	*Dal-kok-me!* strike thyself!	*Dal-kok-ben!* You two strike yourselves!	*Dal-kok-pe!* You strike yourselves!

ADJECTIVE PARTICIPLES.	GERUNDS.
FUTURE.	
Dal-kok (kin, ko, pe ete), Who will strike himself. *	*Dal-kok-reak, te. re*, Of, by, in striking oneself.
SPECIAL INCOMPLETE PRESENT.	
Dal-kok-kan, Who is striking himself.	*Dal-kok-kan-reak, te, re*, Of, by, in striking oneself now.

* Or themselves etc.

SPECIAL INCOMPLETE PAST. *Dal-koḱ-kan-tahēkan*, Who was striking himself.	*Dal-koḱ-kan-tahēkan-reaḱ, te, re,* Of, by, in striking oneself then.
PERFECT. *Dal-akan,* Who has struck himself.	*Dal-akan-reaḱ, te, re,* Of, by, in having struck oneself.
DECISIVE PLUPERFECT. *Dal-akan-tahēkan,* Who had struck himself.	*Dal-akan-tahēkan-reaḱ, te, re,* Of, by, in having struck oneself.
INCHOATIVE FUTURE. *Dal-koḱ lagit',* Who will be about to strike himself.	*Dal-koḱ, lagit'-reaḱ, te, re,* Of, by, in being about to strike oneself.
INCHOATIVE PRESENT. *Dal-koḱ-lagidoḱ-kan,* Who is about to strike himself.	*Dal-koḱ-lagidoḱ-kan-reaḱ, te, re,* Of, by in being now about to strike oneself.
INCHOATIVE PAST. *Dal-koḱ-lagidoḱ-kan-tahēkan,* Who was about to strike himself.	*Dal-koḱ-lagidoḱ-kan-tahēkan-reaḱ, te, re,* Of, by, in being then about to strike oneself etc.

ADVERBIAL PARTICIPLES.

FUTURE.	*Dal-koḱ-khan,* Striking himself or themselves etc.
SPECIAL INCOMPLETE PRESENT.	*Dal-koḱ-kan-khan,* Striking himself now.
SPECIAL INCOMPLETE PAST.	*Dal-koḱ-kan-tahēkankhan,* Striking himself then.
PERFECT.	*Dal-akan-khan,* Having struck himself.
DECISIVE PLUPERFECT.	*Dal-akan-tahēkan-khan,* Having struck himself.

INCHOATIVE FUTURE.	*Dal-kok-lagit'-khan.* Being about to strike himself.
INCHOATIVE PRESENT.	*Dal-hok-lagidok-kan-khan,* Being now about to strike himself.
INCHOATIVE PAST.	*Dal-kok-lagidok-kan-tahēkan-khan,* Being then about to strike himself.
PRELIMINARY EXPOSTULATIVE.	*Dal-akan-nahī,* Having first struck himself.
PRELIMINARY PERSUASIVE.	*Dal-akan-baṅ,* Having first struck himself.
PRELIMINARY ADMISSIVE.	*Dal-akan-ena,* Having first struck himself.
INFINITIVE.	*Dal-kok,* To strike oneself.
INFINITIVE PERFECT.	*Dal-akan.* To have struck oneself.

IMPERSONAL VERB.

FUTURE.

Tetaṅ-iṅ-a, I shall be thirsty (lit it will thirst me.)

GENERAL INCOMPLETE PRESENT.

Tetaṅ-ed-iṅ-a, I am thirsty.

SPECIAL INCOMPLETE PRESENT.

Tetaṅ-ed-iṅ-kan-a, I am now thirsty.

RECENT PAST.

Tetaṅ-ked-in-a, I was thirsty.

ANTERIOR PAST.

Tetaṅ-led-iṅ-a, I was thirsty.

GENERAL INCOMPLETE PAST.

Tetaṅ-ed-iṅ-tahēkan-a, I used to be or was thirsty.

SPECIAL INCOMPLETE PAST.

Tetaṅ-ed-iṅ-kan-tahēkan-a, I was then thirsty.

INDECISIVE PLUPERFECT.

Tetaṅ-led-iṅ--tahēkan-a, I had been thirsty.

Remark. As impersonal verbs are conjugated in the same way as an active verb in the accusative case (vide page 182) it will not be necessary here to write out the full paradigm.

CHAPTER VI.

OF ADVERBS, POSTPOSITIONS, CONJUNCTIONS AND INTERJECTIONS.

SECTION I —OF ADVERBS.

I. Of time.

Nit, nitok'do, now.
Nahak', presently, soon, (the same day.)
Dara, soon.
Auri, soon, not yet.
Hapen, soon, (not the same day.)
Dhinań, after mid-day.
N'ebētar, now-a-days.
Tehengapa, at present.
Barsiṅorsiń, for the present.
Enanṅok're, a little while ago.
Enbetar, at that time.
Enań, a while ago.
Onre, then.
Onkhon, thence.
Onjok'heck', then, at that time.
Enhilok', on that day.
Teheń, to-day.
Gapa, to-morrow.
Meań, the day after tomorrow.
Endrae, three days hence.
Pher endrae, four days hence.
Hola, yesterday.
Mahnder, the day before yesterday.
Onmahnder, three days ago.
Pahapoho, at the first dawn.
Aṅga, at dawn.
Setak', in the morning.
Berrakap', at sunrise.
Baskeak', at 9 A. M.
Basiam, at 10½ A. M.
Tekin, at 12 noon.
Tekinlorak', at 1 P. M.
Marańtarasiń, at 2 P. M.
Tarasiń, at 3 P. M.
Marańdak'lober, at 4 P. M.
Hudińdak'lober, at 5 P. M.
Jhikjhikaok're, at sunset.
Ayup', evening, at dusk, or nightfall.
Kedok' jom, at 9 P. M.

Singār, at 10 P. M.
Ninda, at night.
Tala ninda, at midnight.
Ghaṭaoninda, at 1 A. M.
Nes, this year.
Kalom, next year.
Satom, two years hence.
Phersatom, three years hence.
Dinkalom, last year.
Holkalom, two years ago.
Mūhkalom, three years ago.
Tis ? when?
Tinre ? when ? (at what time of the day.)
Tis jokeck ? at what time ?
Tinjokheck, at what time (of the day.)
Oka, hilok ? what day ?
Jahatisre, whenever (not to-day.)
Jahatinre, when, at any time (of the day.)
Jahatisjahatis, now and then.
Tishõ, at any time.
Tishõban, at no time.
Tishõ alo, at no time(prohibiting
Tishõ oho, at no time (assuring.)
Sedaere, formerly, in past times.
Jaoge jaoge, repeatedly, always.
Jao hilok, every day, always.
Sinsaṭup', the whole day.
Jaejug, in all ages, always.
Maransimrak, first cock crowing.
Hudinsimrak, second cock crowing.
Dinhilak, day after day, every day.
Pahil, before.
Lahare, before.
Maranre, before.
Tis habick ? how long ? (not to day.)
Tin habick ? how long ? (to day.)
Nin habick, so much as this.
In habick, so much as that.
On habick, so much as that.
Nonhabick, so much as this.
Mit'dhao, once.
Ar mit'dhao, once more.
Mit'din, one day.
Bar sin, two days.
Pe mūhū, three days.
Mit' chando, one month.
Mit' serma, one year.

II. Of Place.

Noṅḍe, here (nearest.)
Oṇḍe, there (further off, or absent).
Hoṇḍe, there (still further off).
Haṇḍe, yonder, (furthest off.)
Note, in this way.
Onte, in that way.
Honte, in that way.
Hante, in that way.
Notere, in this place,
Ontere. in that place.
Hontere, in that place.
Hantere, in yonder place.
Neṅḍe, here (nearest).
Eṇḍe, there (further off,)
Heṇḍe, there (furthest off).
Nete, in this way or direction.
Ente, in that way.
Hente, in that way.
Netere, in this place.
Entere. in that place.
Hentere, in that place.
Okare? where?
Okate? in what direction?
Okasen? Okaseck? in what direction?
Okaṭhen? near what place, or thing?
Okaṭhenre? in the vicinty of what?
Okakhon? whence?
Jahãre, wherever.
Samaṅre, before.
Lahare, maṛaṅre, before.
Sanamṭhen, every where.
Sanamṭaṇḍire, every where.
Okarehõbaṅ, no where.
Beṛhaere, all round.
Muchat're, at the end, finally.
Rachare, outside.
Chotre, above.
Chetanre, upon.
Latare, below.
Noasa, this side.
Hanasa, that side.
No, on, hon, han-parom, on this or that side.
Ne, en, hen-parom, on this or that side.

III. Of Manner and Quality &c.

Nọnka, as this.
Ọnka, as that.
Họnka, as that.
Hanka, as that.
Nẹnka, as this.
Ẹnka, as that.
Hẹnka, as that.
Ninka, as this.
Inka, as that.
Hinka, as that.
Chet'leka? how?
Noaleka, like this, in this manner.
Onaleka, in that manner.
Honaleka, in that manner.
Hanaleka, in that manner.
Nialeka, like this, in this manner.
Inaleka, in that manner.
Hinaleka, in that manner.
Tinak'? how much?
Onak', as much as that.
Nonak', as much as this.
Ninak', as much as this.
Inak', as much as that.

Aḍi, uḍi, much.
Aḍiutạr, very much.
Kaṭich'ktalañ, a little.
Nasenase, a very little.
Baebaete, very gently, slowly.
Hakopako, very quickly.
Dihredihre, very slowly.
Saṭmente, quickly.
Eskar, alone.
Eken, only.
Mit'teqi, together.
Begar begar, seperately.
Otọñ-tainom, one after another.
Sarigi, truly, really, indeed.
Auṛipathauṛi, thoughtlessly, at random.
Onkate, gratis.
Magnite, (Hindi) by request.
Dulaṛkate, lovingly.
Jọrmọṭkate, forcibly.
Eṛekate, falsely.
Algate, easily.
Ote, ọtechoñ, even, just, exactly.
Behaj, extraordinarily, very much.

IV. Of affirmation, and negation.

Hoi, yes.
hẽ yes.
hũ, yes.
ba, baṅ, not, no (asserting.)
alo! not (entreating.)
oho, not (assuring.)

SECTION II—OF POSTPOSITIONS.

Re, in, on, at, while.
Te, into, in, by.
Ṭhen, at, to, by.
Khon, from.
Seck, towards, for.
Sen, towards, for.
Lagit', for.
Lagat', for.
Hotete, through.
Iate, on account of.
Tuluck, with.
Gate, with.
Saõte, with.
Begor, without, except.
Dhabick, till, until, as far as.
Dharick, till, as far as.
Harick, till, as far as.
Mente, for, in order.
Phedre, near.
Sorre, near.
Samaṅre, before, in front.
Maraṅre, before, (time and place.)
Lahare, before (time and place.)
Tayomre, *Tayomte*, behind, after.
Talare, *Motore* in the midst of, among.
Leka, according to.
Reak, *Reaṅ*, about, concerning.
Tarire, under,
Latare, under.
Chetanre, above.

SECTION III—OF CONJUNCTIONS.

Among the principle conjunctions are the following :—

a. Copulatives.

Ar, and ; *ado*, and ; *hõ*, also.

Adverbs are declined like nouns ; as *re-khon* from in ; *ṭhen-khon* from near etc.

b. Disjunctives.

Se, or ; *bańkhan*, or else ; *bańdo—bańdo*—whether—or ; *bichkom*, rather; *hõbań*, nor;—*hõbań—hõbań*, neither—nor.

c. Adversatives.

Menkhan, but ; *enrehõ*, yet ; *rehõ—enrehõ*, although—still

d. Conjunctives.

Adomadom—adomadom, partly—partly.

Jahatisjahatis—jahatisjahatis—sometimes—sometimes.

Eken-bańa-menkhan-hõ, not only—but also ; *hõ—hõ*—as well as also—

e. Causals.

Ente, for ; *te*, *teroń*, *khan*, because, as.

f. Conclusives.

Eṇḍekhan, then ; *onate*, therefore ; *iate*, therefore.

g. Comparatives.

—*Khon*, than ; *leka*, as ; *chet'leka*, *as*.

h. Temporals.

Khan, as ; *khangi*, then.

i. Conditionals.

Khan, if ; *kutkeck*, if, in case.

Concessives.

Rehõ, although.

Finals or Conclusives.

Khajuk, that, in order that, so that.

SECTION IV.—OF INTERJECTIONS.

Interjections in Sonthali are very numerous. Among the principal are the following :—

a. Of Calling.

1. (Addressing men), *e̜!, e̜ho! hĕnda! Henda ho! e̜ go!* ho! holla! firrah!
2. (To women). *e̜* go! *e̜ ayo! ho!* hark!
3. (To young men). *e̜* a! *e̜ baba! ho!* hear! oh!
4. (To young women). *e̜ mo̜i! e̜ na! ho!* hear! oh!

b. Of Surprize and Admiration.

Ayoge! Durre! Uh! Baba re! oh, my! dear me!

c. Of Silence.

Hape! Thirok' me! Hape-kok'-pe! Baibo̜i-pe! hush! be quiet!

d. Of Aversion.

Chho̜i! Cho̜ire! Chhi! fie! for shame!

e. Of Grief and Pain.

Haere! Haerehaere! O haere! Hae, Haehae! ah! *Jarejare!* ah! alas! o sad! woe is me!

f. Of Warning.

Men! Menya! So̜nto̜rme! take care!

g. Of Encouragement.

Ma ma! Bugi bugi! well well!

h. Of Threatening.

Hape! take care! *Bhala!* well, we will see

CHAPTER. VII.

ON THE DERIVATION, AND COMPOSITION OF WORDS.

All words are, in regard to their formation, either *(a)* Primitive, or *(b)* Derivative, (or *c)* Composite.

A. ON THE DERIVATION OF WORDS.

SECTION I.—OF NOUNS.

Nouns are formed from other nouns, adjectives, verbs, and adverbs.

I. By affixing to the word any of the case-signs of the nouns, with the suffixes *ick̕*, *kin*, *ko* (he, they two, they.)

II. By affixing to the word the suffixes *ak̕ ak̕kin*, *ak̕ko*, with or without *tet'* [it, they two, they (things.)]

III. By affixing to the word the suffixes *ick̕ kin*, *ko*.

IV. By leaving the word unaltered and using it as a noun.

V. By affixing to the word the suffix *tet'*.

VI. By affixing *n* to the word.

VII. By infixing *p* after the first syllable of the word, with a vowel homonymous to that of the first syllable.

a. Nouns derived from Nouns.

These are formed:

I. By affixing to any noun the Genitive, Dative, Ablative, or Instrumental case-sign with the personal suffixes *ick̕*, *kin*, *ko*; and the impersonal suffixes *ak̕*, *ak̕kin*, *ak̕ko*, (with or without *tet'*). Each of these may be re-declined like a Nominative, the respective oblique cases of which may again be re-declined.

I. PERSONAL FROM PERSONAL NOUNS.

GENITIVE.

Nom.	*Paṇḍu-ren-ich',*	She of Pandu.
Gen.	*Paṇḍu-ren-ich'-ren-ko,*	Those of her of Pandu.
Instr.	*Paṇḍu-ren ich'-hoṭeten-ko,*	Those by her of Pandu.
Dat.	*Paṇḍu-ren-ich'-ṭhen-ko,*	Those with her of Pandu.
Abl.	*Paṇḍu-ren-ich'-khon-ko,*	Those from her of Pandu.

INSTRUMENTAL.

Nom.	*Paṇḍu-hoṭeten-ich',*	He (or she) by Pandu.
Gen.	*Paṇḍu-hoṭeten-ich'-ren-ko,*	Those of him by Pandu.
Instr. is wanting.		
Dat.	*Paṇḍu-hoṭeten-ich'-ṭhen-ko,*	Those with him by Pandu.
Abl.	*Paṇḍu-hoṭeten-ich'-khon-ko,*	Those from him by Pandu.

DATIVE.

Nom.	*Paṇḍu-ṭhen-ich',*	He (or she) with Pandu.
Gen.	*Paṇḍu-ṭhen-ich'-ren-ko,*	Those of him with Pandu.
Instr.	*Paṇḍu-ṭhen-ich'-hoṭeten-ko,*	Those by him with Pandu.
Dat. is wanting.		
Abl.	*Paṇḍu-ṭhen-ich'-khon-ko,*	Those from him with [Pandu.

Remark. 1 The Accusative is like the Nominative.

Remark. 2 *Gamhar-ren-ko-ṭhenko-khon noa do hech'akana,* this has come from those (staying) with those of gambar village, is actually used.

Ablative.

Nom.	*Panḍu-khon-ich,*	He (or she) from Pandu.
Gen.	*Panḍu-khon-ich-ren-ko,*	Those of him from Pandu.
Instr.	*Panḍu-khon-ich-hoteten-ko,*	Those by him from Pandu.
Dat.	*Panḍu-khon-ich-ṭhen-ko.*	Those with him from Pandu

Abl. is wanting.

II. IMPERSONAL FROM PERSONAL NOUNS.

Genitive.

Nom.	*Panḍu-ak,* (or akkin, or akko,)*	That (or those two, or those things) of Pandu.
Gen.	*Panḍu-ren-ko ak,*	That of those of Pandu.
Instr.	*Panḍu-ren-ko-hotete-ak,*	That by those of Pandu.
Dat.	*Panḍu-ren-ko-ṭhen-ak,*	That with those of Pandu.
Abl.	*Panḍu-ren-ko-khon-ak,*	That from those of Pandu.

Instrumental.

Nom.	*Panḍu-hotete-ak,*	That by Pandu.
Gen.	*Panḍu-hoteten-ko-ak,*	That of those by Pandu.
Instr.	is wanting.	
Dat.	*Panḍu-hoteten-ko-ṭhen-ak,*	That with those by Pandu.
Abl.	*Panḍu-hoteten-ko-khon-ak,*	That from those by Pandu.

Dative.

Nom.	*Panḍu-ṭhen-ak,*	That with Pandu.
Gen.	*Panḍu-ṭhen-ko-ak,*	That of those with Pandu.
Instr.	*Panḍu-ṭhen-ko-hotete-ak,*	That by those with Pandu.
Dat.	is wanting.	
Abl.	*Panḍu-ṭhen-ko-khon-ak,*	That from those with Pandu.

* *or aktet', aktet'kin, aktet'ko,*

ABLATIVE.

Nom.	*Paṇḍu-khon-ak',*	That from Pandu.
Gen.	*Paṇḍu-khon-ko-ak',*	That of those from Pandu.
Instr.	*Paṇḍu-khon-ko-hoṭete-ak',*	That by those from Pandu.
Dat.	*Paṇḍu-khon-ko-ṭhen-ak',*	That with those from Pandu.

Abl. is wanting.

III. PERSONAL FROM IMPERSONAL NOUNS.

GENITIVE.

Gen.	*Paṇḍu-ak'-ren-ko,*	Those of that (land etc.) of Pandu.
Instr.	*Paṇḍu-ak'-ten-ko,**	Those (caught etc.) by that (hook) of Pandu.
Dat.	*Paṇḍu-ak'-ṭhen ko,*	Those with (near) that of Pandu.
Abl.	*Paṇḍu-ak'-khon-ko,*	Those from that (country) of Pandu.

INSTRUMENTAL.

Gen.	*Paṇḍu-hoṭete-ak'-ren-ko,*	Those of that (ship etc.) (made) by Pandu.
Instr.	Is wanting.	
Dat.	*Paṇḍu-hoṭete ak'-ṭhen-ko,*	Those with (near) that by Pandu.
Abl.	*Paṇḍu-hoṭete-ak'-khon-ko,*	Those from that by Pandu.

Remark. Sometimes it is necessary to affix *tet'* after *ak'*, in order to distinguish the noun from an adjective; as, *Paṇḍu-ak'-tet' do bań ńel akat'a* I have not seen that of Pandu.

* This is also used extensively as a Dative, denoting the movement towards something; as *Buru-ten-ko,* those, who go to the hills; *Dak'-ten-ko,* those moving to the water.

DATIVE.

Gen.	*Paṇḍu ṭhen ak-ren-ko,*	Those of that (land etc.) near Pandu.
Instr.	*Paṇḍu-ṭhen-ak-ten-ko,*	Those (fishes) (caught) by that (hook) with Pandu.
Dat. Is wanting,		
Abl.	*Paṇḍu-ṭhen-ak-khon-ko,*	Those from that (river) near Pandu.

ABLATIVE.

Gen.	*Paṇḍu-khon-ak-ren-ko,*	Those of that (ship) from Pandu.
Instr.	*Paṇḍu-khon-ak-ten-ko,*	Those by that (hook) from Pandu.
Dat.	*Paṇḍu-khon-ak-ṭhen-ko,*	Those near that from Pandu.
Abl. Is wanting.		

IV. IMPERSONAL FROM IMPERSONAL.

GENITIVE.

Gen.	*Paṇḍu-ak-reak,*	That of that of Pandu.
Instr.	*Paṇḍu-ak-te-ak,*	That by that of Pandu.
Dat.	*Paṇḍu-ak-ṭhen-ak,*	That with (near) that of Pandu.
Abl.	*Paṇḍu-ak-khon ak.*	That from that of Pandu.

Remark. Land, country, ship, hook, fish etc., are put in brackets, in order to show how the different cases may be applied; as *amem laakat' gadiaren hako buko naprak'a, Paṇḍu-hotete-ak'-renko giko naprak'-a,* the fishes of the tank which you have dug are not large, those of that (tank) (dug) by Pandu are large.

INSTRUMENTAL.

Gen.	*Paṇḍu-hotete-reak̕,*	That of that by Pandu.
Instr. Is wanting.		
Dat.	*Paṇḍu-hotete-ṭhen-ak̕;*	That near (or with) that by Pandu.
Abl.	*Paṇḍu-hotete-khon-ak̕,*	That from that by Pandu.

DATIVE.

Gen.	*Paṇḍu-ṭhen-ak̕-reak̕,*	That of that with (or near) Pandu.
Instr.	*Paṇḍu-then-ak̕-te-ak̕,*	That by that near (or with) Pandu.
Dat. Is wanting.		
Abl.	*Paṇḍu-ṭhen-ak̕-khon-ak̕.*	That from that with (near) Pandu.

ABLATIVE.

Gen.	*Paṇḍu-khon-ak̕-reak̕,*	That of that from Pandu.
Instr.	*Paṇḍu-khon-ak̕-te-ak̕,*	That by that from Pandu.
Dat.	*Paṇḍu-khon-ak̕-ṭhen-ak̕,*	That near that from Pandu.
Abl. Is wanting.		

Among the preceding may be counted ·

a. PATRONYMICS.

These are formed by affixing the genitive inflexion with the pronominal suffixes *ich̕, kin, ko;* as *Paṇḍu,-ren-ko,* the sons, or descendants of Pandu.

b. Gentiles.

These are formed in the same manner as Patronymics; as *Champa-ren-ko,* the inhabitants of Champa; *Sikhar-ren-ko,* the inhabitants of Sikhar; *Jambṛo-ren-ko,* the inhabitants of *Jambṛo* (village).

c. Possessives *(Neuter).*

These are formed by affixing *k̉, ak̉,* or *ak̉teṫ* to the word; as *Paṇḍu-ak̉,* that of Paṇḍu; *Buru-ak̉,* that of the mountain; *Manjhi-ak̉,* the work of the head-man.

II. By inserting *p* after the first syllable with a vowel homonymous to that of the first syllable; as,

Collectives.

Manjhee, a village-head-man. *Ma-pa-njhi-ko,* a collection of village-head-men; *Raj,* a king. *Ra-pa-j-ko,* a collection of kings.

III. By affixing to the word *hoṗoṇ;* as,

Diminutives.

Dhiri, a stone, *dhir-hoṗoṇ,* a little stone; *Oṛak̉,* a house, *Oṛak̉ hoṗoṇ,* a little house; *Kumba,* a hut, *Kumba-hoṗoṇ,* a little hut.

IV. By affixing to the word *teṫ*; *as,*

Abstracts.

Ṭhakur-teṫ-iṅ badae-orom-akaṫ-tae-a, I have asertained his divinity (from *Ṭhakur,* God).

Manwa-tet' baṅ bujhau-let'-tae a, boṅga-leka-gi-ṅ aikau-kedea, I could not discover his humanity (any humanity in him) I thought him to be a god.

V. By infixing *t* or *n* after the first syllable with a vowel homonymous to that of the first syllable ; as, *ṅu-tu-m,* a name (from *ṅum,* to call by name). *Lu-tu-r,* the ear (from *lur,* to hear ; but which is lost in the Sonthal language). (Compare *lur-e,* to listen, in Danish and *laur-en,* in German).
U-nu-m, immersion, (From *um,* to bathe).
Da-na-pal, a cover, (from *dapal,* to cover:)
Ha-na-rup', a cover, (from *harup'* to cover up.)
E-to-hop', beginning, (from *ehop'* to commence.)
Su-nu-m, oil, may belong to this class ; but *sum* does not exist in Santhali.

Besides these there are a few words formed by prefixing *a* ; as *a-ṅu,* to give to drink *(trænken)* from *ṅu,* to drink. *A-jo,* to feed, (from *jom* to eat.)

The formations of this fifth class are very few.

b. Nouns derived from Adjectives.

Nouns are formed from adjectives in four ways :

I. By affixing the impersonal affixes *ak', ak'kin, ak'ko ;* as

a. Inanimate Concretes.

Hende-ak' iṅ hataoa, I will take the black (things)
Ketech'-ak'kin iṅ hataoa, I will take the two hard (things.)
Arak'-ak'-ko gi bugia, The red ones are good.

II. By affixing the personal suffixes *ich', kin, ko ;* as,

b. Animate Concretes.

Hende-ko iñ hatao ko a, I will take the black ones (Beings.)
Pond-kin bugi do bañ kan akin, The two white ones are not good.

III. By affixing *tet'* ; as,

c. Abstracts.

Hende-tet', The blackness.
Pond-tet', The whiteness.
Marañ-tet', The greatness.

IV. By using the adjective as a Noun ; as, *Nunak' hamal-te bae langak'-a' ?* Will he not get tired by such a weight ?

e. Nouns derived from Verbs.

Nouns are formed from verbs by affixing the impersonal affixes *ak', akkin, akko,* the personal suffixes *ich', kin, ko,* and the substantive suffix *tet'* to any verbal base, or adjective participle, in any tense, case, voice or form.

a. From the uninflected verbal Bases.

Get'-ak' (akkin, akko),	The cut thing.
Get'-ich' (kin, ko),	The cut Being.
Get'-tet',	The cut (itself.)
Get'-ocho-ak',	The thing caused to be cut.
Get'-ocho-ich',	The Being caused to be cut.

Remark. When duality is required to be expressed *kin* is added to the *ak'*; and when Plurality, then *ko* is affixed to show the inanimate Noun ; as *get'-ak' kin,* the two cut things ; and substituting *kin,* or *ko* for *ich'* to show the animate Noun.

Get'-ocho-tet',	The caused cut (itself.)
Gedok-ak,	The thing to be cut.
Gedok-ich,	The Being, who will cut himself.
Ge-dok-tet',	The cutting oneself.
Get'-ochok-ak,	The thing to be caused to be cut.
Get'-ochok-ich,	The Being to be * caused to be cut.
Get'-ochok-tet',	The about-to-be caused cut.†
Geget'-ak, (akkin, akko,)	The cutting thing.
Geget'-ich, (kin, ko,)	The cutting Being=the cutter.
Geget'-tet',	The cutting (itself.)
Get'-okcho-ak,	The thing causing to be cut.
Get'okcho-ich,	The Being causing to be cut.
Get'okcho-tet',	The causing to be cut.
Geget'okcho-ak,	The thing causing to cut.
Geget'okcho-ich,	The Being causing to cut.
Geget'okcho-tet',	The causing to cut.
Gedogok-ak-(akkin, akko,)	The thing to be cut.
Gedogok-ich,	The Being, who will cut himself.
Gedogok-tet',	The cutting oneself.
Get'ochogok-ak,	The thing to be caused to be cut.
Get'ochogok-ich,	The Being about to let himself be cut.
Get'ochogok-tet',	The letting oneself to be cut.

* Or the Being, who will let himself be cut.

† Or the about-to-let-oneself be cut.

Gepet'-ak̄kin,	The two things cut together.
Gepet'-kin,	The two Beings, who have cut one another.
Gepet'-tet',	The (mutual) cut (itself.)
Gepet'ocho-ak̄kin,	The two things caused to cut or be cut together.
Gopet'ocho-kin,	The two Beings caused to cut one another.
Gopet'ocho-tet',	The being caused to cut together, or one another.
Gepedok̄-ak̄kin,	The two things to be cut together.
Gepedok̄-kin,	The two Beings who will cut one another.
Gepedok̄-tet',	The being about to cut together, or one another.
Gepet'ochok̄-ak̄kin,	The two things to be caused to cut together.
Gepet'ochok̄-kin,	The two Beings to be caused to cut one another.
Gepet'ochok̄-tet',	The being about to be caused to cut together or one another.
G.k̄pet'-ak̄kin,	The two things which will cut together.

Remark. In the above manner any adjective participle of any tense case or form may be formed into a Noun; as *Dal-ket'-ko-a-kin* they two, struck them—*Dal-ket'-ko-kin,* they (two) who struck them; *Mak'-akat'-a-e,* he has cut—*Mak'-akat'-ak'kin* the two things which have been cut.

Verbs formed from any of the cases of the nouns may again be re-formed into nouns in the above manner; as *Paṇḍu-then-ko,* they near Pandu—*Paṇḍu-then-ok'-kan-ko,* those who are joining Pandu.

Geǩpet'-ich,	The Being who will cut (something) together.
Geǩpet'-tet',	The cutting together.
Gepet'-oǩocho-aǩ,	That which causes to be cut together or cut one another.
Gepet'oǩcho-ich,	He who causes to be cut together or cut one another.
Gepet'oǩcho-tet',	The causing to be cut together, or to cut one another.
Geǩpet'oǩcho-aǩ,	That which causes to cut together.
Geǩpet'oǩcho-ich,	He who causes to cut (something else) together.
Geǩpet'oǩcho-tet',	The causing to cut together.

b. From the Inflected Adjective Participles.

Ṅur-ad-e-aǩ, That which fell upon him (Dat.)
Get'-akat'-aǩ, That which they have cut.
Get'-akat'-ko, They, who have cut or been cut.
Ṅel-let'-ko-kin, They two who saw them.
Dadal-kan-ko, They who are striking.
Sereṅlagidoǩkan-ko, They, who are about to sing.
Dhasao-en-aǩ, That which fell down (house.)
Rorakat'-aǩ, That which has been spoken.

c. From Verbs formed from the substantive cases.

Paṇḍu-ṭhen-oǩ-kan-ko, They, who are going over to Pandu.
Paṇḍu-ren-ked-e-ko, They who made him Pandu's.
Hor-ten-akad-e-ko, They who have sent him (out) on the road.

N̓ur-akan-tahen-ak̓, That which has fallen.

At'-len-tae-ak̓, That which is his, which was lost (but found again.)

The cases may be declined and made verbs of *ad libitum,* and such verbs may again be formed into Nouns, as shown above, and re-declined *ad infinitum.* Each tense in its participial form is a verbal base, and may be converted into a Noun by affixing, *ak̓, ick̓, or tet'.*

d. Nouns derived from Adverbs.

Nouns are formed from Adverbs either by affixing *ak̓, ak̓kin, ak̓ko, ick̓, kin,* and *ko,* or by inserting *n* between the adverb and the above terminations.

a. WITHOUT THE INSERTION OF *n.*

N̓it'-ak̓. That of now (Germ. *Das. Jetzige*) (from *nit',* now.)

N̓it'-ko, Those of now (Germ. *Die Jetzigen.*)

Teheń-ak̓, That of today (Germ. *Das. Heutige*) (from *teheń,* to day.)

Teheń-ko, Those of today (Germ. *Die Heutigen.*

Meań-ak̓, That of the day after to morrow (Germ. *Das. Uebermorgende*) (from Meań the day after tomorrow.)

Meań-ko, Those of the day after tomorrow (Germ *Die Uebermorgenden.*)

b. WITH THE INSERTION OF *n.*

N̓ọṇḍe-n-ak̓, That of this place *(Das Hiesige)* (from *nọṇḍe* here.)

N̓ọṇḍe-n-ko, Those of this place *(Die Hiesigen.)*

Ọṇḍe-n-ak̓, That of that place *(Das Dortige)* (from *ọṇḍe,* there.)

Oṇḍe-n-ko, Those of that place *(Die Dortigen.)*

Hoṇḍe-n-ak̕, That of that place *(Das Dortige)* (from *hoṇḍe* there.

Hoṇḍe-n-ko, Those of that place *(Die Dortigen.)*

Haṇḍe-n-ak̕, That of that place *(Das. Dortige.)* (from *haṇḍe,* yonder.)

Haṇḍe-n-ko, Those of that place *(Die Dortigen.)*

Hola-n-ak̕, That of yesterday *(Das Jestrige.)* (from *hola,* yesterday.)

Hola-n-ko, Those of yesterday *(Die Jestrigen.)*

Hĕ-ak̕, That which is promised (from *hĕ* yes.)

SECTION II.—OF PRONOUNS.

Pronouns are formed in the following ways:

1st. Personal pronouns take the prefix *a,* which means it, or it is; as *a-ko,* it is they; *a-(i)ch̕,* it is he. (This *ch̕* is a contraction of *ich̕,* he, as *ń* is a contraction of *iń,* I,); as, *Dal-a-ko,* to strike it is they=they will strike.

2nd. Demonstrative pronouns are formed from demonstrative bases and the abridged personal pronouns; as,

No-i, This (from *no,* here, and *i,* he=here he=this)

On-kin, Those two, (from *on,* there, and *kin,* they two.)

Hon-ko, Those (from *hon,* yonder, and *ko,* they.)

Han-a, That (from *han,* yonder. and *a,* it.)

Remark. Nouns may be formed from Prepositions by affixing *n*; as *chetanre,* above, upon *chetan-re-n-ko,* those above.

These are however nouns in the genetive case, and may be treated as such.

3rd. Demonstrative pronouns of similarity are formed from the other demonstrative pronouns by affixing *ka*, like, with a *n*, and in certain instances adding *a n* to the demonstrative base; as,

No-n-ka-n, Such as this (from *no* and *ka.*)
On-ka-n, Such as that (from *on* and *ka.*)
Ni-n-ka-n, Such as this (from *ni* and *ka.*)
Hi-n-ka-n, Such as that (from *hin* and *ka.*)

The derivation of pronouns as well as adverbs presents very much, that is interesting and assists considerably in tracing and comparing Santhali with other languages.

SECTION III.—OF ADJECTIVES.

Adjectives are formed from Nouns, other Adjectives, Verbs and Adverbs.

a. Adjectives formed from Nouns.

Adjectives are formed from Nouns:

1*st.* By affixing the impersonal suffixes *ak̃, ak̃kin, ak̃ko,* and the personal suffixes *kin* and *ko* to any of the five cases (Genitive, Instrumental, Dative, Ablative and Locative) in connection with the Nouns (vide formation of Nouns from Nouns); as,

Paṇḍu-ren-kiñ hoṛon, The two sons of Pandu.
Hasa-reak̃ kaṇḍa, The earthen vessel (from *hasa*, earth.)
Ṭhakur-hoṭete-n-ko hoṛ, Men (created) by God=God-created men.
Paṇḍu-ṭhen-ko peṛa, The friends with Pandu.

Panḍu-khon-ko peṛa, The friends, from Pandu.
Sadom-te-n-ko hoṛ, The men on horse-back.

2nd. By affixing *an* (possessed of) to a Noun; as,

Up'-an hoṛ, A hairy man=a man with hair.
Daṛe-an, Having strenght=strong (from *Daṛe* strenght.)
Herel-an, Having a husband (from *herel,* a man.)
Sakam-an dare, A tree having leaves (from *Sakam,* leave.)
Achel-an hoṛ, A man possessing riches=rich.

3rd. By affixing *lek, leka, lekan;* as,

Pargana-lek Dahṛi, a hat (topi, turban) meet for a District-chief.

Kuṛi-leka-ti, a hand like that of a girl (Germ. *jungfräuliche.)*

Ạimại-lekan hoṛ, a man like a woman=womanish.

4th. By affixing *selet';* as

Hasa-selet' buluṅ, salt mixed with earth.
Harket-selet'-rạskạ, joy mixed with trouble.

5th. By affixing postpositions and adverbs; [*ad libitum*]; as

Buru-chetan ato, a village upon a hill
Aksar-begor hoṛ, a man without bow and arrows.
Dare-latar hoṛ a man under a tree.
Panḍu tayom hoṛ the man after Pandu.

6th. By using Nouns adjectively; as,

Bir ṭhãi a jungly, or woody place (from *bir,* forest)
Botor ṭhãi, a dangerous place (from *botoṛ,* fear)

Remark. An, lek, leka, lekan, selet' are mostly in use in forming adjectives from Nouns, hence they have been treated separately from the other particles. *Re, te, khon, then* (in the formation of the cases) are nothing more than postpositions.

Umul ṭhũi, a shadowy place (from umul, shadow.)
Daṛe hoṛ a strong man (from *daṛe*, strength, power)

b. Adjectives formed from other Adjectives.

Adjectives are formed from other adjectives by affixing *lek*, *leka*, *lekan*, *Machha*, *ṅoḱ*, *an* and *selet'* ; as,

Huḍiń-lek-hoṛ, a person worthy to te deemed small.
Huḍiń- lekan * *hoṛ*, a person appearing small
Huḍiń-machha hoṛ, a person rather small.
Huḍiń-ṅoḱ hoṛ, a person rather small (less in degree than the the above.)
Hende-lekan merom, a black-looking goat.
Hende-machha merom, a dark-some goat.
Hende-ṅoḱ merom, a goat, which is a little dark
Hende-an merom, a goat with black spots.
Hende-selet'-araḱ sadom, a dark-red horse.

c. Adjectives formed from Verbs.

Adjectives are formed from verbs :

1st. By dropping the final *a* of any tense in any case, voice, form, gender and number (vide formation of Nouns from verbs) ; as,

Dal-hoṛ a struck man (from *dal* to strike)
Dal-oḱ hoṛ a person about to strike himself
Dadal hoṛ, a striking man.
Dapal hoṛ, a fighting man
Dal-ochoḱ hoṛ, a person to be struck.
Ṅam-og-oḱ, obtainable (from *ṅam* to find)

* *leka* for inanimate and *lekan* for animate Nouns.

Dal-ked-e-ko hoṛ, the men, who struck him.
Dal-e-kin hoṛ, the two men, who will strike him.
Ran-ad-e-tae-ko ojha, the doctors who gave medicine to him, who is his.
Dal-iń-lagit' hoṛ, the person about to strike me.
Gock' akad-e hoṛ, the person whom they have killed.
Ńel-og-ok', visible (from ńel, to see.)

2nd. By affixing *lek*, or *leka*, or *lekan* to any of the adjective participles; as
Dal-e-lek hoṛ, a person worthy to be struck.
Gock'-lekan hoṛ, a person like dead.

d. ADJECTIVES FORMED FROM ADVERBS AND POSTPOSITIONS.

Adjectives are formed from adverbs in the same manner as Nouns are (which see) viz. by affixing *ak'*, *akkin*, and *ko* with an insertion of *n* in some cases and in others without it; as

Nonḍe-n-ko hoṛ, the people of this place (from *nonḍe* here)
Teheń-ko hoṛ, the people of to day
Enbetar-ko hoṛ, the people of former times.
Hola-n-ak' roṛ, the word of yesterday (*Das gestrige Wort*).
Chetan-ko hoṛ, the persons upon or above.

SECTION IV.—OF VERBS.

Verbs are formed from Nouns, Adjectives, Adverbs and Postpositions and by affixing voice, case, form, tense-signs and the pronominal suffixes:—in short, Nouns, Adjectives, Adverbs and Postpositions may all be treated as verbal bases.

a. Verbs formed from Nouns.

Hoṛ-ked-e-a-ń, I have made a man of him.

Hoṛ-ok'-kan-a-e, he is becoming a man.

Dahṛi-ad-e-ań, I provided him with a hat.

Bahu-an-a-e, he took to himself a wife.

Bohu-ocho-ad-e-a-kin, they two allowed him to take a wife.

Hoṗoṇ-ked-e-ań, I made him (my) son, *i. e.*, gave him existence.

Paṇḍu- ṭhen-ked-e-ań*, I made him (to be) with Pandu.

Paṇḍu-ren-akad-e-ako, they have made him (to be) Pandu's,

Paṇḍu-ṭhen-ok'-kan-a-e, he is going over to Pandu's (opinion etc.)

b. Verbs formed from Adjectives.

Hende-ket'-a-ń, I made it black.

Hende-k'-kan-a, it is becoming black.

Hende-ad-e-a-ń, I put black on him.

Marań-ochok'-kan-a-e, he is being made great.

c. Verbs formed from Adverbs.

Hẽ-ket'-a-e, he said yes, confessed, or consented.

Hẽ-ad-e-a-ko, they said yes to him, promised him.

Bań-ket'-a-e, he said no, denied.

Bań-ad-e-a-ko, they said no to him, refused him.

Bań-at'-tiń-a, it made no to mine, *i. e.*, I would not.

Note-ked-e-a-ń, I removed him hither.

Hante-akad-e-a-ko, they have removed him thither.

Chet'leka-ked-e-a-pe? What have you done with him.

---

* Any of the cases in connection with the Nouns may be treated as a verbal base.

d. Verbs formed from Postpositions.

Tuluj-ok-kan-a-e, he is going to accompany (*tuluch,* with.)
Sej-ok-kan-a-e, he is drawing near (*sech* towards.)
Tayom-tek-kan-a-e, he is getting behind (*tayom te* behind.)
Laha-te-k-kan-a-e, he is getting in front.

SECTION V.—OF ADVERBS.

Adverbs are formed from other parts of speech :

1st. By affixing *te, kate, leka,* and *gi.*

2nd. By doubling the word itself.

3rd By inserting *ke* between two words or a doubled one.

4th. By prefixing or affixing various particles to other words, in order to form adverbs of time and place.

a By affixing *te, kate, leka* and *gi;* as,

Alga-te ńam-ok-a, it can *easily* be had (*alga,* easy, light.)
Phasiara-kate e hataoket'a, he took it deceitfully (*phasiara* to deceive.)
Herel-leka sahaok-me! Suffer like a man=in a manly way.
Sari-gi-ń ńel-laka, I really saw it (from *sari,* true, real.)

b. By doubling the Word.

Herem-herem e rora, he speaks sweetly (*herem,* sweet.)

c. By infixing *ke.*

Siń-ke-siń, day by day.
Siń-ke-ńinda, day and night.
Chando-ke-chando, month after month.

d. By prefixing or affixing certain particles to other words in order to form adverbs of time and place.

Nonde, here (from *non*, here and *di*, place.)
Onde, there (from *on* there, and *di*, place.
Note, hither (from *no* here, and *te*, to.)
Hante, thither (from *han*, yonder, and *te*, to.)
Ende, there (from *en*, there, and *di*, place.)
Nete, thither (from *ne*, here, and *te*, to.)
Nebetar, now-a-days (from *ne*, this, and *batar*, time.)
Enbetar, at that time (from *en*, that, and *batar*, time.)
Endrae, three days ago (from *en*, that, and *darae*, approach.)
Hol-a, yesterday (from *hol past*, and *a*, *it*, that.)
Sam-an-re, before (from *sam*, front, *an*, of, and *re*, in.)

B. On the Composition of Words.

Compound words, especially verbs, are of very frequent occurrence in Santhali, and they afford great facility for expressing one self with ease and precision.

They are principally of three kinds, namely, *Compound Nouns*, *Compound Adjectives* and *Compound Verbs.*

I. COMPOUND NOUNS.

These are of two kinds: 1st., Nouns joined to Nouns, and 2nd adjectives joined to Nouns; as.

a. Nouns joined to Nouns.

Manjhi-era, the village chief's wife, (from *Manjhi*) chief, and *era*, wife.

Oṛak-boṅga, a house-god (*oṛak*, house, *boṅga*, a god.)

Ato-manjhi, the village Manjhee (*ato* a village.)

b. Adjectives joined to Nouns.

Maraṅ-buru, the great height, or great mountain.

II. COMPOUND ADJECTIVES.

These are of two kinds ; 1st., Nouns preceding adjectives, and 2nd., Adjectives joined to other adjectives ;

a. Nouns preceding Adjectives.

Ṭhakur-ḅarabari, equal with God.

b. Adjectives joined to Adjectives.

Hendẹ-arak, black-read=brown.

III. COMPOUND VERBS.

Such verbs are formed : 1st. By joining a verb and a noun; 2nd., By joining a verb and an adjective; 3rd., by joining two verbs; 4th., By joining a verb to an adverb 5th., By joining a verb and a postposition ; 6th., By affixing certain particles to the verbs ; as

a, Verbs joined to Substantives.

Asul-hoṛ-ked-e-a-ṅ, bringing him up I made a man of him.

Dal-lẹṭẹck-ket'-ko-a-e, striking them he subdued them.

b. Verbs joined to Adjectives.

Dal-hendẹ-ked-e-a-m, thou didst strike him black.

Arup'-ponḍ-ket'-a, he washed it white.

c. Verbs joined to Verbs.

Dal-ṅir-ked-e-a-e, he made them run by striking them.
Halaṅ-samṭao, to pick up (from *halang* to take up.)

d. Verbs joined to Adverbs.

Dal-noṭe-keṭ'-a-e, he struck it hither.
Jok̇ hante-keṭ'-a-e, he swept it hither.

e. Verbs joined to Postpositions.

Dal-tuluch̆-ked-e-a-ko, they made him to join by striking him.

f. Verbs joined to certain Particles.

The most frequent of these are *dara, tora, oṭo, agu, hoṭ', goṭ', ṅok̇, baṛich̆, boṭech̆; as,*

Dal-dara-kad-e-a-ṅ, I struck him in coming.
Dal-tora-kad-e-a-ko, they struck him in going (away.)
Dal-oṭo-kad-e-ko, they struck him and left him behind.
Anjom-ague-me! Go and hear (and bring the heard back.)
Ṅel-agui-me! Go and see (and report about the things seen.)
Dal-goṭ'-ked-e-a-ko, they struck him immediately.
Dal-hoṭ'-ked-e-a-ko, they struck him quickly.
Dal-ṅok̇-ked-e-a-ko, they struck him a little.
Dal-baṛich̆-kad-e-a-ko, they almost struck him.
Dal-boṭech̆-ke-ṅ-a-ko, they might perhaps strike me.

These particles are used very extensively and idiomatically. The meaning of *dara* is, that something takes place in coming, or in the course of time up to the time in which it is spoken; *tora,* means that something takes place in going away from a certain place; *oṭo,* means that something is done and left behind in that state; *agui*, means that one shall go to another place and effect something and bring the result back; *gọt'*, means, immediately; *họt'*, means quickly; *ńok̕*, means a little; *baṛick̕*, means almost; and *bọtẹok̕*, means possibly.

It should be borne in mind that the *last* word of the compound verb is inflected, not the first. This appears natural in most cases; but in connection with certain words it is perplexing at first; as,

Ńel-gọck̕-ked-e-a-ń, I saw him die.
Ńel-kombṛo-ked-e-a-ń, I saw him steal.

This would at first appear to mean: seeing (him) I killed him—seeing (him) I stole him, as *gọck̕-ked-e-a-ń* means I killed him, and *kombṛo-ked-e-a-ń*, I stole him; but the meaning is of course *Ńel-ked-e-a-ń*, *gọck̕* (*gojok̕*) I saw him die.

The following examples will serve to illustrate the manner in which Santhal verbs are joined and used: *Get'-topa*, to cut off; *ńel-tap'*, to see through; *chapat'giḍi*, to throw away; *laga-oḍok̕*, to drive out; *kuṭam-ader*, to strike in or into *(einschlagen)*; *ọr-oṛẹck̕*, to tear in pieces; *sen-ọtọn*, to go after=follow.

There are other compound verbs, as the "Jingling verbs," in which the first word is the real, and the second only a kind of echo: as, *akut'-bakut'*, etc. Here *akut'* is the real word and means to be in a hurry.

PART II.

SYNTAX.

CHAPTER I.

OF SUBJECT AND PREDICATE.

As the reader is supposed to be acquainted with Grammar, and consequently to know that a proposition consists of a subject and predicate; that the subject is either grammatical or logical; that the grammatical subject is either a noun or some other word used substantively (as pronouns, adjectives, infinitives, etc.); that the logical subject consists of the grammatical subject with its modifications; that the subject is either simple or compound; that it may be modified by a noun, or by an adjective; that the Predicate likewise is either grammatical or logical; that it may be either simple or compound; that it may be modified by a noun or adjective; etc.: it is therefore hardly necessary to say much about the agreement of subject and Predicate; still, as every language has some peculiarities, it may not be out of place to make a few remarks.

SECTION I.—OF THE SUBJECT.

The Santhal language has the peculiarity, in regard to the subject of a sentence, that the suffixes are always added to the subject-noun.

a. SIMPLE SUBJECT.

Paṇḍu-e chalaoen a, Pandu he went away; *Oṛak̕ ńuren-a,* the house it fell down.

b. SUBJECT MODIFIED BY A NOUN IN THE SAME CASE; as, *Ale Pargana ko le chalak̕-a,* we Parganas we will go.

c. SUBJECT MODIFIED BY A NOUN IN THE GENITIVE; as, *Paṇḍu-reak̕ duluṛ marań-a,* the love of Pandu is great. *Hoṛko-reak̕ edre baṛae orom-en-a,* the anger of the people was apparent.

d. SUBJECT MODIFIED BY AN ADJECTIVE; as, *Bugi hoṛko ko hech̕-en-a,* the good people came.

SECTION II.—OF THE PREDICATE.

This is either a verb alone, or the *copula* "*kana*" with a noun, adjective, adverb or postposition.

a. SIMPLE PREDICATE; as, *Hejuk̕-a-e,* he will come; *Chalao-en-a-ko,* they went away.

b. PREDICATE MODIFIED BY A NOUN; as, *Rińjaule eṇech̕-a,* we will play *Rinjau* (a game).

c. PREDICATE MODIFIED BY AN ADVERB; as, *Jaoge-e hejuk̕-a,* he always comes.

d. PREDICATE MODIFIED BY AN ADJECTIVE; as, *Marań ńelok̕kanae,* he appears great

---

Remark. The adjectives may of course be modified by adverbs, which again may be modified by other adverbs, etc.

SECTION III.—OF CONGRUENCE.

a. Concord of the Verb with its Nominative.

The verb, when in connection with the common gender, agrees with the subject noun, which stands in the nominative, in gender, number, and person;* as *Paṇḍu-e-chalao-en-a,* Pandu, he went away; *herelkin kin hecḱ-en-a,* the two men they have come; *qimqiko ko sen-en-a,* the women have gone—but when the verb stands in the neuter gender, it shows neither number nor person; as *oṛaḱ-dhasao-en-a,* the house fell down; *oṛaḱ kin* (not a second *kin.* as is the case in the common gender,) *dhasao-en-a,* the two houses fell down; *oṛaḱko dhasao-en-a,* the houses fell down.

Several subjects regarded collectively always take respectively plural suffixes, and the verb is always in the plural; as, *sadomko, ḍaṅrako, setako, sukriko-ko gocḱ-en-tiń-a,* my horse, oxen, dog and pig have died. It is not at all necessary in Santhali that there should be more than one horse, &c., in order to affix the plural suffix to each subject respectively.

A collective noun is always followed by the verb in the plural, as, *horgad ko hejuḱ-kan-a,* the multitude they are coming, *i. e.,* the multitude is coming.

If among many subjects one is to be rendered prominent, *that* subject is put in the instrumental case and takes

* With the exception of, when the subject-noun is put in apposition to either 1st and 2nd person dual or plural; for in this case the noun takes the suffix of the 3rd person, as *herelko-le,* or *herelko-pe hech'-en-a,* we or you men have come.

the plural suffix, as, *Pargana-te-ko ko heck-en-a*, the Pargana with others came.

If there be more than one nominative of different persons, then they are all put in the instrumental case and take the 1st person dual or plural in the verb; as *am-te, iń-te, oni-tebon chalak a*, you, I and he, we will go.

b. CONCORD OF THE ADJECTIVE WITH THE SUBSTANTIVE.

Many adjectives terminating in *a* take *i* in the feminine gender; as *koṅka herel*, a foolish man; *koṅki qimqi*, a foolish woman.

When the two subjects differ as to sex, and form their predicate by an adjective terminating in *a*, then the adjective is always repeated denoting the respective genders; as *Koṛa Koṛiko aḍi ko koṅka koṅki akana*, the boys and girls have become very foolish.

The adjectives may take the dual or plural suffixes; but then the suffixes are generally omitted from the substantives; as, *am-ren-kin koṛa aḍikin hara-en-a*, your two boys have grown very much. But the adjective and adjective pronouns generally undergo no change, the substantive assuming for the most part the suffixes.

The participles however in the oblique cases always take the infixes. (*Vide* participles.)

When the genitive case takes the suffix *ick* and stand substantively, it denotes a feminine; as, *Panḍu-ren-ick*, she who is the wife of Pandu. This is not the case when *ik* is affixed to other cases. (*Vide* page 33.)

e. Concord of the relative with its Antecedent.

As a rule in Santhali, the relative pronoun, which, when in the common gender, is either a personal or a demonstrative suffix or interrogative pronoun used relatively, precedes the correlative; as, *Onkoko hech̀-len, onko doko okaena?* What has become of them who came (here); *Okoekoko chalak̀-a, onko baṛe ko roṛma,* let them speak, who will go; *Hani-m dal-kede, oni baṛe ń el-e-me,* have a look at him whom you struck; *Onẹ-m men-ket',* that which you said; *Onẹ kin ko ideket',* those two things which they took away. *(Vide* page 38.)

The relative and correlative pronouns agree in number and gender with their nouns.

The Participles are most extensively used as relatives; as, *dal-le-ko hoṛ,* those persons whom they may strike, *ńel-led-e-m,* (he) whom you saw.

The correlative very often follows immediately after the relative; as, *onẹ ona-m agu-ket',* that which you brought; *nok̀oe noa,* that which;

At other times the correlative is put last in the sentence, as, *Oni ko dal-ked-e, oni, kangiae,* he whom they struck, he it is; *ẹn serma-m ńel-lede, oni kan gi-a-e,* he is the man whom you saw at that time.

CHAPTER II.

OF NOUNS AND CASES.

SECTION I—THE NOMINATIVE AND VOCATIVE CASES.

a. THE NOMINATIVE.

The nominative is the case of the subject; as, *Pandu-e-ruaḱ-kan-a*, *Pandu* is sick; *kuṛiko doko hecḱ-ena*, the girls have come.

b. THE VOCATIVE.

The vocative is the case of address; as *E, Pandu!* oh *Pandu!*

Ayo-go! Oh mother! *Henda Baba!* Hear!

SECTION II—OF THE GENITIVE CASE.

This case is used very extensively. It is used to indicate:

1. Connection; as *Siokkoreaḱ nahel,* the plough of the ploughers.
2. Possession; as *Iń-aḱ oṭ,* my soil; *Am-ren sadom,* your horse.
3. Origin; as *Paṇḍu-aḱ-ol,* the writing of Pandu.

Some of the most common of its applications are as follows:—

a. Difference, as *ona ar noa-reaḱ aḍi begar,* there is great difference between this and that.

b. Price; as *mit' ṭaka-reaḱ kichricḱ,* a rupee worth of cloth.

c. Material, as, *hasaren,* made of earth; *meṛhet'-reaḱ,* made of iron.

d. Age; as *turui serma-ren,* six years of age.

e. Use; as *tahen-reaḱ,* for staying in (as a *ṭhãi,* place.

f. Size; as *mõṛe moka-reaḱ kichricḱ,* a piece of cloth five hands long.

g. Instead of the Dative; as *ṭhakur-ren bairi,* an enemy to God; *Pandu-aḱ, e roṛ-et'-a,* he speaks for Pandu.

h. It is further used where we in English would use *about, reading, against;* as *Panḍu-reaḱ, baṅ badaeakat'-a,* I do not know about Pandu; *Amaḱ iṅ kaṛi-akat'-a,* I have sinned against you.

SECTION III—OF THE INSTRUMENTAL CASE.

This case denotes:

1. The agent; as *Ṭhakur-ṭhen sanam benao-en-a,* all things are created by God.
2. The means; as *Pandu-hotete-ṅ banchao-en-a,* I was saved by Pandu.
3. The Instrument; as *ṭengocḱ te-ṅ maḱ-ket'-a,* I cut with the axe.
4. Association; as *Panḍu-te ko ko chalao-en-a,* Pandu with others went away; *haṛam buḍhi-te-kin kin kaphariaoḱkan-a,* the old man and the old woman, (*i. e.,* husband and wife,) quarrel with each other.
5. Possession; as *Dulaṛte perecḱ hoṛ,* a man full of love.

SECTION IV.—OF THE DATIVE CASE.

This case denotes :

1. A direction towards something; as *Paṇḍu-ṭhen chalaǩ-me!* go to Pandu! *Bir-te chalaǩ-me!* go to the jungle.
2. Near, or with; as *Paṇḍu-ṭhen menaǩ-a,* it is near or with Pandu; *dare buṭa-ṭhen menaǩ-a,* it is near the root of the tree.
3. Ablative relation; as *Panḍu-ṭhen-i ńam-ket'-a,* I got it from Pandu. (*Vide* dat. in connection with the verb.)

SECTION V.—OF THE ACCUSATIVE CASE.

This case denotes the direct object, and is mostly used in connection with the infinitive; *Panḍu dadal iń ńel-led-e-a,* I saw him striking Pandu, *i. e.,* I saw that he struck Pandu.

SECTION VI.—OF THE ABLATIVE CASE.

This case denotes :

1. Separation (from); as *Panḍu-khon e hecǩ akan-a,* he has come from Pandu; *Ragdha-khon e daṛ-ket'-a,* he ran away from Raydha.
2. Comparison; as; *Panḍu-khon Jogot e marań-a,* Jogot is greater than Pandu.

Remark 1.—When the dative noun is followed by the verb in the dative case, then the former loses its dative sign as *Panḍu-ń emad-e-a,* I gave it to Pandu.

Remark 2.—The accusative suffixes in connection with the verbs are very extensively used.

Remark 3.—This case, in Santhali, is not used to denote the instrument as it does in Latin. We could not, for instance in Santhali, (nor in any Indian language) translate "oculis videmus" with the Ablative, but should have to use the instrumental case.

SECTION VII.—OF THE LOCATIVE CASE.

This case denotes that something is, or is done, in a certain place, and must in English be translated by *in on*, etc.; as *orak'-re menaea,* he is in the house; *parkom-re e gitiakana*, he is sleeping on the bedstead.

CHAPTER III.

OF PRONOUNS.

Very little needs to be added regarding pronouns, in addition to what has already been said in the chapter on Pronouns. (*Vide* page 23.)

SECTION I.—OF PERSONAL PRONOUNS.

Strictly speaking, only *iń, am, ach'; alań, aliń, aben, akin; abo, abon, ale, ape, ako,* with their respective suffixes are real Personal Pronouns—*oni, onkin, onko, ona, onakin, onako* being demonstrative Pronouns.

Ach', akin, ako, meaning self, selves, are often used as he, they.

Remark 1.—It should be observed that the locative case is strictly confined to a resting in or on something. Whenever a motion towards or into is to be indicated then the dative case must be used; as *dak'-te-ń gidi-khadleked-e-a,* I threw him into the water.

Remark 2.—A constructive case may be added to these 8 cases—namely, a case to which any adverb or postposition may be affixed; as *Pandu-talare, Pandu-tuluch', etc.* As however the noun does not change, it is not different in form from the nominative, and accusative cases, and needs therefore no special enumeration.

Indirect speech is unknown in Santhali, hence in subordinate sentences, where in English we use the 3rd person the Santhal uses the 1st person; as, he said that he would not go under any circumstances, *oni-e-men-ket'-a okalekatehõ ba-ń chalak-a,* he said, I will in no wise go.

Ack can only be used for self in the 3rd person—for 1st and 2nd person *te* is affixed to the personal Pronouns; as *ack-e-chalak-ma !* let him go himself; *iń-teń* (or *ińtegiń*) *chalak-a,* I will go myself; *am amte chalak me !* go yourself! *Te* may also be affixed to *ack, akin, ako.*

The Santhal language has no honorefic pronouns, nor are the personal pronouns used as such to any body but a person who either is related or by mutual consent is counted as related to the speaker by marriage. (*Vide* page 24).

SECTION II.—OF POSSESSIVE PRONOUNS.

Ren is used as a genitive-sign, when the noun in the nominative is an animate object, and *ak, an, reak, rean,* are used when the noun in the Nominative is an inanimate object; as *Ińren hopon,* my son; *iń-ak orak,* my house.

Tet', and the genitive suffixes are often used instead of the possessive Pronouns; as *hopon-tet',* or *hopon-tae,* his son; *orak-tam* your house; *hopon-tiń* (or *hopon-iń,)* my son. (*Vide* page 34).

Remark. Tet' is used with all persons and also with inanimate objects as self; as *iń tet',* I myself; *am-tet',* you yourself; *Pandu-tet',* Pandu himself.

SECTION III.—OF DEMONSTRATIVE PRONOUNS.

The difference between *noi* and *ni*, *oni* and *ini*, etc., is that *ni*, *ini* and *hini* convey the idea of *the same*; as *ini kangea*, it is the same person.

This difference is also observable between *onkan* and *enkan*. (*Vide* pages 36 and 37.)

SECTION IV.—OF INTERROGATIVE PRONOUNS.

The difference between *okoe* and *ohele* is, that the first inquires into *who* one is; and the second into *what* he is; as *okoe kanae?* Who is he? *chele kanae?* What is he? *Oka* and *ohet'* are used for inanimate objects. (*Vide* page 37.)

SECTION V.—OF RELATIVE PRONOUNS.

Relative Pronouns have been fully explained at pages 38 and 39, therefore there is no need of further explanation here

---

CHAPTER IV.

OF VERBS.

SECCTION I.—OF THE VOICES.

A. THE ACTIVE VOICE.

The active voice is either transitive or intransitive.

1. *Transitive;* as *hako-ń sap-ko-a*, I will catch fish; *orak-iń benao-a*, I will build a house.

2. *Intransitive;* as *daṛket'-a-e,* he ran away; *achhim-ket'-a-ko,* they sneezed.

B. The Reflexive voice.

This voice is used to express:

1. That the subject acts upon itself; as *dal-ok-kan-a-e,* he is striking himself; *abukokkanae,* he washes himself (hands or feet.)

2. That something takes place with the subject, or that it is in a certain state; as *gujuk-kan-a-e,* he is dying.

3. Passivity; as *ir-og-ok-kan-a,* it is being cut (*dhan*); *dal-ocho-k-kan-a-e,* he is being struck; *ńel-ok-kan-a-e,* he is to be seen.

4. That the subject does something for itself; as *bachhao-joṅ-a-e,* he will choose for himself; *agu-joṅ-kan-a-ń,* I am bringing for myself; *Dal-ocho-joṅ-kan-a-e,* he is causing to be struck for himself;

C. The Reciprocal Active.

This voice denotes the bringing of two objects into mutual action; as *dapal-ket'-a-e,* he struck (something) together, (from *dal,* to strike); *ńapam-kat'-kin-a-e,* he got them two to find one another, *i. e.,* to meet, (from *ńam* to get); *ńepel-ocho-at'-kin-a-e,* he allowed them two to see one another, *i. e.,* to meet (from *ńel* to see);

D. The Reciprocal Reflexive.

This voice denotes:

1. Reciprocal or mutual action *directly*; as *dapal-ena-kin*, they two struck one another; *ńapam-ena-ko*, they found one another, *i. e.*, met; *dapram-ena-ko*, they met one another (from *daram* to come towards.)

2. Reciprocal or mutual action with respect to one another; as *chepet'-joṅ-kan-a-ko*, they consult (quietly) for themselves; *epem-joṅ-kana-ko*, they give one another.

E. The deponent voice.

This voice has no special form, it is only the reflexive voice with active signification; as *hoṛo-ko-gr-ok-kan-a*, they sow rice; *hoṛo-ko ir-ok-kan-a*, they cut (or reap) rice; *chet'-em-ńam-kan-a?* What do you want? (from *ńam* to get.)

From the above it will be seen what a facility the Santhal voices, in connection with the cases and causatives, afford for expressing one'self with precision. Greek, which is one of the most refined of languages, and has more voices than most of the Indo-Germanic tongues, is far inferior to Santhali in this respect. In Santhali we have separate forms for the accusative and dative cases middle voice; whereas in Greek we have only one; as *dal-ok-a-ń*, I will strike myself; *ńam-joṅ-a-ń*; I will find for myself. τύπτομαι, I strike myself; εὑρίσκομαι, I find for myself. In Santhali we have separate forms for reciprocal and causal action, whereas in Greek we have to use the same (only) form in the middle voice; as *ṛopoṛ-a-ń* (from *ror* to speak,) I will discourse (speak mutually with another person); *Gidrako-ń chet'ochojoń-a,* I will cause or get the children to be taught; *διαλέγομαι,* I discourse; *διδάξασθαι τοὺς παῖδας,* to get the children instructed for one'self (Germ. *Sich die Kinder unterrichten lassen*).

The Santhal voices, in connection with the cases and causatives, are so precise that no doubt as to the exact meaning is possible.

SECTION II.—OF TENSES.

FUTURE TENSE.

This Tense is used to express, 1*st*, FUTURITY; as *gapa-ń-chalaǩ-a,* I shall go to-morrow; *ba-ń-dal-me-a,* I will not strike you (thee); *rapudoǩ-a,* it will break.

2*nd*. GENERAL STATEMENTS; as *Ṭhakur sanam ko khoṇe maraṅ-a,* God is greater than all; *Paṇḍu-ae-a* (dat. case,) he is *Paṇḍu, i. e.* he is called, or his name is *Paṇḍu*; *aḍi-e-daṛe-aǩ-a,* he is very strong.

3*rd*. HABIT OR CUSTOM; as *lahare le abukoǩ-a, eṇḍete-enale jom-a,* we first wash our hands and then we eat; *noa burure serma-ke sermale sendrae-a,* we hunt every year on this mountain.

4*th*. *Present* AND *Past* ACTIONS IN *vivid* NARATIVES; as *chaṭ, chando re aḍile sendrae-a, baskeaǩ jomkate burute le-chalaǩa buruphed tiokate, tingukate ṭama-le rue, tirio-le oroń-a, saḍetet'anjomkate Disom hoṛ ko jar-waǩ-a, jarwamit'*—

kate burute le dejoḱ-a ar jelko le goćḱ-angi—in the month of Chait we *hunt* very much :—Having taken our breakfast we *go* to the mountain ; arriving at the foot of it, we stand and play on the drum and *blow* the flute, hearing the sound of which, the people of the land *come* together, we *ascend* the mountain and kill a lot of deer. (Regarding *goćḱ-angi*, *vide* Reflexive voice, dative case, contingent tense) *Peṛakoṭhen tahēkanre aḍi jutiṅ aikaulaḱ-a :—setaḱre beret'-kate burute le ehalaḱ-a, sahan sakam le aguea, bugite le dakaea utuea, jomale, ar ayup'enkhan kulhi muchat'te senkate bugite le sereṅa, enećḱ-a-le, ar enećḱmokoṅ lenkhan le gitien-gi*—when I was with (my) friends I was very much pleased :—After having risen in the morning we *used* to go to the mountains to fetch wood and leaves, to cook rice and vegetables and eat (when we came home) and in the evening we *used* to go to the end of the village to sing and dance, and being tired thereof we would go to bed.

5th. HYPOTHETICAL PRESENT ; as *hor bachoṅ baḍae. Bam baḍaekhan iṅ laiama nahaḱ: Noṇḍekhon senkate Hasapathar sećḱtem chalaḱa, Ṭhakurpuratem rakap'a, gaḍa paromkate Horinsiṅ em ṅela, ona ato senbagiaḱte Deocham tioket'-gi*—I do not know the road *(Ichweissja (choṅ) nicht den Weg)*. If you do not, I will soon explain it to you : Starting from here you *go* in the direction of Hasapather, *enter* Thakurpura, passing the river you *see* Horinsing, and leaving that village behind you, you reach Deocha.

THE GENERAL INCOMPLETE PRESENT.

This tense is used to express in a general far-fetched way an act which has commenced and is not finished, without laying any stress on the present moment; as *Ṭhakur-e-ńel-et'-bon-a,* God sees us, *i. e.,* he has not ceased to see us (not particular now); *apuń-nit'-dhabich-e-kamiet'-a,* my father worketh until now; *nebetar horo-le-rohoe-et'a,* at this time we plant rice. (No stress being laid on the present moment, for in that case the Special Incomplete Present would be used; as *bohok' adi hasoediń-kana,* my head is paining me very much now) This tense is never used like the English Present Indefinite to express general truths, or habits, *i. e.,* actions done now and then, hence we could not translate the English, "God punishes the sinner," with, *Ṭhakur kạkạiko-e-ḍanḍomet'-ko-a;* for that would mean: God has commenced and has not ceased to punish certain sinners; but we would have to use the Future and say; *kạkạiko Ṭhakur-e-ḍanḍom-ko-a.* This tense can only be used when something is actually taking place.

THE SPECIAL INCOMPLETE PRESENT.

This tense ought—1*st,* to be strictly confined to the present moment, when used in the *General Form,* Active; as *dal-el-e-kan-a-ko,* or *dal-e-kan-a-ko,* they are striking him *now.* 2*nd* it is used to express, that something is being tried to be effected, but is failing; as *mit'ṭań marań hako e sab-e-kan-a, menkhan ba-e sap-dare-ae-a, onte note-e phente pherech kan-a,* he is trying to catch a large fish but cannot, (because) he is dodging.

In the Reservative, Intensive and Continuative Forms as well as in the Reflexive Voice and Dative Case, which have no General Incomplete Present, this Tense is used for both the Present Tenses, but can never be used as an Indefinite Present; as *Thakur e ńel-ka-bon-kana,* God looks or is looking on us; *sisikana-e,* he learns now-a-days, or just now, to plough; *jomaќ e emabonkana,* he gives us always or just now food; *kamiakaetahen kan-a-e,* he is continuing to work; *ruaќ kan a e,* he is sick.

The difference between the Future, the General Incomplete Present and the Special Incomplete Present, (when the Future also is used as a Present Tense) is this: the *Future* is used when something is done now and then, under certain circumstances; as *noa burure pe sendraea sepe bańa?* Do you hunt on this mountain (or hill), or do you not? *Jahatis-jahatis le sendraea, Jahatisjahatis do bańa,* sometimes we do and sometimes we do not; the General Incomplete Present is used when something has actually commenced, but is not yet completed, without laying any stress on the present moment; as *apuń nit'dhabicќ e kami et'-a,* my father worketh until now—and the Special Incomplete Present, when something is being done just now; as *dal-et' ko kana-e,* he is striking them now.

RECENT PAST.

This tense is used—*1st,* to express past time, as having once taken place, without any reference to the time of our speaking: it thus corresponds with the Greek Aorist and the Latin Historical Perfect, and is therefore the narrative tense; as *Pargan udo chet' e menket'a? Chet' bae men, bugigi e men ket'a.* What said the Pargana? What should he say, he spoke well, *i. e.*, to my satisfaction.

2nd. As a sequence to the Anterior Past; as *aḍi sener e mak' laka, okoe chọ ko idiket'*, he cut a lot of "rollas," who may have taken them? *Enañ ko hech' len-a, chalao-enako*, they came in the forenoon, but have gone away; *hǫlkalom mit' ṭañ diko hǫpǫn iñak' barea kichrich' e komṛolaka, ñam-ruaṛ ket'añ.* The year before last a Hindu stole two pieces of cloth from me, but I got them back. *Bae dạṛ lak' a? Dạṛ let' giae, sap kedeañ*, did he not run away? (Yes) he ran away indeed, (but) I caught him.

3rd. It is used to denote events, which have happened just now or recently; as *jom ket' añ*, I have taken my food; *hech' ena ko*, they have come; *chalaoenako*, they have gone.

4th. To express actions past, which have abiding effects; as, *gọch' enae*, he has died, *i. e.*, is dead; *bagi ked iñae*, she has left me; *tis e bagi ket' mea?* When did she leave you? *Aḍi din re*, long ago.

THE ANTERIOR PAST.

This tense is used to express—1*st*, actions performed in the past, but afterwards revoked or neutralized; as *Senlenako*, they went (but they have returned); *tọlledeako*, they tied or had tied him (but he was let loose again); *bagiledeae-*

heck ruar enae, she left or had left him, but she has returned; *goc lenae*, he died (Jesus) (but is not dead); 2*nd*, actions which took place long ago, but have now lost their importance; as *kora jokhech iń nel ledea*, I saw him in youth; *hapramko noako bako ńel laka*, our forefathers did not see these things; 3*rd*, actions which took place anterior to other actions in the past; as *birre mit' tań kūl hopon iń nel le dea, ona teń heck ena*, I saw the young of a tiger in the forest, therefore I have come; *bae bugiledińa adoń bagikedea*, he did not cure me, therefore I left him; *auri gujukre adi e saset' lena*, he suffered much before he died.

THE PERFECT.

This tense is used—1*st*, to call attention to *the fact*, that something has taken place in the past and remains in its effects, *i. e.*, connects the past with the present; as *tolakadeako*, they have tied him; *kiriń-akadeań*, I have bought him; *Dapalakaoat'ań*, I have covered it up. It corresponds therefore in this respect with the English Perfect.

2*nd*. To denote, that something took place sometime ago and remains in its effects; as *holań kirińakadea*, I bought him yesterday; *mahnder hilok ko sap'akadea*, they caught him the day before yesterday, (and have got him.)

3*rd*. To express that something took place long ago, but has not been altered, *i. e.*, remains in its effects; as *holkalom' ko hajot akadea*, they imprisoned him two years ago (and he is still in prison.)

The difference between the Recent Past, the Anterior Past and the Perfect presents a great many difficulties, and nothing is easier for the European than to use the Recent Past for the Anterior and *vice versâ*, and the Perfect for the Recent Past. An example taken from the Creed will show the principal difference between these three tenses: *aṛ, (iń patiaoakana) oniren hopon aboren kisũṛ Jesu Masire oni Dhorom Jiu hoṭete e gaṛhaolen, ardaicℏ Mariakhoṇ e janam len, Ponti Pilat tarire e harket' sasetlen, paṭakhuṇ-ṭire e khiljalat', ocholen, goclℏene, topaledeko, hanapurite e-ũṛgulen, pe mũhũhiloℏre gocℏkokhoṇ e beret'ruaṛen, sermate e dech en, Ṭhakur sanamdaṛe apareaℏ etomsecℏre e duṛup'-akan. Gaṛhaolena* and *janamlena*, here the Anterior Past is used, are because the event took place long ago; *saset lena, khiljalat'ocho lena, gocℏ lena, topaledeko, ũṛgulena,* here the Anterior Past is used, because he suffers no more, is no more on the Cross, is no longer dead, is not in the grave, has returned from hades. *Beret'ruaṛena, decℏ ena,* here the Recent Past is used, because he has not returned to the grave and has not re-descended to hades, hence the Anterior Past could not be used in these two instances; for if we said *beret' ruaṛ lenae,* it would mean that he rose but has died again; and we could not say *gocℏ ena,* for that would imply, that he has not risen. *Duṛup'akanae,* he has seated himself and is sitting, here the perfect is used to show that he is still sitting.

A few more examples will further illustrate the difference between these tenses: *Tọl ledeako, chikate choc raṛaen ?*

They tied him, how may he have got loose? *Tolkedeako, ar ohoe dardarelena,* they have tied him, he cannot run away any more now; *sarigi ko tolakadea, bam patiaokkhan, endekhan senkate ńeleme,* indeed they have tied him, if you do not believe it, then go and see him.

Sap'ledeako, they caught him (but he has got lose).

Sap'kedeako, they caught him (historically true), and so far as I know he has not got lose.

Sap'akadeako, they caught him, and he is in their hands.

In the Reservative Form, and the Dative Case, there is only one form for both Recent and Anterior Past, and the meaning in each instance must therefore be gathered from the connection.

THE GENERAL INCOMPLETE PAST.

This tense is formed by adding *tahēkan, was,* to the Geneneral Incomplete Present. It denotes—1*st,* that something was being done in the past, without laying any stress on the concurrence of other actions; as *laiet' tahēkanae,* he was saying, *i. e.*, he, (on a certain occasion) said (*among other things*) so and so.

2nd. It is used to express habits or customs in the past; as *sedaereń sendraet'tahēkana, nitokdoń haramena,* in former times I used to hunt, (but) now I have grown old; *perakothen tahēkanre, jel adiń gocliet'-kotahēkana,* when I was staying with (my) friend I used to kill lots of deer.

THE SPECIAL INCOMPLETE PAST.

This tense is used to denote:

1*st.* That a certain action was going on, without being completed, when another event took place; as *senerińmamaǩkan tahēkana, onre mit'ṭań kūl e bhiṛkaokedińa,* I was cutting rollas when a tiger frightened me.

2*nd.* That something was being tried, but failed; as *sabekan-tahēkanań, phaskaoenae,* I was trying to catch him, but he got off.

In the Reservative Form and in Dative this tense is also used for the General Incomplete Past.

THE INDECISIVE PLUPERFECT.

This tense is formed from the Anterior Past by adding *tahēkana.* It is used to denote:

1*st.* That something has occurred before some other event in the past time, but which had been altered again; as *ape auri pe hejuǩ regi e unumlen tahēkana,* he had fallen into the water before you came (but was no longer there when you came); *gocǩledetahēkanań, eskarente ko eṛekedińa,* I had killed him (before another hit him,) but being alone (and the friends of the other being many) they cheated me (of him, I did not get him.) Here it is used as a Pluperfect.

2*nd.* It precedes the Anterior Past, which again is followed by the Recent Past, which again may be followed by the Present Tense; *Koelede tahẽkanań, bae anjom-laka, onateń hecḱ ruarena, ar nekem ńelińkana,* I requested him (to do so and so,) but he did not listen, therefore I have come back, and you see me here. (Here it is used as a past tense.)

3rd. It is used as a Past Conditional; as *Am alom hecḱlenkhan iń tuńledetahẽkana;* if you had not come I would have shot him; *mak ledetahẽkanań, menkan bań makledea,* I would have killed him, but did not do it (on account of such and such a thing.)*

THE DECISIVE PLUPERFECT.

This Tense is formed from the Perfect by adding *tahẽkana.* It is used:

1st. To denote that a certain action had taken place and remained in its effects, when another action took place in the past; as *meromiń senńamkedea, tolakade tahẽkanako,* I found the goat, they had tied her; *perako then iń sen lena, menkhan ruak hor-e gocḱakantahẽkana jiwet'do bań senńamledea,* I went to (my) friends, but the sick person had died (and was dead), I did not find him alive.

2nd. It is used as an Incomplete Past with verbs, the Perfect of which have the meaning of the Present Tense; as *durup'akan tahẽkanae,* he had seated himself and was sitting = was sitting; *sap'akadetahẽkan-ako,* they had caught him = they where holding him.

---

* The above may also be translated: I had *almost* shot him, *i. e.,* I was on the point of shooting him.

The great difference between the two Pluperfects is, that the Indecisive denotes that something had been done, but had been neutralized, when another event took place in the past whereas the Decisive denotes that it continued effective; as *unumlen tahĕkanae,* he had sank into the water but had come up again; *unumakantahĕkanae,* he had sank into the water and was still there.

INCHOATIVE FUTURE.

This tense is used to express that something will be or is about to be done; as *senoḱ-lagit'-e,* he is about to go soon; *dạṛlagit'-ko,* they are intending to run away soon. When this tense is used it implies that the action will not take place immediately; as *umoḱ lagit'-ko,* they intend to be baptized, *i. e.* have made up their minds for it and it will not be long before they will be baptized.

INCHOATIVF PRESENT.

This tense is used to denote that the action is going to take place immediately, or is on the very point of being executed; as *umoḱ lagidoḱ-kanae,* he is now about to be baptized, (in a few moments it will take place); *merom ko gojelagidoḱ-kana,* they are just now about to kill a goat.

INCHOATIVE PAST.

This tense is used to denote that a certain action was just on the point of being executed, when another event took place; as *jẹl-iń tuńe lagidoḱ-kan-tahĕkan-re mit'ṭań chĕṛe-e uḍao-gọt'ena, onate-e dạṛket'a,* just as I was about to shoot a deer a bird flew up and frightened him away.

THE OPTATIVE.

This tense (or rather mood) is used to express:

1*st.* Option; as *ṇoa chaōrick em emkiṅa? Maente hatao me,* would you give me this plaited cowtail? Well take it; *(Germ nimm es doch); am bam hatao khan, eṇḍekhan em em kiṅa?* If you will not take it, will you give it to me? *Noko moṭore okoeṭam hataokea? Noiṭaṅ hotaokea,* which of them will you take? I will take this.

2*nd.* Condition; as *am em sen lenkhan iṅ senkoka,* if you will or would go or have gone, I will or would go or have gone. It must however be born in mind that this tense even when used as a Conditional, retains its optative signification and must not be confounded with the Conditional (tense). This will be obvious from the following examples: *Am noam em liṅ khan, iṅ hatao kea,* if you would give me this, I would accept of it. *Noam emkiṅ-khan aḍiṅ raskakoka,* if you *only* would give me this how glad would I be!

THE CONDITIONAL.

This tense is used to express actions conditionally in connection with negative particles (in participles and gerunds also without them); as, *aloe dal liṅ khan, ọhọṅ dal lea,* if he had not struck me I should not have struck him; *amem sen-len-rehō, ọhọ giṅ sen lena,* even if you went I should not go; *ọhoe heckruaṛlena, tinak em menlerehō,* he will not come back, in spite of all you may say.

THE CONTINGENT.

This tense is used to express a hypothetical future or present; as *sener mamak̇ birte chalaotalaṅ me. Paset' kul e hejuk̇ adoe goch̀ kedingi? Ohoe goch̀lema, am ṭhen e hech̀lenkhan, ṭaṅgatem mak̇ daram kedegi, adoe daṛtap' engi,* go to the forest and cut us some saplings. Perhaps the tiger may come and then he *will kill* me? No he will not kill you—if he should come to you, well then you simply *strike* at him with your axe and he *runs* away. Here *kill, strike,* and *runs* are in the Contingent Tense (or mood). *Kami baṅ ṅamlekhan adoṅ hech̀ruaṛengi,* if I should not get work, well then I *come* back; *gapa baṛe hejuk̇ me, setak̇, ado laṅ jomket'gi, birte laṅ chalaengi, sener laṅ mak̇ket'gi, ado oṛak̇te laṅ hech̀ ruaṛengi, gitich̀ angilaṅ,* come very early to morrow (morning), then we will take our food (together) go to the forest, cut saplings, return home and go quietly to bed.

This tense is formed from the Recent Past by eliminating the final, "a" and substituting "*gi.*" It is always used to express some imaginary future action and must be translated in English sometimes by the Future Indicative, sometimes by the Indefinite Present Indicative, and at other times, by the Future Potential.

THE PRELIMINARY FUTURE.

This tense is used to express that something will take place before another event in the future; as *noṇḍe laṅ jirao angi, eṇḍete laṅ ehop'a,* we two will first rest here a little, then we two will commence—, *hape, peṛaṭhen-iṅ bolo lengi eṇḍete laṅ chalaka,* wait, I will first call in at my friend's and then we will go; *babon jiraoka? Noa gaḍa bon paromlegi,* shall we not rest? We will first cross the river.

THE PRELIMINARY EXPOSTULATIVE.

This tense is used in retorting, *i. e.*, exposing the fallacy of an argument or the unreasonableness of a demand; as *kombṛo chakbape aguledea? Onile saple nahĩ, eṇḍe-nahĩ-le aguea,* why did you not bring the thief? We must first catch him and then we will bring him; *noko hoṛ kuṛhia-kante ko rengejok kana, aloko kuṛhia len khan oho ko rengech lena. Tisem ṅel kuṛhia-akat lea? Amdo aḍim baḍaea le kuṛhiak-kana mente. Dak-lenahĩ eṇḍe nahim arjaoa,* these people are very lazy, therefore they are poor; if they were not lazy, they would not be poor. When have you seen us lazy? You know much about (I suppose) whether we are lazy or not: It must first rain, and then you will earn (riches).

This tense (or rather mood) is always used when a person is angry with another for expecting or demanding what is unreasonable.

THE PRELIMINARY PERSUASIVE.

This tense ought perhaps rather to be called the Preliminary Corrective, or Modificative, as it is used to remind or persuade the speaker, that what he imagines to be easy of accomplishment, really requires the adoption of some preliminary measure which may prove unattainable or impracticable; as, *nes aḍiṅ arjaoa. Ṭhakur bhoṛ emlembae,* this year

I shall earn much. God must first give you his blessing, (and then you will earn much); *birte senkate adi jelkoń tuńgoch-koa. Ńelńam leko-bam,* going to the woods I will shoot a lot of deer. You must first see them; *nonde adiutar ul menaka, delabon joma. Darete dech-dare-len-babon,* here are lots of mangoes let us eat. We must first be able to climb the tree.

THE PRELIMINARY ADMISSIVE.

This tense is either used to express an admission that something must be done previously to the act proposed by another, or, in simple statements, that something must be done previously to something else; as *kombro chalk bam aguledea? Onin sap'dare le nahāń aguea. Hē, sap'le enam.* Why did you not bring that thief? I must first be able to catch him and then I will bring him. Yes (that is true) you must first catch him; *sihuri tinrebon tioga,'? Auria, gadabon paromle ena,* when will we reach Sewry? Not yet, we must first pass the river.

THE CONTINUATIVE FUTURE.

This tense denotes:

1st. Continuative futurity; as, *auri e hēg reń dal-aka-e tahen-a,* I will continue to strike him till he confesses.

2nd. Indefinite Present; as, *behaj ko āt-a, diko hopon do, aurim em-ako-re, ko ruket'-aka-m-tahen-a,* the Hindus are very troublesome, they continue to scold you till you give them.

3rd. Dubious Perfect; as *okoekope añjom-akae-tahen-khan, ma rorpe!* Whoever of you may have heard it, say on!

THE CONTINUATIVE PRESENT.

This tense denotes that something has commenced and is being continued up to the time of speaking; as *Siṅsatup iñ kami-akae-tahen-kan-a, enrehõ ba-e ṅatum-ak'-tiñ-a,* I have been working the whole day, still he does not recognize it (praise me).

THE CONTINUATIVE PAST.

This tense denotes that something had commenced and was being continued in the past; as *mit' lagateṅ kami-akae-tahēkan-a, enrehõ ayup're heck'-kate e ruhet'-got'-ked-iñ-a,* I had been working without intermission, still he came and scolded me in the evening.

THE PRELIMINARY BENEDICTIVE.

This may be used both as a Preliminary Benedictive and a Precative; as, *Jaekorarko ñel tiolekomam, aurim gujuk' redo!* Mayest thou first see grandchildren before thou diest! *Gook' len mam, ende te amak' achel iñ hataoa,!* Mayest thou first die, and then I will take thy riches!

This mood may also be used when we in English would use *that* or *in order that*; as *auri gujuk're jaekorar ko e ñel-lekoma. Onaiate Thakur e soñ juticHakaoadea,* God has prolonged his life, in order that he may see grandchildren before he dies.

Remarks. This tense is seldom used.

THE PRELIMINARY IMPERATIVE.

This mood is used to express preliminary orders, wishes and requests; as, *Duṛup' len me eṇḍetem chalak' a,* sit first down, and then you (thou) may go.

THE BENEDICTIVE.

This mood is used in the same manner as Preliminary Benedictive, with the exception of the preliminary idea; as *gujuk'mam*! Mayest thou die! *Marańok'mam*! Mayest thou be great! *Ńurok'mam, onateń ọchọgket'a,* I took it away in order that you may or might fall.

THE IMPERATIVE.

This is used to express a command, will, order etc; as *chalak' me!* Go! *Hejuk' me!* Come!

The future tense with *gi* is used as a mild Imperative; as *hejuk' giam,* you (then) must come (don't say no).

THE CONTINUATIVE BENEDICTIVE.

This is used in the same way as the other Benedictive, only with the addition of continuation; as *ṛua-akan-tahen-mam!* Mayest thou continue to be sick!

THE CONTINUATIVE IMPERATIVE.

This is also used in the same way as the General Imperative with the addition of continuation; as *auriń hẹck'-ru-*

Remark. The Benedictive is used extensively in dependent sentences, where we would use *that, in order that,* etc., in English.

aṛ-oǩ-re, ṅonḍe duṛup'-akan-tahen-me! Remain sitting here till I come back!

SECTION III.—OF MOODS.

As the Benedictive, Imperative, Conditional, Contingent, and Optative have all been treated of in connection with the tenses, we have here only to treat of the Indicative, the Subjunctive, and the Infinitive,—

A. Indicative.

This mood is used in independent assertions and questions; as *chalaǩ-a-ń*, I will go; *hečh-en-a-e*, he came; *maraṅ-kan-a-e*, he is great; *bae dal-ko-a*, he will not strike them; *chet'-em-ńel-ket'-a?* What did you see? *Tinaǩ-em-ńam-ket'-a?* How much did you get?

B. Subjunctive.

This mood is used to express an action, *objectively* possible, as conceived by the mind. It stands between the Indicative, the actual, and the Optative or conditional, the *subjective* possible, and is *always* used whenever there is no positive reality on the one hand, and yet not a mere subjective possibility on the other; for, in the first case, the Indicative is used, and in the latter, the Conditional, or Optative.

The difference in form between the Indicative and Subjunctive is that the latter leaves out the final "*a*."

The Subjunctive may be used *with* or *without* prefixed or affixed particles. The most common particles used in connection with this mood are *khan*, if or *when*, *choṅ*, possibly, *paset'*, perhaps, *baṛe*, may or oh that! *Hutkeck*, in order.

They are used in the following way:—*Dal-khan-e*, if he will strike; *dal-ket'-khan-e*, if he (really) struck; *Paset'-ko dal-ked-e*, perhaps they struck him; *paset'-e bagi-me*, perhaps he may leave you; *bagi-ked-e-choe, chet' choṅ*, he possibly has left her; *oni-baṛe-e hejuk*, may he (or, oh, that he would) come! *Khajuk-e baḍae*, that he may know. *Edrekate ar-e dal-me, enḍekhan chet'-em men-a?* Getting angry and he *strikes* you, what will you then say? *Ma ko kurumuṭuma, jahaļekate kami ko sąt*, let them work hard *that they may* finish the work.

When *chōṅ* is affixed to the verb it might be called *the Potential mood;* but as the termination of the verb is the same, with the exception of the particle, it is more correct to call it *The Subjunctive with choṅ.* The following examples may serve to show the different form and meaning of the mood: *Dal-a-ko*, they will strike; *ar-ko-dal*, and (in case) they strike; *Dal-ke-a-ko*, they would strike; *Dal-le-khan-ko*, in case they should strike.

C. Infinitive.

As Santhali is extraordinary in its grammatical structure in other respects, it may be expected to be so likewise with regard to the Infinitive, and such is the case; for not

---

Remark. *Choṅ*, when affixed to subjunctive may also have an asserting meaning; *as chaba-ket'-cho-ṅ*, well, I have finished it. (*Germ. Ich habe es ja vollendet.*)

only has this remarkable language an *Infinitive for each voice, form, causative, case, number and person, but also for each tense.*

The forms of the Infinitives are the same as those of the Adjective Participles. Some of these Infinitives are of frequent, others of rare occurrence. Among the common, are the Future Infinitives, General and Intensive Form, and the Perfect, the second and third of which generally are used as pure Infinitives, whereas the first is more used like the Sanscrit Infinitive or the Latin Supine.

The Infinitive may be used :

1. As the subject of a sentence ; as

Dadal do bañ bugi-a, it is not good to strike.
Tutuñ do algak-a, it is easy to shoot.

2. As the Predicate.

Laichugli hõ gogoch, to backbite is also to kill.
Dhorom tahen gi bugi tahen, to live religiously is to live well.

3. As the Object.

Dadal barick gi lè metak kana, we call it bad to strike.
Dularochok gi sanae kana, he wishes to be loved.

ACCUSATIVE WITH INFINITIVE.

The accusative with Infinitive is constructed in two ways :

1. By prefixing the Infinitive; as *kokombro iń ńel-led-e-a,* I saw him steal; *dadal iń ańjom-akad-e-a,* I have heard him strike.

2. By infixing the Infinitive, as *ńel-kombro-ked-e-a-ń,* I saw him steal; *ańjom-dal-ked-e-a-ń,* I heard him strike.

It is only the Future Infinitive of the General Form, *i. e.,* the bare root, which can be used in the second instance, whereas the Future Infinitive of the Intensive Form and the Infinitives of any of the other Tenses may be used in the first mode of construction; as *dadal e menakaoad-iń-a,* he has told me to strike; *Dar-ket' ko men et'-a,* they say that (he) ran away (they say (him) to have run away); *goch-akan ko men et'-a,* they *say* that he has died, they say (him) to have died; *hech len iń ańjom-lak-a,* I heard that he had *come,*—I heard (him) to have come.

The simple root, (*i. e.,* the Future Infinitive of the General Form,) is, with the exception of being infixed, as shown above, used more like the Latin Supine in *um* or the Sanscrit Infinitive; as, *sadom kiriń iń hech akana,* I have come to buy a horse; *dak agu iń kolakadea,* I have sent him to fetch water; *sadom tol-e e met-ad-iń-a,* he told me to bind (him) the horse.

D. Of Participles.

The Santhal language has two kinds of participles,—the adjective or relative, and the adverbial or absolute.

Remark. It should be observed that any of the abridged Pronouns may be affixed to the Infinitive to show the person and case; as, *em-ae e metadiń-a,* he told me to give him; *dal-ko e metadea,* he told himto strike them.

I. THE ADJECTIVE OR RELATIVE PARTICIPLES.

These are used: *a.* To express an attribute to a substantive; as *dadal hoṛ*, a striking man; *jọrọk-kan met'*, a weeping eye; *chalak hoṛ*, a man about to go; *dal hõṛ*, a struck man; *añjom roṛ*, a heard word; *hejuk kan hõṛ*, a coming man; *b.* To express an attribute to a substantive relatively; as, *ńel-dal-ledeko hõṛ ko mendaṛeaka*, the men who saw him strike are able to say; *heck len ko hõṛ*, the men who came; *senokko hõṛ do okaenako?* What has become of the men who will go; *ńel-lede ko hõṛ*, the men who saw him; *janhe dadal hoṛ*, the man who will thrash out *janhe; hola gọcken hoṛ*, the man who died yesterday; *gọk-ke-tam hoṛ chak bam metadea?* why did you not ask (tell) him, who would have carried your? (*dhan.*)

These Participles may also be used substantively; *ran-ad-e-tiń-ko*, they who gave medicine to him, who is mine; *họpọnak hapa reckket'-tae-tiń-ko*, they who took away his stick, (he) who is my son; *ńel-kedetińko*, they who saw him, who is mine; *dal gọck-ked-e-ko*, they who killed him; *ńel-ked-iń-pe*, you who saw me; *dal-let' me-ń*, I who struck thee.

The Santhal language, as already has been shown in the paradigms of the verb, has a participle for each tense. A few examples showing how they are used may not be superfluous:—

Remark. It should be observed that the 3rd person singular takes the suffix *ich'*, instead of e, when the Participle stands substantively; as *emat ko-ich'*, he who gave them.

FUTURE.

Chalak̇ hor̤ hoho̤-ae-me! Call the man who is to go.

Hane tor̤a senok̇ hor̤ tam! Yonder is the way you shall go.

GENERAL INCOMPLETE PRESENT.

Añjomet' hor̤ chak̇ em ruhed-e-kan-a? Why do you scold the man who listens? *Sahan mak̇-et'-ko hor̤ chak̇ iñ edre ako-a?* Why should I be angry with those (men) who cut wood?

SPECIAL INCOMPLETE PRESENT.

Atiñ-et'ko-kan hor̤ do okoe? Who is he who is feeding them (the cattle.)

RECENT PAST.

Halañ-ket' hor̤ ñumeme! Name the person who took it up!

ANTERIOR PAST.

Dor̤-let' hor̤ e ruar̤ ena, the man who ran away has returned.

PERFECT.

Sap'-akad-e hor̤ bugi ñ metaekana, I call the man good who has caught him.

GENERAL INCOMPLETE PAST.

Kombr̤o et' tahẽkan tale hor̤iñ sap'akad-e-a, I have caught the man who used to steal our (dhan.)

SPECIAL INCOMPLETE PAST.

Ñel-e-kan-tahẽkan hor̤ agu-epe! Bring the person who was seeing him (when he did it.)

INDECISIVE PLUPERFECT.

Jol-led-e-tahēkan hor iń ńel-ledea, I saw him who had bound him (released again).

DECISIVE PLUPERFECT.

Durup' akan tahēkan hor ko iń ńel tiok'-ket' koa, I got to see those who had seated themselves (and were sitting.)

II. THE ADVERBIAL OR ABSOLUTE PARTICIPLES.

These Participles are used very much like the Latin Participle when it is an abridged sentence, and like the Ablative; as:—

Absolute; as *chaekhon odoń-enkhan, champa-le tiok'-ket'-a,* having left Chae, we arrived in Champa; (compare *Aristides, patriā pulsas, Lacedæmonem fugit.*)

Pargana beret'-enkhan, ale hō le hech ena, the Pargana having risen, we also came (home), (compare *Pythagoras, Tarquinio superbo regnante, in Italian venit.*)

Hejuk'khan, ma hech ocho ae pe, (if) coming, let him come: *Dal-ed-e-khan em chika-e-a,* striking him, what can you do? *Ńel-ede-kan-khan ohom okodare-lea,* seeing him (now), you cannot hide him;

Remark. In the above manner the participles of any tense, case, causative, voice, form, number and person may be used.

Remark. In English these participles cannot always be rendered literally, as we have not a special participle for each tense, like in Santhali. Words like *as when after*, etc. must be used with the verb in the indicative.

Sen lagidok̇ kan khan ma e chalak̇ ma! Being about to go, (well) let him go! *Gọk̇ák̇kaoat'me khan, bae emam-a?* Having promised you, will he not give you?

E. OF GERUNDS.

The Gerunds are used to express the action of the verb as an abstract substantive-idea (Substantivbegriff); and are declined like other nouns. The Santhal language has one gerund for each tense. These gerunds partake of a *two-fold declension*: 1st, they partake, like the Infinitives and Participles, of the FOUR CASES IN CONNECTION WITH THE VERB; as *dal*, to strike; *dal-ae*, to strike for him; *dal-tae*, to strike his; *dal-e*, to strike him; and 2nd, THEY PARTAKE OF THE EIGHT CASES IN CONNECTION WITH THE NOUNS; as *dal-akat'*, they having struck; *dal akat'-reak̇ pọrhọ*, the benefit of having struck; *dal-akat'-te*, by having struck; *dal-akat'-ṭhen*, near where one has struck; *dal akat'-khọn*, from having struck; *dal-akat'-re*, in having struck.

The gerundial concretes are also declined like the abstracts; as *heċk akan-ko-ṭhen chalak̇ me!* Go to those who have come! *Irakat'-ak̇-khon idi me*, take from the cut (dhan.)

The instrumental case of the future Gerund is often used like an Infinitive; as *hejuk̇te ge hoyok̇-tama*, you must come!

The locative case gives very often the idea of *with regard to;* as *dal-kedeań dal-re-do.* With regard to striking, I struck him.

The future Gerund of the Reservative Form is used very extensively as an adverbial participle; as *dal-ka-te,* striking or having struck.

SECTION IV.—OF CASES IN CONNECTION WITH THE VERBS.

As already stated, (p. 44), the verbs are influenced by four cases, the Nominative, the Genitive, the Dative, and the Accusative.

A. The Nominative.

The Nominative is the case of the subject, which always, in the common gender, is an abridged pronoun, and affixed either to the final *a* and consequently stands last in the sentence, or to the last word before the verb; as *dal-ket'-a-le,* we struck; *hecḱ-en-a-ko,* they have come; *ale-ren hǫpǫn-ṭhen-ko hecḱ-akan-a,* they have come to our son; *am-hotete-ń bańchao-en-a,* I was saved by you.

B. The Genitive.

This case is used to express:

1st. Possession; as *agu-ket'-tam-a-ko,* they have brought yours; *kombṛo-akat'-tiń-a-ko,* they have stolen mine.

2nd. Origin; as *ńel-akat'-tae-a-ń ǫl,* I have seen his writing.

3rd. Behalf *of, or for;* as *kami-ka-tiń-me,* work for me; *roṛ-tabon-ma-ę!* Let him speak for us!

4th. Dative relation; as *dharao-tae-a-ń,* I owe (to) him;

johar-tabon-me! Be greeted (to us) (Germ. *Sei uns gegrüsst.*)

5th. Opposition, against; as *ạdiń kạ̣i-akat'-tam-a,* I have sinned *against* you.

6th. Accusative relation; as *ańjom-tiń-'ne!* hear me!

c. The Dative.

This case is used, where we in English would use the prepositions *to, for, on, towards, with, against,* etc; as *hecŘ-ad-iń-a-e,* he came to me; *benao-ad-e-a-ń,* I made for him; *tọl-ad-e-a-ko,* they tied on him; *ti-e-tiar-ad-iń-a,* he stretched the band towards me; *edre-at'-ko-a-e,* he got angry with them; *hiṣka-ad-iń-a-e,* gheot a spite against me.

d. The Accusative.

This case is used to express:

1st. The direct object; as *agu-ko-m!* bring thou them *Ńel-ket'-ko-a-ń,* I saw them; *dal-e-m-e!* strike thou him!

2nd. Ablative sense; as *ṭańga-e recŘ-ked-ińa,* he took the axe *from me; mõṛe ṭaka e aguked-iń-a,* he took five Rupees *from me; tinaŘ em agu-iń-a?* how much will you take from me?

3rd. English genitive; as *pe poisa e eṛeked-iń-a,* he cheated me of five pice.

The last two are examples of a double object, like in English: The judge fined him five Rupees.

SECTION V.—OF THE FORMS.

a. The General Form.

This form is used in a general way, like the only form in English; as *dal-a-ń*, I will strike; *gocȟ-ked-e-a-ko*, they killed him; *kiriń-ked-e-a-ń*, I have bought him; *ńel-ked-e-a-ko*, they saw him; *ańjom-ket'-a-ń*, I heard it.

b. The Reservative Form.

This form denotes an action by which the object is brought into a certain state, in which it is allowed to continue, so as to be available for any ulterior purpose. It is used where in German they would use *an, auf, hin, etc.*; as *ańjom-kaǩ-me!* listen to it! *(Höre es an!)* (that you may give evidence, in case it should be necessary), *Ńel-kad-e-a-ko*, they saw him *(Sie sahen ihn an)* (and left him in that state); *kiriń-ka-ko-ań*, I will buy them up; *(Ich werde sie auf kaufen)*; *gocȟ-ka-ko-kan-a-ko*, they are killing them; *(sie schlachten sie hin)* (and let them lie.)

c. The Intensive Form.

This form denotes an effort to effect what the verb implies; as *ńa-ńam-kan-a-e*, he seeks (to get) (from *ńam*, to get); *ńam-et'-kan-a-e*, is the general form and means, he is getting,—*ńe-ńel-kan-a-e*, he is looking; *ńel-et'kan-a-e*, he is seeing,—(the latter is the general form) *hako ko sa-sap'-kan-a*, *(ha-ko-sap-et'-ko-kan-a,)* they are catching fish, (the latter is the general form.)

d. The Continuative Form.

This form denotes continuation, and is formed from the Reservative Form ; as *ńel-akaetahen-a-e,* he will continue to see.

e. The Repetitive Form.

The Repetitive form has a general form ; as *dal-dal-ke-dea-le,* we repeatedly struck him, a reservative one ; as *dal-dal-kad-e-a-le,* we repeatedly struck him and left him,—an intensive one ; as *dak-dal-kana-le,* we are trying to get ready with striking,—and a continuative form ; as *ńel-ńel-akae-tahen-pe,* continue to see ! It frequently has the same meaning as the general form.

The second part of a compound verb is also repeated ; as *ropor-babarae from ror* to speak, and *barae* to be engaged in.

CHAPTER V.

OF THE ARRANGEMENT OF WORDS AND CLAUSES.

SECTION 1.—OF WORDS.

The general arrangement, when the most of that parts of speech are to be included, is as follows :—

1. The vocative.
2. The genitive.
3. The adverb.
4. The adjective.
5. An accusative noun.
6. The instr. dat. or abl.
7. A negative.
8. A nominative suffix.
9. The root of the verb.
10. The causative.
11. The tense-sign.
12. The acc. or dat. suffix.
13. The auxiliary present tense-sign.
14. The auxiliary past tense-sign.
15. The genitive suffix.
16. The 2nd gen. suffix.
17. The final "a"
18. A conjunction.

As: E. baba, hoponren aḍi, marań, sukri, onihotete, ba-ko gocḱ-ocho-ed-e-kan-tahēkan-tae-tam-a-menkhan, enḍekhan phasiara metań-me, hear, if they were not causing the very large pig of your son's to be killed by him, then you may call me a deceiver.

The following may serve as examples on shorter sentences:

Nom. *Panḍu-e chalaḱ-a,* Pandu he will go.

Gen. *Panḍuren hopon-e chalaḱ-a,* Pandu's son will go.

Instr. *Panḍren hopon ińhotete-e banchaoena,* Pandu's son was saved by me.

Dat. *Panḍu Jogot-then-e-chalaḱ-a,* Pandu he will go to Jogot.

Acc. *Panḍu Jogot dalal-e-reben-a,* Pandu will be willing to strike Jogot.

Abl. *Panḍu Jogot-khon-e hecḱ-en-a,* Pandu he came from Jogot.

Loc. *Panḍu oraḱ-re menae-a,* Pandu is at home.

SECTION II.—OF CLAUSES.

The Santhal language leans towards putting the subordinate before the principal clauses, but this is by no means invariably done; as *okoeko ko chalak'-a, onko bar̤e ko heck'-hod̤ok'-ma,* those who will go let them come at once; *okare-m, tahena, ona bar̤e lại-me,* say, where you will stay; *oni-m dal-akad-e-te, adi-m bar̤ick'akat'-a,* you have done very wrong in having struck him (or that thou hast struck him,)—but it is also allowable to say: *Anjom-akat'-a-ń, heck' akanae,* I have heard, that he has come; *chalak'-a-bon, bae heck'-len-khan,* if he does not come, we will go, etc.

In vivid descriptions, etc., the clauses are loosely connected, *i. e.*, without a conjunction.

In relative clauses the final "a" ought to be omitted; as *oni hola-m ńel-led-e (not ńelled-e-a) oni do okaena?* What has become of him whom you saw yesterday? *Or okaenae: oni hola-m ńel-led-e,* what has become of him whom you saw yesterday? This is much more elegant and certainly more correct than to say: *oni hola-m ńel-led-e-a, oni do okarc,* for the latter means literally: you saw him yesterday, what has become of him?

P. S.—THE PROSODY WILL BE TREATED IN A SEPARATE VOLUME.

Remark. Adverbs and Postpositions are fully explained elsewhere.